DEFINING
VISUAL RHETORICS

§

DEFINING
VISUAL RHETORICS

§

Edited by

Charles A. Hill
Marguerite Helmers
University of Wisconsin Oshkosh

First published by Lawrence Erlbaum Associates, Inc., Publishers
10 Industrial Avenue
Mahwah, New Jersey 07430

Reprinted 2009 by Routledge

Routledge

270 Madison Avenue
New York, NY 10016

2 Park Square, Milton Park
Abingdon, Oxon OX14 4RN, UK

Cover photograph by Richard LeFande; design by Anna Hill

Library of Congress Cataloging-in-Publication Data

Defining visual rhetorics / edited by Charles A. Hill, Marguerite Helmers.

p. cm.

Includes bibliographical references and index.
ISBN 0-8058-4402-3 (cloth : alk. paper)
ISBN 0-8058-4403-1 (pbk. : alk. paper)
1. Visual communication. 2. Rhetoric.   I. Hill, Charles A.   II. Helmers,
Marguerite H., 1961–   .
P93.5.D44   2003
302.23—dc21

2003049448
CIP

To Anna,
who inspires me every day.
—C. A. H.

To Emily and Caitlin,
whose artistic perspective inspires and instructs.
—M. H. H.

Contents

Preface

A few years ago, we noticed a major shift in the field of rhetoric, one in which an increasing amount of the discipline's attention was becoming focused on visual objects and on the visual nature of the rhetorical process. The phrase *visual rhetoric* was being used more frequently in journal articles, in textbooks, and especially in conference presentations. However, it seemed equally obvious that the phrase was being used in many different ways by different scholars. There seemed little agreement on what exactly scholars intended when they used the term, and no reliable way to distinguish the work being done under the rubric of "visual rhetoric" as a coherent category of study.

Some scholars seemed to consider visual elements only in relation to expressing quantitative relationships in charts and graphs. Others concentrated solely on the ubiquity of visual elements on the Internet, which might give the impression that visual elements are important only in online communication. Much of the more culturally oriented work was based in art history and art theory, sometimes using the terms *visual rhetoric* and *visual culture* to refer to artistic images exclusively. In still other cases, the use of the word *visual* included *visualizing,* the mental construction of internal images, while other scholars seemed to use it to refer solely to conventional two-dimensional images. Add those scholarly pursuits to the study of print and film advertising, television, and cinema, and suddenly a new field of inquiry emerged, rich with possibility, but sometimes puzzling in its breadth.

The larger problem was not that rhetoricians were analyzing a wide variety of visuals—we saw this diversity of efforts as exciting and productive. The problem was that there seemed to be very little agreement on the basic nature of the two terms *visual* and *rhetoric.* To some, studying the "visual" seemed to consist solely of analyzing representational images, while to others, it could include the study of the visual aspect of pretty much anything created by human hands—a building, a toaster, a written document, an article of clothing—

making the study of "visual rhetoric" overlap greatly with the study of design. To still others, the study of visual rhetoric seemed to necessarily involve a study of the process of looking, of "the gaze," with all of the psychological and cultural implications that have become wrapped within that term.

Scholars engaged in visual analysis have also (with notable exceptions) largely neglected to discuss the ways in which their work is truly rhetorical, as opposed to an example of cultural studies or semiotics. What seems clear is that the turn to the visual has problematized any attempts to distinguish between these methodologies, blurring further what were already quite fuzzy and often shifting boundaries between them. But while it would make little sense to try to draw any rigid boundaries between these methodologies, we think it is still useful to ask of any scholar what aspects of his or her work make it legitimate or useful to label such work "rhetorical."

As we thought about the definitional problems surrounding the study of visual rhetoric, it became immediately clear that the appropriate response was *not* to try to "nail down" the term, to stipulate a set of definitions that all rhetoricians would agree to abide by (a naïve notion, to say the least). Rather, we thought that it would be more interesting and productive to have scholars working with visuals discuss the definitional assumptions behind their own work, and to exemplify these assumptions by sharing their own rhetorical analyses of visual phenomena. Our own assumptions behind this approach are two-fold. First, any discussion of definitions from which one is operating is necessarily post-hoc; that is, one discovers such definitional assumptions through the work, rather than explicating them (even to oneself) before approaching a scholarly project. Second, at this very early stage in the contemporary study of visual rhetoric, we assume that people are more interested in writing about and in reading about specific scholarly projects than in lengthy arguments about definitions.

We asked each contributor to this book to explain how his or her work fits under the heading of, and helps define, the term *visual rhetoric*. Using this approach, we hoped to capture the diversity of the work being done in this area while providing—for readers and, by extension, for the rhetoric community— some explanation of how this wide variety of work can be seen as complementary and part of a coherent whole. Our goal is not to promote any particular claims about what terms such as *visual* and *rhetoric* and *visual rhetoric* should or must mean. Rather, we want to prompt readers to think about, and to talk to each other about, what these terms mean to them and what they *could* mean—about how they can be productively used in creative ways to explore a broad range of phenomena, but without being diffused to the point where they lose their explanatory power.

We intend this book for anyone who is involved in or interested in such conversations. This includes not just those who are working explicitly on projects in visual rhetoric, but anyone interested in the rhetorical nature of visuals or in the disciplinary issues surrounding the increasing overlap between methodologies (rhetoric, semiotics, cultural studies) and disciplines (rhetoric, communication, art theory, etc.) by which and in which visual phenomena are studied. It is, perhaps, this refusal to be restricted by disciplinary and methodological boundaries that many of us working in this area find so exciting about visual rhetoric, and we hope that the chapters in this volume exemplify that inherent breadth and diversity, and that they express some of that excitement.

ACKNOWLEDGMENTS

All books are collaborative efforts, and thanks are due to many individuals who assisted in the preparation of this one. First and foremost is Linda Bathgate at Lawrence Erlbaum Associates, whose belief that visual rhetoric was a developing area of rhetorical study led directly to the production of this volume. Debbie Ruel at Erlbaum provided us with valuable editorial assistance in the production of the manuscript. Robie Grant created the indexes. Richard LeFande was enthusiastic when we contacted him about the use of his photo as a cover piece. Peggy O'Gara at Corbis helped us secure the use of Thomas P. Franklin's September 11, 2001 photograph for the Introduction. Anna Hill developed several striking cover designs, and conversations with Anna about art history and graphic design played no small part in the original inspiration for this collection.

The Faculty Development Board at the University of Wisconsin Oshkosh funded research that led to the development of parts of this work. In addition, the authors gratefully acknowledge the assistance of the Alberta Kimball Endowment at the University of Wisconsin Oshkosh. Large sections of the Introduction to this work were completed during a summer seminar on literature and the visual arts, sponsored by the National Endowment for the Humanities and held at the Boston Athenaeum in 2002. The seminar group, led by Director Richard Wendorff, included Anna Arnar, Laura Bass, Megan Benton, Ellen Garvey, Michelle Glaros, Christine Henseler, Margot Kelley, Jim Knapp, Lori Landay, Vincent Lankewish, Jennifer Michael, Peter Pawlowicz, Laura Saltz, and Thaine Stearns. All of these colleagues deserve praise for their insightful observations, without which this work would not have taken the shape that it did.

We thank our colleagues in the English Department for their friendship, encouragement and support, as well as for stimulating conversations about the use of images in rhetoric and literature pedagogy, and our students, who traveled with us as we explored some of the initial ideas behind this volume.

Introduction

Marguerite Helmers
Charles A. Hill

In this book, we study the relationship of visual images to persuasion. But where do we begin? Which images do we select to tell our story or to prove our case? Which authors do we cite as pioneers in the field of visual rhetoric? We could extend ourselves as far back in time and place as ancient Egypt and cite the role of hieroglyphs in conveying meaning and recording memory. Or we could call up the painted caves at Lascaux. We could invoke the famous example of Xeuxes' painted grapes that tricked the birds into pecking at them. Or we could fast forward to the stained glass windows of medieval churches and the role they played in educating the peasantry about Biblical texts. We could name the exuberant paintings of the Hudson River School of American painters, whose images helped to broaden people's imaginations and pushed them westward across the country, or survey images from *Life* magazine or *National Geographic* and discuss how they shaped a national consciousness of America's place in the world. Any of these visual artifacts could shed light on the primary question that drives the essays in this volume: How do images act rhetorically upon viewers?

This inability to begin comfortably, much less securely, at a point in time with a particular class of images was a cue to begin the work of defining visual rhetorics. Images surround us in the home, at work, on the subway, in restaurants, and along the highway. Historically, images have played an important role in developing consciousness and the relationship of the self to its surroundings. We learn who we are as private individuals and public citizens by seeing ourselves reflected in images, and we learn who we can become by transporting ourselves into images. We refer to our sense of our own personality as a *self-image*, and we critique celebrities and politicians when they tarnish their images with poor judgment. Yet images are treated with distrust; in Western culture, images have often been placed in a secondary and subordinate relationship to written and verbal texts and the potential dialogy between images and words has been especially neglected. "One of the crucial media-tions that occurs in the history of cultural forms is the interaction between verbal and pictorial modes of representation," writes W. J. T. Mitchell. "We rarely train scholars, however, to be sensitive to this crucial point of conflict, influence, and mediation and insist on separating the study of texts and images from one another by rigid disciplinary boundaries" ("Diagrammatology" 627). Mitchell's caution, about which we will have more to say later, provides us with a rationale for undertaking this type of interdisciplinary work. For this book, we invited contributions from authors who situate themselves at the crossroads of more than one discipline, and we have chosen to survey a wide range of sites of image production, from architecture to paintings in muse-ums and from film to needlepoint, in order to understand how images and texts, both symbolic forms of representation, work upon readers.

Rhetoricians working from a variety of disciplinary perspectives are begin-ning to pay a substantial amount of attention to issues of visual rhetoric. Through analysis of photographs and drawings, graphs and tables, and motion pictures, scholars are exploring the many ways in which visual elements are used to influence people's attitudes, opinions, and beliefs. There is a diversity in these efforts that is exciting and productive, but which can also be confusing for those who are trying to understand the role of visual elements in rhetorical the-ory and practice. Some people seem to think of visual elements only in relation to expressing quantitative relationships in charts and graphs. Other scholars concentrate solely on the ubiquity of visual elements on the Internet. Much of the more culturally oriented work is based in art history and art theory, giving the im-pression that, when speaking of "visuals" and "images," we mean artistic artifacts exclusively. In English studies, there is no vocabulary for discussing images, or per-haps we might say that there are so many disciplinary-specific vocabularies that we in English have to borrow extensively. In fact, despite his assertion that "transferences from one art form to another" are "inescapable" ("Spatial Form" 281), Mitchell encourages cross-disciplinary rhetoricians and cultural critics to de-velop a "systematic" method for investigating the relationship between arts and words in order to avoid charges of "impressionism" ("Spatial Form" 291). This systematic approach would demand a theoretical basis and a set of terms com-mon to the field of visual rhetoric. One of the most important lessons from the Sister Arts Tradition in literary studies from the late 1950s is that "A student of the sister arts must learn to work twice as hard" (Lipking 4), training as a scholar in two disciplines—linguistic and visual—in both primary and secondary materi-als. Mitchell's warning draws attention to the institutional fact that, just as ear-nestly as we seek to join the study of verbal rhetoric with the study of visual material, so also others earnestly seek to separate the disciplines from "contami-nation," a perception that the study of images is soft or non-rigorous because images are commonly construed to be illustrative and decorative. In order to counter what has been called a *paragonal* relationship between word and im-

age—a struggle for dominance over meaning between verbal and visual discourse—we suggest that readers and scholars working with visual rhetoric
attend to the notion that word and image are used by writers and illustrators to
accomplish different aims. Printed verbal material is conveyed to us in visual
forms, whether electronically or through traditional paperform methods. Thus
rhetoric encompasses a notion of visuality at the very level of text; it is mediated
by visuality, typography, even the somatic experience of holding the book or
touching the paper.

Art historian Barbara Stafford draws attention to the ways that images are
often considered to be subordinate to written text, logical argument, and
truthful exposition: "In spite of their quantity and globalized presence, for
many educated people pictures have become synonymous with ignorance, illiteracy, and deceit. Why?" (110). In "Material Literacy and Visual Design,"
Lester Faigley explores a similar point, citing an 1846 poem by William Wordsworth that, with characteristic Romantic era angst, bemoans the initial publication of the *Illustrated London News* in 1842. Wordsworth's concern is with
progress: It was the word that raised the English from their earliest beginnings
to an "intellectual Land." The image, because it is mute, or "dumb," cannot express either truth or love, but rather has a profound national and psychological
effect of reverting the country "back to childhood." He concludes his poem
with the exclamation, "Heaven keep us from a lower stage!" Faigley's essay re-
captures the notion of progress, however, and records the irrepressible movement of images into our society through various technologies from the
printing press to the World Wide Web.

Where, then, should the rhetorician who is interested in analyzing visual
images begin? What bodies of scholarship are essential to master? What terms
should rhetoricians adopt? Are some images more suitable than others for the
study of images in rhetorical theory?

As we worked together to identify a suitable cover image for this volume,
these questions surfaced. The image we chose to represent a volume of work
on vision and representation had to be multilayered and complex, but not so
detailed as to be inscrutable or to require excessive verbal explanation. On the
other hand, the image had to foster verbal discourse, debate, argument, and
thoughtful reflection while in itself having a visual impact. Furthermore, we
believed the image could not be tied too strongly to one event because its own
rhetorical work was to represent the themes that the authors in this book address: vision, revision, representation, media, memory, presence and absence.
Richard LeFande's (cover) image of a photograph held against the Manhattan
skyline spoke to these themes, while drawing attention to the strongest visual
event of this new century: the devastation of the World Trade Center in New
York City on September 11, 2001.

Points of crisis in American culture since the Vietnam War have been visually
recorded and widely disseminated to the public. The use of television cameras

and the evening news to broadcast the battles of Vietnam gave it the name "the living room war." The Gulf War two decades later was a visual event of a slightly different sort. Anchormen broadcasting with bombs falling over their shoulders became symbolic of the real presence of the media in our lives. The use of infrared and computerized piloting devices by the military became symbolic of the depersonalized gamesmanship of an advanced technological war. In both cases, though, just as with September 11, 2001, the spectator was able to experience the exceptional power of visual media to create "simultaneity," a national consciousness of being together as a community (Anderson 132; Baty). Writing about September 11 in "Images, Imaging, Imagination," Annick T. R. Wibben expresses the conundrum of televised access:

> We all have images stored in our eyes (how does this differ for those who saw the events on TV and those that were in NYC or DC?). We are bombarded by ever more images by the media (how does the replay and information overload numb us to the effects of particular images?).... We were all there, but yet we weren't. We saw it, but saw nothing. We kept uttering this isn't real, while knowing that it was. We witnessed death, yet we saw no bodies, no blood. (Wibben)

One of Benjamin Barber's main points in his influential book *Jihad vs. McWorld* is that information technologies (audio, visual, film, print, and electronic) "inevitably impact culture and politics and the attitudes that constitute them" (74). The "infotainment telesector"—the connection of technologies, news, and entertainment (60), comprised of "those who create and control the world of signs and symbols" (79)—is something like a universal country without borders. As Wibben indicates, significant facts about images and their interpretation and important questions about the relations of all images to human mediation emerged from the September 11 attacks. Strong national symbols such as the eagle and the flag are liberally in use in the popular and mass media as a means of gathering together the imagined national community, and to these patriotic and sentimental images the twin towers of the World Trade Center have been added in the way that the red poppy came to symbolize the First World War. Together, these symbols form an expressive syntax for what Barber calls American "monoculture," a "template," a "style" that exemplifies a certain lifestyle—but in turn begins to demand "certain products" (82). Symbols resist individualistic interpretation because they are overdetermined by customary usage, embedded so frequently in conventional discourse that they rarely take on a reflective, individual meaning. As Edwards, Strachan and Kendall point out in their contributions to this book, national symbols are employed as a visual shorthand to represent shared ideals and to launch an immediate appeal to the audience's sense of a national community.

At the same time, though, a strong populist movement to remember individuals and their unique testimony resists the immediate temptation to impose a Master Narrative on the 9/11 tragedy. In his commemorative poem, "The Names," U.S. Poet Laureate Billy Collins stressed that the memory of September 11 is a memory of proper names, "spelled out on storefront windows" and "printed on the ceiling of the night." Maureen Daly Goggin demonstrates that the need to individualize by inscribing one's presence is not unique to this time or place in history; women in the 17th century used their needles to illustrate their histories. While the media may hark the "attacks on America," the families and friends of those killed or wounded in the attacks remember names, faces, and their own stories of where they were on the morning of 9/11.

Thomas Franklin's photograph (Fig. I-1) of three New York City firefighters raising a flag over the rubble of the World Trade Center on September 11, 2001, illustrates the possible modes of interpretation and the resistance to interpretation that a single image may have in our interpretive lives.

One of the ways that we understand this photograph is through its reference to other images. Thus, one of the ways that images may communicate to us is through intertextuality, the recognition and referencing of images from one scene to another. The reader is active in this process of constructing a reference. If the reader is unaware of the precursors, the image will have a different meaning, or no meaning at all. We first saw the photo by Thomas E. Franklin now known as *Ground Zero Spirit* on September 12, 2001, the day after the World Trade Center collapse. Immediately, we were struck by its obvious resemblance to the famous photo of U.S. Marines raising the flag at Iwo Jima. Thomas Franklin himself notes that he saw the three men raise the flag and thought "Iwo Jima." Our students even make this association, knowing no more about the battle in the Pacific than the name "Iwo Jima." The immediate distribution through newspapers and magazines gave the image an instant power and authority over the interpretation of the day's events. Institutions such as news media and magazines implant "modes of knowledge in each individual, family, and institution" (De Lauretis 15), and the knowledge that was imparted to the American public about 9/11 was not that of sorrow or loss, but of resilience and triumph.

Acknowledging that the title *Ground Zero Spirit* affects the interpretation of the image, we refer to Franklin's photograph by this name in this essay. As a documentary photograph, the image is untitled. Because we address the image as a slice of time, a moment frozen from a historical sequence, and because we also discuss the three firefighters as actors, we have chosen to distinguish the photograph as an object and icon by referring to it by its commodified designation. Having said this, we should also acknowledge that the image itself is more easily recognizable than either its name or the facts of its production. Our students are unsure if the firefighters raised the flag on 9/11 or some later date, and it's clear that the exact date doesn't matter to the effect

FIG. I.1.   *Firefighters at Ground Zero*. Photograph by Thomas E. Franklin, 2001. Copyright © 2001, *The Record* (Bergen County, N.J.). Reprinted by permission of Corbis.

of the photograph. It is the act captured on film that matters. The three men raising the flag do have proper names, of course—George Johnson, Dan McWilliams, Bill Eisengrein—and due to the popularity of the photograph, their individual names are now protected by copyright and licensing agreements; however, in viewing the photograph, their names are less important than their symbolic value as "firefighters." They intended to use the American flag as a sign to rally the spirits of those working amidst the rubble of the Trade Center. McWilliams had been working at Ground Zero since late in the morning on September 11, when he was called to evacuate. He saw the flag on the yacht the *Star of America* docked at one of the piers on the Hudson River, to the west of the Trade Center site. It was an immediate symbol. He was, in the words of the Bergen County *Record*, where the photograph was originally published, "inspired." "Everybody just needed a shot in the arm," McWilliams later noted (Clegg). The flag was raised on a flagpole emerging from the rubble at the site at 5:01pm in the afternoon of September 11. Photographer Franklin was at Ground Zero all day, despite threats to arrest him. He commented later that the photo "just happened," although he immediately recognized the pose of the firefighters as being similar to the pose of the Marines in Joe Rosenthal's Iwo Jima photograph. "It was an important shot," Franklin explained. "It told of more than just death and destruction. It said something to me about the strength of the American people and of these firemen having to battle the unimaginable. It had drama, spirit, and courage in the face of disaster" (Franklin, "Photo of a Lifetime").

When the photograph was published the next day, its impact was powerful and immediate, seized at once as a symbol by millions. *Newsweek* cemented the photograph's popularity and significance by running the Ground Zero photo as the cover image for the September 24, 2001 issue. "I have just received my Sept. 24 issue, 'After the Terror,' wrote Jodi Williams to *Newsweek*:

> I haven't even had time to read it yet, but I wanted to say thank you for the cover picture. I have wondered what the icon of this event would be and am pleased with your choice. In showing the flag being raised out of the rubble, you have chosen a positive image—the strength and resilience of Americans, and the specific bravery of those members of the NYPD and FDNY who risked and sometimes lost their lives in the hope of saving others.

The simple composition of the image is both essential and non-essential to the meaning. The fact that there are three figures involved in the flag raising, rather than two or five, invokes the Christian Trinity of Father, Son, and Holy Ghost. Inscribing the Trinity over the rubble of the Trade Center offers a corrective to the "Islamic fundamentalism" of the ad hoc pilots of the aircraft that blasted into the buildings in the morning. The immediate symbolic value of the American flag encodes "appropriate" and conditioned responses of patriotism, loyalty, and invincibility. Whenever an image of the flag appears, the American public associates it with such abstract ideas—even if individuals do not respond to it emotionally. The colors of the flag have symbolic meaning: red for valor, white for innocence, and blue for justice. When the American flag was created, it was designed to represent ideas rather than a monarchy or a particular religion. By the early decades of the 20th century, the flag was recognized as denoting freedom and democracy. In being designated a national symbol, the flag is synecdochic. To defend one's country and people, and possessions, is synecdochically known as "defending the flag." It is the embodiment of national spirit, a shorthand for the words of the Pledge of Allegiance (to the flag): "liberty and justice for all." Furthermore, like any icon, the flag becomes meaningful to the public through repeated imaging and storytelling. "[I]t is useful to remind ourselves that nations inspire love, and often profoundly self-sacrificing love. The cultural products of nationalism"—poetry, painting, song—"show this love very clearly in thousands of different forms and styles" (Anderson 120). In Franklin's image, the flag's importance is emphasized because it occupies the central axis of the photograph. The diagonal placement of the flagpole across the ground of the rubble physically cuts across the devastation with something whole, purposeful, strong, and integrated. It marks the connection to an imagined community called "America" that, in turn, recognizes the photograph as symbolic.

New York firefighters were the first on the scene and were inside the towers when they collapsed, leaving 343 firefighters dead. The rubble—the background to this photograph—provides meaning to the image, for it is this "ground" of rubble, which encompasses half of the scene but does not intrude on the activities of the men, that gives meaning to the figures' resilient action. They are not rescuing or digging out here, but taking time to reflect on the spirit that gives meaning and purpose to the activities at Ground Zero. It is because the men stand in the foreground that the photograph achieves its power. Imagine a different photograph, one taken through the rubble, framing the men, dwarfed by the gothic arcs of the burning, decaying steel, or, as seen through the charred cruciform windows of buildings adjoining Ground Zero. Decreasing the physical relationship between men and rubble would decrease the importance of the working man, the New Yorker, in overcoming disaster. It would place disaster in the foreground and as the protagonist of the photograph. In fact, photographers such as James Nachtway, Anthony Suau, Susan Meiselas, and Gilles Peress made images such as these; yet these images failed to become icons.

When Joe Rosenthal's image of the Marines raising the American flag on Mount Suribachi appeared in 1945, the photograph immediately symbolized the triumph over adversity and death that the Marines had encountered in taking the island. Karal Ann Marling and John Wetenhall write that the "act of planting a flagstaff meant: enemy terrain captured, the highest point seized—triumph" (73). Thus, the meaning of the American flag in this context depends on a notion of an enemy, the adversary who held the ground initially. "Rosenthal's picture spoke of group effort, the common man—working in concert with his neighbors—triumphant. The very facelessness of the heroes sanctified a common cause" (73). Similar meanings are associated with *Ground Zero Spirit* as well. Franklin's photograph of the three firefighters shifts the emphasis from military might to the exemplary actions of common men. The three are self-assured and attentive to duty. Hands on hips, focused on the stars and stripes of the rising flag, they don't cry over the disaster behind them, but stoically resolve to raise the symbol for their lost and living comrades as an indication that there is courage in the collective will of the nation. Like its precursor in the Pacific a half-century earlier, this flag in New York City "calls the audience to the task of building their society in the same manner as the men in the picture, through sacrifice and coordinated labor" (Hariman and Lucaites 372).

As Marling and Wetenhall point out, "[T]he Stars and Stripes took on a new symbolic weight during World War II .... Beginning with the Memorial Day parade in Washington in 1942 ... flags appeared everywhere and, thanks to [President FDR's] example, the display of Old Glory on private homes, businesses, and commercial products became common practice" (76). The ability of the flag to grace a private home meant that everyone could partake of its meaning, share its association, mark the national community. The 1946 Congressional Flag code made the flag a religious object, with rules for devotion. The flag unified a country that was based on diversity; without allegiance to a common religious goal, the country could focus on patriotism, on protecting the country that allowed individual and collective freedom to flourish. The flag aspires, pushes upward, and lifts the spirit, as Marling and Wetenhall comment (204). Furthermore, it is itself an intertextual symbol, "a field of multiple projections," as Robert Hariman and John Lucaites describe:

> Such projections include direct assertions of territorial conquest and possession, totemic evocations of blood sacrifice, demands for political loyalty to suppress dissent, representations of consensus, tokens of political participation, articulations of civil religion, ornamental signs of civic bonding amid a summer festival, and affirmations of political identity and rights while dissenting. Given the rich intertextuality of the iconic photo, it is unlikely that only one of these registers is in play, and probable that any of them could be activated by particular audiences. (Hariman and Lucaites 371)

At a simple denotational level, however, there are questions about Franklin's *Ground Zero Spirit* that cannot be answered without association to Rosenthal's photograph from Iwo Jima. For example, abstracting ourselves from immediate history, how do we know, on the basis of the photograph alone, that the three firefighters are *raising* the flag? Is it not possible that they are lowering a flag left standing amidst the ruins of the Trade Center? Secondly, without the context of the photograph and the immediate, collective memory of the events of September 11, there are no indications that the photograph takes place in New York City, amidst the rubble of the former World Trade Center, or in September 2001. The necessary historical detail that contextualizes the photograph also gives the photograph its profound meaning. Furthermore, the *Ground Zero Spirit* photograph is significant because it is like and unlike Iwo Jima. Rosenthal's Marines gaze at the ground, struggling enmasse to plant the flag on inhospitable, rocky, and unwelcoming ground. *Ground Zero's* men gaze at the flag, adjusting its folds and presentation, very much aware of its meaning for the workers at the site. It is this attentiveness that provides interpretive clues. McWilliam's and Eisengrein's hands are on the flag; they look up at its folds. Iconographically, to look downward is to lower, and lower the spirits of the spectator. Looking up, as in the Renaissance images of the Madonna and the saints, represents hope. The attention of Johnson, McWilliams, and Eisengrein attests to the need to raise the flag as a symbol on this day.

Rosenthal's photograph was compared to other works of American patriotic art: Archibald M. Willard's *The Spirit of '76* (1876; 1891) and Emanuel Gottlieb Leutze's *Washington Crossing the Delaware* (1851), both of which employ, like Franklin and Rosenthal's images, triangular formats. In both *Spirit of '76* and *Washington Crossing the Delaware*, the American flag occupies the central axis of the painting and is the highest physical point of the image. In a now-famous editorial from February 1945, the Rochester *Times-Union* compared Rosenthal's photograph to DaVinci's *Last Supper* and drew attention to the structural gesture in which "the outstretched arms and the foremost man's left leg leads the eye directly to the flag." The writer continues:

> Oddly, though, the eye does not rest there. A slight breeze is stirring, not enough to unfurl the folds of the flag, but enough to enlist the forces of nature on the side of the Marines who are hurrying to raise the staff. So the eye, turning back to a line parallel to the outstretched arms, follows the blood-red stripes to the entirely empty space in the upper right where the flag, in just a moment, will be. Few artists would be bold enough to make empty space the center of their picture. And yet this bit of art from life has done just that. In that space is a vision of what is to be. (qtd. in Marling and Wetenhall 204)

There are, however, three versions of Franklin's photograph, which complicates the analysis. In the first, the original, the tip of the flag pole is visible. The men occupy the lower one third of the image. The flag is directly centered over the rubble. The second version is cropped; the top of the flag pole is not visible, the flag moves slightly closer to the top of the image space, and the men occupy half of the picture. The United States postage stamp commemorating "heroes" further crops the image, so the men occupy more than half of the image space. Trimming the visible picture space thus alters the meaning of the image, moving from a struggle of the individual in the face of adversity to a new hero that is not superhuman, but a common man.

Following the original appearance of Franklin's photograph in the Bergen County *Record*, it began to appear in other locations, in both borrowed and direct representations. *Newsweek* chose one of the cropped versions for its cover on September 24, 2001, thus establishing the picture's popularity. Franklin won several awards as a photojournalist. By the 1-year anniversary of 9/11, the *Record* established a special website to accommodate requests for use of the photograph. Its reprint could include buttons, pins, mugs, cups, cards, CD covers, clothing, stationery, needlework, jewelry, mousepads, posters, rubber stamps, sculptures, and computer wallpaper. Franklin reports that he began collecting authorized and unauthorized uses, "carved pumpkins, Christmas ornaments, miniature statues, key chains, paintings, tattoos, humidors, clocks, watches, light switches, snow globes, and leather jackets" (Franklin, "Sept. 11"). The photograph "has been spotted in places like prisons, barns, front lawns, fake dollar bills, tree ornaments, chocolate bars, bumper stickers, light switches, billboards" (Szentmiklosy). The U.S. Post Office released its Heroes 2001 postage stamp on June 7, 2002, affixing a seven-cent surcharge to benefit the Federal Emergency Management Agency.

A proposal for a life-sized memorial of the three men created for the FDNY Brooklyn headquarters caused controversy, when the men were physically altered to represent the multicultural "spirit" of New York rather than the individuality of Johnson, McWilliams, and Eisengrein. This is a battle of specificity and symbolism. Johnson, McWilliams, and Eisengrein view their act as a specific contribution to history. It was their choice to intervene at this moment and they would like to be remembered as the men who took the initiative. John Bradley, Rene Gagnon, and Ira Hayes, the surviving members of the Marines who raised the flag at Iwo Jima, became celebrities after the Rosenthal photo achieved popularity. They recreated the flag raising in cities across the United States for the war bond fund-raising tours. Gagnon was offered a contract from Hollywood. Although Johnson, McWilliams, and Eisengrein eschew publicity, they consented to allow Madame Tussaud's to recreate their flag raising into wax for the New York museum because it was the action and spirit that was represented and not their own selves. Yet their fight to retain control over the image as an act of historical particularity is partially in vain, because their act was symbolic and strong symbols like the flag immediately transcend their historical context. As the letter to the editors at *Newsweek* attests, Americans were waiting for a symbol, and this was it.

As with any work of art (or photojournalism) in the age of mechanical reproduction, the question of what the photograph means depends on its dissemination and reception. *Ground Zero Spirit* is in such demand that a strict licensing agreement is employed to control its appearance on commercial— and academic—projects. In the world of image studies, the paragonal contest between word and image is here exemplified, with word winning. Legal discourse restricts how the image is received by the public, placing the image into certain contexts where it can be viewed. Some artist/interpreters have avoided the licensing fee by creating an image that echoes but does not reproduce Franklin's photograph. Is this plagiarism? Or intertextuality?

A potent critique of the photograph, for its absence, its denotation and connotation, has come from the Women firefighters of New York City. While the temporal fact that three men raised an American flag at Ground Zero exists ontologically, the *idea* that three White men (and not women, gays, or Blacks) could represent work at Ground Zero, but also the community of "America" and its spirit, seemed to test the capacity of imaging to be inclusive. The photograph functions, with the absence of women, as a powerful persuasive device that women did *not* exist at Ground Zero. Lt. Brenda Berkman of the New York Fire Department, in remarks made at the National Women's Law Center's 2001 Awards Dinner in Washington, DC, listed the roles that women played in the immediate rescue at Ground Zero: firefighter, EMT, police officer, ambulance driver, nurse, doctor, construction worker, chaplain, Red Cross worker, and military personnel:

> The reality is that women have contributed to the aftermath of the World Trade Center attack in every imaginable way. But the face the media has put on the rescue and recovery efforts in New York City is almost exclusively that of men. Where are the pictures or stories of Captain Kathy Mazza shooting out the glass in the lobby of one of the towers to allow hundreds of people to flee the building more quickly?

In becoming the iconic image of 9/11, *Ground Zero Spirit* imprints an idea of heroism on the collective consciousness of Americans, and that idea is entirely male. Ultimately, it must be read for what is absent as much as for what is present. As the women firefighters in New York—the 25 out of 11,500—attest, the representation of the males in the photograph is fact, evidence of the discriminatory policies of the FDNY against hiring women. That the losses at the Trade Center were male "reflects the way the FDNY has tested and hired over the past two decades," writes Terese Floren, editor of WFS Publications, but it does not attest to "the merits or failures of women firefighters." Berkman returns to the issue of representation: "When we were growing up, we did not see any women role models in firefighting and the trades" (qtd. in Willing). That *Ground Zero Spirit* exemplifies the male ideal is disturbing in the long run because it represents rescue work as the domain of men. Berkman's point is important, yet even she, like the three men themselves, does not realize the full measure of the photo's significance: The image relies on the interpretant, the mental representation that is individuated for each viewer. The photo *means*, not because Johnson, McWilliams, and Eisengrein were there physically, but because they represented the millions who were there only "in spirit"—or perhaps more accurately, and to echo Wibben's thoughts, those who were there due to electronic and print media.

One of the important concepts for any discussion of the role of the viewer in images is the relationship between viewing and time. Images work on us synchronically and diachronically. Synchronically, we view the image that represents the present. Diachronic viewings are slightly more complicated, for we view an image that represents the past and was created in the past, but we also view contemporaneous images with a knowledge of their precursors and their previous meanings. "As American attitudes and values changed, so the public estimate of the Iwo Jima motif shifted from near adoration to neglect and back again to a patriotic pride mingled with nostalgia for the lost age of unambiguous heroes" (Marling and Wetenhall 196). Intervening in the history of the image was the suspicion over the military fostered by Vietnam and, even earlier, post-war films that were critical of the violence of war. The nostalgia for the masculine American hero is evident again in the Ground Zero photograph, in which the flag raisers are common men, focused on their duty and, symbolically, on their country. Some of the commentary following the attacks of 9/11 praised the return to the "unambiguous hero" of the 21st century. However, just as the fiction was in place in 1945, it is again in place. Heroes are manifestations of national desire.

In the introduction of this visual text, we have drawn upon a text that is popular, widely imitated, photojournalistic, and symbolic in order to introduce key ideas about the problems of vision and representation and in order to introduce key terms—*paragonal, intertextual, interpretant*—which we explain further a bit later. We have also, after much debate, decided to reproduce the newly famous photograph by Thomas E. Franklin, despite it being readily available to readers' consciousness due to its reproduction and extensive distribution. In addition, there is evidence from psychologists and historians who have studied memory and "flashbulb" memories that "the *distortion* of memory traces" occurs at the level of the interpretant, at the moment that the visual image or event is encoded (Winter and Sivan). In other words, our memory of the photograph may habitually encode distortions. According to Winter and Sivan, this is a frequent predicament with visual memory:

> [I]nterference operates either by manipulating major so-called "facts" and/ or by introducing key interpretive terms which have clear-cut resonances for the *semantic memory* of the individual and are, of course, culture-dependent. The result is a new script which integrates pieces of information brought to bear upon the interpretation of the event. As we all know, such new scripts may vary dramatically from the original memory, let alone the event itself. (13–14)

As David Campbell commented in the online edition of *INFOinterventions*, "what we saw on television on September 11 wasn't what the event was like. The event was much more horrific than the impression conveyed by the television pictures" (in other words, if you were *there*, physically present). The caution is well placed in the context of a discussion of visual rhetoric: As readers of image texts, we must always be aware that the photograph does not reveal the truth. And while intertextuality can be a positive means of enabling interpretation through comparison of the image at hand to a previous image, it can also be a means of negating the veracity of memory by introducing image texts that have very little to do with the events of a particular time and place. This aspect of what Henry Louis Gates calls *signifying*—texts talking to one another, repetition, revision—is introduced below.

I. INTERTEXTUALITY

Although there is not space here to do justice to Gerard Genette's fascinating study of intertextuality titled *Palimpsests*, an overview must suffice to gather interest in his work for visual rhetoricians. Genette prefers the term *transtextuality* to *intertextuality* and he defines this quality of a text as "all that sets the text in a relationship, whether obvious or concealed, with other texts" (1). By "concealed," Genette intends to invoke the subtle allusion, or the palimpsest, that which is hidden behind the writing rather than directly articulated within it. The palimpsest, a paper on which one written text has been effaced and covered by another, represents writing again, written upon twice. Intertextuality is "a relationship of copresence between two texts or among several texts," writes Gennette (1), but it is only one of five modes of allusion that can bring an occluded precursor to the fore. Readers of this text may find it useful to see these acts of copresence delineated as "forms of transtextuality." In Genette's categorization, intertextuality alone refers to quoting (with or without quotation marks), plagiarism, allusion, and the perception by the reader of the relationship of one work to another. *Paratextuality* indicates the presence of material around the primary text, but in which the text is embedded: the framing acts of title, subtitle, preface, illustration, book covers, dust jackets, and the setting of the book that is dependent on external conditions, which the readers cannot ignore. (See Philippe Lejeune, Calinescu for excellent readings of paratextuality.) *Metatextuality* moves outward to consider the effects of commentary and critical relationships posed between one text and another. *Hypertextuality* indicates a level of dependence between texts: Text B is unable to exist without Text A. At this point, Gennette's work borrows from that of Peirce's concept of the *index*, and further, as we note later, echoes Jacques Derrida's description of the *trace* as a mark that points to the past and the future. Finally, in a play on words, Gennette's concept of *architextuality* indicates a generic classification of the text or object that must result from paratextuality. In other words, the library classification of a text with call letters as a PR or an HQ depends on the degree to which the text is like other texts. Similarly, the description of a photograph as a family snapshot or a work of photojournalism such as *Ground Zero Spirit* indicates the existence of outside factors in classifying the object. The categories, it is evident, are interrelated and fluid. One object may move, over time, from one architextual category to another.

II. PEIRCE ON SEMIOTICS

In the late 19th century, the philosopher Charles Sanders Peirce articulated several theories of signs and representation that have continued to influence rhetoricians. Peirce's theory derived from John Locke's *Essay Concerning Human Understanding*, in which Locke proposed that the study of "semeiotic" (now commonly referred to as "semiotics") would afford a theory of knowledge. Peirce's conviction was phenomenological: Things exist in a reality outside of what we perceive or think about them. His background in the natural sciences caused him to search for a logical, scientific method that would not be confused by what he termed "beliefs." Three theories of signs emerge in his philosophy of logic as semiotic, and each of these theories is parsed in detail, but the one that is used most frequently by rhetoricians to discuss both language and images is the triadic theory of icon, index, and symbol. Peirce's distinctions are useful to rhetoricians because they establish a formal terminology for considering different types of imagistic sign systems, from representational, through diagrammatical, to allegorical.

Two levels of terminology establish the relationship of sign to referent. At the first level, Peirce contended that a sign stands in for an Object; it "tells about" its Object (100). He gave this sign the name *representamen*. The *representamen* is rhetorical; it "addresses somebody, that is, creates in the mind of that person an equivalent sign" and this equivalent sign is called the *"interpretant"* (Peirce 99). The interpretant represents an idea that Peirce called "the ground of the representation" (qtd. in De Lauretis, *Alice* 19). The *interpretant* is thus a mental representation; it is not a person. Thus, both *representamen* and *interpretant* relate to the same Object. In using the work of Peirce to establish a semiology of art, Mieke Bal and Norman Bryson contend that the interpretant is associative and connotative. "The interpretant is constantly shifting; no viewer will stop at the first association" (189). Nonetheless, this does not mean that interpretants are unique; interpretants are shot through with "culturally shared codes" (De Lauretis 167). "Interpretants are new meanings resulting from the signs on the basis of one's habit. And habits, precisely, are formed in social life" (Bal and Bryson 202). At this point, ideological constructions of gender enter into the creation of the interpretant.

Once these terms are understood, they facilitate understanding Peirce's distinction between icon, index, and symbol. This trio of signs is not graded or hierarchical; rather, each term describes ways that different types of images may be understood. The icon may be abstract or representational; it possesses a character that makes it significant. A vacation photograph and Charles Schultz's Snoopy are icons, but so is a pencil streak indicating a geometric line. The Object does not have to exist, for it is easy enough to visually represent an alien from "outer space" or a solar system even though we have not seen either. Peirce refers to the icon as an image.

The index, on the other hand, depends on the existence of the Object to have left what Jacques Derrida, in *Dissemination*, would later call a "trace." Therefore, the indexical image holds an existential relationship to its Object and often raises in the viewer a memory of a similar Object. The classical example of an indexical sign is a bullet hole. The interpretant indicates, "here is a hole in the front door" and relates the hole to other holes, but not to the Object (a bullet making the hole) because the Object—the bullet and the gun—are missing. In Roland Barthes' words, the index "points but does not tell" (62). Peirce describes the index as a diagram.

The symbol is the most abstract of the three sign types. It depends on the *interpretant*, that is, the mental representation in the mind's eye. Therefore, the symbolic image holds a conventional relationship to its Object that is not contingent on resemblance. "The act of interpretation ... brings [the symbolic sign] to life," write Bal and Bryson (192). Peirce calls the symbol a metaphor.

Ground Zero Spirit operates on all of these levels. As an image/icon, at the literal level, the three men who raise the American flag are performing a common action in American civil society. Thus, denotationally, their action is recognizable to that group that Benedict Anderson called "the imagined community." Memory of similar flag raising ceremonies, of the soaring existence and the dreadful collapse of the Twin Towers of the World Trade Center, of the deaths of hundreds of firefighters and rescue workers moves the image into the realm of indexical and diagrammatic sign, for the index points to the prior existence of these Objects, even though they are not directly visible within the frame of the photograph. Metaphorically, the idea of the firefighter in American culture carries symbolic weight; their triangulated pose evokes the memory of the Marines at Iwo Jima, of courage under fire, of American ideals of toughness, grit, and masculinity. Again, while Peirce does not propose his levels of signs as a hierarchy, *Ground Zero Spirit* fulfills all aspects of his taxonomy, making the photograph appealing, disturbing, popular, contentious, and powerful.

III. BARTHES ON SIGNS

A third linguistic approach to the study of images derives from the work of the French linguist Ferdinand de Saussure, whose published lectures titled *A Course in General Linguistics* provided the foundation for the study of signs in French thought of the late 20th century. It is neither practical nor theoretically sound to reduce Saussure's ideas to a single thesis, but we will focus here on his system of linguistic differences between words, or signs, which was adopted and further explicated by Roland Barthes. According to Saussure, understanding is established by difference; practically speaking, we understand *cat* because *cat* is different from *dog*. The names are merely arbitrary, established by social and linguistic convention, rather than having any existential link to the object itself. Barthes extended this refusal to name to the differences between literature and painting. "Why not wipe out the difference between literature and painting," he asked, "in order to affirm more powerfully the plurality of 'texts'?" (55). The question is not as polemical as it may seem. Barthes raised it in the context of his analysis of Balzac's short story *Sarrasine, S/Z*, a treatise that set out to exhaustively identify the codes that comprise written work and the experience of reading it. Rather than seeking to overthrow two disciplines, textual studies and art history, he wanted to parse vision and experience as semiological.

Thus, both paint and word refer not to an external reality, but "from one code to another" (55). Reality is always framed by codes that determine what the writer or painter looks at—what they believe is worthy of vision and representation—and what mode of representation they select to describe that reality (such as the selection of word or image, but also of poetry, Cubistic canvas, film, etc., what Barthes terms a "code of the arts" [55]). As Hariman and Lucaites acknowledge in their discussion of Rosenthal's Iwo Jima image, the frame created by the boundaries of the photograph "marks the work as a special selection of reality that acquires greater intensity than the flow of experience before and after it" (366). As Andrea Kaston Tange demonstrates in this book, 19th-century middle-class homemakers selected socially coded home design items to represent their position in society. Quite literally, these objects conveyed the meaning of their lives. Rather than depict reality accurately, or event impressionistically, the creator assembles and arranges "blocks of meaning" so that the description becomes yet another meaning. Rather than reveal truth or provide understanding, the poem or the image offers yet another meaning. The import of Barthes' insights for the study of visual rhetoric is that the assembling of these "blocks of meaning" is a rhetorical act. Furthermore, Barthes reminds us to avoid seeking the transparent, definitional relationship between image and referent. While an image may index something exterior (that which is "real"), "it points but does not tell" (62).

For the rhetorician studying visual material, Barthes' work is significant in instructing us to continue following the chain of signifiers and connotations. *S/Z* alone is rife with words that reference fluidity, movement, and instability, words such as "layering," "agglomeration," "sequentiality," "dynamic," and "infinite thematics." Just as Peirce allowed for an infinite series of connotations in his concept of the interpretant, so also does Barthes' thesis allow for an infinite series of meanings built from blocks of text. "Visual *representation* gives way to visual *rhetoric* through subjectivity, voice, and contingency," comments Barbie Zelizer. With photojournalism, or with other representational media, we are able to project "altered ends" for the representations we see. This insertion of the spectator's desires for the future is like the tense in verbal discourse, as tense can locate a moment into the past (that which has already happened and cannot be changed; visual *representation*), the present (what

Zelizer terms the "as is"), or the future (the moment of possibility that Zelizer calls the "as if"). Rhetorically, "as if" has the greatest power because it directly involves the spectator and depends on the spectator's ability to forecast and manipulate contingencies in order to create a meaning.

This sophisticated reading between disciplines—between linguistics, rhetoric, and photojournalism—offers the next step to the Sister Arts Tradition as a bridge between disciplines. We must offer a caution, nonetheless. Certainly, the idea that verbal and visual modes of representation could be understood as symbolic practices, each with a signifying grammar, is a powerful argument for the founding of a visual rhetoric. Yet it denies the fact that verbal and visual representation work with particular media that also, in themselves, signify. A daub of paint is existentially different from a stitch with silk thread, and each has its own mode of conveying meaning. One of our projects as visual rhetoricians is to differentiate ourselves from semiology by studying material as rhetoric. What does the character of and texture of pencil on paper or a smooth and reflective wall with names etched into its face impart to the meaning that the spectator takes from the object?

VISUAL RHETORIC, AN INDISCIPLINE

In a commentary published in *Art Bulletin*, Mitchell explores the problems of a discipline that could be termed "visual culture studies." Primarily, Mitchell's concern is that visual culture is by its very nature interdisciplinary. In explicating the image through verbal media, scholars occupy two spaces of inquiry. "On the one hand," he writes, "visual culture looks like an 'outside' to art history, opening out of the larger field of vernacular images, media, and everyday visual practices in which a 'visual art' tradition is situated, and raising the question of the difference between high and low culture, visual art versus visual culture" ("Interdisciplinarity" 542). On the other hand, Mitchell continues, art history has always engaged issues of spectatorship, pleasure, and social relations, the interests of theorists of cultural studies. The positive outcome of this interdisciplinarity is that "visual culture is ... a site of convergence and conversation across disciplinary lines" (540). The more negative aspects are that more conventional disciplines argue to claim the new work, to institutionalize it as a concept or field of study, or argue for its insubstantiality, the very pluralism that gives it meaning diluting its impact.

Thus, Mitchell proposes a term that we feel describes the cross-disciplinary work of visual rhetoric, the mingling of verbal and visual emphases, and the exciting possibilities for inquiry. That term is *indiscipline*. Mitchell locates the "indiscipline" "at the inner and outer boundaries of disciplines," sites of inquiry characterized by "turbulence or incoherence": "If a discipline is a way of insuring the continuity of a set of collective practices (technical, social, professional, etc.), 'indiscipline' is a moment of breakage or rupture, when the continuity is broken and the practice comes into question" ("Interdisciplinarity" 541). The breakage in this sense occurs within the interdiscipline, when "the way of doing things" is restated so many times, in so many new ways, that there is no coherence—nor is there a way to return to a pre-critical moment prior to when two or more disciplines merged.

The type of paradigm shift that Mitchell captures with the term "indiscipline" is occurring at this very moment across the humanities. The previously unquestioned hegemony of verbal text is being challenged by what Mitchell labels the "pictorial turn" (*Picture Theory*)—a growing recognition of the ubiquity of images and of their importance in the dissemination and reception of information, ideas, and opinions—processes that lie at the heart of all rhetorical practices, social movements, and cultural institutions. In the past decade, many scholars have called for a collaborative venture, in essence for the *disciplining* of the study of visual phenomena into a new field, variously labeled visual rhetoric, visual culture studies, or "image studies" (Roy Fox). This proposed new field would bring together the work currently being accomplished by scholars in a wide variety of disciplines, including art theory, anthropology, rhetoric, cultural studies, psychology, and media studies. Barbara Stafford argues that the current situation, in which researchers and scholars in varied disciplines study the production, dissemination, and reception of images independently, is counterproductive, at best, and ultimately unsustainable:

> It seems infeasible, either intellectually or financially, to sustain multiple, linear specializations in art, craft, graphic, industrial, film, video, or media production and their separate histories. Instead, we need to forge an imaging field focused on transdisciplinary *problems* to which we bring a distinctive, irreducible, and highly visual expertise. (10)

Disciplines provide structures and conventional practices for supporting, disseminating, and responding to projects based on a common area of inquiry, and these structures and conventions can be highly productive by increasing efficiency, sharing ideas among scholars, and enhancing the credibility of individual studies as well as of the discipline as a whole. An important part of the work of any discipline is to develop common terminology, with fairly settled definitions of the terms that the discipline recognizes as important for doing its work. But disciplinary conventions also filter and constrain, and disciplines are defined by their boundaries—as much by what topics, questions, and practices are *not* accepted as part of the disciplinary discourse as by those that are. At this early point in the history of image studies, it may be too soon to settle on accepted practices, disciplinary conventions, and perhaps even on terminological definitions.

When we solicited contributions for this volume, we asked all of the contributors to think about and to express in their chapters their own definitions of

the term *visual rhetoric*. We deliberately did *not* set out to develop a single definition of visual rhetoric that we would try to persuade others to accept; rather,
we wanted to collect definitions from which individual scholars were working. We felt, here at the beginning of what may prove to be a renaissance of image studies, that collecting some of these definitions and allowing individuals
to demonstrate how their own ideas and assumptions about the term influence their work would provide more heuristic value than trying to settle on a
single definition.

Some of the contributors have answered our call very explicitly; others
have implied more than expressed their notions of the term *visual rhetoric*. But
all of them attempt to explicate and demonstrate methodologies for analyzing various types of visual texts. It is important, at this point in the history of
visual studies, to collect a wide range of such methods, examining the explicit
and implicit theoretical stances behind them, before disciplinary conventions
begin to restrict the kinds of work that disciplinary structures will reward.

In some ways, the contributors' responses indicate a surprising level of
agreement. At one level or another, every contributor rejects the notion that a
clear demarcation can be drawn between "visual" and "verbal" texts. In almost
every chapter, the reader will find some discussion of the ways in which the visual and the verbal bleed over into each other's territory. In popular film
(Blakesley), political cartoons (Edwards), captioned photographs (Finnegan),
needlepoint samplers (Goggin), advertisements (Hope), political campaign
films (Kendall & Strachan), statistical graphs (Kostelnick), and in some of
Blair's examples of "visual arguments," we see visual and verbal expression
working together in an effort to prompt a desired response from the audience.
Stroupe discusses this blending of the visual and the verbal explicitly in his discussion of "hybrid" literacies.

The chapters by Kaston Tange and by Dickinson and Maugh push the definition of visual rhetoric to include the study of constructed spaces, but even
here we see the importance of verbal text for a rhetorical process that seems, at
first glance, dominated by the visual. Dickinson and Maugh discuss the verbal
text on a Wild Oats store's display signs, text that explicitly points out the
global nature of the commercial enterprise, even while the visual and spatial
design of the store works to emphasize a sense of "locality." And Kaston
Tange examines the ways in which home design and images of home life in
Victorian culture reflected dominant ideologies, assumptions about which
were disseminated largely through written texts. Finally, Helmers' analysis of
the rhetorical nature of visual art points out the necessity of verbal discourse—in particular, the ways in which narrative discourse is used—to comprehend, to interpret, and to respond to works of an entirely visual medium.

Of course, others have argued before us that words and images most often,
perhaps inevitably, work together in persuasive discourse, and that a "visual
turn" in scholarly work in the humanities should not ignore the insights into

the primary influence of language on all human enterprise, including the dissemination of, interpretation of, and response to visual texts. James Elkins argues perhaps most explicitly and forcefully against any sharp demarcation between words and images, insisting that "the word–image opposition is ... demonstrably untrue" and persists largely because it "correspond(s) to institutional habits and needs" (84). In this volume, though, the contributors do not stop at arguing that visual and verbal modes of communication work together in complex ways; rather, they offer analyses of the workings of these interrelated modes in a wide variety of rhetorical situations.

A glance at the table of contents will demonstrate that the contributors to this volume analyze a wide variety of visual modes of communication. One of our aims, of course, was to demonstrate some of the many kinds of texts that could be considered instances of visual rhetoric. However, it is also important to note the wide variety of rhetorical situations in which these texts are operative, with their attendant variety of rhetorical methods, motives, and cultural assumptions. A hint at this variety can be gleaned merely by noting the different physical sites in which these texts are located—for example, political conventions, editorial pages, movie theatres, art museums, suburban food stores, government documents, as well as the Victorian drawing room and, as in Goggin's examination of needlepoint, orphanage schools in the 19th century. This wide range of texts, rhetorical situations, and sites of praxis supports our point that it may be premature to begin constructing the boundaries that would define a "discipline" of visual studies in the formal sense. Perhaps, at least for awhile, it would be more productive to continue pushing against existing disciplinary boundaries and to maintain the "indiscipline" status, continuing to question all current practices while developing new ones. This may be a romantic idea, and it may be impractical, as Stafford argues, to maintain this undisciplined stance for long, but it is, we believe, both necessary and desirable to maintain the current unsettled state of visual studies for at least the near future.

Perhaps the most useful possible outcome of a volume such as this—one that attempts to capture a small part of the wide range of work that is possible when a field begins to take seriously the study of images as important cultural and rhetorical forces—is that it makes explicit the seemingly infinite range of possibilities for those who are interested in studying rhetorical transactions of all kinds. It is this openness, this resistance to closure, that drew us to the field of rhetoric in the first place. And, as we hope the chapters in this volume demonstrate, every new turn in the study of rhetorical practices reveals yet more possibilities for study, for discussion, for wonder. The visual turn is just the latest of these, but it has revealed a seemingly inexhaustible supply of new questions, problems, and objects of study—so many that any one volume can contain only a tiny fraction of the possibilities. Knowing that one has barely touched on the range of possibilities in a vast new area of inquiry is humbling, but tremendously exciting. It is, perhaps, the best of all possible worlds.

WORKS CITED

Anderson, Benedict. *Imagined Communities: Reflections on the Origin and Spread of Nationalism*. 1e. London: Verso, 1983; 1991.

Bal, Mieke, and Norman Bryson. "Semiotics and Art History." *Art Bulletin* 73.2 (June 1991): 174–208.

Barber, Benjamin. *Jihad vs. McWorld*. New York Times, 1995.

Barthes, Roland. *S/Z: An Essay*. Trans. Richard Miller. New York: Farrar, Straus and Giroux, 1974.

Baty, S. Paige. *American Monroe: The Making of a Body Politic*. Berkeley: U of California P, 1995.

Berkman, Brenda. "Remarks of Lt. Brenda Berkman, FDNY at the National Women's Law Center's 2001 Awards Dinner, 'Celebrating the Many Roles of Women,' 14 November 2001." Women in the Fireservice, Inc. (WFSI). <http://www.wfsi.org/BerkNWLC.html>. 12 September 2002.

Calinescu, Matei. *Rereading*. New Haven: Yale UP, 1993.

Campbell, David. "Imaging the Real, Struggling for Meaning." *INFOinterventions*. 6 October 2001. <http://www.watsoninstitute.org/inforpeace/911/campbell_imaging.html>.

Clegg, Jeannine. "Flag-raising was 'shot in the arm,' The three firefighters who hauled up the flag." *The Record*. 14 September 2001. <http://www.groundzerospirit.org>. 19 September 2002.

Collins, Billy. "The Names." The Poetry and Literature Center of the Library of Congress. 6 September 2002.<http://www.loc.gov/poetry/names.html>.

De Lauretis, Teresa. *Alice Doesn't: Feminism, Semiotics, Cinema*. Bloomington: Indiana UP, 1983.

—. "The Violence of Rhetoric: Considerations on Representation and Gender." *Semiotica* 54.5 (1985): 11–31.

Derrida, Jacques. *Dissemination*. Chicago: U of Chicago P, 1981.

De Saussure, Ferdinand. *A Course in General Linguistics*. Trans. Roy Harris. London: Duckworth, 1983.

Elkins, James. *The Domain of Images*. Ithaca: Cornell UP, 1999.

Faigley, Lester. "Material Literacy and Visual Design." *Rhetorical Bodies*. Ed. Jack Selzer and Sharon Crowley. Madison: U Wisconsin P, 1999.

Floren, Terese M. "Too Far Back for Comfort." Women in the Fireservice, Inc. (WFSI). No date. <http://www.wfsi.org/Toofarback.html>.

Fox, Roy F. "Image Studies: An Interdisciplinary View." *Images in Language, Media, and Mind*. Ed. Roy F. Fox. Urbana, IL: National Council of Teachers of English, 1994. 3–20.

Franklin. Thomas E. "Getting the Photo of a Lifetime." *The Record*. 13 September 2001. <http://www.groundzerospirit.org>.

—. "Sept. 11, Not a Photograph, Changed My Life." *North Jersey.com*. 11 September 2002. <http://www.northjersey.com>.

Gates, Henry Louis. *The Signifying Monkey: A Theory of Afro-American Literary Criticism*. New York: Oxford UP, 1988.

Genette, Gerard. *Palimpsests: Literature in the Second Degree*. Trans. Channa Newman and Claude Doubinsky. Lincoln: U Nebraska P, 1997.

Hariman, Robert, and John Lucaites. "Performing Civic Identity: The Iconic Photograph of the Flag Raising on Iwo Jima." *Quarterly Journal of Speech* 88.4 (November 2002): 363–392.

Lejeune, Philippe. *On Autobiography*. Trans. Katherine Leary. Minneapolis: U of Minnesota P, 1989.

Lipking, Lawrence. "Quick Poetic Eyes: Another Look at Literary Pictorialism." *Articulate Images: The Sister Arts from Hogarth to Tennyson* Ed. Richard Wendorf. Minneapolis: U of Minnesota P, 1983. 3–25.

Locke, John. *An Essay Concerning Human Understanding.* Ed. Roger Woolhouse. New York: Penguin Books, 1997.

Marling, Karal Ann, and John Wetenhall. *Iwo Jima: Monuments, Memories, and the American Hero.* Cambridge: Harvard UP, 1991.

Mitchell, W. J. T. "Diagrammatology." *Critical Inquiry* 7.3 (Spring 1981): 622–633.

—. "Interdisciplinarity and Visual Culture." *Art Bulletin* 70.4 (1995): 540–544.

—. *Picture Theory: Essays on Verbal and Visual Representation.* Chicago: U of Chicago P, 1994.

—. "Spatial Form in Literature: Toward a General Theory." *The Language of Images.* Ed. W. J. T. Mitchell. Chicago: U of Chicago P, 1980. 271–99.

Peirce, Charles Sanders. *Charles S. Peirce: The Essential Writings.* Ed. Edward C. Moore. New York: Harper, 1972.

Stafford, Barbara Maria. *Good Looking: Essays on the Virtue of Images.* Cambridge, MA: MIT Press, 1997.

Szentmiklosy, Chris. "Photographer Discusses Famous Sept. 11 Photo." *The Mosaic.* <http://northjersey.com>.

Wibben, Annick T. R. "9.11: Images, Imaging, Imagination." *INFOinterventions.* 6 October 2001. <http://www.watsoninstitute.org/inforpeace/911/new/article.cfm?id=25>.

Williams, Jodi. Letter to the Editor. *Newsweek.* 1 October 2001.

Willing, Linda. *Beyond Ground Zero.* Women in the Fireservice, Inc. (WFSI). No date. <http://www.wfsi.org/Berkman2.html>. 19 September 2002.

Winter, Jay, and Emmanuel Sivan. *War and Remembrance in the Twentieth Century.* Cambridge UP, 1999.

Zelizer, Barbie. "The As If of Visual Rhetoric." Paper delivered at Visual Rhetoric, Bloomington, IN, 6 Sept. 2001.

CHAPTER ONE

The Psychology of Rhetorical Images

Charles A. Hill

The range of visual elements that could be considered rhetorical is vast, as evidenced by the many types of visuals that are examined and analyzed in the chapters of this volume. The rhetorical analysis of visuals could be extended even further, to include types not directly addressed in this volume, including landscapes and public memorials. It is exciting and important that the field of rhetoric is taking account of so many different types of visuals, partly because doing so helps us understand how rhetorical elements work in forms of expression that are not obviously and explicitly persuasive. For my purposes in this chapter, I will concentrate on representational images—visuals that are clearly designed to represent a recognizable person, object, or situation— while recognizing that such images constitute only a subset of the types of visual elements that could be productively examined as rhetorical elements.

Most rhetorical studies of images, including many of the ones in this volume, focus on a specific genre, medium, method of distribution, or rhetorical purpose for which images are often used. Most of the insights now available to us about the rhetorical nature of images have come from these types of studies. In this chapter, though, I intend to approach the rhetorical study of images from a slightly different direction. I begin with a question that is both broad and simple in its formulation: How, exactly, do images persuade? In other words, how do representational images work to influence the beliefs, attitudes, opinions—and sometimes actions—of those who view them? To be sure, many practitioners (e.g., advertisers, political consultants, and other professional persuaders) instantiate, in their daily practice, a variety of principles about how to take best advantage of the persuasive power of representational images. Any good undergraduate course in marketing, advertising, or public relations includes some discussion of specific methods for using images to influence viewers' opinions, beliefs, and actions. These principles and methods are based mostly on past practice, and sometimes on experimental studies that demonstrate the relative effects of a number of variables on the persuasiveness of visual appeals. But a full theoretical treatment of visual persuasion will involve not only identifying individual variables that appear to strengthen visual appeals in certain situations, but also attempts to explicate the processes by which images exert their rhetorical influences.

Cultural studies of visual rhetoric constitute one type of attempt to understand how visual appeals operate. In these types of studies, scholars analyze the ways in which culturally shared values and assumptions are utilized in persuasive communication, and how these shared values and assumptions influence viewers' responses to mass-produced images. The psychological approach that I take in this chapter is not meant to replace or to compete with cultural or textual studies, but merely to address the phenomenon from a different perspective. Neither is it meant to denote a set of processes that are entirely distinct and separate from the cultural and social processes that are explored so well in some of the other chapters in this volume, for psychological processes and cultural practices are inextricably linked. At the very least, cognitive processes may be said to be the mechanisms through which the influences of culture operate. Therefore, although it may be useful to explicate them separately, psychological and cultural influences on individual response and action are not, in reality, distinct and separate. While I take psychological processes as my starting point for this discussion, I also discuss the influence of shared cultural values in an attempt to demonstrate how the cultural and psychological work together in the persuasive process. Ultimately, a comprehensive theory of visual persuasion will need to incorporate the insights gathered from a variety of viewpoints and methodologies, including cultural, psychological, and textual studies, and attempt to explicate how the mechanisms identified by these different methodologies work together in the production of, reception of, and response to persuasive images.

To ask how images work to influence viewers' beliefs, attitudes, and opinions is ultimately to ask about the very nature of images and about how people respond to them. Conventional wisdom says that representational images tend to prompt emotional reactions and that, once the viewer's emotions are excited, they tend to override his or her rational faculties, resulting in a response that is unreflective and irrational. Psychological research suggests that this conventional explanation of the rhetorical power of images is broadly accurate in outline, though inadequate for explaining how persuasive images work.

More importantly, the simple description of the power of rhetorical images as "emotional" has contributed directly to the relative neglect of such images by the fields of rhetoric and argumentation, a neglect that has only recently begun to be corrected. Argumentation scholars, especially, have always been concerned not just with describing the ways that persuasion can occur, but also with discovering and promoting methods of persuasion that are epistemically useful and valid (van Eemeren 38). If images, by their nature, prompt irrational and unreflective responses, then they are best avoided rather than studied closely, and they certainly have no place in the classroom, where the goal is to help students develop useful and sound reasoning habits.

Until recently, the scholar interested in the serious study of rhetorical images faced a problem. If one accepted the description of visual input as being largely "emotional" in nature, then rhetorical visuals would be largely dismissed as not worthy of serious study. The interested scholar would then be faced with the task of explaining that people respond to visuals in much the same way as they respond to verbal arguments, an assertion that would deny much of the psychological research into persuasive images, not to mention the everyday experience of nearly everyone who deals with images in persuasive contexts. (This perceived need has also contributed to the adoption of linguistic terms for the study of images in an attempt to capture for images some of the cachet that has largely been reserved for verbal elements, a tendency which has, I believe, led to some misleading assertions about the nature of visual communication.) Only recently, now that simple binary distinctions such as "emotional vs. rational" have been problematized in the theoretical literature and demonstrated as invalid by much of the empirical research into cognitive and neurological processes, has it become acceptable to treat rhetorical images as objects worthy of serious study without feeling the need to deny their largely emotional nature.

IMAGES AND RHETORICAL PRESENCE

As argued above, simply applying methods and concepts designed specifically for verbal language to persuasive images is not the most productive or accurate way to develop a methodology for the study of visual rhetoric; doing so often results in misleading (or sometimes simply useless) assertions about the ways in which persuasive images work. However, many rhetorical concepts already exist that were not developed exclusively for the study of verbal elements, and it makes sense to begin a study of rhetorical images by mining these concepts to see what insights they may offer that could be applied to such images. One such concept that seems especially applicable to the study of images is the concept of *presence* as discussed by Chaim Perelman and Lucie Olbrechts-Tyteca (*The New Rhetoric* 115–120). Perelman and Olbrechts-Tyteca recognize that most rhetorical situations are complex, and often involve two or more advocates stating their respective cases, attempting to win adherence from audience members who are simply trying to determine what they should believe and how they should feel about the issue at hand. In many of these situations, the audience is faced with a bewildering array of elements to consider—elements that may include statistics, charts and graphs, anecdotes and other narratives, items of physical evidence, and abstract ethical and philosophical arguments. Each of these elements can be potentially important for convincing audience members to accept a particular viewpoint, but the individual rhetor is faced with the danger that any particular element may be forgotten or get drowned out in a sea of information, anecdote, and argument. To counteract this danger, a good rhetor will attempt to prompt audience members to focus their attention on the specific elements that the rhetor thinks will most benefit his or her case.

Convincing people to change their minds or to take a stand, especially on important policy issues, can be exceedingly difficult for several reasons. For example, many controversial issues are very complex, and arguments about such issues may involve assertions about facts and principles that not every novice audience member may feel confident to evaluate. We also know that factors external to the argument can greatly influence the effectiveness of any rhetorical appeal. For instance, audience members will often be influenced by the tone in which the arguments are expressed and by various traits of the arguers that might influence judgments about their credibility and sincerity. And the effectiveness of any particular appeal on any complex issue will be greatly affected by how much the appeal supports or conflicts with the beliefs, values, and assumptions that the audience members already hold about relevant topics. Many psychological studies of persuasion have found that, when faced with opposing verbal arguments, a reader or listener will usually accept the one that reflects or reinforces his or her already-held opinions and assumptions (see, for example, Evans; Johnson-Laird and Byrne; Kuhn; Lau, Smith, and Fiske; Voss et al.). People often accept and come to defend a particular viewpoint, not because they have carefully thought through and evaluated the available alternatives, but because they identify with other people holding the same position (Burke) or because challenging or denying the position would challenge their own self-concept (Cederblom). With all of these factors coming into play, it is easy to see that any particular appeal, no matter how logically valid or relevant, may become insufficient, almost even irrelevant to the success of the larger argument.

The challenge for a rhetor defending any particular position or forwarding any particular proposal is to make the elements in the situation that are supportive of that position or proposal stand out for the audience members, to make these elements more salient and memorable. This can be done partly by the simple act of explicitly naming and pointing out those elements: "By the very fact of selecting certain elements and presenting them to the audience, their importance and pertinency to the discussion are implied. Indeed, such a choice endows these elements with a presence" (Perelman and Olbrechts-Tyteca 116).

Presence, as the term is used by Perelman and Olbrechts-Tyteca, refers to the extent to which an object or concept is foremost in the consciousness of the audience members. Skillful rhetors attempt to increase the presence of elements in the rhetorical situation that are favorable to their claim because they know that elements with enhanced presence will have a greater influence over the audience's attitudes and beliefs. But presence is not a binary phenomenon;

the rhetor's goal is not merely to create some presence where before there was none, but rather to endow the elements in the situation that are favorable to the rhetor's case with as much presence as possible. In fact, the rhetor's ultimate goal, whenever possible, is to make the relevant object, concept or value fill the audience's entire "field of consciousness" (118). In other words, when particular elements are given enough presence, they can crowd out other considerations from the viewer's mind, regardless of the logical force or relevance of those other considerations. The rhetor's hope is that this process will prompt audience members to accept his or her claim based on one or two pieces of powerful, vivid evidence, and not stop to think about issues such as the relevance or actual importance of the evidence, or about what other arguments and opinions should be brought into the equation and weighed before making a decision.

Several verbal forms can be used to increase the presence of an object, idea, or person, but the desired element receives the greatest amount of presence from being directly perceived; an object or person is most present to us when we can see it directly (117).[1] (The most effective way to increase an object's rhetorical presence is to make it physically present—to actually bring it into the room—but, of course, this is often not possible.) The phenomenon of *presence* is inherently linked to visual perception. It has often been remarked that a picture of one starving child is more persuasively powerful than statistics citing the starvation of millions. In Perelman and Olbrecht-Tyteca's terms, the one child depicted in a photograph becomes undeniably more "present" to us, whereas the million individual children whose tragedy and suffering are summed up in a statistic are not. Although we can all recognize this phenomenon from our own experiences, it is difficult to explain why this should be so.

If we assume that we are talking mostly about photographic images, then we could say that the suffering portrayed in the photograph carries more epistemic force than a verbal description because the existence of the photograph proves the existence of its subject. As Barthes points out, a photograph is, by definition, a captured reflection of an object or person that actually exists or that existed at one time, so the photograph at least proves the existence of the person or object, no matter how much the circumstances surrounding that existence may be manipulated in the darkroom. (Let us bracket, for the time being, any discussion of the new digital image manipulation techniques that make such an assertion far from certain.) In Peirce's terms (239–240), a photograph is an "index" (as opposed to the other types of signs, "icons" and "symbols"). Unlike icons and symbols, indexical signs would not exist if their objects did not exist, so the very existence of the sign proves that its object also existed. (Other indexical signs include bullet holes and footprints.) Messaris argues that the indexical aspect of photographs and of videotaped evidence helps define the ways in which people respond to them.

Such an argument assumes that people reflect on the nature of evidence to an extent that would prompt a line of reasoning something like this: "The starving child depicted in the photograph must be real, while the statistics could be inaccurate, misleading, or even made up. Therefore, it is rational to place more weight on the one 'real' child in the photograph." But empirical evidence, as well as everyday experience, suggests that powerful images do not prompt such rational reflection. Besides, we do not really disbelieve that the children in the statistics exist; yet somehow, the child in the photograph seems more "real" to us, and the photograph is much more likely to prompt a visceral, emotional response.

My point here is supported by the fact that visceral reactions to visual input are not limited to photographic images. In fact, rhetorical presence does not necessarily rely on actual seeing. In many rhetorical situations, displaying the actual object, person, or event under discussion—or a representational image of it—is not practical. In these situations, Perelman and Olbrechts-Tyteca advise the rhetor to use concrete, descriptive words and specific terms in their verbal arguments, because doing so helps the audience members construct a mental image of the object or event being depicted: "The more specific the terms, the sharper the image they conjure up, and, conversely, the more general the terms, the weaker the image" (147). When direct visual perception of the desired element is not feasible, then using concrete language to help the reader or listener construct a mental image can be quite effective for enhancing the presence of the favorable rhetorical element. And words are symbolic, not indexical—they neither rely on nor prove the actual existence of the object, person, or situation that they purport to represent.

THE PSYCHOLOGY OF RHETORICAL IMAGES: HOW VISUALS WORK TO PERSUADE

Psychological studies have confirmed the common assumption that, in general terms, images tend to elicit more emotional responses while print messages tend to elicit more analytic responses (Chaudhuri and Buck). But this easy identification of the visual with the emotional response and the verbal with rational responses is clearly too simplistic. Some visual appeals are highly rational (e.g., bar graphs, line graphs and other visuals designed to demonstrate statistical relationships). And psychological studies demonstrate that words can also elicit highly emotional responses. In particular, these studies support Perelman and Olbrechts-Tyteca's contention that imagistic and concrete words prompt emotional responses more than non-concrete and non-visual words (Campos, Marcos, & Gonzales). We commonly speak of readers constructing a "mental image" while reading a narrative or descriptive text, and neurological studies show that this occurs quite literally—i.e., reading a descriptive text can actually activate the same parts of the brain used to process visual images (Howard et al.; Rebotier; Sinatra). These mental images can result in emotional responses similar to those that are prompted by the viewing of actual pictures.

Because imagistic language can prompt mental imaging and therefore elicit emotional responses, it seems likely that using such language would increase the rhetorical effectiveness of the message. The relationship between the creation of mental images through reading text and the process of developing or revising one's beliefs and attitudes based on these mental images has been studied by psychologists as the concept of *vividness*. In psychological studies, *vivid information* is identified as information that is emotionally interesting and concrete (Nisbett and Ross). (Of course, describing vivid information as "emotional" is a bit of a tautology, because one of the questions that psychologists study is whether such information prompts more emotional responses than non-vivid information.) *Vivid information* takes the form of concrete and imagistic language, personal narratives, pictures, or first-hand experience. Vividness is a matter of degree, of course, but the most vivid type of information would be an actual experience (being attacked, being involved in an accident, etc.), and the least vivid type of information would be information that one is exposed to by reading or listening to abstract, impersonal language and statistics. A comprehensive continuum of vividness might look something like this:

Most Vivid Information	actual experience
	moving images with sound
	static photograph
	realistic painting
	line drawing
	narrative, descriptive account
	descriptive account
	abstract, impersonal analysis
Least Vivid Information	statistics

Several experiments have demonstrated, not surprisingly, that vivid information tends to prompt more emotional reactions than non-vivid, abstract information. (Scientists are allowed to take nothing for granted, so psychologists often seem compelled to experimentally test even rather obvious assertions.) In other words, the more vivid the information, the more likely it is that the information will prompt an emotional response from the receiver (Campos et al.). Vivid information also seems to be more persuasive than non-vivid information. In experiments, pictures have been demonstrated to be more persuasive than text and "personal case stories" built on personal narrative to be more persuasive than "abstract impersonal information"

(Block and Keller). In a study using a simulated jury trial, the participants tended to vote in favor of the disputant who presented his or her case using vivid (i.e., image-evoking) language (Wilson, Northcraft, and Neale).

Baesler points out that, although many studies have shown vivid evidence to be more persuasive than non-vivid information, several other studies have found no persuasive advantage for vividness. In fact, Frey and Eagly found that vivid text may be even less persuasive than non-vivid text under some circumstances. Such inconsistent results are not uncommon in persuasion research (as a glance through O'Keefe's review of the research makes clear), and such inconsistencies usually mean that more complex research designs are needed, designs that attempt to ferret out some of the dizzyingly complex relationships between the many factors that help to make up any rhetorical situation. The results of a study that utilized a more complex design than most (Smith and Shaffer) suggest that vivid language makes a persuasive message easier to comprehend and more likely to be remembered, but only if the vivid elements are clearly and explicitly relevant to the message itself. If the vivid images are not clearly relevant to the claim being made and to the particular argument being forwarded, then the images may make the argument more difficult to process and to remember by distracting the viewer from the argument being presented. And arguments that are incomprehensible or not remembered have no chance to influence a recipient's opinions or beliefs.

Overall, the more sophisticated research designs tend to support the notion that vividness enhances persuasiveness. Vividness itself, like any single persuasive trait, will not make a bad argument convincing, but it will, if properly employed, enhance the persuasiveness of a reasonably strong position. And operationally speaking, vividness is almost a direct synonym for visualization, whether one is creating mental images through the use of concrete language or actually presenting a visual image to a viewer.

Vividness, emotional response, and persuasion have all been shown to correlate with each other (Chaudhuri and Buck), but just asserting this fact does not explain *why* imagistic language and actual images are more persuasive than abstract verbal arguments, and it does not explain the role of emotions in this process. Researchers have proposed several models to try to explain exactly how this relationship between vividness, emotional responses, and persuasion works in the mind. For example, some psychological theories of persuasion distinguish between two types of cognitive processing: "systematic processing," which is "contemplative, analytic, and responsive to the argumentative quality of the message," and "heuristic processing," which "occurs whenever an individual relies on some shortcut decision-making rule to construct an attitude toward the persuasive advocacy" (Dillard and Peck 462). The very language that Dillard and Peck use to describe these two cognitive strategies indicates that they place a higher value on systematic processing. Certainly, instructors of argumentation would prefer their students to be "contemplative" and "analytic" when making a decision on a controversial issue and to attend to "the argumentative quality of the message" when deciding whether or not to accept the arguer's claim, and we would be disappointed (though not surprised) to find that our students were instead relying on "some shortcut decision-making rule" (462). Nevertheless, people tend to choose a heuristic processing strategy when one is available because it is faster than systematic processing and requires less cognitive work.

It is likely that verbal text, because of its analytic nature (being made up of discrete meaningful units) and because it is apprehended relatively slowly over time, is more likely to prompt systematic processing, while images, which are comprehended wholistically and almost instantaneously, tend to prompt heuristic processing. Therefore, these psychological models might explain why vivid images tend to overpower verbal arguments in a decision among opposing or controversial claims. In short, because our minds prefer to take the fastest and easiest route to making a decision, and because images or imagistic texts offer shortcuts toward the endpoint of making a decision, then images (or, to a lesser extent, imagistic, concrete language) will prompt the viewer to make a relatively quick decision, largely ignoring the more analytical, abstract information available in verbal form.

Vivid Information and Emotions

But using terms like *heuristic processing* almost seems like a strategy to avoid discussing the difficult concept of *emotions*. And saying that people "choose" or tend to "prefer" to make decisions based on their emotional responses (if that is, indeed, what heuristic processing refers to) also seems misleading, since powerful, visceral responses to emotional images and vivid stories hardly seem like a choice that one has made. In short, although descriptions of cognitive laziness and a preference for cognitive shortcuts might be useful for helping to explain how images affect us, a full understanding of the rhetorical power of images necessitates a discussion of emotion. Vivid images are valued by rhetors and derogated by some argumentation theorists because they tend to elicit strong emotions, and we do not need to perform psychological experiments to know that strong emotions will often overcome and even inhibit analytical thinking.

Many psychologists consider emotions to be a cognitive recognition of and response to a physiological reaction to some external stimulus (Dillard and Peck). In other words, when we recognize (perhaps on some preconscious level) a potential danger, that recognition results in a range of physiological responses (our hair standing up on end, increased adrenaline flow, etc.). Our brain recognizes these responses and interprets them in a way that we recognize and label as an *emotion* (e.g., anger, fear, sadness). According to some theories, then, an emotion is little more than a recognition of these physiological responses (de Sousa 40, 51). (De Sousa recounts William James' famous dictum, "We do not weep because we are sad, but rather we are sad because we weep.") These physical responses that we call emotions are generally considered to be evolutionary adaptations that help us deal quickly and decisively with dangerous situations.[2]

It's relatively easy to understand how some of the more basic emotions (e.g., fear, anger) might be evolutionarily designed to help us deal with sudden potential dangers. Emotions such as these arise quickly and claim all of our attention; it is virtually impossible to ignore them or, in many cases, to even think about other matters until these emotions have been resolved. If the purpose of the emotional response is, as some psychologists believe, to direct our attention to a nearby danger, then it makes sense that we would be programmed to react quickly and decisively, without taking the time to analyze the situation and evaluate all of the information that might be potentially relevant. (By the time we accomplished such an analysis, it might be too late to eliminate or avoid the danger.)

When we hear or read a description of a far-away danger (far away in either location or time or both), then we have the luxury of taking our time in deciding whether or how to act. But when we are exposed to visual information, our body reacts much as it would if the danger represented in the image were actually present. Our evolutionary response kicks in, and we are prompted to make a quick decision and to take action without an extensive amount of analysis. In evolutionary terms, the existence of realistic representational images has been a relatively recent development, so the tendency to respond differently to emotional stimuli that are clearly representational images—and therefore posing no immediate danger—rather than actual, nearby dangers has not yet developed.

Although the primal emotions may be a result of an evolutionary response to personal danger, the specific stimuli that trigger these emotions can be personally and culturally conditioned. For example, fear is perhaps the most primal (and, evolutionarily speaking, the most useful) emotion of all. But the specific stimuli that trigger fear (i.e., what one is actually afraid of) will vary widely across cultures and even across individuals within a culture. As Patricia Greenspan puts it, emotions tend to "spill over and to fix on objects resembling their appropriate objects in incidental ways" (18), resulting in some highly idiosyncratic fear responses. (I know several people who report being deathly afraid of circus clowns.)

Evolution can explain the existence of the more basic emotions, but it seems clear that powerful cultural forces help to define such complex emotional responses as guilt, love, and envy, and even more so when we consider even more complex concepts, such as *nationalism* and *prejudice*—concepts that are based on conscious reasoning of a sort, but that also rely on emotional responses for their power and that, I would argue, are largely defined by their attendant emotions. (Similarly, there are certainly denotative definitions of concepts such as *motherhood* and *freedom*, but definitions that do not include a consideration of the emotional responses culturally bound to such words cannot fully describe what they *mean* to us.)

These concepts, which we might call cultural values, are continually exploited in persuasive discourse for the emotional weight they contain. In many persuasive appeals that use images, the images elicit emotions largely because these images instantiate one of these values, and evoking one of these cultural constructs causes the emotions that are linked to it to be instantiated. Because of the evolutionary origin of emotional responses (as responses to signs of immediate danger), those of us who have internalized the value are prompted to respond instantaneously and without the benefit of a sustained rational analysis, even though the emotional complex we are responding to is culturally determined.

Professional persuaders—politicians, attorneys, marketing experts, etc.—exploit the linkage between emotions, values, and particular images by creating associations between those images and abstract values that the persuader wishes to make more present to the audience. We commonly say that a waving flag can stir "feelings of patriotism." However, *patriotism* is an abstract and complex concept that I am calling a "value," not a feeling. In actuality, a three-way relationship is being brought to bear, between the image (the flag), the value of patriotism, and the emotions that are schematically linked to that value. So an emotional reaction can be prompted even by abstract symbols of complex concepts. Once the association between a particular image and a value is created and internalized, the image becomes a symbol for the abstract value and can be used to trigger its associated emotions. This helps explain the immense amount of emotional attachment that many Americans have with the American flag, an attachment that has even led to attempts to make desecration of the flag a federal crime—and that has made the *Ground Zero Spirit* photograph the dominant symbol of the 9/11 tragedy.

Building Connections: The Transfer of Emotions

Discussions of rhetorical presence do not generally take into account psychological research on vividness and emotion, and psychological research reports do not mention the work of Perelman and Olbrechts-Tyteca. But both rhetorical theorists and psychologists studying the process of persuasion are essentially addressing the same questions, attempting to explain why certain types of assertions tend to have extraordinary persuasive power in a rhetorical situation, sometimes to the point of crowding out other, seemingly relevant and important information. No matter which methodology or theoretical lens they apply to this phenomenon, scholars seem to agree on two things. First, persuasive elements that instantiate strong emotions in the audience tend to have an extraordinary amount of persuasive power. Second, this phenomenon seems to be related to visual perception. Information that is expressed either in visual form or in a verbal form that promotes the construction of mental images is more likely to instantiate these emotions and to be given additional persuasive weight.

But using images to persuade is not, of course, as simple as showing the audience an image and reaping the benefits that result. In fact, Kjeldsen argues that the persuasive power of vivid images is shortlived, and is not really effective for convincing someone to change his or her beliefs over the long term. Surely there are situations in which someone succumbs to an emotional appeal, only to have his or her newfound conviction fade as the triggered emotions fade. In other words, an emotional appeal will often result in a new conviction or acceptance of a controversial claim only so long as the triggered emotions last. For many persuasive purposes, this will render an emotional appeal useless and may even result in a backlash if the audience member later begins to feel that he or she has been emotionally manipulated.

But many persuasive messages are part of long-term persuasive strategies; the most obvious examples are political and advertising campaigns. The producers of such campaigns may have no expectation that any particular message will convince the audience members to vote for the desired candidate or to buy the product being sold. Instead, they expect that the series of messages will work together, constructing an overall image and set of schematic relations that will convince the audience member to take the desired action. The objective in such campaigns is not to prompt a powerful temporary response, but to build up, over time, a schematic connection between the product or candidate and a set of positive values that will prompt the reader to think favorably of the product. The overall goal is to prompt members of the target audience to develop positive feelings toward the product or the candidate (and a political candidate is, in essence, the "product" that a political campaign attempts to sell). This can be accomplished by continually displaying visual associations between the product and some object or symbol that is already schematically tied to a positive value (thereby taking advantage of the emotional responses that are already associated with that value).

For example, an insurance company may include the famous picture of marines raising the flag on Iwo Jima in its promotional literature, in the hope that the image and the emotions that it evokes in the viewer will become associated with the insurance company. As Kenneth Burke points out, using the image allows the company to appropriate these emotions and values without having to explicitly argue for their relevance (87). Since the relationship between the insurance company and the attitudes and feelings associated with the image is not stated, there is no explicit argument to be refuted, and the implied connections are not likely to be questioned or challenged. (In chapter 2 of this volume, Anthony Blair makes a similar point in his discussion of the

Pepsi commercial "with the giggling children and frolicking puppies.") Such connections can be developed through verbal argument, especially through the use of concrete visual language, but using actual images (which increases the level of *vividness* and, therefore, *presence*) is almost universally considered by professional persuaders to be advantageous when it is feasible to do so.

What makes such identifications insidious is precisely the fact that we usually don't think about them. Roy Fox claims that advertisers generally don't want to *persuade* people to buy their products, because persuasion implies that the audience has given the issue some thought and come to a conscious decision. Instead, advertisers want to *transform* people. They want to compel people to buy a product without even knowing why they're buying it—as a visceral response to a stimulus, not as a conscious decision. And this is best done through images.

This description of the development of an automated, unthinking response sounds suspiciously like classical conditioning, in which animals are trained through repetition to associate an emotional or autonomic response to an initially unrelated stimulus. Unflattering images of Pavlov's dogs salivating at the sound of a bell come to mind, and many of us would no doubt like to think that we are not so easily manipulated. Nevertheless, classical conditioning has been shown to work in humans, and research with advertisements has demonstrated the phenomenon that psychologists call *affect transfer*, wherein an emotional response from an unrelated object or event is transferred to the product being sold, simply by showing an image of the product, followed by an image of the emotional object or event, and repeating the procedure many times (Kim and Allen). Again, what bothers many of us about this procedure is that our attitudes, opinions, and even our actions are influenced without any conscious processing on our part. In fact, most people are probably convinced that such manipulations do not work on them. But advertisers and political consultants know otherwise.

Using images to develop connections between initially unrelated concepts does not necessarily involve the use of emotional subject matter (Kim and Allen), and images can even be used to prompt sustained, analytical thinking (Scott). Images, like verbal text, can be used to prompt an immediate, visceral response, to develop cognitive (though largely unconscious) connections over a sustained period of time, or to prompt conscious analytical thought. This is not to say that there is no meaningful distinction between the rhetorical use and cognitive processing of images and verbal text—far from it. Rather, although verbal discourse can be used to prompt listeners and readers to create "mental images," to instantiate values and stir up strong emotions, actual images tend to be more efficient forms for accomplishing these goals. This is what excites professional persuaders and frightens many academic scholars about rhetorical images.

But rather than continuing to avoid consideration of rhetorical images, we must come to terms with them. By applying relevant theoretical concepts and psychological research to the study of persuasive images, we can learn more about how and why images are so rhetorically effective. Perhaps more important, we may learn how to use images to prompt sustained reflective thinking instead of using them to discourage it. Simply avoiding the study of rhetorical images is not only impractical (because they are so ubiquitous), but doing so would, in effect, constitute an effort to banish emotional and aesthetic concerns from the study of rhetoric and communication.

Rhetorical images are ubiquitous, powerful, and important. We need to embrace them, not only as scholars, but also as educators, and teach students to use them effectively and responsibly. Doing so does not require us to abandon our intellectual values, but perhaps to re-examine them a little, to reflect on the assumptions behind them, and perhaps to express and apply those values and assumptions a bit more carefully and thoughtfully.

NOTES

1. Discussing presence as a matter of holding up objects to look at or of prompting listeners or readers to construct a "mental image" may make it seem as if presence applies only to actual physical objects or people. However, presence can also be imbued in abstract ideas or values, either by explicitly invoking them or by creating a relationship between the idea or value and a concrete image or object, as I discuss later in this chapter.
2. See Ronald de Sousa, *The Rationality of Emotion*, for a description and critique of the physiological theory of emotion. De Sousa argues that emotions are rational more so than physiological constructs. My own view is that the range of constructs that we classify as *emotions*—everything from panic and rage to envy and nostalgia—cannot be explained by any one set of processes. There may be some common mechanisms involved in all types of emotions, but feelings of nostalgia or envy over another's material wealth are clearly more culturally defined than the more primal moment of panic that might be triggered by the sight of a snake in one's path while walking in the woods. Yet we typically label all of these responses as different types of emotions.

WORKS CITED

Baesler, E. James. "Persuasive Effects of Story and Statistical Evidence." *Argumentation and Advocacy* 33 (1997): 170–175.

Barthes, Roland. *Camera Lucida: Reflections on Photography*. Trans. Richard Howard. New York: Hill and Wang, 1981.

Block, Lauren G., and Punam Anand Keller. "Effects of Self-Efficacy and Vividness on the Persuasiveness of Health Communications." *Journal of Consumer Psychology* 6 (1997): 31–54.

Burke, Kenneth. *A Rhetoric of Motives*. Berkeley, CA: U of California P, 1969.

Campos, Alfredo, Jose Luis Marcos, and Maria Angeles Gonzales. "Emotionality of Words as Related to Vividness of Imagery and Concreteness." *Perceptual and Motor Skills* 88 (1999): 1135–1140.

Cederblom, J. "Willingness to Reason and the Identification of the Self." *Thinking, Reasoning, and Writing.* Ed. E. P. Maimon, B. F. Nodine, and F. W. O'Connor. New York: Longman, 1989: 147–159.

Chaudhuri, Arjun, and Ross Buck. "Media Differences in Rational and Emotional Responses to Advertising." *Journal of Broadcasting and Electronic Media* 39 (1995): 109–125.

De Sousa, Ronald. *The Rationality of Emotion.* Cambridge, MA: MIT P, 1987.

Dillard, James Price, and Eugenia Peck. "Affect and Persuasion: Emotional Responses to Public Service Announcements." *Communication Research* 27 (2000): 461–495.

Evans, Jonathan St. B. T. *Bias in Human Reasoning: Causes and Consequences.* Hillsdale, NJ: Lawrence Erlbaum Associates, 1989.

Fox, Roy F. "Where We Live." *Images in Language, Media, and Mind.* Ed. Roy Fox. Urbana, IL: National Council of Teachers of English, 1994: 69–91.

Frey, Kurt P., and Alice H. Eagly. "Vividness Can Undermine the Persuasiveness of Messages." *Journal of Personality and Social Psychology* 65 (1993): 32–44.

Greenspan, Patricia S. *Emotions and Reasons: An Inquiry into Emotional Justification.* New York: Routledge, 1988.

Howard, Robert, et al. "Seeing Visual Hallucinations with Functional Magnetic Resonance Imaging." *Dementia and Geriatric Cognitive Disorders* 8 (1997): 73–77.

Johnson-Laird, P. N., and R. M. J. Byrne. *Deduction.* Hillsdale, NJ: Lawrence Erlbaum Associates, 1991.

Kim, John, and Chris T. Allen. "An Investigation of the Mediational Mechanisms Underlying Attitudinal Conditioning." *JMR: Journal of Marketing Research* 33 (1996): 318–328.

Kjeldsen, Jens E. "Visual Rhetoric—From Elocutio to Inventio." *Proceedings of the Fourth International Conference of the International Society for the Study of Argumentation* (June 16–19, 1998). Ed. Frans H. van Eemeren, Rob Grootendorst, J. Anthony Blair, and Charles A. Willard. Amsterdam: SIC SAT, 1999. 455–460.

Kuhn, D. *The Skills of Argument.* Cambridge: Cambridge UP, 1991.

Lau, R. R., R. A. Smith, and S. T. Fiske. "Political Beliefs, Policy Interpretations, and Political Persuasion." *Journal of Politics* 53 (1991): 644–675.

Messaris, Paul. *Visual Literacy: Image, Mind, and Reality.* Boulder, CO: Westview P, 1994.

Nisbett, Richard E., and Lee Ross. *Human Inference: Strategies and Shortcomings of Social Judgment.* Englewood Cliffs, NJ: Prentice-Hall, 1980.

O'Keefe, Daniel J. *Persuasion: Theory and Research.* Newbury Park, CA: Sage, 1990.

Peirce, Charles Sanders. *Peirce on Signs: Writings on Semiotic by Charles Sanders Peirce.* Ed. J. Hoopes. Chapel Hill: U of North Carolina P, 1991.

Perelman, Chaim, and Lucie Olbrechts-Tyteca. *The New Rhetoric: A Treatise on Argumentation.* Trans. John Wilkinson and Purcell Weaver. Notre Dame: U of Notre Dame P, 1971.

Rebotier, Thomas Paul. "Vision and Imagery: The Role of Cortical Attractor Dynamics." *DAI: Dissertation 1999* 59 (1999): 5129.

Scott, Linda M. "Images in Advertising: The Need for a Theory of Visual Rhetoric." *Journal of Consumer Research* 21 (1994): 252–273.

Sinatra, Richard. *Visual Literacy Connections to Thinking, Reading and Writing.* Springfield, IL: Charles C. Thomas, 1986.

Smith, Stephen M., and David R. Shaffer. "Vividness Can Undermine or Enhance Message Processing: The Moderating Role of Vividness Congruency." *Personality and Social Psychology Bulletin* 26 (2000): 769–779.

van Eemeren, Frans H. "The Study of Argumentation as Normative Pragmatics." *Text* 10 (1990): 37–44.

Voss, J. F., R. Fincher-Kiefer, J. Wiley, and L. N. Silfies. "On the Processing of Arguments." *Argumentation* 7 (1993): 165–182.

Wilson, Marie G., Gregory B. Northcraft, and Margaret A. Neale. "Information Competition and Vividness Effects in On-line Judgments." *Organizational Behavior and Human Decision Processes* 44 (1989): 132–139.

CHAPTER TWO

The Rhetoric of Visual Arguments

J. Anthony Blair

This book is about visual rhetoric, and this chapter is about visual arguments. I take it as part of my task, then, to address the relationships among these three: rhetoric, argument, and the visual. How can there be visual arguments when arguments as we usually know them are verbal? And if there can be visual arguments, what is their rhetorical aspect? Because arguments are supposed to be tools of persuasion and rhetoric is often thought of as including (but not exhausted by) the study and use of the instruments of persuasion, I begin by exploring the relationships among rhetoric, argument and persuasion. Then I turn to the difficulties and opportunities that present themselves when considering visual argument in particular. The chapter ends by taking up the question: What does being visual add to arguments?

Rhetoric and argument have been associated since antiquity, and in that connection arguments have traditionally been thought of as verbal phenomena. Aristotle, one of the earliest in European culture to study rhetoric systematically, identified the art of rhetoric with knowledge of modes of persuasion (*Rhetoric* 1354ᵃ 13-14). The method of persuasion, he held, is "demonstration," and demonstration's instrument is the *enthymeme*, which is a form of argument (*Rhetoric* 1355ᵃ 5-6). An Aristotelian enthymeme is an argument in which the arguer deliberately leaves unstated a premise that is essential to its reasoning. Doing so has the effect of drawing the audience to participate in its own persuasion by filling in that unexpressed premise. This connecting of the audience to the argument is what makes the enthymeme a rhetorical form of argument.[1] But next, Aristotle took it for granted that the agent of persuasion is the orator, and from that it follows on his conception that the principal tool of persuasion must be the orator's medium, namely, language. So, according to one of the earliest and most influential accounts, the material to which rhetoric is to be applied is verbal argument.

The conception of rhetoric as essentially about speech has remained with us to this day, although it has become more and more contested. As recently as

41

a decade ago, the French rhetoric scholar, Olivier Reboul, restricted rhetoric to the use of language to persuade: "Here, then, is the definition we propose: rhetoric is the art of persuading by means of speech."[2] Because non-argumentative speech, or non-argumentative properties of speech, can be persuasive, Reboul's definition does not make a necessary connection between rhetoric and argument, but it certainly does envisage speech as essential to rhetoric. In the introductory chapter of their book on contemporary perspectives on rhetoric, Sonja Foss, Karen Foss and Robert Trapp urge a broader conception, proposing to "define rhetoric broadly as the uniquely human ability to use symbols to communicate with one another," and they explicitly mention as one possible instance, "an artist presenting an image on canvas"—in other words, visual rhetoric (11). Even so, on the very next page they make this concession to the tradition: "We believe that the paradigm case of rhetoric is the use of the spoken word to persuade an audience" (12).

One task, then, is to explain how rhetoric may be conceived as extending beyond the boundaries of the verbal, its *terra cognita* since antiquity, so as to include as well the visual; in other words, to show how there can be *visual persuasion*. That task is taken up in the other chapters of this book, so I do not need to address it in detail. A second task, assuming there can be a rhetoric of the visual, is to make the connection between visual persuasion and argument—to see how there can be visual arguments.

PERSUASION

This might seem to be a simple matter. In the first place, the power of things visual to persuade us, to shape our attitudes, and even our beliefs and actions, seems obvious. However, from this perspective a lot hinges on how "persuasion" is understood. It was Reboul's view that rhetorical persuasion consists in *causing* someone to believe (*"faire croire,"*) by means of speech (5). Now, if we drop the connection with speech in order to allow for the possibility of visual rhetoric, but retain the understanding of persuasion as a cause of changes in belief (and let's add changes in attitude, or in conduct), then what sorts of causal instruments will we allow to count as persuasion?

Persuasion cannot be just any manner of influencing a person. Imagine (what might already be possible, for all I know) that by manipulating neurons or implanting electronic circuits in a human brain, neurosurgeons could produce changes in the beliefs, attitudes, and behavior of the person whose brain is modified in this way. The rapist loses his anger and misogyny; the pedophile no longer has erotic interest in children; the self-sealing unreason of the Holocaust denier and of the conspiracy theorist disappears. Would we then classify such brain surgery as persuasion? As rhetoric? Surely not, but if not, then—assuming persuasion is a kind of cause—what marks persuasion off from other kinds of causal factors affecting beliefs, attitudes or conduct? If rhetoric is to retain its connection with persuasion, the concept of persuasion requires attention.

We have just seen that not all causes of behavior count as persuasion. What seems to be a necessary ingredient in persuasion as a kind of cause of behavior change is that the person persuaded assents to the pressure of the vector of influence. The person consciously assents, and that implies that he or she is free to resist the causal influences. We do not consider the neurosurgeon's implant to be persuasion because going along with its influence is not subject to the agent's control. Other examples reinforce this point. The robber's gun *is* persuasive, just because we can choose to comply with his demand under its threat or, foolishly, to resist. There was a time when if a woman stuck her tongue in my ear, she could pretty well do with me as she would. Her seduction was persuasive, because it was possible to resist it; my assent was under my control. In both cases of persuasion, the assent was not compelled, precisely because the capacity to resist the influences was present.

The narratives we formulate for ourselves from visual images can easily shape our attitudes. Think of scenes of midtown Manhattan during rush hour. The energy and excitement will be hugely attractive for many; the disorder and cacophony will be repulsive to others. And presumably messages expressed visually can be resisted no less than other kinds. Your heart goes out to the grief-stricken parents of children killed in war or terrorist attacks, shown on TV news video clips, but you can also ask hard questions about whether those parents might have put their children in harm's way. Also there will be borderline cases. We learn from color specialists that rooms painted in different colors tend to cause different reactions. Certain blues are cool, certain greens are relaxing, certain reds are warm and comforting. Shall we then speak of the rhetoric of wall paint? On one hand, the colors have their effects unconsciously; on the other hand, once we know about their effects, can't we resist or compensate for them? So perhaps the rhetoric of color is a legitimate subfield; it's not a clear call either way. Visual persuasion, then, is clearly a growing concern.

Persuasion and Argument

However, just as not all influences that result in changes of behavior count as persuasion, visual or otherwise, so too not all cases of persuasion count as arguments. Consider the examples just used. To speak of the robber's gun as an "argument" is to make a joke or use a metaphor, even though it is persuasive (or for a sensible unarmed person, it ought to be persuasive). It is reasonable to hand over your wallet or purse, but the robber has not presented an *argument* for doing so just by pointing his gun at you. My fantasy woman's seduction might have been persuasive, but stimulating an erogenous zone does not constitute an *argument*. Such a stance might puzzle rhetoricians because, as Scott

Jacobs has put it, "rhetorical theorists have ... tended to think of *any* mode of communication as argument if it functions to gain assent" (263). But Jacobs continues: "And that just will not do .... not all symbolic inducements are arguments, and arguments are not the only way of gaining assent" (263). What distinguishes arguments from other kinds of "symbolic inducement"? It has to do with how they function. Arguments supply us with *reasons* for accepting a point of view. The fact that certain propositions are deemed true, probable, plausible or otherwise worthy of acceptance, is considered to provide a reason, or a set of reasons, for thinking that some claim is true, some attitude is appropriate, some policy is worthy of implementation, or some action is best done. Here is Jacobs again: "Arguments are fundamentally linguistic entities that express with a special pragmatic force propositions where those propositions stand in particular inferential relationships to one another" (264); and he continues, in a note appended to this sentence:

> The canonical form that I have in mind here is captured in the speech act of assertion. Among other things, in making an argument one commits to defending the truth of a complex of propositions and to undertaking to get the hearer to accept the truth of one proposition (call it the standpoint) as being justified by the truth of other propositions (call those the arguments). (Jacobs, note 4)

Arguments are traditionally associated with speech, either written or oral, for a couple of linked reasons. First, because the reasons they use are propositions. Second, because propositions are standardly expressed by sentences in languages. A proposition is what is expressed by a sentence that has a *truth value*, which is to say that it is either true or false (unlike, say, a command, a request, a promise or a question). In presenting an argument (of the simplest possible form), someone *asserts* that some proposition, B, is true (1) because some other proposition, A, is true and (2) because B follows from or is supported by A. *Asserting* is a kind of action, paradigmatically a speech act, whereby the assertor takes responsibility for the truth of the sentence she or he asserts. Just as when you promise you take responsibility for doing what your promise commits you to do, so when you assert or make a claim (for example: "The AIDS epidemic is over." or "Democratic administrations are, historically, as likely to go to war as Republican administrations."), you take responsibility for its truth, and may legitimately be asked to produce your evidence for your claim. But photographs or paintings or cinematic images or video images do not seem, on the face of it, to be capable of being true or false. They might be moving, funny, clever, or beautiful (or their opposites), but to call them "true" or "false" seems to be, at best, using a metaphor, and at worst, just inappropriate. "Visual argument," then, seems to be a solecism.

Visual Argument?

To be sure, no one owns the word *argument*. It is entirely possible to use the word to refer to any form of persuasion whatever and thus simply to reject outright Jacob's ruling: "But that just will not do." After all, who is *he* to say? However, such a dismissal of Jacob's point carries a cost. If you use the word *argument* in a different way, so that it is not tied down to reason having and reason giving, or to propositions with their truth values, then you lose contact not only with argumentation scholarship but also with the way the concept of argument has functioned historically and the way it works in standard English, or in any corresponding language. You are then really talking about something different from argument in anything but a stipulated sense of the concept.

This is an important theoretical point. Words and concepts have meanings in historical contexts; they are situated in the conventions of their usage communities. To be sure, community conventions, including conceptual and linguistic ones, can change, and often should. But if words are stretched too radically, they break their connection to their anchorage and drift anywhere, meaning anything. A good example is *democracy*. The former Soviet Union called itself a democracy because its government claimed to represent the best interests of its people. But if a totalitarian dictatorship or oligarchy can count as a democracy by self-definition, then the concept of democracy has lost its connection to rule by (as well as for) the people. Almost any system of government can then count as a democracy, and the word *democracy* has lost its value as designating a distinctive type of political system. The theoretical point I am making can also be used equally to justify the introduction of new terminology. In trying to remove the sexism that is built into the language, why not, for example, just get used to thinking of postmen and stewardesses as *both* female and male? The answer many feminists gave was that it was important to make the break from conventions that needed changing, and so completely new terms were needed, "letter carrier" and "flight attendant," that had none of the old associations of being exclusively male, or exclusively female, occupations. With respect to the concept of "visual argument," I am trying to urge that we be cautious about stretching the concept of argument too far, for similar reasons. We might like the idea of calling any kind of visual persuasion an argument, but unless we can make a connection to the traditional concept, it would be best not to stretch the term *argument* to that extent. If there is no real connection, let's just use a new term, and leave *argument* to the domain of the verbal.

So the issue of whether there can be visual arguments is uninterestingly settled by simply declaring any instance of visual persuasion to be an argument. It is much more interesting if it turns out that, in spite of their historical association with language, arguments *in the traditional sense* can be visual as well as verbal. It is much more interesting if it can be shown that visual communications can be a legitimate tool of rational persuasion. Now, some hold that there can be no visual arguments or visual uses of arguments in the traditional sense of *argument*,[3] and if they are right, then visual rhetoric cannot include visual arguments and there is no place, in this book or anywhere else, for a discussion of the rhetoric of visual arguments.

There are two central reasons offered against the very possibility of arguments being visual. One is that the visual is inescapably ambiguous or vague.[4] The other is related to the fact that arguments must have propositional content, and the apparent fact that visual communications do not. Both of these objections have been answered.[5]

The vagueness objection runs as follows. Arguments aim to move us by appealing to considerations that we grant and then by showing that the point of view at issue follows from those concessions. If it is not at all clear, because of vagueness or ambiguity, what considerations we are granting, or what is supposed to follow from what we grant, then we cannot tell what we are being asked to concede, and we cannot decide whether to agree or whether the alleged conclusion follows. The process is impossible if the appeal is vague or ambiguous. Thus vagueness or ambiguity makes argument impossible.

The answer to the vagueness or ambiguity objection is simply that these features inhabit spoken and written arguments as well as visual communication, if not to the same extent. Indeed, they are common enough in verbal arguments that we have identified as fallacies with their own names— *equivocation* and *vagueness*—such moves if they impede the goals of argument. However, not every case of ambiguity or vagueness is considered a flaw in a verbal argument or in communication in general. So long as everyone can tell from the context what is really meant by such potentially ambiguous communications as an advertisement stating, "Bathing suits 40% off" (*amphiboly*), a sign saying "Slow School" (*accent*), a notice stating, "All donors have contributed $1,000" (*division*),[6] there is no mis-communication whatsoever. Then the use of such statements in arguments would not be fallacious. Similarly, vagueness, far from always being fallacious, is necessary for efficient communication. We do not expect a speaker or writer to be more precise than is needed for the purposes of his or her communication in any context. If someone asks what the population of Canada is in order to compare it to that of the Netherlands, a number rounded off to the nearest million is precise enough. But such a degree of vagueness about population size would be unacceptable in a census report. When you are asked your age, you are not expected to answer to the minute, the hour, the day, or the week—just to the year, which is pretty vague but entirely precise enough for most purposes. It is relevant that children often identify their age to the half-year. That is because at a young age, with freedoms and other perceived advantages increasing with age, half a year makes a big difference, and so there is a (perceived) point to the greater precision. Vagueness in diplomatic language is essential to maintaining good relations between states: The vagueness of statements made by the Secretary of State in news conferences is studied and necessary. So, on one hand, although either vagueness or ambiguity can in some circumstances be a flaw in an argument, they are risks that verbal argument manages to negotiate. Their presence in visual arguments, therefore, does not constitute an in-principle objection to arguments communicated visually. Moreover, because many so-called "visual" arguments are in fact mixtures of visual and verbal communication, their verbal content can (and often does) function to disambiguate them or make them sufficiently precise. (More will be offered on this point that "visual" arguments are usually mixed "visual plus verbal" arguments.) On the other hand, the presence of ambiguity and vagueness in verbal arguments is very far from always being objectionable, so once again, their presence in visual arguments cannot be a reason for rejecting the possibility of such arguments in principle. And finally, as we will see in a moment, it is simply not true that all visual arguments are vague or ambiguous. The visual is not inexorably vague or ambiguous.

The other principal objection to the possibility of visual arguments is that visual communication does not have truth values, and so cannot convey propositions, whereas argument requires propositions in order to perform its role. I have already alluded to this point.

Typically, arguments have as their primary purpose to influence people to change their beliefs, other attitudes or conduct. Arguers do this, first, by appealing to commitments their audience already has, and, second, by showing (or alleging) that these beliefs, attitudes or behavior also commit that audience to accept the modified or new belief, attitude or conduct being advanced. The "object" of a commitment will be a sentence or proposition that is capable of being true or false. My belief (in 2003) that India and Pakistan possess nuclear weapons is a cognitive attitude I have toward the proposition expressed by the sentence "India and Pakistan possess nuclear weapons." If those countries don't have nuclear weapons at the time, my belief is false; if they do, it's true. And it's got to be one or the other. For it to be possible for visual arguments to occur, it would have to be possible for visual images to be true or false—to have truth value. But a photograph or photographic collage, or a piece of film or a series of visual images (as in a TV commercial), or a painting or sculpture, are not "true" or "false." The meaning conveyed is not propositional. Therefore such visual communications, however they work, cannot express arguments. In whatever manner they achieve their rhetorical effects, it cannot be by the use of visual *arguments* because the essential components or arguments —propositions—cannot be expressed visually.

There are at least two replies to this "no-propositions" objection. One is to grant that for arguments aimed at changing beliefs, propositions are essential, but then to show that it is possible to express propositions visually. To establish this possibility, all that is needed is one actual case. Here is one. There is a famous pre-World War II cartoon by the British cartoonist David Low in which an evidently complacent Englishman is depicted in a lawn chair reading a newspaper, sitting directly beneath a jumble of precariously balanced boulders rising steeply above him. The bottom boulder, sticking out but wedged under and holding up the rest, is marked, "Czecho." Sitting directly on it are boulders marked "Rumania" and "Poland" and together they support a large boulder labeled "French Alliances," which in turn supports a huge boulder labeled "Anglo-French Security." A thick rope is attached to the out-thrust end of the "Czecho" boulder and pulled up overhead and out of sight. Clearly a strong pull on that rope would dislodge the "Czecho" boulder, causing the rest to come crashing down on the Englishman below. The cartoon's caption reads, "What's Czechoslovakia to me, anyway?"

Low is arguing that to regard the fate of Czechoslovakia as having no consequences for England is mistaken. The reason Low offers for this proposition is the conditional proposition that if Czechoslovakia were to fall to Germany, that would initiate a chain of events (the fall of Poland and Rumania), which would result in the fall of the French alliances and eventuate in the collapse of Anglo-French security and that would have disastrous consequences for England.[7] I have just expressed Low's visual argument in English and in doing so have expressed two propositions—his conclusion and his premise. It was, at the time, either true or false that "to regard the fate of Czechoslovakia as having no consequences for England is mistaken," and that "if Czechoslovakia were to fall to Germany, that would initiate a chain of events (the fall of Poland and Rumania), which would result in the fall of the French alliances and eventuate in the collapse of Anglo-French security." (The argument has the unexpressed premise that "the collapse of Anglo-French security would have a major impact on England.") In short, to the objection that propositions cannot be expressed visually the reply is that because it has been done in Low's cartoon, it is possible. (Notice that there is no ambiguity or vagueness whatsoever about Low's meaning.)

A second reply to the "no-propositions" objection is to point out that arguments are used for primary purposes other than to cause belief change. We also use arguments with the intention of changing the attitudes, or the intentions, or the behavior of our audience. The structure of the arguing process is the same. The arguer appeals to attitude-, intention- or behavior-commitments of the audience, and tries to show that they commit the audience to the new attitude, intention or behavior at issue. But attitudes, intentions and conduct do not have truth value. My preference for the Democrats over the Republicans isn't true or false; I just have it. Perhaps it is ill-advised, perhaps I have no good reason for it ("we've always been Democrats"); what it is *not* is false (or true). Yet because we do offer reasons to people to change their attitudes, intentions and behavior, it is clear that there can be (even) verbal arguments in which not all the components are propositions. Not all arguments must be propositional. Hence, even if it is true that (some) visual images do not express propositions, it does not follow that they cannot figure in arguments.

If these two replies to the "no-propositions" objection do not lay it to rest, I will take it that at least they shift the burden of proof. And combined with the replies to the "vague or ambiguous" objection, they clear from our path the general theoretical objection that visual arguments are not possible, and leave us free to consider the rhetorical properties of visual arguments.

Here let me add a stipulation. Although there can exist purely visual arguments, most communications that are candidates for visual arguments are combinations of the verbal and the visual. The words might be in print (as in cartoons), or voiced (in the case of television or film). When I refer to "visual" arguments in what follows, I mean to include these combinations of verbal and visual communication. By "verbal" arguments I will mean exclusively verbal arguments, with no visual element.

Visual Arguments Versus Other Types of Persuasion

If it is correct to distinguish visual persuasion from visual argument, presumably visual argument is one type of visual persuasion among others. The question then becomes, what distinguishes visual argument from other types of visual persuasion?

My suggestion is that what differentiates visual argument is the same as what differentiates argument in general. To be an argument, what is communicated by one party to another or others, whatever the medium of communication might be, must constitute some factor that can be considered a reason for accepting or believing some proposition, for taking some other attitude[8] or for performing some action. A test of whether such a factor is present is whether it would be possible to construct from what is communicated visually a verbal argument that is consistent with the visual presentation. This verbal construction would in no way be the equivalent of the visual argument, precisely because it could never adequately capture the evocative power of the visual element in the original presentation of the argument. However, it would abstract from the visual presentation the component that constitutes a reason for the claim being advanced.

Some of the best examples of visual arguments are the political advertisements made for television. One of the classics is the Democrats' anti-Goldwater spot run during the Presidential race between Lyndon Johnson and Barry Goldwater in 1964. Here is a description of what became known as "The Daisy Ad" (available on the Internet at www.cnn.com/ALLPOLITICS/1996/candidates/ad.archive/daisy_long.mov).

This chilling ad begins with a little girl in a field picking petals off a daisy, counting. When the count reaches ten, her image is frozen and a male voice commences a militaristic countdown. Upon the countdown reaching zero, we see a nuclear explosion and hear President Johnson's voice: "These are the stakes, to make a world in which all God's children can live, or to go into the darkness. Either we must love each other or we must die." Fade to black. White lettering. "On November 3rd vote for President Johnson."

The purpose of the ad—remember, this was at the height of the Cold War —was to suggest that Goldwater was trigger-happy about the use of the H-bomb, and thus that to elect him would be to place the nation in grave peril. The ad did not mention Goldwater. It was thus a kind of visual enthymeme, requiring the viewing public to supply Goldwater as the alternative to Johnson. Never mind that the ad was an indefensible slur on Goldwater; it was brilliant. It conveyed the impression that Goldwater might, on something as arbitrary as a whim (the mere chance of which petal was plucked last), engage the nation in a nuclear holocaust, thus causing the destruction of everyone, including the innocent children who pluck daisies playing "s/he loves me; s/he loves me not." The inference that it would be a danger to the national interest to elect Goldwater follows straightforwardly.

I have just expressed in verbal form the *reasoning* of the ad, but to be clear let me set it out even more explicitly.

Goldwater might, on something as arbitrary as a whim, launch a nuclear holocaust.

Such a holocaust would cause unspeakable horror for everyone, including innocent children.

Hence, it would endanger the national interest to elect Goldwater.

To repeat, I do not for a minute suggest that this verbal expression of the argument is equivalent to the visual argument. For one thing, a number of equally plausible alternative verbal renditions of the argument are available. For another, and more importantly, this verbal extraction leaves out completely the enormously evocative power of the visual imagery and symbolism of the actual visuals making up the ad. For instance, the juxtaposition of the child in its innocence and the nuclear mushroom cloud has huge pathetic force that words cannot capture. However, what the verbal construction does succeed in doing is identifying how the visual ad contained within it a reason for not voting for Goldwater. And that, I contend, is what made the Democrats' attack ad an argument.

If this account is correct, then visual arguments constitute the species of visual persuasion in which the visual elements overlie, accentuate, render vivid and immediate, and otherwise elevate in forcefulness a reason or set of reasons offered for modifying a belief, an attitude or one's conduct. What distinguishes visual arguments from other forms of visual persuasion is that in the case of the former it is possible to enunciate reasons given to support a claim, whereas in the case of the latter no such element is present. Thus we can see that the "Daisy" ad was conveying an argument against supporting Goldwater.

The Visual Difference

The advantage of visual arguments over print or spoken arguments lies in their evocative power. Part of this power is due to the enormously high number of images that can be conveyed in a short time. Television commercials today show between one and four *dozen* different moving visual images in a 30-second spot. We have no trouble processing that much visual information, whereas it would be impossible to express 30 different propositions verbally in 30 seconds, and even if it were not, it would be far beyond normal human capacity to process them. Visual images can thus be used to convey a narrative in a short time. Recall the Coca Cola commercial shown during the 2002 Winter Olympics in Utah, in which an awkward youth wins the heart of an elegant female figure skater against the competition of several older handsome young men by giving her a Coke at the end of her program. The story is told with ingredients of poignancy, sexiness and humor—all in 30 seconds—and although (I would argue) this commercial is not an argument, it does illustrate the narrative capacity of the visual.

Another factor is the sense of realism that the visual conveys. My students, for example, year in and year out tell me that television news is better than print news in the respect that with television news they can see for themselves what happened whereas with print news they are told by a reporter, and so have only second-hand access to the events depicted. I believe that this impression is quite mistaken. A lot of TV news pictures are file footage, but even video of the actual event being reported is limited to a small number of camera vantage points and angles, and a very few seconds of footage, and the video is packaged with voice over and cut aways. Besides that, each TV news "item" on network news programs, and often on local news programs too, is a carefully crafted "story." It is deliberately assembled with a beginning (a problem or question), a middle (information, opinions) and an end (resolution of the problem or answer to the question, followed by dénouement, the outcome). The result is that the "reality" is a selected perspective presented in a highly structured or filtered way. Nevertheless, my students are under the impression that the visual gives them direct access to what is visually portrayed in a way that print does not, and their impressions are what matter so far as the power of the visual is concerned.

The visual element in visual arguments is most significantly a *rhetorical* dimension, rather than *logical* or *dialectical*. Understanding the dialectical dimension of arguments to be the process of interaction between the arguer and interlocutors who raise questions or objections, we can see that visual arguments lack this dialectical aspect. The visual makes an argument in the sense of adducing a few reasons in a forceful way. It might contain or present a *didactic narrative*—a story that supports a point. But it does not permit the complexity of such dialectical moves as the raising of objections in order to refute or otherwise answer them. This is a serious deficiency in what Ralph H. Johnson has called the "manifest rationality" that ought, ideally, to characterize argumentation. Johnson's suggestion is that when we try to convince others using arguments, we ought to mention the objections to our views that we know about and explain how we would answer these objections. There should be no suppressed problems with our case. Johnson is calling for a kind of "truth in arguing"—a "full disclosure" policy. If his ideal is one we ought to try to meet, and if visual arguments cannot, as it seems they cannot, incorporate this "dialectical" dimension of challenge and response, then visual arguments will always fall short of dialectical rationality.

Understanding the logical dimension of arguments to be the support that the reason(s) offered provide for the viewpoint that is supported by them, we can see that visual arguments supply simple, minimalist support. The verbal expression of the argument will have one or two premises, tending to be more or less syllogistic in structure. The logic of the argument will not be complicated or subtle.

Understanding the rhetorical dimension of arguments to consist of the various facets of its situatedness, it is plain that the visual is above all rhetorical. To be effective, the visual properties of a visual argument must resonate with the audience on the occasion and in the circumstances. The visual symbolism must register immediately, whether consciously or not. The arguer must know and relate not only to the beliefs and attitudes of the intended audience, but also to the visual imagery that is meaningful to it. The arguer needs also to be sensitive to the surrounding argumentative "space" of the audience, because so much of the argument must remain tacit or unexpressed. Visual arguments are typically *enthymemes*—arguments with gaps left to be filled in by the participation of the audience. The anti-Goldwater "Daisy" ad is a clear example, with Goldwater the clear target of the ad but never mentioned in it. So the arguer has to be able to predict the nature of the audience's participation. Given the vagueness of much visual imagery, the visual arguer must be particular astute in reading the audience. Thus in a variety of ways, visual arguments rely particularly on the rhetorical astuteness of the arguer for their success. We may say, then, that visual arguments are distinguished by their rhetorical power. What makes visual arguments distinctive is how much greater is their potential for rhetorical power than that of purely verbal arguments.

Why Argue Visually?

One reason for using visual arguments is that there is no alternative way of giving the argument permanence. In a largely oral culture with little literacy, verbal arguments have only as much endurance as their currency in the oral tradition. Thus we see the didactic visual arguments chiseled in the granite "decorations" of the great European medieval cathedrals. A striking example is the sculpture of the damned going to hell and the saved going to heaven to be found in the tympanum over the south transept door of the high gothic cathedral. The damned are depicted in graphic detail, being led or herded naked down to the right, their bodies twisted in grotesque contortions, their faces distorted and their open mouths screaming in pain. They are shackled, flames lick at them, devils prod them with pitchforks, and some are tossed into great cauldrons of boiling liquid. The saved, on the other hand, troupe triumphantly upward to the left, clad in gowns, their faces smiling with delight, with those at the top being welcomed to heaven. The message is clear: These are the fates awaiting the virtuous and the vicious upon their respective deaths. The obvious implicit premise is that no one would want the fate of the damned and anyone would want the fate of the saved. The tacit conclusion follows straightforwardly: Be virtuous and refrain from vice. Many of these depictions of the argument have so far lasted, unmodified except by the weather, for over 700 years. They are fixed in stone no less effectively than had they been fixed in print.

Besides giving this moral argument a permanence, its visual expression communicates something unavailable to the verbal version, whether it is communicated orally or in writing. No words can convey the horrible fate of the damned or the ecstatic beatitude of the saved as dramatically, forcefully and realistically as do the stone carvings. It is one thing to hear a description of these respective fates; it is quite another, far more vivid and immediate, to *see* them with your own eyes. So here is another reason for conveying an argument visually: one can communicate visually with much more force and immediacy than verbal communication allows.

I think there are two related reasons for the greater force and immediacy of the visual. First, visual communication can be more efficient than verbal communication. In order to convey and evoke emotions or attitudes, the verbal arguer must rely on his or her oratorical powers to cause the audience to exercise its sympathetic imagination. There are three opportunities for failure in such communications: The arguer can fail to be effectively evocative, the audience can refuse to cooperate in the imaginative exercise, and the audience can, even if trying, fail in its imaginative task. In the case of visual arguments, these three chances to misfire reduce to one. The creator of the visual expression of the argument can fail to give adequate or appropriate visual expression to the feelings or attitudes to be conveyed, and in that case, the advantages of the visual expression of the argument are lost. However, should the visual expression succeed—as the medieval cathedral tympanum sculptures do so marvelously—then the audience cannot help but become involved, and in just the way the arguer intends. Hence the arguer does not have to rely on either the cooperation of the audience or its powers of sympathetic imagination. In this respect, then, visual argument is likely to be more efficient than its verbal counterpart.

What takes the need for the cooperation and competence of the audience out of the visual argument equation—and this is the second reason for the greater force and immediacy of the visual—is the power of visual imagery to evoke involuntary reactions—reactions that must be consciously countered by the recipient if their power is to be at all defused. Evidence of this power is today found most pervasively in movies and in television commercials. The power of visual imagery in commercials is actually confirmed empirically, at least for national TV advertising campaigns, though movies are increasingly also tested on focus groups prior to their release. The effects of various symbols are well-known and much exploited. For instance, images of young children and young animals evoke immediate sympathy in adults. Several years ago Pepsi ran a commercial that consisted of nothing else than two little boys (clearly twins, maybe 3-year-olds) and three or four puppies from the same litter at their ungainly stage of locomotion, frolicking together across a slightly sloping lawn. The puppies were jumping up to lick the boys' faces, the little boys were giggling with delight, and both the boys and puppies were tumbling together and getting up and running down the slope. The kids and the puppies were utterly adorable, and any adult viewer who wasn't a sociopath couldn't help smiling and responding, "Ohhh, they're so cute!" What the commercial had to do with choosing Pepsi is not my point at the moment. The point is that this imagery, however it might be explained, evoked a powerful involuntary response in the normal viewer.

It seems plausible that there is an evolutionary advantage to having the caring and protective responses of the adults of most species that are triggered by the young of their own or even other species biologically hard-wired in them. The hard-wiring seems indisputable. I have seen a pair of robins hatch and feed a starling nestling along with their own, and cowbirds are notorious for taking advantage of this response by laying their eggs in other birds' nests and having them raised by those other birds. We have all heard of nursing mothers of various mammal species taking on the nurture and care either of other offspring of their own species or the offspring of other species. Notice how advertisers often rely on this response by showing cute babies, both human and those of other animals, in commercials in which there is no plausible connection between the baby and the product. (Such appeals are *pathetic appeals*—appeals to the sympathy or emotional responses of an audience.)

Other kinds of symbolism, such as the authority of the physician or scientists used in pain-killer or indigestion-remedy commercials that is conveyed by actors dressed in white lab coats with a stethoscope around their necks, clearly have learned, conventional associations. (This is an *appeal to ethos*—an appeal to the character or stature of a person or a role to lend credibility to what is portrayed.) Yet others are mixtures of learned and biological responses, such as heterosexual responses to the appearance of members of the opposite sex considered beautiful. Sexual attraction is presumably at least partly hard-wired, although there are clearly social factors in sexual attraction that are culturally variable. Lean or stout, short or tall, tattooed or clear-skinned, pierced or unadorned—these are variations in sexual attractiveness that any student of other cultures, or indeed of our own, are bound to notice. The point is that our responses—learned, innate, or a combination of the two—are used by advertisers, and their effectiveness in advertising is well tested.

Thus, the use of such symbolism in visual arguments can almost guarantee the ethotic and pathetic rhetorical influences that the arguer intends. And all it takes to accomplish these rhetorical effects is the flash of a series of visual images.

For as long as we have had near-universal literacy and a tradition of print, verbal arguments have been as permanent as we might wish them to be, and in fact have greater permanency than the evanescent television screen or the movie. So the motivation for visual arguments has not in our time been the advantage of fixing the argument in a stable medium. The evocative power of visual means of communication, especially television (but also movies, pictures in magazines, and posters or billboards) is what has recommended the visual as a medium of argument.

Genres of Visual Argument

Traditional rhetoric as applied to arguments was concerned with the means of giving the greatest possible persuasive power to the written or spoken word. It did not seek to replace the propositional content of argument, but to position it so as to be maximally forceful. The same goes for rhetoric as applied to visual arguments. My contention is that visual persuasive communication cannot ignore or set aside prepositional content and continue to count as argument. Argument requires the giving and receiving of reasons. However, visual media offer rich means for generating forcefulness for arguments expressed visually. Let us consider briefly some of the different genres of visual argument, and some of their tools and deficiencies.

I have already given an example of a political cartoon used to make a visual argument. Cartoons are distinctive because they permit an explicitness and precision of meaning found in few other visual genres. The convention that allows for labeling, and the abilities of cartoonists to capture the distinctive visual traits of well-known public figures, and the opportunity that caricature provides for exaggeration, all enable their messages to be unambiguous. To be sure, a great deal more than that is going on in cartoons, as Janice Edwards in her chapter on the visual rhetoric of cartoons (chapter 8, this volume) makes clear. The multilayered meanings and associations of various visual cultural icons generate powerful resonances around simple pen-and-ink drawings.

When the cartoonist is making an argument (and not every cartoon is intended as an argument), the points asserted visually have a particular forcefulness and credibility when such iconic imagery is used, and the means used can be analytically identified, as Edwards (chapter 8, this volume) shows in applying Perlmutter's (1998) list of list of ten characteristics of photographs of outrage that can give them iconic status.

Films empower arguments visually largely by means of the construction of credible narratives. When a movie is making an argument (and by no means is every film intended as an argument), it tells a story that makes the argument's cogency seem inevitable. Oliver Stone's *JFK* made the case that there was a conspiracy to assassinate President Kennedy and to cover up the conspiracy. In telling that story, it made the characters who believed in a conspiracy highly credible, and those who denied it highly unbelievable. The film made the argument forcefully by presenting a narrative in which that conclusion was the most plausible interpretation of the events portrayed. *Black Hawk Down* is a more current example. It makes the case that the U.S. attempt to capture a local warlord in Mogadishu during the Somalia intervention was an ill-conceived plan by portraying dramatically the horrible consequences that snowballed from just one thing going wrong (a soldier falling out of a helicopter during the initial attack). The idea of narratives functioning as arguments is familiar to us all. To give just one example, our countries often justify their foreign policies in terms of narratives, the only plausible resolution of which is the policy being defended. Thus the "Communist conspiracy" was a narrative that justified Cold War policies. More recently, the Muslim fundamentalist threat epitomized by the attacks on the World Trade Center and the Pentagon on September 11, 2001, were woven into a narrative that justified the Bush administration's "war on terrorism." To call these arguments narratives is not to call them fictions or to challenge their legitimacy, although they might be open to such challenges. The point is, rather, that as narratives they tell stories that have "logical" resolutions, and hence function as arguments. Because pictures, and especially films, both fictional and documentary, are wonderfully suited to telling believable stories, they provide an excellent medium for visual argument by means of narrative construction.

What the visual element adds to film or video, over, say, a novel or short story, or over documentary prose alone, is that with film or video, we don't just imagine the narrative, we "see" it unfolding before our eyes. Seeing is believing, even if what we are watching is invented, exaggerated, half-truths or lies.

The third and last type of visual argument that I want to discuss is advertising, and television advertising in particular. For the most part, we watch TV to relax, as a diversion from our working lives. Television commercials thus invade our private space and time and reach us when we tend not to be alert and vigilant. Although we can control which programs we view, we cannot control which advertisements accompany those programs and it takes an effort to "mute" the commercials. Moreover, advertisers can and do predict with a high degree of accuracy the demographics of the audiences of any program, and so they design their messages to exploit the vulnerabilities of the members of that demographic group. Combine with these factors the huge influence of repetition, and the attraction of the visual as the medium of influencing choice becomes obvious.

My view of whether TV ads are visual arguments is not widely shared. My initial point was to emphasize the evocative power of visual communication. This power is thus available for visual arguments, whether static (print) or dynamic (television). But that does not imply that all uses of visuals in persuasion are cases of visual arguments. It strikes me that although magazine and television visual advertising often presents itself as more or less rational persuasion aimed at influencing our preferences and actions, what is in fact going on in the most effective ads is that the actual influence is accomplished behind this façade of rationality.

Whether or not even to call it persuasion strikes me as moot, because it is not clear that we have the capacity to reject the influence. When I think of a rich custard cream sauce or creamy chocolate mousse, foods I adore, I cannot help but salivate. (I am salivating as I write this description! Try thinking about tastes you love without having your mouth water.) The only way to avoid it is not to think of these foods. It might be that especially television advertising is for most of us what chocolate mousse is for me—something whose influence can be avoided only if we avoid exposure to it. If that is true, it is more like the surgeon's brain implant than even the robber's gun. And then it is not persuasion, but unconscious causation, and so not rational persuasion, and so not argument, visual or otherwise.[9]

The Pepsi commercial with the giggling children and frolicking puppies was, I want to argue, not a visual argument at all. It merely evoked feelings of warmth and empathy, which were then associated with the brand. The objective of the advertiser, I expect, was to cause the audience to feel good about the commercial, and then transfer that good feeling to the brand. Presumably the hope (and probably it was an empirically confirmed conviction) was that the good feeling about the brand would cause shoppers to reach for Pepsi on the supermarket shelf when buying soda for their families. There was no reason of any kind offered for preferring Pepsi to alternative colas or other types of soda. To insist that this commercial be understood as an argument strikes me as to be in the grip of a dogma, the dogma that all influence on attitudes or action *must* be at least persuasion if not its subspecies, argumentation. What premises could possibly be reconstructed from the advertisement? That drinking Pepsi causes little kids and puppies to be cute? Absurd. That Pepsi, like you and I, thinks little kids and puppies are cute and so we, the consumers, should favor Pepsi over other cola brands or types of soda, which don't think kids and puppies are cute? Far-fetched. Stupid as we consumers might be, we are not complete idiots. Given the choice between interpreting this commercial as a completely stupid argument, on one hand, and as not an argument at all but an attempt to influence us via our psychological associations with young children and puppies, on the other, any principle of interpretive charity points to the second alternative as by far the more plausible.

By the way, this sort of visual influence through association and the power of visual symbols is not restricted to advertising. Consider another, more mundane, example. Every evening on network television news broadcasts, when the broadcast turns to federal political news from Washington, a reporter stands against the backdrop of the White House or the Capitol and reads his or her report (with cutaways edited in, to be sure). The White House and the Capitol are not just buildings. They are powerful symbols, conveying the immense authority and prestige of the institutions of the Presidency and the Congress. Thus these visual images lend to the television reporter, by association, some of the authority of those political institutions, thereby adding to his or her credibility. These backdrops are visual rhetorical devices that render the message conveyed more believable or persuasive. They lend *ethos* to the reporter. However they are not arguments. No argument is offered to show that the reporter is credible or authoritative. If the reporter were to say, "I am standing in front of the White House, and it follows from this fact that you should take my report or opinions seriously," we would on that basis *not* take him or her seriously. The symbols do their work precisely by making contact with our unconsciously held, symbol-interpreting apparatus, not by engaging our capacity to assess reasons and their implications.

What typically happens in TV commercials and other visual advertising is that there is a surface "argument," usually supplied by the accompanying verbal text or voiceover. This argument is usually thin, offering little by way of reasons for preferring the product in question to similar products sold by competitors, or for liking that brand name. What does the influencing is the psychological appeal. Charles Revson, the founder of Revlon, is reported to have once said, "I don't sell cosmetics; I sell dreams." Advertising agencies use social science research (or do their own) into the current values and aspirations, the dreams and fantasies, *of their target markets*. What's hip? What's cool? What's *bad*? Their ads then use actors or celebrities dressed and behaving in ways that embody those values, aspirations, dreams and fantasies. We viewers transfer our identifications with the commercials to the brand or product. We want this brand or product because we think of ourselves as like the person in the commercial, doing the kinds of things done in the commercial. No reasoning occurs here at all. Think of the old Marlboro cigarette ads. A billboard with a picture of a cowboy with a tattoo on a horse smoking a cigarette. Visual influence? Absolutely. Visual argument? None.

So my view is that although TV commercials and other kinds of visual advertising might seem to represent the epitome of visual argument, in reality they constitute a poor case for their existence. I cannot claim that no TV commercial can reasonably be construed as an argument. On the contrary, I construed the Democrats' "Daisy" political ad against Goldwater as a visual argument. But "visual" plus "influence" does not add up to "argument" in every case.

CONCLUSION

It is time to sum up. Are visual arguments possible? It might seem not, since argument is paradigmatically verbal and essentially propositional, and visual images are often vague or ambiguous. However, we saw that vagueness and ambiguity can be managed in verbal argument, and so are in principle manageable in visual communication; moreover not all visual communication is vague or ambiguous. As well, propositions can be expressed visually no less than verbally. Argument in the traditional sense consists of supplying grounds for beliefs, attitudes or actions, and we saw that pictures can equally be the medium for such communication. Argument, in the traditional sense, can readily be visual.

It does not follow that visual argument is a mere substitute for verbal argument. The spoken word can be far more dramatic and compelling than the written word, but the visual brings to arguments another dimension entirely. It adds drama and force of a much greater order. Beyond that it can use such devices as references to cultural icons and other kinds of symbolism, dramatization and narrative to make a powerfully compelling case for its conclusion. The visual has an immediacy, a verisimilitude, and a concreteness that help influence acceptance and that are not available to the verbal.

While granting the persuasiveness of visual argument, we saw that in logical terms, its structure and content tends to be relatively simple. The complications of the dialectical perspective are not easily conveyed visually, and the result is that visual argument tends to be one-sided, presenting the case for or the case against, but not both together. Qualifications and objections are not readily expressed. Where visual argument excels is in the rhetorical dimension.

Rhetoric as related to argument, we saw, is the use of the best means available to make the logic of the argument persuasive to its audience. In communicating arguments visually, we need to attend particularly to the situation of the audience. What is the setting, and how does it introduce constraints and opportunities? What visual imagery will the audience understand and respond to? What historical and cultural modes of visual understanding does the audience bring to the situation? Visual arguers will answer these questions in creating their visual enthymemes, thus drawing the viewer to participate in completing the construction of the argument and so in its own persuasion. When argument is visual, it is, above all, visual rhetoric.

NOTES

1. For a recent, insightful discussion of the rhetorical role of the enthymeme, see Christopher W. Tindale.
2. *"Voici donc la définition que nous proposons: la rhétorique est l'art de persuader par le discours."* Olivier Reboul, *Introduction à la Rhétoric* 4.
3. For example, David Fleming, in "Can Pictures be Arguments?"
4. Strictly speaking, ambiguity exists when there are two possible meanings, and the context makes it impossible to determine which the author (or image creator) intended. The difficulty with visual images is more often that there is any number of possible interpretations, and there is no way to determine which of them was intended or indeed if any particular one of them was intended, and this phenomenon is properly termed *vagueness*, not *ambiguity*. The headline, "Lawyers offer poor free advice" is ambiguous, absent further contextual specification; "Coke is it!" is vague.
5. See David S. Birdsell and Leo Groake, "Toward a Theory of Visual Argument," and J. Anthony Blair, "The Possibility and Actuality of Visual Arguments," for fuller discussions of these points.
6. These examples come from S. Morris Engel, *Analyzing Informal Fallacies*, a book whose treatment of fallacies is now out of date.
7. I borrow the example from Leo Groarke, "Logic, Art and Argument."
8. I say, some "other" attitude, because it has become widely agreed among philosophers analyzing the concept of *belief* that beliefs are a kind of attitude themselves (a type of "propositional attitude").
9. I am setting aside for purposes of this discussion the enormous influence of music in television advertising. From the perspective of a study of persuasion, the role of music must be given a central place.

WORKS CITED

Aristotle. *Rhetoric*. Trans. W. Rhys Roberts. *The Complete Works of Aristotle*. Ed. Jonathan Barnes. Princeton: Princeton UP, 1984.

Birdsell, David S., and Leo Groarke. "Toward a Theory of Visual Argument." *Argumentation and Advocacy* 33 (1996): 1-10.

Blair, J. Anthony. "The Possibility and Actuality of Visual Argument." *Argumentation and Advocacy* 33 (1996): 23-39.

Engel, S. Morris. *Analyzing Informal Fallacies*. Englewood Cliffs, NJ: Prentice-Hall, 1980.

Fleming, David. "Can Pictures be Arguments?" *Argumentation and Advocacy* 33 (1996): 11-22.

Foss, Sonja K., Karen A. Foss, and Robert Trapp. *Contemporary Perspectives on Rhetoric*. Prospect Heights, IL: Waveland P, 1985.

Groarke, Leo. "Logic, Art and Argument." *Informal Logic* 18 (1996): 105-129.

Jacobs, Scott. "Rhetoric and Dialectic from the Standpoint of Normative Pragmatics." *Argumentation* 14 (2000): 261-286.

Johnson, Ralph H. *Manifest Rationality: A Pragmatic Theory of Argument*. Mahwah, NJ: Lawrence Erlbaum Associates, 2000.

Perlmutter, David D. *Photojournalism and Foreign Policy: Icons of Outrage in International Crisis*. Westport, CT: Praeger, 1998.

Reboul, Olivier. *Introduction à la Rhétoric [Intoduction to Rhetoric]*. Paris: PUF, 1991.

Tindale, Christopher W. *Acts of Arguing, A Rhetorical Model of Argument*. Albany, NY: State U of New York P, 1999.

CHAPTER THREE

Framing the Fine Arts Through Rhetoric

Marguerite Helmers

We learn from our construction of the past what possibilities and choices once existed.—Gerda Lerner, *Why History Matters*

PHILOSOPHY! Sure Guide to limpid Truth!—Benjamin Martin

Within the vast field of objects that can be looked at, certain objects have been elevated to a special class, the fine arts. What are the *fine arts*? As objects of shape, form, and material, the fine arts encompass sculpture, paintings, pottery, textile design, drawings, and prints. As ideas, over time, they have been constructed as a category of things worth preserving and viewing. They derive from the imagination, rather than serve as illustration, entertainment, or propaganda. There appears to be a certain agreement about what constitutes that which is "great," an attribute "which defines and distinguishes certain works from other forms of art" (Perry 15). These works edify. They please. In this chapter, I explore the persuasive qualities of painting as a fine art.

No discussion of rhetoric and the visual arts can begin without allusion to the Sister Arts tradition in literary studies. The founding maxim, fostering rich debate over the centuries, is Horace's declaration in the *Ars Poetica*, "Ut pictura poesis," [as a painting, so also a poem]. The 18th century German writer Gotthold Lessing amplified and took issue with Horace's construction. His own contribution can perhaps be termed the most significant critical dictum over the ages, for Lessing sought to keep the arts separate, warning that painting is an art of spatiality, whereas poetry is an art of time. As Richard Wendorf comments, however, "Lessing and a host of subsequent theorists have warned of the dire effects of these critical distinctions, but writers and painters have always been fascinated by the relations that serve to join words and images" (1361).

While the investigation of the Sister Arts was practiced from the 18th century onward (mostly notably by Walter Pater and John Ruskin in 19th century Britain), it remained for the 20th century American literary critic Jean Hagstrum to explicitly establish a critical tradition. Hagstrum announced his intent to apply the techniques of literary criticism to the analysis of visual depiction in literature in the 1958 text titled *The Sister Arts*. His primary concern focused on poetry that employed the rhetorical trope of *ekphrasis*, the art of description. Aside from his magisterial study of the arts, Hagstrum also coined the term *pictorialism*, which referenced a specific type of verbal depiction in literature, that which created pictures in the mind's eye of the reader. Since Hagstrum's work appeared, there have been many critics working fruitfully at the intersections of ekphrasis, pictorialism, poetry, and painting. Much of that work turns on the rhetorical ability of the writer to call forth pictures in the mind of the reader; thus its subject matter and the critical explications of the critics are valuable to any rhetorician working at the intersection of visual arts and language. Yet the critical products of that tradition bear little resemblance to what rhetoricians are now investigating and to the conclusions they draw. Therefore, I offer a brief exposition here of how rhetoric creates its own set of questions about reading the visual arts.

The primary difference between the Sister Arts tradition and visual rhetoric is that rhetoricians are not working with correspondences between written works and visual images, so much as they are asking how visual images are themselves carriers of meaning. To borrow from Tony Blair's work (chap. 2 in this volume), visual images are construed not as capable of arguments, but as invested with the ability to offer audiences propositions. A second important difference is that the images rhetoricians study are not limited to the Western canon of the fine arts as are the images offered through the Sister Arts tradition, but range through some of the more popular arts such as advertisements, printmaking, and photography. Third, visual rhetoricians consider the temporal and spatial implications of context: the ways in which the meaning of a single image can alter dramatically due to placement, context, cropping, and captioning.

Rhetoricians point to Kenneth Burke as an early visual rhetorician. In his 1966 publication, *Language as Symbolic Action*, Burke encouraged scholars to analyze all symbolic forms, including "mathematics, music, sculpture, painting, dance, architectural styles" (28). Thus, rather than search for correspondences between the word and the image (poetry and painting), a rhetoric of the visual abstracts both text and image to the level of signs. Such a practice moves away from—but does not violate—Lessing's contention that one essential difference between poetry and painting is the medium. To adopt another famous phrase, in Burke's configuration, it is the message and the act of communication that is more important than the medium. Another essential difference between the theories is that rhetoric does not focus on correspondences between the arts, but on the image itself as a carrier of meaning.

Yet, because it is rhetoric and rhetoric is situational, a visual rhetoric cannot hope to be a unified theory. Just as different painters can be credited with authoring different visual styles, different spectators approach viewing at different times, in different spaces, and with varying degrees of prior experience and access to information. A *visual rhetoric* is a frame of analysis for looking and interpreting. As James Heffernan notes, drawing from Ernst Gombrich, "looking at a picture can often take a good deal of time" because it involves "scanning, remembering, anticipating, correcting, and confirming impressions" (97). Looking is further complicated by the human desire to possess, to bring the object into our own life story or narrative, to account for witnessing something extraordinary, moving, or meaningful, or perhaps merely popular. Martin Jay notes that the word "theater" has the same root as theory or theoria, "to look attentively, to behold" (23) and James Elkins extends looking to possession, as in "searching" and attempting to bring something into one's field of vision or narrated self: "There is no looking without thoughts of using ... owning ... appropriating, keeping, remembering and commemorating" (Elkins 22). Looking is always framed by past experiences and learned ideas about how and what to see. "Just looking" is never innocent, nor is it ever final.

Many of the insights in this essay derive from art history; thus, art historians may find the discussion here to be rather abbreviated and somewhat mundane. I must stress that the discussion is directed at rhetoricians turning to the visual field, who, in the process of investigating aspects of visual culture, might question how, even whether, given the Sister Arts tradition, the fine arts can be analyzed rhetorically. In attempting to discuss rhetoric and the fine art of painting, I set into play three elements: the spectator, the space of viewing, and the object that is viewed. Meaning is not located in the object itself. Nor is it found in the spectator's well of previous experiences. Meaning derives from the interplay of these elements and is not limited to expressive or persuasive modes of response. Visual rhetoric provides a theoretical crucible for investigating responses to the visual arts, ultimately unhinging the traditional dynamic of pleasure/expressiveness (what Louise Rosenblatt termed an *aesthetic response*) and function/persuasiveness (Rosenblatt uses the term *efferent response*) in favor of a dialogic, transactional viewing.

I am going to assume for the purposes of this chapter that the rhetorical capacities of works of art extend beyond aesthetic or expressive response (I will set aside the idea of pleasure for the time being). My assumption is that it is agreed in academic circles, and as Rosenblatt demonstrated some 65 years ago, that meaning can be found in a work without recourse to a supporting document. Nonetheless, I am going to assert that there are types of misreadings that locate readers in interpretative spaces that are interpretively misleading. The exhibit "Facing Nature," which I discuss in the second half of this essay, is one such space. In order to test our responses and make a decision about whether an interpretation is a misreading in the sense that it is an intentional reading against the grain (a powerful position, as in Griselda Pollock's work) or a misreading in the sense that it presents a proposition about the past that is not supported by other works of the time, we must set ourselves a "Charge" as viewers. We must ask what we know and what we need to know before we even begin an analysis.

READERS AND HISTORY

As David Lowenthal notes, although the past could be said to exist in the present through memory, history, and relic, "The ultimate uncertainty of the past makes us all the more anxious to validate that things were as reputed" (191). *Validation* amounts to construction of the past to be investigated. It is not that there are no independent facts about the past, but that the researcher is instrumental in selecting the area to explicate and illuminate. We are always rewriting history, comments cultural critic Slavoj Zizek. We read the past as a symbol of "historical memory ... retroactively giving the elements their symbolic weight by including them in new textures—it is this elaboration which decides retroactively what they 'will have been' " (56). The *past* is a gap that readers must fill with that which they know at the time of viewing the artistic work. Reading the past offers the readers choices: build a meaning around the evidence presented on the canvas from existing knowledge or continue to investigate the circumstances of creation of the work.

Yet, in trying to recover the past, we produce misreadings because we infuse the past with our desires. For example, I list some misreadings of Joseph Wright of Derby's 1767 painting, *An Experiment on a Bird in the Airpump* in a previous study of his work (see Helmers, "Painting"). These ranged from interpreting the natural philosopher at the center of the canvas as a Frankensteinian "mad scientist" and believing that the young girls in the lower right corner were being stereotypically represented as weak females. As David Bleich illustrated in his study of readers of literature, *Readings and Feelings*, misreadings enable us to learn about the readers themselves; however they don't tell us much about the past. Griselda Pollock's *Vision and Difference* used a psychoanalytical model to interrogate paintings of Dante Gabriel Rossetti, but the analysis is largely hypothetical. Working with the analysis that Pollock started, Lynne Pearce posits two types of readers of art in her work on Rossetti and the pre-Raphaelite Brotherhood. One is a "naïve viewer," whose primary interest is in representational content. The other is a "knowledgeable" viewer (like Pearce herself, or Pollock) who is versed in technical conventions of paintings. Pearce favors the former, for that viewer, through her "technical illiteracy," has "the possibility of making for the picture a narrative of her own choosing" (33). Whereas the knowledgeable viewer is enslaved by interpretive explanations (34), the naïve viewer has opened a liberating space for the subjects of the painting: they may be who they "*might be*" rather than what they "ought to be" (43). Furthermore, narrative liberates painting and viewer from controlling regimes of explanation, of "consensual symbolism" (Pearce 34).[1] Alberto Manguel, in a recent book titled *Reading Pictures*, connects reading the artistic work to reading the print work, but he also warns that some narratives may provide us with misreadings based on prejudice, as well as misreadings based on compassion:

> When we read pictures—in fact, images of any kind, whether painted, sculpted, photographed, built or performed—we bring to them the temporal quality of narrative. We extend that which is limited by a frame to a before and an after, and through the craft of telling stories (whether of love or of hate), we lend the immutable picture an infinite and inexhaustible life .... We construct our story through echoes in other stories, through the illusion of self-reflection, through technical and historical knowledge, through gossip, reverie, prejudice, illumination, scruples, ingenuity, compassion, wit. No story elicited by an image is final or exclusive, and measures of correctness vary according to the same circumstances that give rise to the story itself. (13)

Narration animates the static representations of a work of art. Because the viewer must supply dialogue and sequential action, "he or she becomes complicit with the designer in telling the story, creating a discourse, and ... defining a cause that generates the narrative that will unfold" (Lewis 33). Suzanne Lewis deftly illustrates how the reader is implicated in telling the story of the Norman Conquest of England 1066 by translating the sequential images of the Bayeux Tapestry. Employing narrative theory, Lewis establishes rhetoric as a form of narrative and visual persuasion based on conventions of representation, tropes, and formalized addresses to audiences that, in turn, engenders reaction and reflection. She is not particularly concerned with persuasion, primarily because the outcome of the battle that the tapestry represents is always known and the hero is never in doubt: William (who is known to history as "the Conqueror") will always win the Battle at Hastings. It is important, however, that the viewers of the tapestry be engaged in a ritual process of viewing that allows them to re-animate the important history and situate themselves within a new reign following the death of Edward the Confessor and the battle for the throne between British Harold and Norman William. The Bayeux Tapestry "can best be seen as an imaged performance text played out on a newly constructed, transitional 'stage' for court audiences with residual Anglo-Saxon ties as well as strong Norman sympathies" (Lewis 5). Thus, the ritual process of viewing allows the spectators to re-imagine the past and create stories about the images. Nonetheless, despite being "witnesses" to the historical events represented in the tapestry, the viewers of the Bayeux Tapestry over time lost the capacity to remember those events. They had to supply their memories with a store of twice-told tales and, eventually, written materials (like Lewis's own book) that identified main characters and significant turning points in the tale. Without access to some frame of reference, the tapestry's suasive qualities are diminished, if not nullified.

There is a significant body of art historical work that is sociological in nature that can influence a rhetorical analysis. This type of inquiry, identified with Arnold Hauser's *The Social History of Art* (1951) and often termed "materialist art history" (Perry 8), focused attention on written documents, such as exhibition reviews, rather than on the biography of the artist or on the aesthetic properties of a work or the tradition of connoisseurship that stressed the value of a particular work (Perry 9). An early rhetoric of the arts that is sociological or materialist in focus can be identified in Gombrich's influential work, *The Story of Art* (1950). Gombrich asserted that no matter the era, artists were faced with practical problems that they needed to solve in order to create their works. All artistic production is the result of decisions made by the artist and is created for particular audiences (12): "They were made for a definite occasion and a definite purpose" (13).[2] Gombrich's argument removed painting from an idea of "expression" to a cultural problem that is indicative of rhetorical questioning. Human agency and choice are essential as mediators between differing expectations and visual concepts. Contemporary art historian Michael Baxandall makes a similar point. He expresses the painter's rhetorical imperative as the painter's "Charge." The Charge derives from the painter's need to act, "a relation between the object and its circumstances" (42). The Charge must also take into account the painter's "Brief," "local conditions in the special case," or "objective circumstances" (30). Together, Charge and Brief make up the particular circumstances in which the image is created, but they also take into consideration the painter's mind or attitude toward the job or technique. From the many resources and possible attitudes presented, the painter must make selections; thus, as Baxandall sees it, painting is primarily a rhetorical act. Just as the artist worked within a cultural situation that shaped the work of art, the viewer operates from within a cultural situation that enables particular responses at particular times. Viewing is a transactional process.

My intent, in this chapter, is to expand the notion that viewing is a transaction enacted within a cultural moment through two specific examples of the ways in which language-based acts create "frames" for viewing art. While the physical frame is obviously one device that can be isolated for analysis, in this piece I would like to expand the idea of "the rhetoric of the frame" into a textual and culturally situated metaphor so that it more closely resembles the type of rhetorical work in which scholars in English and communications engage. To draw language from Marxist critic Louis Althusser, what type of spectator is "hailed" by paintings?[3] And if hailing results in a moment of "reification," in which the subject recognizes that he/she is being addressed, are the spectators paused in a moment of self-other recognition by technique, subject, frame, gallery, catalogue, audiotour, or guidebook? Rhetorically speaking, this moment of recognition is the transaction between spectator and painted subject in which something draws our attention.

Lynne Pearce states that representation is itself a mediating device, a frame; the spectator witnesses reality through the intervening vision of the artist. Spatially and temporally, that vision of the artist also engages—or "frames"— a moment in time, a moment in the life of the subject of the representation, whether that subject is Jesus Christ, the Virgin Mary, or Sir Brooke Boothby. A rhetorical reading, then, engages the spatial and the temporal, contrary to, once again, Lessing, who isolated painting as a spatial art and textual works as temporal. If the spectator is able to animate the spatial through the deployment of cause and effect, before and after, then the spectator is temporally enacting a narrative. In particular, then, it is narrative framing devices that occupy my attention in this essay.

Once again, viewing is not quite as innocent as I would make it seem in this discussion, for just as soon as one offers narrative as the framing device *du jour*, it is easily parsed into the question of authority: whose narrative? As I demonstrate in the two sections that follow, this question has real consequences for the position of the spectator in relation to the art on display. Eventually, one is forced to confront issues of power. Curators have power over both the art and the spectator. Historians and critics, through their own (and I should add *valid*) inquiry, have the power to shape the ways that a text is received. Our own narrative explanations, the artist's reflections gleaned from letters and diaries, the museum's explanatory notes, all engage in a struggle between word and image, between the supremacy of the text as a narrative and the effects of the visual. This *paragonal* struggle is even embedded at the heart of the disciplinary naming device visual/rhetoric. It is my hope that rhetoricians are flexible enough to open the space between medium and technique and message and text.

FRAMES I: WINDOW PAIN

In a darkened room, a scientist (known at the time as a natural philosopher), dressed in the conventional loose fitting red robe of the alchemist, works an airpump, a vacuum, in which a white bird has been placed. Around him are gathered eight figures: a young couple, a young man, a middle-aged man comforting two young girls, an elderly man directing his gaze at an illuminated bowl at the base of the airpump, and a small boy at the window. This is the scene of *An Experiment on a Bird in the Airpump* by Joseph Wright of Derby.

Despite Benedict Nicolson's assertion that "A beautiful lucidity informs everything Wright did; … The spectator is never left in any doubt" (1), what does a spectator actually know about the painting, given a historical distance of 250 years and only the evidence of the framed canvas and its mounting in the Sackler Room of the National Gallery in London? Even Nicolson uses "lucidity" in a double sense: as the light of the candle for which Joseph Wright was so

FIG. 3.1. Joseph Wright of Derby, 1734–1797, British. *An Experiment on a Bird in the Airpump* (1768). Oil on canvas, 182.9 × 243.9 cm. Presented by Edward Tyrrell, 1863, National Gallery, London.

famous and in its metaphorical sense as the light of knowledge, or insight. The current exhibition space tells us very little. Wright's *An Experiment* is located between the Constables and the Gainsboroughs as an example of a certain period in British art. What is compelling, nonetheless, is that the painting itself poses questions through character and action and because of the remoteness of the scientific experiment being conducted. Otto Von Guerlicke and Robert Boyle invented the airpump, simultaneously and apparently independently, in Holland and Britain during the mid-17th century. It continued to be a familiar instrument of scientific inquiry well into the 19th century. The principle behind it was simple and the instrument's design was elegant. Air was pumped out of a glass chamber in which a lighted candle or a rodent was placed in order to demonstrate the necessity of air to life. Common enough in Wright's time, but in ours, who but a chemist or historian has heard of an airpump prior to their exposure to the painting? Who is familiar with the works of Joseph Wright? Certainly, the spectator need not be a historian of science or fine arts in order to create a meaning from the painting, but once the meaning is created, many unanswered questions remain. What is the irregular object within the glass bowl at the base of the pump? Are these people members of a family? Why is it so dark in the room? From the crucible of aesthetic and efferent readings, initial responses tend toward the aesthetic and expressive: *feeling* that the bird is being treated cruelly or believing that there is something powerful about this painting.

A second tendency, when viewing *An Experiment*, is to see the painting as a window onto the past, a documentary illustration of life in the mid-18th century. In fact, traditionally, the audience construed the physical frame around the canvas as a "window" into the image. Looking through the frame of exhibition at the framed canvas involves an *ekphrastic* moment that refers to a moment or moments of offstage action. Although we, like the art patrons of the 18th century, look on the painting in a gallery, we imagine by the "mind's eye" what has happened to the bird, supplementing evidence with our own fears for its safety and our desire for its well being. These mental activities stretch us into the room where the experiment takes place and back to the earliest time, to the (fictional) moment when the experiment was conducted. Although the painting is viewed in the present, spectators are drawn into an early industrial past in which familiar markers of place and occasion are absent. A spectator's Charge, to employ Baxandall's configuration, is to select an interpretation of the painting that brings the painting into their own story, their time, place, and moral system of meaning. Spectators whom I observed in the National Gallery often do just this, making moral judgments about the consequences of the experiment addressed to other spectators in "now" time, but also addressing their judgments to the past.

Living in London in the 1750s, Joseph Wright was situated in a milieu of inquiry. In works published in the last 15 years, Iaian Pears and Lisa Jardine have detailed the developing importance of sight, seeing, and collecting visual objects in the 18th century. Printing, engraving, painting exhibitions—even the demonstration and sale of telescopes and microscopes—contributed to the expanding knowledge of the natural and artistic world. Men of wealth and position took to the continent for the Grand Tour that would expand their acquaintance with the arts and letters. Lacking a tradition of religious art and oil painting, British painters traveled to Italy to learn the techniques of the masters Raphael, Rubens, and Titian. Returning to Britain, they began to create an artistic class in society, one that encountered paintings not in Church, for that flirted dangerously with Catholicism's purported idolatry, but in academies and in the home. Painting entered the public sphere as a commodity and a means of social and economic exchange. The painters of the 18th century were dependent, to great extent, on a wealthy merchant class or members of the aristocracy for purchase. Gombrich draws attention to the "momentous change" brought on by the establishment of academies of art in Paris and London in the latter half of the 18th century:

> [A]nnual exhibitions became social events that formed the topic of conversation in polite society, and made and unmade reputations. Instead of working for individual patrons whose wishes they understood, or for the general public, whose taste they could gauge, artists had now to work for success in a show where there was always a danger of the spectacular and pretentious outshining the simple and sincere. (380)

"Perhaps the most immediate and visible effect of this [shift in visual performance] was that artists everywhere looked for new types of subject-matter" to catch the spectators' eyes (Gombrich 380). Artists of the time were "desperate" to "grab visitors by the lapels with dramatic or topical subjects, strong colors, inventive compositions, or—in the case of portraits—famous, glamorous, or notorious sitters," writes art critic Richard Dorment (32). Exhibitions crowded paintings together, frames touching, ceiling to floor and the exhibition floor could be just as crowded. As an anonymous writer in the London newspaper *The Morning Chronicle* of May 1, 1780 claimed, "Public exhibitions, which are usually the subject of public conversations, become matters of interest to every man who lives in the world, and wishes not to appear ignorant of what passes in it" (*Royal Academy Critiques*). Pears amplifies this idea in *The Discovery of Painting*: "The picture increasingly took on many aspects of being an intellectual fetish: from having a function as an illustration of, or commentary on, religious devotion and worship ... the picture itself became the object of commentary and discussion .... by which individuals and groups measured themselves" (242). Artists played to the demands of the public, as well. Thomas Gainsborough wrote that the artist must "conform to the common Eye" and choose subjects that the public "will encourage, & pay for" (qtd. in Dorment 35). It follows then, that, rather than painting from his inner lights (a Romantic era notion that post-dates Wright's time by 30 years or more), Wright consciously worked within canons of artistic expectation that framed his own situation as an artist within a powerful system of status and commodity exchange.

Complicating this issue further were the art critics of Wright's time, whose overwhelming concerns were with mimetic qualities of the art (did they reflect *reality* accurately) and with the ability of the paintings to be narrated. Appropriately—in a rhetorical gesture that joins the physical site of display to active reception—the paintings were frequently called "performances." For example, a reviewer in London's *Morning Post* in May 1780 commented on the general lack of "technical terms of the arts," but asserted that they were unnecessary when one could speak about paintings "from that effect on our judgment produced by a comparison between nature itself and the imitations of nature." Likewise, reviewers reported stories of the exhibition itself. A 1781 report testifies to the power that "likenesses" can have on the viewer:

> Last Friday in the Royal Academy, a young lady of fortune was so affected with a portrait that resembled her sister lately deceased, that she was obliged to withdraw from the rooms, and has since continued extremely ill. As there is nothing which captivates the senses, heightens the affections, or elevates the ideas, more than painting, it is no wonder that a striking likeness of a deceased friend or relation, suddenly appearing, should excite the most painful emotions. (*Royal Academy Critiques*)

This agreement between the power of representation and the power that was manifest in a universe created by God is not to be overlooked. In the 18th century, God as Author had yet to be replaced by science, although scientific advancement in England gradually opened up a space for secular and religious debate. Citing Ronald Paulson's work on Wright, Murray Roston positions Wright at the center of the changing ideology of his time and singles out *Airpump* for its "sad awareness of the mutual exclusiveness of the older beliefs and the new" (246):

> What strikes the art historian most forcibly is the painter's reversion to the chiaroscuro techniques of Caravaggio to deepen the effect of mystery in what is supposedly a rationally conducted experiment. Yet one must acknowledge that such mysterious responsiveness to the emotional implications of the demonstration rather than its overt theme, the acquiring of empirically tested knowledge, would seem to undercut the purpose of the painting. (Roston 246)

The question then is where Wright's sentiments lie, with the advent of science as the "Guide to limpid Truth," as one of Wright's contemporaries phrased it, or with the older belief in the God the Father and the Great Chain of Being.

Roston ultimately sides with science and technology to read the painting as a "displacement of traditional faith by the rationalism of the laboratory" in which God lies the "victim" (250). Yet, deconstructively, Roston's reading of the situation of *An Experiment* is a misreading, for it is based on a traditional iconographical reading of the bird in the receiver as a dove, rather than as the cockatoo that Wright actually painted. Extrapolating that the bird is a dove, the traditional artistic symbol for the Holy Spirit, does shift interpretation to the religious. Seeing the bird as a cockatoo, however, aligns Wright more closely with the works of his neighbors in Holland, who were so fastidiously concerned with the lush details of daily life and the exotic riches brought back from the travels of explorers. In addition, our knowledge of Wright changes. We can envisage him as a materialist painter, concerned with the details of his own time and the economic and social conditions of his surroundings in mid-century, rather than a painter of timeless theological ideals.

The periodical press and natural philosophers on the traveling lecture circuit through the country fostered the dissemination of scientific thought in the 18th century. As Simon Schaffer points out, the traveling scientist was a showman whose "task was to exploit control over these powers to draw out and make manifest the theological and moral implications" of the experiments for the audience (5). Drawing on the legacy of theater and performance, the spectacle of science was used to enlighten and entertain. Joseph Wright—like the traveling showmen—"publicized and exploited" the new developments in science. His scientist enjoins us to "behold," drawing from a popular poetical gesture of the 18th century. Not only did the century establish itself as a society of the spectacle, but also there existed a pervasive attitude to teach moral and general "improving" principles. As John Warltire, one of the other popular scientists and itinerant lecturers of the age noted, "the Business of EXPERIMENTAL PHILOSOPHY is to enquire into and investigate the Reasons and Causes of the Various Appearances in Nature; *and to make Mankind wiser and better.*" Hence, to look and to see were signally important in order to understand. For proper effect, the audience itself had to be appropriately "enlightened" already, precluding the general classes of society. The importance of this is that Wright was familiar with the lectures, the subsequent publications by the traveling philosophers, the experiments, the equipment (his airpump is an exact replica of Benjamin Martin's own portable table model, circa 1765), and their popular interest among men of learning. And, if we borrow from Roston, we might say as well that Wright was a knowledgeable reader of the theological implications of his subject.

The price for admittance to a philosophical lecture was above that which a working man or woman could pay, approximately 2.5 guineas for a public lecture; for a private course, 3 guineas per person. The number of people at a private experimental lecture was kept small. John Theophilus Desagulier, for example, offered his lectures in coffee houses or in private homes. Philosophers usually published the full text or a synopsis of their lectures in book form. Benjamin Martin, an 18th century natural philosopher, inventor, writer, and showman published an instructional book on using the portable table air-pump titled *The Description and use of a new, portable, table air-pump and condensing engine* (1766). His description of the types of experiments also includes a morally improving discourse. The book is intended to:

> elevate the rational Mind above the low Pursuits of sensual Amusements, and the little Dignity than can accrue to human Nature from all the Documents of a Play or a Romance. False Taste, and Pedantry should be banished to the Climes of Superstition and Despotism; and genuine Erudition fought for from the BIBLE of NATURE only in this *Newtonian* Age.

To publicize his ideas further, Martin published an edition of *The General Magazine of the Arts and Sciences, Philosophical, Philological, Mathematical, and Mechanical* that used a conventional dialogue between fictional and emblematic characters, one Cleonicus, a young man returned home from university, and his curious and sensitive sister, Euphrosyne. In two volumes, it is the first that contains the dialogues *The young GENTLEMEN'S and LADIES PHILOSOPHY; or a particular and accurate SURVEY of the Works of NATURE, by way of DIALOGUE; illustrated by Experiments and embellish'd with Poetical Descriptions.* Martin's publication adds another element to Wright's Brief: Women of good standing were educated in science as well as the polite arts of drawing, languages, and music. As Cleonicus explains to his sister, the fortunes of their parents allowed them both to partake of a good scientific education:

> Tis our Happiness that we have Parents whose Fortune enables, and whose Temper inclines, them to bestow on us Education, and to train us up to truely honourable and polite Life. I have all the Advantages of the University, and you of the Boarding-School. (Dialogue I, 1)

The conceit of the dialogue is that, whilst at home, Cleonicus will teach Euphrosyne the wondrous experiments he has learned while away. "Philosophy ... is a peculiar Grace in the Fair Sex; and depend on it, Sister, it is now growing into a Fashion for the Ladies to study Philosophy"[4] (Dialogue I, 1).

Among the scientific experiments that the pair daily conducts are experiments with the airpump. Martin had developed his own airpump and, in something of a marketing ploy, he advertises its superiority within the pages of the dialogue. Martin's chief development to the pump was that his did not leak; therefore, the experiments were much more successful than those conducted in previous models. As he explains in *The Description and use of a new, portable, table air-pump and condensing engine*, one of the most spectacular experiments involved placing a small animal under the glass receiver, such as a kitten, a rabbit, or a bird. Of course,

> An ANIMAL (as Rat, &c.) being put under the Receiver, when the Air begins to be exhausted, shews Signs of Uneasiness and Pain; as you continue the Operation, the Animal convinces you of encreasing Pain and Agonies, 'till at length it expires in the utmost Convulsions. (XLI, 28)

Martin warns, the *"tender-hearted"* may find this experiment too horrific, and the scientist should resort to using the pig's bladder "to convey the intended Ideas, *without torturing the Animal for Amusement."*

Martin's narrative hands us an explanation for the painting, a piece of writing that verifies not only the actions of the group assembled in Wright's dim chamber, but also of the emotions suffered by the women in the room. Yet, without Martin's convenient text, how much of this struggle between life and death is evident in the painting? To what extent is the foray into educational and scientific documents of the time necessary? As we can see, traditional art history, such as the statements and interpretations offered by Nicolson and Roston, is inaccurate, but our own ideas of the painting suffer from similar inaccuracies. We all begin with the basic equipment of the canvas, the exhibition space, the "already-said" (such as a knowledge that the painting is well-known), the human tendency toward emotion, and the ability to situate this scene within a sequence or narrative. The struggle between life and death in captivity, ascribed in this painting to the bird, is a narrative that is familiar to us all, and was familiar in Wright's own time through, if not other sources, the medium of the Bible. However, the vehicle for this death, the airpump itself, is an arcane, unfamiliar object that requires some technical knowledge. The fact of its appearance in this painting points to something significant: The painting yields readily to rhetorical inquiry because of its documentary nature. It is a window on its time by its refusal to engage in timeless allegory. Its existence argues for the power of painting to be reflective of society, to argue for the potential of human works to better society.

FRAMES II: INTERFACING NATURE

An exhibition of airpumps at the Science Museum of London argues that scientific understanding was an imperative for the people of the 18th century because it was an avenue to democratic understanding. "The upheavals of the English Civil War in the 1640s," the exhibit text argues, "had caused many people to question accepted thinking about religion, society and nature." One of the primary advocates for the beneficent uses of scientific inquiry was Joseph Priestly, the educator and philosopher. Priestly was also a member of the Lunar Society, a group of West Midlands manufacturers and propertied men who gathered monthly to discuss new developments in science and with whom Wright associated. Priestly is remembered, however, as an anti-royal. Sympathetic to the French Revolution, he argued that the new science and new scientific instruments were agents of greater knowledge and democratic change that should make the English monarchy obsolete. Sweeping societal improvements were a hallmark of the 18th century. Poverty, hard work, low wages, and a lack of education were believed to be overcome by efficient, machine-led ways to improve work and profits. The exhibition seeks to contextualize the work of science in the 18th century in a cohesive narrative, providing artifacts to concretize the narrative. At the same time, the machines themselves are visual artifacts requiring a text to explain their operation and dramatize their significance. Like the painting, *An Experiment*, artifacts refuse to be "lucid." The narrative provided by the Science Museum is comforting because of its certainty and ability to define and provide evidence. Yet, it is important to remember that this exhibition situates the airpump within a fiction, a narrative about the past that determines what "will have been" (Zizek 56).

Exhibitors rely on cultural and visual memory to bring unfamiliar objects and representation into a discourse of intelligibility that is shared among groups. Such "shared consciousness" as visual memory has been termed "collective memory" by the French sociologist Maurice Halbwachs. According to Halbwachs' thesis, memory thus operates at the cultural rather than the personal level. "Unlike personal memory, whose authority fades with time," writes Barbie Zelizer, interpreting Halbwachs' work,

> the authority of collective memories increases as time passes, taking on new complications, nuances, and interests. Collective memories allow for the fabrication, rearrangement, elaboration, and omission of details about the past, often pushing aside accuracy and authenticity so as to accommodate broader issues of identity formation, power and authority, and political affiliation …. We find memories in objects, narratives about the past, even the routines by which we structure our day. (3)

Furthermore, collective memory allows societies to agree on what is important, what should be saved, and what should be commemorated. It is a negotiated process. Societies are frequently engaged in a discourse about the past and its preservation and these debates are based on what Jean Francois Lyotard identified as the common understanding of a Master Narrative.

In many ways, the place to begin when discussing the work of art may not even be within the exhibition space itself, but in the mall bookstore, the campus poster shop, or the parking lot of the museum, places where the meaning of art is negotiated and where art is transmitted as a commodity such as a calendar, poster, or billboard and where the initial idea of an object as "fine art" is apprehended. To paraphrase Matei Calinescu's work on rereading, even before we enter the space of exhibition, we have developed "certain expectations" about what we will see and we are "better informed about it than [we] might suspect" (42). However, a familiar warning surfaces from Calinscu: the information derived from the multifarious and ambient sources "may well turn out to have been misleading" (42).

Art museums generally use some form of textual material to reference, explain, or contextualize paintings or artifacts on display. In this section of the essay, I want to continue the emphasis on painting, but focus on the exhibition space and its composed narrative. My contention is that exhibitors are powerful mediators in the reception of texts. Curators exert immense power in arguing that certain works of art should be preserved because of the cultural work they do. Furthermore, through the so-called "blockbuster exhibit" (for example, the traveling Edouard Manet or Ansel Adams shows) they create a cultural and visual memory that establishes the value and meaning of objects.

"Facing Nature," a retrospective of oils, watercolors, illustrations, and engravings ranging from Homer's early work as a freelance "artist-reporter" in New York City through his reclusive years in the Adirondacks was mounted at the Denver Art Museum in March, 2001. It is the exhibition philosophy and the experience of walking through the exhibition that provide the opportunity to consider the way that "Homer" and "Art"—or in fact, any "artist" and "works"—are represented within the space of the museum. I place quotation marks around the painter's name and around the artistic product in order to illustrate my contention that what we experience in the space of the art museum is a way of seeing that is authored, not by the artist, but the curators.

A story of a trip through the four galleries of "Facing Nature" should sound something like a traveler's tale, a narrative. Spectators were directed to move through a "tour" of the American past, to see new sights and to pause to contemplate the natural world as represented in the 19th century paintings. Reading material memory and the rhetoric of exhibition spaces demands that all signifiers be examined, from ambient noise to the announced "subject" of the exhibition. This broadened question of how the past is displayed is engaged here. This exhibition revealed that a spectator's Brief includes codes of performance and display related to our time. The exhibit did not challenge the spectator's sense of moving from, say, a mall bookstore into a museum. Instead, it superimposed conventions of commercial display upon the art exhibition.[5]

Curators arranged the exhibit "Facing Nature" chronologically and thematically, taking a biographical approach to the painter's work. Visitors began with the Civil War and moved through seacoast paintings, through works depicting fishermen and hunters. Interpretive side panels that explain the historical significance of the works and provide background to the author's life are traditional in museums. The Denver Art Museum added to these ordinary, familiar elements. A curved wooden bench fronted seascapes, mounted on pale blue walls. Visitors might rest there to contemplate, not the sea, but representations of the sea in its beauty and its forbidding terror. In the words of Richard Grusin, "Nature provides the prior condition for the ... mimetic aim" of the exhibition (419) and is understood as something "pre-existent" and "represented." Three chiseled boulders two to three feet in height angled from corners of this exhibit space. Passing beyond this room into the environment of the sportsmen, one could rest again on a rustic, camp-style, twisted birch or willow bench. A long, low table in front of the bench held copies of art manuals on Homer and other American naturalist painters. A copy of Henry David Thoreau's *Walden* was tucked amidst these works. A wooden rowboat rested again the far wall of the room, before a contemporary, Home-Depot style wall mural of a mountain lake. Into it several children climbed, bringing paper and pencils to draw, not Nature, but strange monsters from the 20th century. Several wooden easels and artist's benches were grouped together beyond the boat, and children, again, occupied these easels. These props "staged" the exhibition. They transformed the art into a theatrical space where the audience could enact roles. The mind's eye allowed the spectator to imagine oneself as a tourist along the coast of Maine or a hunter tracking a deer in northern New York woods. The distance between spectator and art was thus reframed by contextualizing the artworks as windows onto a natural environment and into the past. The props also made a direct, physical connection to the nostalgic props for sale outside the space of the exhibit at the gift shop. The Denver Art Museum's special Winslow Homer gift shop, like most of the major museum gift shops, commodifies art and memory by selling wicker creels and wooden duck decoys that relate thematically to the subjects of Homer's paintings and give tangible presence to the two-dimensional paintings.

One common feature of exhibitions at major museums is the audiotour. In this exhibition, the audiotour involved not only a voice interpretation of the paintings, but folk-inspired music, of the type popular following the Ken Burns documentary, *The Civil War*. A guitar plucked simple melodies; a violin etched dance tunes. The music echoed Homer's position as an American artist, and thus performed a subtle political function in situating Homer as a historian of the American past—rather than, say, positioning him in relation to his European contemporaries. It also reinforced the dominant conception that his works are about the (clichéd) "simpler time" in the past, a time before industrial progress and immigration altered the sensibilities of the country and its people, a time before electric guitars and amplification. Yet, even without the audiotour, the room was not silent. A persistent soundtrack washed about the separate galleries. Seagulls cried as water rushed against the rocks on the Gloucester, Massachusetts coast; crickets ticked amid the Adirondack scenes. The museum had used an ambient sound nature track to recreate nature within the walls of culture. The marketing material about the exhibit draws attention to these innovative techniques in museum display:

Visitors will feel as if they are immersed in Homer's world, as they experience several sensory elements designed to create an atmosphere consistent with Homer's works. The galleries provide an intimate feel and incorporate ambient sound, environmental objects and artifacts, interactive areas with easels to draw on and a life-size boat to sit in. (*Winslow Homer*)

The effect was like being in a film. Spectators were scenic "extras," placed on a set, given props, and asked to react to the fictions as if it were all real. The sounds of wind rustling the leaves, of the plopping of a trout into a dusky pool, of the birds chirping in the oak leaves nearly convince us that we are there in a mythic and Arcadian past. There was a conscious decision to involve spectators in a narrative of anti- or pre-urban life in this exhibition.

One of the more interesting complications of the curators' theatrical approach to "Facing Nature" is that American art historians consider Homer a narrative painter. Homer trained himself as an illustrator of society events and leisure activities for popular magazines. His first works in oil were scenes of Civil War camp life, which he drew from his experiences as a pictorial correspondent for *Harper's Weekly*. From these early paintings, through his late works depicting hunters, trackers, and fisherman, there is a trajectory of narrative action. Life is suspended between two points in a story, the past and the future. His actors, like the boys in *Snap the Whip*, are moving toward a conclusion that is—and always will be—outside the frame (see Fig. 3.2). He paints "in prose" notes Geoffrey O'Brien, and about his paintings there is "a persistent sense of incompletion" (15–16). The spectator in our time reads the end of the narrative in their present.

One of the reasons that rereading a past becomes so easy in this exhibition is that Homer believed that his descriptive scenes should speak for themselves; he was, according to Nicolai Cikovsky, "reticent almost to the point of secretiveness about the meanings of his creations" (qtd. in O'Brien 15). Yet, as Robert Poole notes (citing David Tatham) Homer does "speak to people across the years": "The outcome is always in doubt ... Homer felt that viewers had an obligation to participate in the painting ... His point was to raise more questions than answers" (Poole 95, 98).

The result is that the paintings introduce storytelling for viewers, who retell the events of the painting and assign psychological motives to the characters. Even Poole, Associate Editor of *National Geographic*, can be found adopting the storytelling mode:

What happens to the brook trout leaping clear of the water? Does the hook give way? Or the deer swimming across a blue pond on a glorious October day, pursued by hunter and hound. Does the buck escape? What did that guide hear that caused him to turn his head away from the viewer? (95)

As Poole says, "Homer's range covers a whole world of emotions, like those of an accomplished actor, and the New York crowd that Poole observed at an

FIG. 3.2. Winslow Homer, 1836–1910, American. *Snap the Whip* (1872). Oil on canvas, 22 × 36 in.; 55.88 × 91.44 cm. Collection of the Butler Institute of American Art, Youngstown, Ohio.

exhibition warms to him. They point. They smile and poke their noses into the paintings" (84). The exhibition in New York was theater. In Denver, the curators added the props and the soundtrack. Painting becomes performance art, a Happening for the new century.

Michael Baxandall reminds readers that "we explain pictures only in so far as we have considered them ... Most of the better things we can think or say about pictures stand in a slightly peripheral relation to the picture itself" (1, 5).

As he explains, what art historians and observers have to say about a painting is more a representation of their own thinking about the painting. Thus, the adjectives "glorious" (Poole), "tranquillity" (Poole), even "realist" are concepts into which "Homer" is placed by his critics (as the metonymic representation of his oeuvre). Baxandall claims that the personal interferes to some extent with historical understanding, a particularly post-structuralist claim. Yet Baxandall's comment is useful in the examination of "Facing Nature," because the personal must reassert itself within powerful governing narratives designed by the curators of the exhibit. The sounds of wind and sea "soundscaping," designed to affect the emotions and draw the imagination, either are resisted or are assumed into the interpretation of the paintings as, again, "realist windows" on the world.

To some extent, Tony Bennet points out, all exhibitions and collections are dialogues between presence and absence, cultural capital (in the sense of value added) and the everyday. "What can be seen on display," he notes, "is viewed as valuable and meaningful because of the access it offers to a realm of significance which cannot itself be seen" (35). The settings in which the displayed objects are placed, furthermore, help to insert the viewer into the more significant realm through representation. In other words, a gallery designs its space to reflect the value it places on its objects. The National Gallery in London is somber, tasteful, and serious. The Guggenheim in New York City is open, spacious, and architecturally significant in order to validate architecture as art itself.

The paintings, sculpture, or natural history collections that are on display are meant to be "seen through," Bennet asserts (35). The problem is that only certain members of the class system are envisioned to have the ability to see through to the "appropriate socially coded" level of seeing. This level of seeing places the art works into a historical, thematic, cultural arrangement—in other words, class distinction allows those with greater cultural capital to discern that there is a rhetoric to exhibitions. Museums become instruments of social control and of class division. They are places to separate the "popular" from the "more significant." The irony, then, is that Homer would be championed as a painter of the popular while exhibited in the traditional realm of the elite. The accouterments of this exhibit refashion the museum as common ground rather than elite space.

Raymond Williams, the British cultural critic, has described "culture" in the earliest sense of use as "husbandry, the tending of natural growth" ("Cul-

ture" 87). Eventually, Williams notes, "culture" came to represent symbolic
systems of expression, such as literature, art, music, and philosophy rather
than natural production. Ironically, these two senses of the word are at work in
the exhibition "Facing Nature." Within the space of the exhibit, Nature is the
occluded term: We are facing culture as we sit on the benches and gaze at the
oiled sea.

In many ways, then, the two subjects of this chapter are similar because
they connect the natural world with the manufactured. If we agree with Williams, this is because "the idea of nature contains, though often unnoticed, an
extraordinary amount of human history" ("Ideas" 67). Human perception is
at the center of human endeavor, to such an extent that human emotion and
the human timeline circumscribe natural and cultural productions. Nature is a
stage for human action, on which dramas of command, conquest, domina-
tion, and exploitation are played, as they are without a doubt in *An Experiment
on a Bird in the Airpump* and "Facing Nature."

FRAMES III: STAGES

Perhaps the previous case studies were a lengthy way of restating James
Heffernan's assertion that the most "suggestive moment" of a painting is the
midpoint, "the point from which past and future action may be inferred as
cause and consequence of the action portrayed" (109). As he admits, this point
can never deliver "more than a partial meaning" (109) and it overlooks the
spectator's own visual memory. In addition, narrative is acknowledged by
many critics as playing a role in the interpretation of paintings, yet it is not specifically theorized. As we saw, Pearce uses narrative as the mode of inquiry of
her naïve viewer, but narrative itself is neither naïve, straightforward, or transparent. Tone and meaning depend on the axis of inquiry or the frame in which
the painting is viewed. Also, the notion of the naïve spectator, she who narrates, is problematic because, although naïve about painterly symbolism, the
spectator may be quite sophisticated with narrative options, learned from the
realm of the visual and verbal cultural imaginary: film, television, drama,
dance, poetry, novel—even vacation photography and advertisements.

Drawing on the work of Michel de Certeau, cultural critic Marcia Pointon
notes that the fascination with the past also constructs a "stage" on which we
place characters and actions. "Because our access to the object, a painted canvas, is immediate, what is represented on that canvas seems, by extension, historically graspable" (Pointon 9). In theater, as well, we focus on different
characters as they come to the fore; this conception allows us to understand
different lines of sight in painting and authorizes something of an inquiry-
based spectatorship in which the spectator raises questions and hypotheses. As
in literary studies, the painting/text can never be just one picture or have a single meaning, because its construction depends on an unlimited variety of fac-

tors such as, for example, the inclination and/or capability of individual spectators to create mental pictures—as well as their beliefs, outlooks, and impressions—the particular historical moment, the prevailing ideology, the composition of the audience, the ambient and intentional conditions that surround looking (Moore 66, note 7). Looking indicates the way things could be rather than proving the way things are.

The rhetorical meaning of a painting, then, appears to depend on perception and reception. Prior knowledge and the context of viewing the object will condition perception. Reception depends not only on emotion and structures of feeling, but also on the framing devices and cultural expectations being created by the area of display. In the case of *An Experiment*, for example, focusing our sight on the bird in the airpump may lead us to read the painting as an allegory of life and death, that is, unless the bird is mistakenly identified as a dove. In the latter case, the painting will become a Christian allegory, referring directly to the place of God and redemption in a secular society. If we move our gaze to the right and become interested in the little girls who appear so fearful, we might find that they are powerful girls indeed, for we have been directed to pity by their glances. On the other hand, if we see the central figure of the natural philosopher as a commanding figure of evil and science gone awry, we would have to eventually admit to a modern misreading of the figure of the scientist in 18th century culture, for this figure is not the Dr. Frankenstein of myth, but more likely an earnest traveling teacher, displaying the necessary connection of breath to life. One of the faults of the fully framed exhibition, "Facing Nature," was its refusal to allow readings and misreadings to surface amid the spectators. "Facing Nature" offered the stage and the offstage action succeeded in redrawing the spectator, as well.

In conclusion, visual rhetoric as a method for studying the fine arts must allow space for inquiry-based spectatorship. Interpretation is a process of accrual in which past experiences merge with the evidence of the canvas to construct a meaning. Nonetheless, that meaning will change over time as the memory of the viewing event is recalled and the image is revisited in different settings.

NOTES

1. Although I will be advocating Pearce's claim that the naïve viewer has a certain liberty of interpretation that is valid, I am concerned by Pearce's argument that animating a character in paint is liberating for the character, for it appears that we bring a new level of surveillance and control to the image by having the textual subject "think what we wish her to think" (Pearch 43).
2. Pollock's explanation of purpose is that the male viewers were enacting fetishistic scopophilia.
3. My thanks to Lori Landay for this observation.

4. There is also a need to tame the potentially errant woman, for Euphrosyne is not only the Muse of Good Cheer, but was often equated in 18th century iconography with Bacchanalian revelry. She is potentially licentious, and thus the discipline of science and the power of Enlightenment Reason, in addition to Euphrosyne being located in the home, would hold her to the path of goodness.
5. See the review of the new book, *Art on the Line*, for a comment by Richard Dorment on how we must be retrained to see things as they were in the past.

WORKS CITED

Althusser, Louis. *Lenin and Philosophy, and Other Essays*. Trans. Ben Brewster. London: Monthly Review Press, 2001.

Baxandall, Michael. *Patterns of Intention: On the Historical Explanation of Pictures*. New Haven: Yale UP, 1985.

Bennett, Tony. *The Birth of the Museum*. London: Routledge, 1995.

Bleich, David. *Readings and Feelings: An Introduction to Subjective Criticism*. Urbana, Illinois: National Council of Teachers of English, 1975.

Burke, Kenneth. *Language as Symbolic Action: Essays on Life, Literature, and Method*. Berkeley, CA: U of California P, 1966.

Calinescu, Matei. *Rereading*. New Haven: Yale UP, 1993.

Dorment, Richard. "*Art on the Line: The Royal Academy Exhibitions at Somerset House, 1780–1836*, Ed. David H. Solkin." *New York Review of Books* 49 (13 June 2002): 32–36.

Elkins, James. *The Object Stares Back: On the Nature of Seeing*. San Diego: Harcourt Brace, 1997.

Gombrich, Ernst. *The Story of Art*. Englewood Cliffs, NJ: Prentice Hall, 1950; 1995.

Grusin, Richard. "Representing Yellowstone: Photography, Loss, and Fidelity to Nature." *Configurations* 3.3 (1995): 415–436.

Hagstrum, Jean H. *The Sister Arts: The Tradition of Literary Pictorialism and English Poetry from Dryden to Gray*. Chicago: U of Chicago P, 1958.

Halbwachs, Maurice. *The Collective Memory*. Trans. Francis J. Ditter, Jr. and Vida Yazdi Ditter. New York: Harper and Row, 1980.

Hauser, Arnold. *The Social History of Art*. New York: Knopf, 1951.

Heffernan, James A. W. "Space and Time in Literature and the Visual Arts." *Soundings: An Interdisciplinary Journal* 70 (Spring-Summer 1987): 95–119.

Helmers, Marguerite. "Painting as Rhetorical Performance." *JAC: Journal of Advanced Composition* 21.1 (Winter 2001): 71–95.

Homer, Winslow. *Facing Nature*. Denver Art Museum. 4 April 2001. <http://www.denverartmuseum.org/homer/homer_exhibition.html>.

Jardine, Lisa. *Ingenious Pursuits: Building the Scientific Revolution*. New York: Nan A. Talese, 1999.

Jay, Martin. *Downcast Eyes: The Denigration of Vision in Twentieth-Century French Thought*. Berkeley: U of California P, 1993.

Lerner, Gerda. *Why History Matters: Life and Thought*. New York: Oxford UP, 1997.

Lessing, Gotthold. *Laocoön: An Essay on the Limits of Painting and Poetry*. Trans. Edward Allen McCormick. Baltimore: Johns Hopkins UP, 1984.

Lewis, Suzanne. *The Rhetoric of Power in the Bayeux Tapestry*. Cambridge: Cambridge UP, 1999.

Lowenthal, David. *The Past is a Foreign Country*. Cambridge: Cambridge UP, 1985.

Lyotard, Jean Francois. *The Postmodern Condition.* Trans. Geoff Bennington and Brian Massumi. Minneapolis, MN: U of Minnesota P, 1984.

Manguel, Alberto. *Reading Pictures: A History of Love and Hate.* New York: Random House, 2000.

Martin, Benjamin. *The Description and use of a new, portable, table air-pump and condensing engine. With a select variety of capital experiments, which, together with different parts of the apparatus and glasses, are illustrated by upwards of forty copper-plate figures.* London 1766.

—. *The General Magazine of the Arts and Sciences, Philosophical, Philological, Mathematical, and Mechanical: Under the following Heads, viz. I. The young GENTLEMEN'S and LADIES PHILOSOPHY; or a particular and accurate SURVEY of the Works of NATURE, by way of DIALOGUE; illustrated by Experiments, and embellish'd with Poetical Descriptions.* London 1755.

Moore, Jeannie Grant. "'In My Mind's Eye': Postmodern (Re)visions of *Hamlet.*" *Hamlet Studies* 22 (2002): 40–76.

Nicolson, Benedict. *Joseph Wright of Derby: Painter of Light.* 2 vols. New York: Pantheon Books, 1968.

O'Brien, Geoffrey. "The Great Prose Painter." *The New York Review of Books* 43 (29 February 1996): 15–16, 18–19.

Pearce, Lynne. *Woman, Image, Text: Readings in Pre-Raphaelite Art and Literature.* Buffalo: U of Toronto P, 1991.

Pears, Iaian. *The Discovery of Painting: The Growth of Interest in the Arts in England, 1680–1768.* New Haven: Yale UP, 1988.

Perry, Gill. "Preface." *Academies, Museums, and Canons of Art.* Ed. Gill Perry and Colin Cunningham. New Haven and London: Yale UP, 1999.

Pointon, Marcia. *Strategies for Showing: Women, Possession, and Representation in English Visual Culture, 1665–1800.* New York: Oxford UP, 1997.

Pollock, Griselda. *Vision and Difference: Femininity, Feminism, and Histories of Art.* New York: Routledge, 1988.

Poole, Robert. "American Original." *National Geographic* 194.6 (December 1998): 72–101.

Priestly, Joseph. *An Essay on a Course of Liberal Education for Civil and Active Life.* London: C. Henderson, 1765.

Rosenblatt, Louise. *Literature as Exploration.* New York : Modern Language Association of America, 1938; 1995.

Roston, Murray. *Changing Perspectives in Literature and the Visual Arts, 1650–1820.* Princeton, NJ: Princeton UP, 1990.

Royal Academy Critiques &c. Vol. 1. 1769–93. London.

Schaffer, Simon. "Natural Philosophy and Public Spectacle in the Eighteenth Century." *History of Science* 21 (1983): 1–43.

Warltire, John. *Analysis of a Course of Lectures in Experimental Philosophy; With a brief Account of the Most necessary Instruments used in the Course, and the Gradual Improvements of Science.* Exeter: R. Trewman, 1767.

Wendorf, Richard. "Visual Arts and Poetry." *The New Princeton Encyclopedia of Poetry and Poetics.* Ed. Alex Preminger and T. V. F. Brogan. Princeton: Princeton, UP, 1993. 1360–64.

Williams, Raymond. "Culture." *Keywords.* New York: Oxford UP, 1976; 1983.

—. "Ideas of Nature." *Problems in Materialism and Culture.* London: Verso, 1980. 67–85.

Zelizer, Barbie. *Remembering to Forget: Holocaust Memory Through the Camera's Eye.* Chicago: U of Chicago P, 1998.

Zizek, Slavoj. *The Sublime Object of Ideology.* London: Verso, 1989.

CHAPTER FOUR

Visual Rhetoric in Pens of Steel and Inks of Silk: Challenging the Great Visual/Verbal Divide

Maureen Daly Goggin

As the chapters in this volume so well demonstrate, attempting to define visual rhetoric is slippery business. Highly contestable, the term *visual rhetoric* is invoked to describe a broad range of diverse scholarly interests. These include, for example, "narrowly, the study of the design of texts on pages," to "more generally, the study of all visual signs, including the semiotics of graphic arts, television, and other media" (Bernhardt 746), to a broader study of "visual and material practices, from architecture to cartography, and from interior design to public memorials" (Lucaites and Hariman 37). Yet, however disparate and decidedly contested definitions of visual rhetoric are, they nevertheless share a tendency to draw a hard-line distinction between rhetoric of the *word* and rhetoric of the *image*, that is, a dichotomy between the *visual* and the *verbal* features of textualized objects. In this chapter, I argue that the relationship between rhetoric of the word and rhetoric of the image is far more fluid both on synchronic and diachronic levels than the divide permits. This relationship is contingent on social, cultural, economic and technological domains in which existing semiotic resources for both creating/transforming and circulating/consuming meanings shift along axes of accessibility, purposes, subject positions, material conditions and practices.

What contributes to the propensity to bifurcate rhetoric of the *word* and rhetoric of the *image*? There are no doubt several contributing factors. Among the strongest, for the purposes of this chapter, is that current theories of meaning and communication continue to privilege logocentric approaches and perspectives even as they treat an ever-wider range of semiotic artifacts and practices apart from the scripted, printed and digital pages. In calling for

new ways of thinking about semiotic systems, Gunther Kress makes a powerful case for the hegemony of logocentricism:

> The focus on language alone has meant a neglect, an overlooking, even a
> suppression of the potentials of all the representational and communica-
> tional modes in particular cultures; an often repressive and systematic ne-
> glect of human potentials in many of these areas; and a neglect equally, as a
> consequence, of the development of theoretical understandings of such
> modes .... Or, to put it provocatively: the single, exclusive and intensive focus on
> written language has dampened the full development of all kinds of human poten-
> tials. (emphasis added, "Design" 157)

The continued bifurcation of visual and verbal aspects of rhetoric in subtle,
and sometimes not so subtle, ways reifies the *words*—written language—as a
measure against, and somewhat above, all other potential resources for representation and communication. Thus, it tends to blind us to theorizing and historicizing other kinds of semiotic resources and practices. As a result, the
divide severely limits *what* counts as rhetorical practice and *who* counts in its
production, performance and circulation.

VISUALIZING THE VERBAL, VERBALIZING THE VISUAL

In both a literal and figurative way, a rhetoric of the written word is *visual*, distinguishable from other forms of symbolic representation by the sense of
sight.[1] Both images and words on script, print or digital pages engage the eyes.
When images and words appear together in one discursive space, they operate
synergetically. In this sense, written verbal rhetoric *is* visual rhetoric. In both
performance and circulation, such rhetoric is better contrasted with other
semiotic practices that engage senses apart from the visual, such as those of
touch as in Braille, or the ear as in audio performances whether live or recorded, or the tactile / ocular (e.g., the body and sight) as in sign languages or,
in the German term *Gebärdensprache*, gesture language.

   If we shift attention to the material practice of creating/transforming
semiotic meaning, the clear divide between image and word becomes even
fuzzier. This shift raises important questions regarding the semiotic resources
for any given rhetorical situation. Anthony Giddens distinguishes between
two kinds of semiotic resources, what he terms "allocative" and "authoritative." The former refers to the raw materials and technologies for transforming material into cultural meaning. The latter refers to the capacity to control
allocative resources, that is, access to and skill with materials and technologies. As Kaufer and Carley, drawing on Giddens, point out, "the author's authoritative resources consist of knowledge and position in the sociocultural
landscape, the sociocultural inheritance with which the author is currently

vested and brings to any current transaction" (137). For Giddens, it is the inter-action between allocative and authoritative resources that permit meaning makers to exert influence over social structures. In this dynamism, semiotic re-sources are best understood as multiple complexes of technological condi-tions and sociocultural landscapes that overlap like Venn diagrams. Of course, certain material conditions and landscapes have been (and continue to be) more privileged than others. Because certain groups of rhetors have been barred from particular positions in dominant sociocultural landscapes—pri-marily because of their class, gender, race, ethnicity, and sexual orientation—they have had limited, and at times, no access to either dominant allocative or authoritative resources. Forced to work with alternative allocative resources on the margins of hegemonic sociocultural landscapes or in alternative spaces, their discourses have typically been rendered invisible.

As Kress notes, "the issue of materials through which the semiotic mode is realized is crucial for two reasons: because of their representational potentials, and because of their cultural valuations" ("Multimodality" 191). In other words, the materiality of constructing meaning is contingent on material re-sources, cultural values and cultural positioning. These factors, however, shift in response to kairotic conditions of time and place as well as technological, economic, social, political and cultural forces. In short, complex contextual forces both permit and limit resources, valuations and positioning, thus foster-ing certain material practices while limiting others, and, as a result, both culti-vate and restrict the range of possible rhetorical participants and the rhetorical artifacts to which praxis may give rise or even be recognized.

All discursive practices may be best understood as material practices. That is, for visual rhetoric, material surfaces (paper, stone, clay, canvas, metal, digital space) are marked with a tool of some sort that releases a physical substance such as ink or lead, or scratches, etches, carves or molds signs, or translates key-strokes into electronic impulses and so on. The technologies of each vary in per-mitting some possibilities for representation while constraining others. In addition, access to technologies also varies tremendously. Moreover, the cul-tural, social and political expectations for how particular kinds of meaning may be represented (and, thus, "seen" or made visible) shapes what kinds of repre-sentations are permitted. That is to say, the materiality of semiotic practices and artifacts is socially, culturally and politically constructed (Street 170). The ques-tion is: If all discursive practices are material practices, what is the range from all available material practices that may be understood as meaning-making? Is it the case that all material practices hold the potential to serve as semiotic re-sources? Can hammering a nail into drywall, for example, be understood as a meaning-making activity? Under what circumstances might such an act be per-ceived as semiotic? What are the features that identify a material practice as a meaning-making, knowledge-generating endeavor? Given the longtime schol-arly privileging of the "word" in limited material terms—primarily scripted, printed and, more recently, digital pages—other kinds of semiotic material practices have been left under-, if not un-theorized.

How do we begin to understand the rhetorics of those who have been denied access to spaces in dominant sociocultural landscapes with little or no access to particular allocative resources? How do we study the rhetorical practices and works of those who have turned to alternative allocative resources and have worked on the margins of privileged sociocultural landscapes, or in landscapes that are not recognized? Needlework offers a powerful place to look for alternative semiotic resources and acts of meaning making.

In this chapter, I explore needlework as a semiotic practice, and more specifically, the history of sampler making to demonstrate the ways in which the relationship between rhetoric of the word and rhetoric of the image is much more fluid than is typically theorized, and as a way to make visible rhetorical practices and performances that have remained largely outside the dominant scholarly gaze. By tracing the discontinuities both in the praxis of sampler making and the circulation of samplers, I show how the interdependent relationship between image and word shifts historically, contingent on the medium, the technological domain, the web of other semiotic practices in which a given material practice is situated, the social, political and cultural contexts, and the socialized individual subject positions. Historically, needlework has offered an alternative rhetorical space to those who have been denied participation in dominant discourses by virtue of their gender, class, ethnicity and race. A study of needlework, then, contributes to a richer, more robust understanding of rhetorical praxis and texts.

SEMIOTIC RESOURCES: NEEDLEWORK AS A CASE IN POINT

Needlework as a practice may be best understood as a form of meaningful mark-making—a polysemous system of writing. It incorporates two broad families of writing systems—what Geoffrey Sampson has termed *semasiographic systems* and *glottographic systems*.[2] *Semasiographic systems* are defined as "systems of visible communication ... which indicate ideas directly" (29); e.g., international sign symbols). The other, *glottographic systems*, are those "which provide visible representations of spoken-language utterances" (29); e.g., alphabet systems such as written English). Sampson's distinction between these two families of writing systems helps to account historically for the emergence of very different material practices of graphic representation. However, at the level of production, the distinction between glottographic and semasiographic systems only makes sense when the semiotic resources for inscribing the verbal word differ from those for inscribing other images. The question is: To what degree, and under what material circumstances, do the semiotic resources (both allocative and authoritative) necessary to render alphabetic letters dramatically differ from those needed to render other kinds of images?[3]

In needlework, the semiotic resources for inscribing both glottographic and semasiographic systems are exactly the same. Learning what semiotic resources are available (domain knowledge) and how to use them (procedural knowledge) is part and parcel of knowing how to read and write the *textile*. In the case of embroidery, domain and procedural knowledges can be quite complicated because of the variety of different kinds and combinations of potential materials and the sheer abundance of different types of stitches. Embroidery stitches may be categorized into two major classes. The first, often called color work, consists of stitches typically worked on the surface of the fabric, and may be further classified by their stitch structure into four groups: *flat stitches*, which are straight stitches wrought in varying lengths and directions that lay flat against the surface of the fabric (e.g., back, satin, split, stem, running stitches); *cross stitches*, which are worked with two or more stitches that cross each other in a variety of different ways (e.g., cross stitch, herringbone, long-armed cross, star stitches); *looped stitches*, which are formed by looping the thread on the surface of the fabric and holding it place by a smaller stitch (e.g., chain, feather, buttonhole); and *knotted stitches*, which are made by knotting or twisting the thread on the surface of the textile (e.g., Danish, French and bullion knots). These four classes of stitches can be combined into composite stitches to create more complex textures and effects. The second major class, often called white work, covers three major categories of open work: *cutwork*, in which the background fabric is cut away and filled in by lace-like stitches; *drawn work*, in which individual warp or weft threads of the background are pulled out and stitches are added to create intricate lace patterns; and *pulled thread*, in which the stitches are pulled tightly to leave open areas. Taken together, these two broad families of embroidery stitches account for hundreds of different kinds of stitches (Eaton; Brittain).[4]

As stitches are rendered with differing sizes and kinds of needles, using different numbers, colors and types of threads on different kinds and colors of background fabrics, and are combined into distinct patterns, their potential as a semiotic tool multiplies exponentially. Understanding the function of various kinds of stitches and combinations "gives the embroiderer power to create" (Wearden 130). This power "comes through the embroiderer's familiarity with stitches: with their structure, with the hand movement required to make them and with their seemingly infinite variation" (129). In short, an embroiderer needs know the available means of creating a *text*/ile via choices of appropriate tools, stitches, threads, background materials, colors, motifs and so on.

Early samplers served as crucial spaces for developing and sustaining the complex domain and procedural knowledges of threadwork. However, this practice was radically transformed over time as it participated in a web of other semiotic practices. And it is to a brief history of sampler making that we now turn our attention.

A BRIEF HISTORY OF NEEDLEWORK SAMPLER MAKING

The art of embroidery, including sampler making, dates back thousands of years, and has been found in every region of the world (Dreesmann 7; Huish 9; Wanner-Jean Richard 9). The earliest known sampler, which is currently held at the Museum of Primitive Art in New York, is a Nazca culture Peruvian piece that has been dated *circa* 200 BCE. Given the vast geographical and temporal scope of the history of samplers, I have chosen to concentrate primarily on Western embroidery practices, and more specifically, on English. There is a good reason for such a focus. As textile historian Sheila Paine points out, the original function of needlework was radically transformed in the West over the last several centuries, while "outside of the West … embroidery has remained close to its origin" (7). This transformation is a major concern in this chapter. The earliest known pieces of embroidery that can be attributed to English needleworkers are dated *circa* 850 CE, and are currently preserved at Maeseyck in Belgium (King and Levey 11). However, the material record is sketchy until around the 16th century. Not only do materials wear out or disintegrate over time, but as styles and fashions change, materials are discarded. In addition, some early samplers were most likely disassembled for new projects or for the value of the material used such as gold threads and semi-precious stones. Thus, to limit the geographical scope and given the scanty early material record, I focus primarily on English sampler making from early to late modernity, a time of radical shifts and discontinuities in this practice.

The word *sampler* derives from the Latin *examplum* and the old French *essamplaire* meaning "a pattern" or "an example." In a dictionary compiled by John Palsgrave in 1530, "sampler" was defined as an "example for a woman to work by" (*fo* xxxi). As this definition suggests, early samplers were worked by experienced needleworkers, for both domestic and paid labor[5] purposes, and served as an invention tool similar to that of the commonplace notebook.[6] Samplers provided a space for learning, practicing, recording and creating myriad stitches and diverse motifs in a variety of colors and materials using differing kinds of needles and threads, and a place to turn to for inspiration when creating new pieces of embroidery. For nearly 2,000 years—as far back as the material record takes us—sampler making served as a form of rhetorical invention, the art of generating effective and appropriate material for a particular rhetorical situation as well as the art of making critical judgments about that material (Attridge 21; Kress, "Design" 156; Young 349). In short, early samplers served as the *old* from which the *new* could be refashioned. Under this view, a needleworker then may be best understood as a stitcher-rhetor.

Early Western samplers were generally worked on long, narrow rectangular pieces of fabric that were often stored around an ivory rod or rolled up scroll-like in a workbox, or collected together in a book so that a stitcher-rhetor could refer to them easily for inspiration or recall while working on a new piece. The two most common types were spot and band samplers.

The spot sampler, also called the random spot sampler, contains a variety of randomly placed stitches and geometric and naturalistic motifs. Figure 4.1 depicts a typical mid-17th-century English spot sampler that measures 30 × 11 inches, consisting of geometric and naturalistic designs (a rabbit, a deer, a peacock and various types of flowers) wrought in a variety of intricate flat mass (for filling in areas), shading (for giving depth) and outline (for emphasizing a motif) stitches.

The wide range of different kinds of stitches was typical of samplers from this time. Textile historian Joan Edwards found in her study of 16th- and 17th-century spot and band samplers that each contained on average about 36 different kinds of stitches, although particular combinations of these varied across needleworkers and specific samplers (see also Toller).

The band sampler, as the term suggests, generally consists of a series of repeated band designs that can be used as borders or corners to embellish any number of embroidered items. Figure 4.2 shows a typical mid-17th-century English band sampler containing several complex designs rendered primarily in double-running and knot stitches on linen measuring about 23 × 5 inches.

On early band samplers, the rows of repeated border designs followed no particular order; a needleworker used virtually every spare inch of material, often turning the fabric 90 to

FIG. 4.1. *Circa* mid-17th-century English spot sampler. Courtesy Victoria and Albert Picture Library, Ref. T.234–1928.

180 degrees to squeeze in designs wherever space permitted.

As these figures show, early Western samplers were neither signed nor dated and contained only a semasiographic writing system.[7] Yet, glottographic systems had long appeared on finished needlework projects. A good case in point is the 11th-century Bayeux tapestry, which despite its name is a piece of embroidery, not a tapestry in the precise use of that term as a heavily decorated handwoven cloth. Measuring some 270 feet long and 20 inches wide, it depicts in a combination of embroidery stitches on coarse linen the Norman Conquest of England, beginning with the accession of Edward the Confessor to the defeat and downfall of Harold through both pictorial representations and Latin phrases that run along the top. Told from an obviously pro-Norman point of view, it is generally agreed that it was designed to extol the validity of William of Normandy's claim to the English crown (Brown; Lewis). Since glottographic systems had so long been integral to needlework, it may seem curious that they did not appear in early samplers. However, this perplexing phenomenon can be best understood if we recognize that it is our modernist legacy of privileging the *word* as over and apart from the *image* that calls our attention to the distinction. The fact is that the same stitches—whether from color work or white work—used to render images are also used to render the alphabet; thus, in material terms, stitching glottographic symbols is no different than stitching semasiographic ones. As a semiotic resource, the variety of stitches recorded on a sampler would serve as inspiration and recall equally for both image and word, the latter being treated then as just one of any number of graphic designs.

FIG. 4.2. *Circa* mid-17th-century English band sampler. Courtesy Victoria and Albert Picture Library, Ref. T.185–1987.

DESIGNING THE WORD: RADICAL SHIFTS IN SAMPLER MAKING

By the first half of the 16th century, however, some sampler makers began to incorporate the alphabet in both spot and band samplers, and by the 17th century, it along with numbers was increasingly stitched. The first known Western sampler to include an alphabet is an early 16th-century German spot sampler (Humphrey, personal communication). As Fig. 4.3 shows, in the top left-hand corner, the sampler maker cross stitched in red silk one row of the alphabet minus the J and the U as was conventional until the end of the 18th century; also missing (curiously) is the W. In this *text*ile, the alphabet, consisting of a mix of upper and lowercase letters, appears as one of many spot designs. It sits, that is, among a series of random geometric and naturalistic spot motifs, including religious icons such as Christ on the cross, political icons such as the German Iron Cross, and domestic images such as the house situated behind trees. Interspersed among the spot motifs are random band designs. This sampler is a fine example of a commonplace textile notebook.

Around the time that this German sampler maker was plying her needle, some needleworkers began to sign and date their work even as their samplers continued to serve a heuristic function. In fact, the first known signed and dated English sampler was stitched by Jane Bostocke in 1598; it is also the first known English sampler to include the alphabet. Bostocke's sampler is a transition piece that combines spot motifs, repeated band designs, the alphabet, a signature and date in one place.[8] Like the early 16th-century German sampler in Fig. 4.3, Bostocke's sampler was created as an invention resource. By the late 16th century, sampler makers thus began to incorporate a glottographic system along with a semasiographic one. The question is: Why, after so many centuries of not recording or practicing glottographic signs, even though these appeared elsewhere in domestic, personal, religious and political needlework items, did sampler makers begin to do so?

Among the confluence of forces that operated on this meaning-making practice, two powerful and intertwined influences are important for the purposes of this chapter: the nascent print culture and the Protestant Reformation.[9] In part, sampler making was influenced by, and in turn influenced, the emergent print culture. It is probably no coincidence that it was a German sampler maker early in the 16th-century who stitched the first known alphabet on a sampler because the earliest known charted alphabet appeared in Johannes Schönsperger's, *Ein New Modelbuch*, the first printed pattern book, which rolled off the nascent presses in Germany in 1524 (Lotz; Epstein "Introduction"). The printed glottographic woodcut of the alphabet appears alongside other charted geometric and naturalistic designs, treated as one of a series of design possibilities. Many of these woodcut and engraved designs, and, in particular, the woodcut of this alphabet, were later picked up and reused by other printers in Germany, France and England as pattern books became in-

FIG. 4.3. Early 16th-century German spot sampler. Courtesy Victoria and Albert Picture Library, Ref. T.114–1956.

creasingly popular.[10] These early patterns began to show up in samplers of the same time period, and continued to influence needlework designs up until the 19th century (Parmal 42).

Early pattern books provided only a collection of designs without comments on how to recreate the patterns in needle and thread or on what stitches, colors and materials to use. As Epstein reasons, "this [silence] suggests that the printers assumed prospective buyers were familiar with techniques needed to translate the woodcuts and engravings into embroidery" ("Introduction" 3). In other words, printers assumed that the readers of these books already controlled the semiotic resources (both allocative and authoritative) for reconstructing designs—the kinds of stitches that could be used for particular curves and angles of designs, the various types required for filling in, shading, and outlining of these, and the colors, types of thread, and size and kind of needles for generating threadwork patterns.

Each printed pattern could be rendered in multiple ways on fabric, depending on the materials and stitches used. The only constraints a needleworker had to grapple with were the limits of the material and structure of the stitch for producing particular designs— whether glottographic or semasiographic. For example, although almost any color work or white work stitch may be used to render alphabetic letters and numerals, some stitches are more effective than others at producing clearly defined letters and numbers. Among the more common color work stitches used for letters and numerals are chain, cross, satin and eyelet (Epstein, "Threads" 45–50), for these types of stitches lend themselves to clean rendering of the lines and curves of the alphabet.

Pattern books both influenced threadwork designs and conversely drew their designs from samplers stitched before the advent of print (Epstein "Needlework"). Moreover, the alphabets that appeared on samplers from the 17th century on resonated with the fonts then used by printers, and in some cases, continued to appear on samplers long after they became defunct in printing (Epstein, "Threads" 50–51). Thus, there was an interdynamic relationship between the nascent print culture and sampler making, a relationship that became even more prominent over time.

A second significant force that exerted pressure on sampler making beginning in the 16th century was the emergence of the Protestant Reformation. Particularly influential was Martin Luther's doctrine of justification by faith alone rather than by sacraments, mediation of Church or good works, and his insistence on reading the Bible to give the individual greater and more direct responsibility for salvation. The former tenets challenged, and eventually displaced, religious icons and images like those stitched on the early 16th-century German sampler in Fig. 4.3. The latter doctrine was both contingent on, and buoyed by, the emergence of print technology that made the Bible and other religious texts more widely available. Thus, the two forces of print technology/culture and Protestantism were intertwined, fostering a rise in literacy. The spread of Protestantism in England (with literacy as a byproduct) was secured by Henry VIII when in 1534 he signed the Act of Supremacy, which rejected papal authority and created the Church of England. The tenets of Protestantism were, therefore, fairly well entrenched by the time Jane Bostocke stitched the first known alphabet and text to appear on an English sampler in 1598.

As historians Patrick Collinson, Margaret Spufford, and Tessa Watt, among others, have demonstrated, the Reformation led eventually to a displacement and transformation of religious images, with text increasingly replacing visual imagery. The transformation represented a radical discontinuity, a shift from what Watt terms "images of piety" that "contained few or no words but spoke the complex language of saints' emblems and pictorial conventions ... which the medieval audience had learnt to 'read'" (131). The displacement of religious images occurred gradually in stages, with the first generation of Protestants advocating an "iconoclasm," the substitution of other acceptable (typically more secularized) images for religious ones. Later Protestants advocated what Collinson terms "iconophobia," the "total repudiation of all images" (Watt 117). The bifurcation of word and image, resulting from a changing relationship between the two, was thus both prompted and influenced by cultural and religious politics that were supported by print technology.

Just as words were beginning to overtake images on printed materials, especially ballad broadsides and other cheap print sheets, so too did they begin to appear with increasing frequency on needlework samplers wrought during the same time period. As with print, the shifting relationship between image and word occurred as a gradual series of displacements. Whereas in early samplers, images (in the form of spot motifs and band patterns) dominated, in later samplers, alphabetic and numeric symbols as one of a series of possible patterns were introduced and slowly incorporated. Eventually textual signs overtook images, so that by the 18th and 19th centuries, text dominated English and American samplers. But as with print, the change did not happen all at once. Sampler making was slowly transformed as it participated in a web of other semiotic practices and circulations, especially those of cheap print. Most striking is how strongly sampler designs resonated with those of broadsheets, chap books and other cheap print, and vice versa.

Figure 4.4 depicts a typical 17th-century English broadsheet that was used to line an oak box, *circa* 1630.[11]

This broad sheet consists of a series of bands of alternating geometric and naturalistic motifs with lines of text. The moral inscriptions read in part:

[A] POWERFVL HAND SHALL RVLE THE LAND

SAVE VS O LORD FROM HEATHENS SWORD

FROM EVILL STRAY AND LIVE FOR AYE

A VERTVOVS WIFE GIVES HUSBAND LIFE

[A ?] [?]MAN IS LIKE A SCORPION

As Tessa Watt notes, broadsheets functioned on two levels: on a semiotic level, as an *aide mémoire*, reminding viewers of their moral and national duty, and on an aesthetic level, as decoration, serving as wallpaper and posters in private and public houses, or used, as in Fig. 4.4, to decorate or line other items (Watts 221ff). Here bands of text alternate with bands of secular and religious motifs. Both converge to signify a particular moral, cultural and political stance.

The visual pattern of this common broadsheet shows up on samplers stitched during this time. Figure 4.5 depicts a transitional English band sampler wrought by Margaret Jennings in 1695, in which bands of geometric and

FIG. 4.4. Paper lined oak box, *circa* 1630. Courtesy Victoria and Albert Picture Library, Ref. W.51–1926.

floral designs rendered in both color and white work alternate with bands of text. This sampler closely resembles contemporary common broadsides that may well have adorned the walls of Margaret Jennings's home and certainly would have appeared in public houses (Watt 192ff).

The middle of Jennings's sampler is devoted primarily to bands of white work (the top wrought mainly in pulled stitches and the bottom in cut work), with one band of the alphabet rendered in white satin stitch appearing toward the bottom of this section. In the rest of her sampler, color work bands of text are set off both figuratively and literally by alternating color work bands of designs. The text reads:

LOVE THOV THEE LORD AND HE WILL

BE A TENDER FATHER VNTO THEE

FAVOVR IS DECEITFULL AND BEAUTY IS VAI

N BUT A WOMAN THAT FEARETH THE LORD

SHEE SHALL BE PRAISED GIVE HER OF THEE

FRUIT OF HER HANDS AND LET HER OWN

Here the text functions on two levels: first, as a visual design (i.e., as a band pattern) and second, as a signifier of moral lessons—lessons that strongly echo those advanced in the broadsheet in Fig. 4.4. Jennings engaged the very same semiotic

FIG. 4.5. English band sampler, Margaret Jennings, 1695. Courtesy Montacute House, Goodhart Collection (National Trust), Ref. Sampler No. 51.

resources to construct both image and text, using similar kinds of flat and cross stitches for both. Together, all of the stitching manifested, in Jennings's words, the "fruit of her hands," both image and word serving as a single moral, pious act. Thus, in this case, words *are* images and images *are* words both in terms of the praxis and the artifact; they converge as one act and one semiotic representation that manifests skill in stitching and commitment to piety.

The similarities between pictorial / textual band samplers and broadside sheets call attention to the point that samplers and cheap print were both influencing one another in a web of semiotic practices and circulations. More than mere surface resemblance, however, both also shared a similar substantive use during this time. As Watt notes of cheap print in those days:

> these printed wares [cheap print] were not finished products like gloves or combs, to be used in much the same way by each purchaser. If we are to choose a metaphor from the chapman's pack, print was much more like the "scotch cloth" or "coarse linen," sold by the yard, to be made into something by the buyer. (6)

Similarly, samplers of the 16th and 17th century were not finished products; rather, wrought on the "scotch cloth" and "coarse linen" that was peddled by chapmen, they served primarily as a *means* to an end.

In Jennings's sampler, however, we begin to see the transition of sampler making from invention to creation of finished artifact. Here, although the various designs certainly serve as a repository of complex stitches, the sampler itself serves not just as a means to an end but is beginning to become an end in itself. The shift suggests a difference in purpose from that which came before it, for example, that which guided the samplers depicted in Fig. 4.1 through Fig. 4.3. By the late 17th century, as Jennings was stitching, sampler making was on the cusp of a radical shift from invention to demonstration of knowledge that resulted from a radical displacement of the praxis, the socialized subject position, the purpose and the circulation of the *textile*.

DISPLACEMENT, TRANSFORMATION AND ERASURE

During the 17th century and into the 18th, the purpose of sampler making was substantively transformed from that of an invention tool (as a *means* to another end) to that of demonstration of stitching skill (as an *end* in itself). These changes occurred as sampler making itself was displaced, moving out of domestic and paid-labor spaces and into the schoolroom, and as new roles and subject positions were occupied by needleworkers—novice stitchers beholden to master teachers as opposed to earlier experienced stitchers beholden to their own art.

Two major changes in band samplers over this period reveal the ways in which sampler making was being displaced and transformed. First, the band sampler shifted from a random series of bands squeezed in where space permitted to a hierarchical pattern of bands that moved from simple to more complex stitches. Such purposeful ordering resulted from the fact that samplers were in the process of becoming primarily educational tools rather than resources, and they were increasingly being worked by young novice stitchers rather than experienced needleworkers (Humphrey *Samplers*; Parker). Over this time, as in Jennings's sampler in Fig. 4.5, text was beginning to be incorporated as part of a series of designs. Second, unlike earlier band and spot samplers that recorded contemporary designs, some of the bands that appear on late 17th-century samplers were taken from designs popular in previous centuries (Parmal 8, 14). Since these patterns were not found on contemporary clothing or furnishings of the day, they most likely were worked to demonstrate that one had properly learned how to stitch rather than to record, practice or create designs that could then used for other new creations.

By the end of the 18th century, the displacement and transformation was complete. Sampler making as an invention practice was erased. Samplers primarily became decorative pieces of needlework, square in shape, and suitable for framing and hanging. The displacement-transformation-erasure of sampler making is obvious in Dr. Samuel Johnson's 1799 definition of sampler as "a pattern of work; a piece worked by young girls for improvement" (qtd. in Krueger 8). Some 250 years after Palsgrave's 1530 definition of "an example for a woman to work by," we see that samplers have been transformed into an end product—"a pattern of work"—the subject position has shifted from "woman" to "young girls," and sampler making itself has become an educational exercise—meant to be "worked by young girls for improvement" not only in stitching but in moral, social and intellectual arenas as well (Humphrey, *Samplers* 34). Samplers became, in short, tools of accountability, and in the process, their function as semiotic resources was displaced.

This radical discontinuity is evidenced by a historical study of the kinds of stitches that were sewn. As samplers were transformed into tools of accountability, there evolved a "school style" of stitching. Rather than the rich range of hundreds of diverse kinds of stitches, the scope was increasingly reduced. Textile historian Joan Edwards's study of sampler stitches shows that whereas there were on average about 36 different kinds of stitches on 16th- and 17th-century samplers, by the late 18th and early 19th century, the number shrank to about 20 different types of stitches on average. The scope continued to decrease until, toward the end of the 19th century, nearly the only type remaining was the cross stitch. In fact, this one stitch became so connected with the sampler that it became known as the sampler stitch, and samplers were called cross-stitch samplers. As versatile as the cross-stitch may be, it is a highly truncated semiotic resource with limited uses, serving as only one of numerous surface stitches available to fill in areas. Missing are flat, looped and knotted stitches that help with filling in, shading and outlining designs as well as the more intricate family of white work stitches. Gone also is the flexibility to create composite stitches from various combinations of stitches. In short, in becoming transformed and displaced, sampler making no longer served as invention; rather it served a far more limited function of demonstration of skill, with the knowledge and resources for creating needlework artifacts paradoxically placed further and further away from the rhetor-stitcher. In the process, the severely limited semiotic resources curtailed the range of possibilities for semiotic representations. Sampler makers developed limited domain and procedural knowledges that allowed them to copy some designs but hampered them from developing knowledges that would permit them to create their own designs or textiles.

SEMIOTIC CIRCULATION:
SAMPLERS AS DEMONSTRATION OF SKILL

The relationship between the means of semiotic production and circulation is symbiotic. As the means of sampler making radically shifted, so too was there a discontinuity in the circulation of samplers. In the transformation of the sampler maker's subject position, purposes and semiotic spaces of production, circulation was similarly transformed, moving out of the experienced stitcher's workbox into a more public space of display. Two distinct routes of display emerged to serve differing cultural and socioeconomic groups who undertook sampler making as a tool of accountability, a means of demonstration. Sampler making and samplers themselves were transformed as they began to participate in the burgeoning privileging of the written word over other symbolic representations. That is, the practice and artifact were shaped by both iconoclasm and iconophobia, to use Collinson's terms, and by the resulting logocentrism or "tyranny" of alphabetic bias, to use Harris's phrase. In fact, a preponderance of text over motif is one of the features that distinguishes 18th- and 19th-century English and American samplers from those wrought earlier.

During this time, two broad families of samplers emerged that circulated for different, though related, reasons. The first may be best described as pictorial or decorative samplers, namely, those that we most typically think of today as quintessential samplers, and that most closely resembled broadside ballads, chap books and other printed sheets. Pictorial samplers were stitched to create a decorative picture (e.g., a pastoral or biblical scene) that typically included one or more rows of the alphabet along with one or more verses. Pictures and words were enclosed by a border of flowers or geometric patterns. By the early 19th century, however, it was fairly common for sampler makers to stitch long biblical and moral passages with sparse decorative borders. These pieces, like other contemporary artwork, resonated with the visual layout of cheap print of their day. As Watt notes:

> Painted texts were enclosed within borders of strap-work pattern or Renaissance ornament, borrowing the convention of woodcut borders used in books and on broadsides. The texts themselves were painted in the same black-letter style as the standard typographical font …. [Thus] these media of paper, cloths and walls must be seen together. Not only did they decorate the same rooms, they shared the same themes. Prints give us some idea about the painted cloths and walls which have fallen apart or been destroyed. (192, 193)

Because samplers participated in, and drew on, these same visual/typographic designs, they also provide important clues to the web of semiotic practices Watt describes.

Signed and dated by their maker, pictorial samplers were often framed in expensive and elaborate ways by those in socioeconomic brackets that could afford such luxury. In these, text and image converged into one semiotic currency, as samplers, mounted in prominent spaces on the walls of living and reception rooms, circulated as proof of good breeding, upward mobility, moral fiber, and virtuosity with a needle—though over time the last accomplishment became less and less important than the former ones. These were the refrigerator art of early days. Parents proudly hung these as evidence of their own role in educating their children well in moral, religious, political and secular arenas, and as display of their own wealth.

The second broad family of samplers may be best described as utilitarian works. A variety of more utilitarian types of samplers became popular throughout the 18th century and well into the 19th century: for example, marking, plain sewing, and darning samplers. Marking samplers typically consist of rows of the alphabet and numerals rendered in different typographical fonts; plain sewing samplers consist of typical utilitarian stitching techniques, such as basting, seams, hems, buttonholes and buttons; darning samplers typically consist of a series of different darning techniques used to repair worn spots and holes in a variety of fabrics. To mimic torn and worn-out fabric, needleworkers cut different kinds of holes in the sampler, and then used a variety of different kinds of darning stitches to demonstrate their versatility in mending personal and household items. These plain-stitch samplers served as a domestic and domesticating exercise undertaken particularly, though not exclusively, by young women, especially in the lower classes, to equip them with skills for positions that would enable them to avoid potentially horrific circumstances—an escape well captured by Geraldine Clifford's title, "Marry, Stitch, Die or Do Worse." In turn, these specimens could, and did, circulate as a material *CV*. Thus, like their decorative counterpart, these samplers functioned as a demonstration of skill—an end product. However, this family of sampler making restricted the stitcher-rhetor to skills almost exclusively concerned with the marking or mending of household or clothing materials created elsewhere. In this sense, these stitcher-rhetors had a more limited access to allocative and authoritative semiotic resources than their higher socioeconomic counterparts.

One of the most common of the utilitarian samplers was the marking sampler on which young needleworkers would practice stitching various styles of alphabetic letters and numbers that could be used to mark household and personal items. Figure 4.6 depicts a typical, though beautifully rendered, marking sampler stitched by then 16-year-old Charlotte Eleanor Cullum in 1874 when she was at the Bristol Orphanage.

This piece is one of a number of known marking samplers of fine quality that come from the Bristol Orphanage Schools, founded in the 19th century, where boys as well as girls were required to learn how to sew and knit. The top half of the sampler is devoted to different styles of lettering in both upper and lowercases as well as different styles of numbers similar to typographic fonts then in circulation. The bottom half consists of neatly rendered small decorative motifs (including a cow, a Bible, and several versions of a royal crown) as well as a variety of borders and corner patterns. These motifs may be best understood as secularized, and therefore, safe, iconography. In this, as in other marking samplers, semasiographic and glottographic are not distinguishable on either a means of production or a circulation level. Not only are the means of semiotic production the same but the circulation and its purposes are exactly the same: proof that the needleworker could undertake a variety of stitching projects. In short, utilitarian samplers offered material evidence that the needleworker could embellish and repair a variety of personal and household items—could, in short, stitch word and image with pen of steel and silken ink.

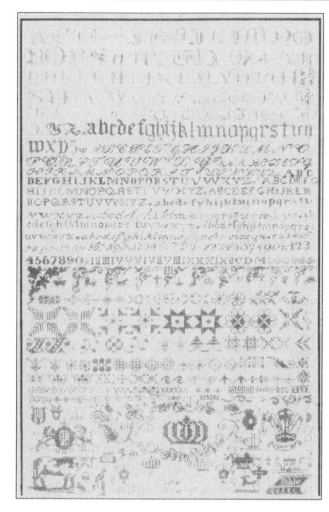

FIG. 4.6. Marking sampler by Charlotte Eleanor Cullum, 1874. Courtesy Witney Antiques, Witney, England, Ref. Cat. No. 36.

HEMMING THE RAW EDGES: SOME FINAL THOUGHTS

I end this chapter with the metaphor of hemming raw edges because hems are not permanent insofar as they can be ripped out, and then either turned up higher to shorten a garment or let down to lengthen it. In samplers, old and new, the edges are hemmed to prevent the background fabric from fraying as an embroiderer plies her needle. Here I offer some final, although not last, thoughts on the slippery and fluid relationship between visual and verbal rhetoric. Like a hem, I leave these open and invite others to engage in the issues I tackle in this chapter.

In tracing some of the discontinuities in the history of sampler making, I have shown how semasiographic and glottographic writing systems converged in both the means of creating and those of circulating needlework samplers, and that the relationship between the two shifted over time. In short, word and image combined to create a visual rhetoric in pens of steel and silken ink. Thus, in this chapter, I have challenged the clear-cut division between rhetoric of the word and rhetoric of the image to contribute to a more complex definition of visual rhetoric. Perhaps, however, we need to reconsider the term, *visual rhetoric*. As Kenneth Burke taught us, terms are filtered through terministic screens that direct our attention to certain aspects and away from others. Bifurcation of word and image—of visual and verbal rhetoric—permits thinking about semiotic production, circulation and artifacts in particular ways but also threatens to render invisible a whole host of other kinds of rhetorical practices, objects and participants because they do not appear on the dichotomized radar screen. Because the phrase, visual rhetoric, has been so saturated by the great divide, perhaps we need another term that will challenge us to consider not only distinctions but convergences between word and image, and that will ask us to both visualize the word and word the visual. We might flip the term, visual rhetoric, to *rhetoric of the visual* to signify that meaning-making material practices and artifacts that engage in graphic representation are visual, whether the graphic is dealing in glottographic or semasiographic systems or both.

In demonstrating the fluidity between image and word on samplers over time, I hope to encourage others to explore all sorts of rhetorics of the visual from a material perspective of semiotic resources and circulations—to use as a starting point, in other words, not the artifact itself but the means of production, and to trace this through the performance of the semiotic work. Doing so requires historicizing the praxis and demonstrating that rhetorical construction, artifact and circulation are pliant, radically shifting over time and place in response to myriad social, cultural, economic, political, and technological forces. Disentangling the strands of influences and the threads woven and distributed—threads combined and recombined—is well worth the effort for helping us to understand the complexities of rhetoric of the visual both in the past and today, and for directing our attention to important alternative rhetorical practices and spaces that have been until now ignored.

NOTES

I want to acknowledge the generous assistance of the following textile historians and keepers who kindly answered numerous questions, shared materials with me, and gave me access to rare samplers: Clare Browne, Curator of Textiles and Dress, Victoria and Albert Museum, London; Edwina Ehrman, Curator of Costume and Decorative Art, Museum of London; Carol Humphrey, Honorary Keeper, Textiles, Fitzwilliam Museum, Cambridge, England; Kathleen (Epstein) Staples, Curious Works Press, Atlanta; Mark

Rogers, House Steward, and Christine Bailey, House Secretary, Montacute House, Somerset, England; Jo Moore, Collections Manager, National Trust, Somerset, England; and Joy Jarrett and Rebecca Scott of Witney Antiques, Oxfordshire, England.

1. See Harris, who argues persuasively that the history of writing is situated in drawing as much as it is in speech. This history has been obscured by what Harris calls a "tyranny" of alphabetic bias (8).
2. On the symbolic significance of embroidered motifs, see Sheila Paine.
3. The separation of visual arts from communicative arts represents a historical discontinuity, a by-product of modernity. Medieval scribes, for instance, created both the illumination and the textual representations in incunabula manuscripts—an intersection well exemplified by the very definition of *incunabula*, which signifies both a "book printed before 1501" and "a work of art or industry of an earlier period" (*Webster's Ninth New Collegiate Dictionary* 611).
4. For a useful history of particular stitches, see Christie's *Samplers and Stitches*.
5. Here I use the term *paid labor* rather than *professional* because concepts and practices surrounding both "profession" and "professional" did not emerge until the 19th-century; see, for example, Burton Bledstein and Randall Collins.
6. On commonplace notebooks, see, for example, Ann Moss, and Susan Miller.
7. Semiotic practices in needlework participated in, and resonated with, the web of those in manuscript and print cultures. As Kaufer and Carley note, "before print, the role of the individual author did not become visible unless a text was found to be a transgression of church or government interests. After print, the author became visible as a property holder" (136). It was at this point that the author's name took on a new role. Related to this was the shift in the trust accorded to written documents during early modernity. As Clanchy points out, only gradually over 200 years between the 12th and 14th centuries were written documents permitted to stand alone without corroborating oral oaths and testimonies or other material proof (e.g., a dagger or ring; *Memory*, "Hearing"). Thus, signing documents held little currency. The shift in status of the written document and authorial claim to it resonates with a shift in the sampler as it took on a new status as "document" rather than as heuristic, though this occurred much later in the textilescape.
8. For an extended discussion of this sampler and its function as a transition piece in the history of sampler making, see Goggin's "*Essamplaire*." Also see Pamela Clabburn and Clare Browne.
9. Given the scope of this chapter, I trace only two of the many forces that converged to radically redefine and transform sampler making. For a discussion of other complex forces, see Goggin's "*Essamplaire*."

10. Most of the earliest pattern books were printed not just for needleworkers but for artisans of any ilk, including those who worked in metal, wood, stone and other media. In this sense, embroidery was but one part of a whole web of semiotic practices. Often the multimedia intent was signaled by the titles. For example, the full title of Nicolas Bassée's 1568 pattern book is: *New Modelbuch. Von Allerhandt Art Nechens vnd Stickens. Jetz mit viellerley Mödel vnnd Stahlen/Allen Seidenstickern/vnd Neterine/sehr nützlich vnd Künstlich Zugericht* [New Pattern Book of all kinds of Forms of Sewing and Embroidery. Now with Many Patterns and Samples/for all Stone Masons/Silk Embroiderers/and Net Makers/ Proven to be Very Useful and Artistic; Epstein, "Introduction" 5–6]. Also see Ciotti, printed in 1596. The popularity of these books for all sorts of artisans is well documented. As Kathleen Epstein points out, between 1524 and 1700, "more than one hundred and fifty different titles were produced ... by various German, Italian, French and English printers" ("Introduction" 3).

11. In separate presentations, both Edwina Ehrman and Carol Humphrey (museum curators and textile historians) first called attention to the similarities in the design features of samplers and broadsides and other cheap printed sheets; Ehrman also used the broadside-lined oak box depicted in Fig. 4.5 as an example in her presentation.

WORKS CITED

Attridge, Derek. "Innovation, Literature, Ethics: Relating to the Other." *Publications of the Modern Language Association* 114 (1999): 20–31.

Bernhardt, Stephen A. "Visual Rhetoric." *Encyclopedia of Rhetoric and Composition: Communication from Ancient Times to the Information Age.* Ed. Theresa Enos. New York: Garland, 1996: 746–748.

Bledstein, Burton J. *The Culture of Professionalism: The Middle Class and the Development of Higher Education in America.* New York: Norton, 1976.

Brittain, Judy. *Step-by-Step Needlecraft Encyclopedia.* New York: Portland House, 1997.

Brown, Shirley Ann. *The Bayeux Tapestry: History and Bibliography.* Suffolk, England: The Boydell P, 1988.

Browne, Clare, and Jennifer Wearden. *Samplers from the Victoria and Albert Museum.* London: V & A Publications, 1999.

Browne, Clare. "Samplers in the Museum's Collection." Browne and Wearden 7–11.

Burke, Kenneth. *Language as Symbolic Action: Essays on Life, Literature and Method.* Berkeley: U of California P, 1966.

Christie, Archibald. *Samplers and Stitches.* 1920. London: Batsford, 1959.

Ciotti, Giovanni Battista. *A Book of Curious and Strange Inventions, called the first part of needleworkes containing many singular and fine sortes of cut-workes, raised-workes, stitches, and open cutworke, verie easie to be learned by the diligent practisers, that shall follow the direction herein contained.* London: J. Danter for William Barley, 1596.

Clabburn, Pamela. *Samplers: The Shire Book.* 2nd ed. Princes Risborough, England: Shire Publications, 1998.

Clanchy, Michael T. *From Memory to Written Record in England, 1066–1307.* Cambridge, MA: Harvard UP, 1978.

—. "Hearing and Seeing and Trusting Writing." *Perspectives on Literacy.* Ed. Eugene Kintgen, Barry Kroll, and Mike Rose. Carbondale: Southern Illinois UP, 1988: 135–158.

Clifford, Geraldine. "'Marry, Stitch, Die or Do Worse: Educating Women for Work." *Work, Youth, Schooling: Historical Perspectives on Vocationalism in American Education.* Ed. Harvey Kamor and David B. Tvack. Stanford: Stanford UP, 1982: 223–268.

Collins, Randall. *The Credential Society: An Historical Sociology of Education and Stratification.* Orlando: Academic P, 1979.

Collinson, Patrick. *The Birthpangs of Protestant England: Religious and Cultural Change in the Sixteenth and Seventeenth Centuries.* New York: St. Martin P, 1988.

Cope, Bill, and Mary Kalantzis, eds. *Multiliteracies: Literacy Learning and the Design of Social Futures.* London: Routledge, 2000.

Dreesmann, Cécile. *Samplers for Today.* New York: Van Nostrand Reinhold, 1972.

Eaton, Jan. *Mary Thomas's Dictionary of Embroidery Stitches.* 1934. Rev. ed. North Pomfret, VT: Trafalgar Square, 1998.

Edwards, Joan. *Sampler Making 1540–1940: The Fifth of Joan Edwards Small Books on the History of Embroidery.* Dorking, England: Bayford, 1983.

Ehrman, Edwina. "Juda Hayle: A Study of an Ipswich Teacher and Her Pupils." Conf. *Sampler Dames in England and America.* Atlanta, GA. 12 May 2001.

Epstein, Kathleen A. "Introduction." *German Renaissance Patterns for Embroidery: A Facsimile Copy of Nicolas Bassée's New Modelbuch of 1568.* Trans. Kathleen Epstein. Austin, TX: Curious Works P, 1994: 3–19.

—. "Needlework and Pattern Books: An Examination of the Relationship Between Stuart Domestic Embroidery and English Pattern Books." *Ars Textria* 12 (1989): 51–63.

—. "Threads of Duty, Threads of Piety: An Analysis of Seventeenth-Century English Band Samplers." MA Thesis. U of Texas at Austin, 1991.

Giddens, Anthony. "Structuralism, Post-Structuralism and the Production of Culture." *Social Theory Today.* Ed. Anthony Giddens and Jonathan Turner. Palo-Alto: Stanford UP, 1987: 195–223.

Goggin, Maureen Daly. "An *Essamplaire Essai* on the Rhetoricity of Needlework Sampler Making: A Contribution to Theorizing and Historicizing Rhetorical Praxis." *Rhetoric Review* 21 (2002): 309–328.

Harris, Roy. *The Origin of Writing.* La Salle, IL: Open Court, 1986.

Huish, Marcus B. *Samplers and Tapestry Embroideries.* 2nd ed. 1913. Rpt. ed. London: B. T. Batsford, 1990.

Humphrey, Carol. Letter to the Author. 7 December 2000.

—. *Samplers.* Cambridge: Cambridge UP, 1997.

—. "Teachers and Traditions, Prints and Pedlars: A Sideways Look at 17th-Century Sampler Groups." Conf. *Sampler Dames in England and America.* Atlanta, GA. 12 May 2001.

Kaufer, David S., and Kathleen M. Carley. *Communication at a Distance: The Influence of Print on Sociocultural Organization and Change.* Hillsdale, NJ: Lawrence Erlbaum Associates, 1993.

King, Donald, and Santina Levey. *The Victoria & Albert Museum's Textile Collection: Embroidery in Britain from 1200–1750.* New York: Canopy, 1993.

Kress, Gunther. "Design and Transformation: New Theories of Meaning." Cope and Kalantzis 153–161.

—. "Multimodality." Cope and Kalantzis 182–202.

Krueger, Glee. *A Gallery of American Samplers: The Theodore H. Kapnek Collection.* New York: Bonanza Books, 1984.

Lewis, Suzanne. *The Rhetoric of Power in the Bayeux Tapestry.* New York: Cambridge UP, 1999.

Lotz, Arthur. *Bibliographie der Modelbücher.* London: Holland P, 1963.

Lucaites, John Louis, and Robert Hariman. "Visual Rhetoric, Photojournalism, and Democratic Public Culture." *Rhetoric Review* 20 (2001): 37–42.

Miller, Susan. *Assuming the Positions: Cultural Pedagogy and the Politics of Commonplace Writing.* Pittsburgh: U of Pittsburgh P, 1998.

Moss, Ann. *Printed Commonplace-Books and the Structuring of Renaissance Thought.* Oxford: Clarendon P, 1996.

Paine, Sheila. *Embroidered Textiles: Traditional Patterns from Five Continents with a Worldwide Guide to Identification.* New York: Thames and Hudson, 1997.

Palsgrave, John. *Lesclarcissement de la Langue Francoyse.* 1530. Facsim. ed. Menston, England: Scolar P, 1969.

Parker, Rozsika. *The Subversive Stitch: Embroidery and the Making of the Feminine.* Rpt. ed. New York: Routledge, 1989.

Parmal, Pamela A. *Samplers from A to Z.* Boston: Museum of Fine Arts, 2000.

Sampson, Geoffrey. *Writing Systems: A Linguistic Introduction.* Stanford: Stanford UP, 1985.

Spufford, Margaret. *Small Books and Pleasant Histories: Popular Fiction and its Readership in Seventeenth-Century England.* Athens: U of Georgia P, 1981.

Street, Brian V. *Social Literacies: Critical Approaches to Literacy in Development, Ethnography and Education.* London: Longman, 1995.

Toller, Jane. *British Samplers: A Concise History.* Chichester, England: Phillimore & Co, 1980.

Wanner-Jean Richard, Anne. *Patterns and Motifs Stitched and Ornamented on Textile Ground: Catalogue of Samplers, St. Gallen Textile Museum.* Trans. Vivan Blandford and Tony Hafliger. St. Gallen, Switzerland: St. Gallen Textile Museum, 1996.

Watt, Tessa. *Cheap Print and Popular Piety 1550–1640.* Cambridge: Cambridge UP, 1991.

Wearden, Jennifer. "Stitches and Techniques." Browne and Wearden 129–135.

Webster's Ninth New Collegiate Dictionary. Springfield, MA: Merriam-Webster, 1987.

Young, Richard. "Invention." *Encyclopedia of Rhetoric and Composition: Communication from Ancient Times to the Information Age.* Ed. Theresa Enos. New York: Garland, 1996: 349–355.

CHAPTER FIVE

Defining Film Rhetoric:
The Case of Hitchcock's *Vertigo*

David Blakesley

> *The death of Hitchcock marks the passage from one era to another .... I believe we are entering an era defined by the suspension of the visual.*
>
> —Jean Luc Godard, 1980[1]

Godard is a great filmmaker, but he may not be a particularly good prophet. He clearly recognized, however, that Alfred Hitchcock—perhaps more than any other director of his time—drew our attention to the power of the visual as an appeal to the audience's desire and as a means of fostering and interrogating identification. Although other directors and cinematographers—Orson Welles and Gregg Toland, for instance—made great advances in cinema in terms of visual technique and representation, it was Hitchcock more than any other who both recognized this power of the visual as an appeal and also turned our attention to the psychological subject of the visual itself. In so many Hitchcock films—especially *Rear Window* (1954), *Vertigo* (1958), and *Psycho* (1960)—the central theme is arguably the psychological consequences of seeing and being seen, or more properly, voyeurism and the objectification that accompanies the desire. So Godard is not wholly wrong; Hitchcock did indeed help define an era in filmmaking when the visual became more than just the primary medium or technique of cinema's appeal, but additionally, and in modernist-fashion, cinema's contested subject.

Since 1980, however, we have not witnessed the end of an era of the visual. On the contrary, we have witnessed a visual turn—especially in the mid- to late-1990s—with tremendous interest in understanding the function of the image in its own right as well as the interanimation of the visual and the verbal in our means of (re)presentation. That focus of critical theory has accompanied similar developments in art and art history, perceptual psychology and neuroscience, cultural studies, and a host of other disciplinary areas. With the gradual emergence of digital filmmaking and on the heels of this visual turn, the contested nature of representational realism has also been examined in many popular films, such as *The Usual Suspects* (1995), *The English Patient* (1996), *The Matrix* (1999), *Memento* (2000), *Minority Report* (2002), and many others. These are films that also make identification an explicit theme. Although we can safely say that all films—as projections and sequences of images—function representationally to some degree, films like these that self-consciously contest the relationships among realism and identity make excellent subjects for the study of film rhetoric and thus for understanding the verbal and visual ingredients of identification.

In critical theory, the rhetorical or linguistic turn of the 1980s became the visual turn of the 1990s. The rhetorical turn had heightened awareness of the ways that our verbal means of representation cannot be easily (or rightly) separated from our ways of knowing. The verbal is implicated in epistemology so fundamentally that any attempt to bring the mirror to nature, to use Richard Rorty's phrasing, must be seen as disingenuous or naïve because we understand the world through mediating symbol systems. In its most general sense, the visual turn simply asserts that symbolic action entails visual representation in the inseparable and complex verbal, visual, and perceptual acts of making meaning. Who we are and what we know suddenly become intertwined with questions about visual representation or about the relationship between what we can see or imagine and what we can know. This visual, or pictorial, turn is closely allied with the rhetorical turn because, in Kenneth Burke's apt phrasing, "A way of seeing is also a way of not seeing—a focus on object A involves a neglect of object B" (*Permanence and Change* 49). Seeing is believing, but believing is seeing as well. In the most detailed working through of the implications of the visual turn for critical theory—*Picture Theory: Essays on Verbal and Visual Representation*—W. J. T. Mitchell explains:

> Whatever the pictorial turn is, then, it should be clear that it is not a return to naïve mimesis, copy or correspondence theories of representation, or a renewed metaphysics of pictorial "presence": it is rather a postlinguistic, postsemiotic rediscovery of the picture as a complex interplay between visuality, apparatus, institutions, discourse, bodies, and figurality. It is the realization that spectatorship (the look, the gaze, the glance, the practices of observation, surveillance, and visual pleasure) may be as deep a problem as various forms of reading (decipherment, decoding, interpretation, etc.) and that visual experience or "visual literacy" might not be fully explicable on the model of textuality. (16)

The interanimation, or interplay, of the verbal and the visual in the context of film interpretation is certainly as complex as Mitchell suggests. In my view, a rhetoric of film would articulate the dimensions of this deep problem, with the aim of suggesting ways through or around some of the central problems that have vexed film critics for a long time—especially the nature of identification and spectatorship as rhetorical processes. In my conclusion, I discuss the visual component of identification specifically to show how film rhetoric elaborates and exploits visual ambiguity to foster identification and thus provides insight into the rhetoric of film as an appeal to desire.

DEFINING FILM RHETORIC

What constitutes *film rhetoric*? With reference to Hitchcock's *Vertigo*, this essay addresses that question by defining four approaches to film rhetoric, each of which reflects and animates our broader understanding of visual rhetoric. These four approaches share interests in identification and persuasion as rhetoric's aims, yet their differences in application reveal substantial disagreement about the nature of film rhetoric or about whether rhetoric itself is any more than a means of textual analysis. In the last 10 years or so, however—and as Thomas Benson notes—rhetorical criticism of film now entails more than attention to its explicitly persuasive dimensions:

> A much broader approach encompasses rhetoric as the study of symbolic inducement, reaching beyond films that are didactic or propagandistic, and employing the whole range of tools common to humanistic inquiry into cultural forms and investigating issues of text, genre, myth, gender, ideology, production, authorship, the human subject, meaning, the construction of cinematic ways of knowing, response, and reception. (620)

In my introduction to the collection, *The Terministic Screen: Rhetorical Perspectives on Film*, I outline four approaches to film rhetoric that I want to summarize and extend here. In the second section of this chapter, I aim to illustrate the approach that I see as encompassing the others to varying degrees—film identification—by showing the ways that *Vertigo* reveals and interrogates the processes of identification that are central to our understanding of rhetoric as the faculty for elaborating or exploiting ambiguity to foster identification itself. That *Vertigo* and other Hitchcock films make identification a central theme has been much discussed in the Hitchcock criticism, especially among feminist theorists, such as Laura Mulvey and Tania Modleski. Nevertheless, I think a conception of identification grounded in rhetoric and in visual rhetoric in particular can help us through the impasse of determining not only the nature of the spectator and spectatorship, but the basis of filmic appeal as implicitly visual and rhetorical, with film's visual elements reinforcing its nature as an appeal addressed to an audience and seeking identification and transformation. A core concept of the approach is that of the terministic screen,

which is a phrase used by Burke to describe how our terms—or more generally the means of representation—direct the attention to one field rather than
another such that our observations of experience (all that can be known) are
implications of the particular terms themselves (*Language as Symbolic Action*
46). I conclude by considering what difference it makes for our interpretation
of *Vertigo* and film generally when we see rhetoric's key term as *identification*
and ground that concept in the visual.

Each of the following *categories—Film Language, Film Ideology, Film Interpre-*
tation, and *Film Identification*—can be thought of as orientations or leanings (in
the sense of attitudes)—rather than precisely defined and practiced philosophical foundations.

Film Language

Advanced in the work of Christian Metz, Stephen Heath and Patricia
Mellencamp, Vivian Sobchack, Stephen Prince,[2] and others, this approach
treats film both semiotically and phenomenologically as a grammatical system of signs, with attention to spectatorship and perceptual processes. Metz's
groundbreaking work in particular has been enormously influential, mostly
for his attempt to develop a sign system for film spectatorship, drawing heavily
from Lacanian psychoanalysis. Metz develops for film analysis the concepts of
the *mirror stage*—the moment of self-recognition and distinction that marks
the immersion into language—and the insistence of the letter in the unconscious—the idea that the unconscious is structured like a language. In tying
this semiotic system to the imaginary (the realm of secondary identification),
Metz shifts our focus to the construction and reception of film and, thus, ways
that film functions both like a language (in its sign system, with cinematic
technique the analogical equivalent of a grammar), but also rhetorically, as an
appeal to or assertion of identity in the audience (Blakesley "Introduction").

Approaching film as a language suggests the possibility that there is a grammar of visual signs that operates predictably and that can be used to generate
an infinite variety of meanings. The elements of film language include but are
not limited to its *visual elements*, which include camera movement, mise-en-
scène (placement in the frame), color, proxemic patterning (spatial relationships among characters and between the viewer and the visual material), the
subjective camera and point-of-view shot, special visual effects, visual editing,
iconic symbolism, visual repetition, and so on. One problem with attempts to
locate the rhetorical in the visual language of film, which obviously shares
with traditional rhetoric an interest in language as a system, has been that—as
Mitchell observes—it has been developed on the model of textuality, without
sufficient appreciation of textuality or visuality as a means of representation
embedded in the social process of human relations, the traditional realm of
rhetoric. In the realm of the textual or the visual, the ideological apparatus has

a determinative influence on what is read or seen at the moment of perception. What we read, as well as what we see, is a product of what we know or want to believe, as much as it is a product of the formal properties of the system observed. The reader/viewer is implicated in the effects and meaning propagated by the visual (and semiotic) system. Traditionally, film ideology has been specified by its explicit content: Films convey messages or shape attitudes that rehearse or challenge ideological pieties and in this sense are representational. What the visual turn suggests, however, is that the medium of the visual functions ideologically as well. The visual composition of the frame, for example, conveys meaningful relationships among components in the frame, and these relationships also transmit or create ideology. *Visual composition* functions rhetorically to the extent that the visual material represented is the expression of value, a choice among alternative means of representation or among the myriad objects that might be represented in the first place. The rhetorical operates at the moment of choice or neglect, when we (viewers, directors) focus on object A and neglect object B. How a subject is filmed is an expression of ideology, and to the extent that this agency positions the viewer, the director, or even characters on screen relative to the filmic content, the film functions rhetorically as an exploitation of that subject's ambiguity.

Metz's insufficient appreciation of the rhetorical/ideological component of perception in his semiotic system nevertheless did not prevent him from making forays into identification and spectatorship—in *The Imaginary Signifier* (1982), for instance—representing a fairly radical departure from his more formalistic articulation of film language.[3] In making such a move, Metz helps us understand more fully the visual nature of identification, about which I will have more to say later in the chapter. *Identification* is, from a rhetorical perspective, the act of asserting or imagining identity between two (or more) dissimilars, on the basis of similitude. As Metz argues, film identification functions in the imaginary, on the secondary (or even third) order of reality that is the film viewing experience. A film appeals to this desire for identification—of the self with others, for example—in an imaginary, symbolic realm, with interesting and complex psychological consequences for the film spectator and for spectatorship generally.

Film Ideology

This approach to film rhetoric views film as serving ideological purposes in both its content, technical apparatus, and distribution mechanisms. It examines film in its partisan aspects, as a kind of "pamphleteering." The task of film criticism is to expose film's complicity with or deconstruction of dominant ideology. Rhetorical analyses (of film, texts, speeches or any other symbolic activity) are typically concerned with both how works achieve their effects and how they make their appeals to shared interests (the margin of overlap) among people. This attention to agency in concert with ideological analysis and critique make this perhaps the most common way to approach a film rhetorically and as an instantiation of rhetoric (Blakesley "Introduction"). In film studies, its practitioners include Bill Nichols, Robert Stam, Barry Brummett, Thomas Benson, and a host of others.[4] As cultural expression, films reveal not only the predispositions of its makers, but they also serve ideological functions in the broader culture (as critique, as hegemonic force, as symptomatic) that can be analyzed as having a rhetorical function, especially to the extent that rhetoric serves as the means of initiating cultural critique and stabilizing cultural pieties (Blakesley "Introduction"). As we will see, this conception of film rhetoric also focuses our attention on identification to the extent that identification is an assertion of a margin of overlap—an identity of values, beliefs, and even bodies and bodily processes—in cases where we are also clearly divided, where common values or beliefs are arguments or propositions as much as they are a pre-existing basis for acting together. In *Vertigo*, ideology functions as a rationalization of male desire and of woman's otherness, voiced, for example, through the "historian" Pop Liebl's naturalized mythology of Carlotta Valdes and Scottie's failed attempt to read Madeleine through that terministic screen.

Film Interpretation

This approach treats film as a rhetorical situation involving the director, the film, and the viewer in the total act of making meaning. Its subject is often the reflexivity of interpretation, both as it is manifest on screen and in the reception by the audience/critic. Like Nichols in his treatment of documentary film rhetoric, J. Hendrix and J. A. Wood, David Bordwell, Seymour Chatman, and Bordwell and Noël Carroll each examine the film experience as a rhetorical situation.[5] Bordwell is perhaps most concerned with the role of the critic in that situation. Chatman attempts to show that film interpretation should account for audience reactions, the formal elaboration and function of genre, and the symbolic representation of meaning on screen. Chatman, however, shies away from rhetoric's role in articulating the situational nature of film (or any text), preferring instead to imagine rhetoric as useful for translating linguistic tropes and forms into their visual equivalents (Blakesley "Introduction").

Film Identification

This approach considers film rhetoric as involving identification and division. Film style directs the attention for ideological, psychological, or social purposes. Identification has been paired with discourses on the postmodern subject in work by critics such as Laura Mulvey, Kaja Silverman, Tania Modleski and many others whose approaches have been influenced by Metz in feminist and psychoanalytic studies.[6] Although the notion of the subject in film studies has received its due share of attention, the meaning of identification, particularly as it functions rhetorically, has yet to be closely scrutinized outside of the psychoanalytic (Oedipal) terministic screen. For Metz, identification occurs in the imaginary realm of the signifier, where film narratives create the conditions for identification to occur in a secondary order of reality. It would be useful, I think, to examine identification in the imaginary as a rhetorical process as well as a semiotic process of decoding and encoding signs. Kenneth Burke saw identification—and with it, the corresponding situation of division—as both the condition and aim of rhetoric. The desire for identification, which Burke calls *consubstantiality*, is premised on its absence, on the condition of our division from one another. There would be no need for the rhetorician to proclaim our unity, Burke says, if we were already identical (*A Rhetoric of Motives* 18–29). Consubstantiality, with its root in the ambiguous *substance* (substance), may be purely an expression of desire, an identity of attitude and act in a symbolic realm, much like Metz's secondary order.

The aim of rhetoric, according to Burke, is identification. From the perspective of the audience, or the spectator, identification functions as desire, as an *assertion* of identities, such that while there may be division or differences among people and characters, we pursue that identification as one way of expressing (or, again, asserting) our consubstantiality. Pushed to its extreme, we desire to become the other, to inhabit that psychological and physical space, to take ownership of some kind, to walk in someone else's shoes for awhile (to put it in more familiar terms).

Film is an especially powerful medium for cultivating this desire for identification, and, of course, not just between film and spectator, but among characters on screen. Hitchcock was especially interested in these processes of identification, foregrounding not only the relationship between viewer and film (so that our own desire for identification is never far from conscious awareness), but also among his characters, many of whom seek identification with a vengeance. In *Vertigo*, as we will see, Scottie's pursuit of Madeleine is an expression of this desire and a response to a challenge to the integrity of his legally sanctioned identity as a police detective. His is a desire to transform the self through the transformation of the other into the self. I will argue that Scottie wants not only to possess Madeleine (thus competing with Gavin Elster and especially the ghost of Carlotta Valdes), but also to be Madeleine, as much as that can be possible. The tangled relations of identity in the film implicate the viewer as well in this search for what we might call an *analogical self*—an identity that is similar but somehow different. In film generally, the projection of the visual field on or from a screen compels our attention this way and that, with the rhetoric of identification manifest as a desire for orientation—for sorting through, arranging, and forming visual cues that are expressions of attitude and identity. For that matter, seeing itself can be conceived as an active, rhetorical process—an assertion of the self on the world and the reverse manipulation of the viewing subject, as James Elkins has suggested in *The Object Stares Back*. In approaching film as identification, we ask, How does film exploit and elaborate our compulsion to see and, consequently, to identify?

THE CASE OF *VERTIGO*

Hitchcock's *Vertigo* is an exemplary case to elaborate the nature and value of each of these approaches to film rhetoric. The story follows John "Scottie" Ferguson (James Stewart), a recently retired police detective, as he tracks the "possessed" wife, Madeleine (Kim Novak), of an old college friend, Gavin Elster (Tom Helmore). Scottie has *acrophobia* (fear of heights) that gives him vertigo, a condition he often discusses with his friend Midge (Barbara Bel Geddes). He learns from Elster that Madeleine is possessed by the spirit of Carlotta Valdes, her great grandmother, who had committed suicide. According to a local San Francisco historian, Pop Liebl (Konstantin Shayne), Carlotta was the mistress of a wealthy and powerful man who kept their child and then "threw [Carlotta] away." Carlotta went mad and ultimately committed suicide. Scottie follows Madeleine throughout San Francisco to see what he can learn. When she leaps into San Francisco Bay, Scottie rescues her. He brings her back to his apartment while she is still unconscious, undresses her, and puts her in his bed. Although startled when she awakens from her "trance," the two have a sexually charged tête-à-tête , then part ways. The next day they meet again when Madeleine returns to thank him for rescuing her. As Scottie and Madeleine try to unravel the mystery of her possession, they fall quickly in love. But at the midpoint of the film, Madeleine apparently commits suicide while in one of her spells by leaping from the tower at the San Juan Bautista Mission. Scottie tries to stop her from reaching the top of the tower but is slowed by his vertigo.

The second half of the film tracks Scottie as he copes with Madeleine's death. He revisits all the locations where he had previously followed her, until one day when he sees Judy Barton (also Kim Novak) pass by on the street. She reminds him of Madeleine, so he persuades her to have dinner with him. The mystery of Madeleine is quickly revealed in a flashback seen from Judy's perspective. She had pretended to be Madeleine for Gavin Elster, with whom she was having an affair. When Judy reached the top of the tower at the San Juan Bautista Mission, she discovered that Elster had killed the real Madeleine, throwing her body from the tower to make it appear that, like Carlotta, she had gone mad and committed suicide. Judy contemplates running away now that Scottie has found her, but then tears up her confessional note, realizing that she loves him. Scottie remakes Judy into his image of Madeleine, making sure that she has the right clothes, make-up, hairstyle, and so on. Eventually, she comes to look exactly like Madeleine. One night when they are getting ready to go out to dinner, Scottie secretly notices that Judy is wearing the same necklace he had seen on Madeleine and in the portrait of Carlotta. Instead of taking Judy to dinner, he takes her back to the "scene of the crime" to force her to admit what has occurred. At the top of the tower, which this time Scottie has been able to reach, Judy confesses. They embrace, but then Judy is startled by a nun emerging from the darkness and falls backward out of the tower and to her death. The film ends with Scottie standing precariously on the ledge.

In my analysis of *Vertigo*, I want to focus primarily on Film Identification, which entails the other three approaches under the terministic screen of rhetorical theory. *Vertigo* positions its viewers, its characters, Hitchcock, and its cinematic style in a matrix of ideological practices and rhetorical appeals analyzable as identification and division. Scottie is a representative figure for the neurosis of pure yet imaginary identification. His madness midway through the film as he falls into the wild zone of the feminine and his relentless re-imag(in)ing of Madeleine/Judy in the latter half of the film are expressions of rhetorical desire, ones that Hitchcock locates in the common desire of seeing and being seen. Throughout the film, Hitchcock employs a variety of visual techniques (Film Language) to focus our attention on the psychological consequences of this desire for identification or identity. I will allude to some of these techniques as I elaborate these mechanisms of identification, in addition to noting instances when our consideration of the film might also slide into considerations of Film Ideology (what does *Vertigo* reveal or repress?) and Film Interpretation. What is the basis of disagreement, for instance, between Mulvey and Modleski on the nature of the spectator of *Vertigo*, and how can this disagreement be mediated by a more textured understanding of identification as a rhetorical process?

Identification becomes a central theme at the very start of the film, as the Saul Bass/John Whitney credit sequence unfolds. The camera shows an extreme close-up of a woman's face (but not Kim Novak's), slightly off-center to the left. Already, we have transgressed the proxemic space of the familiar into the intimate. The camera pans left, until we see "James Stewart" appear above the woman's lips, with the implication, perhaps, that she speaks the name, or rather that he (or his character) will speak for her (see Fig. 5.1). Either way, there is the implicit equation between Stewart's character and woman in this juxtaposition of the verbal and the image that presents or speaks it.

The credit sequence continues with the camera moving slowly up to show the woman's eyes. She looks to her left, then right, as if she feels she is being watched, and then we zoom in to an extreme close-up of her right eye. To this point, there has been just a hint of color visible, but suddenly everything is tinted red as the eye widens in surprise (or fear). The title of the film emerges from her eye, then Alfred Hitchcock's name as director, and then we descend inward as spiral-shaped images begin to slowly rotate and merge with the rest of the credits. There is much that is suggestive about this opening sequence and that sets a mood and a visual theme for the remainder of the film. There is

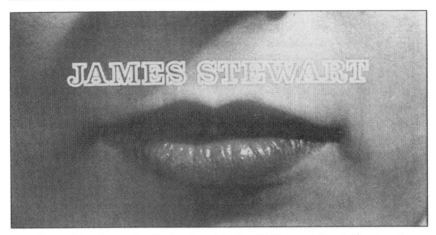

FIG. 5.1. Opening credits, *Vertigo*. Copyright © 1986 Universal City Studios, Inc. Restored Version © 1996 Leland H. Faust, Patricia Hitchcock O'Connell, and Kathleen O'Connell Fiala.

the woman being scrutinized and written upon, in fear of being watched. The close-up is so extreme it is unsettling. The camera pans across the woman's face and then descends into her eye where we see the verbal and the visual intermixed, with the credits juxtaposed to spiraling patterns suggestive of objects seen later in the film, such as the twirl in Carlotta / Madeleine's hair. If we translate this sequence into its literal equivalents, the spectator has not only been watching this woman from an intimate distance but has entered her mind, occupying the most private and inaccessible space of all. Even at this early stage, we have been forced to identify absolutely—we are consubstantial. But that identification has to be earned, as Hitchcock knows, so we retreat from inside, the camera zooming out, and with the pace of the music quickening, there is a cut to the film's opening scene, the rooftop chase. For the rest of the film, Scottie wants to return to that dark space—to find out who Madeleine is, what secrets haunt her, what moves her, and what or who possesses her. Implicated as we are in this identification, Hitchcock appeals to the viewer to want the same.

We next witness the rooftop chase and fall, with a "criminal" dressed in white being chased by a police officer (in black) and Scottie (in grey). The critical moment comes when Scottie can't quite make one jump and nearly falls to the street below. He clings desperately to a drain gutter. We then see two point-of-view shots: one of the police officer reaching out his hand to help Scottie, and the other, when Scottie looks down in a famous example of the dizzying reverse tracking / zoom shot. Even this early in the film, his vertigo is our vertigo. The police officer tries to help, but falls to his death. The criminal escapes. The scene ends with Scottie still clinging to the drain gutter. As Robin Wood shrewdly observes, this opening scene suggests the pattern of the quest for identification to follow in the remainder of the film: the criminal is the Id (which is set free); the police officer is the Superego (which is eliminated); and Scottie is the Ego left hanging (in search of a stable self; 32).

The early insistence on the viewer's identification with the image of the woman—and by extension Woman as a categorical ambiguity—and our identification with Scottie's precarious situation raises a critical issue regarding the role of the viewer and whether Hitchcock has scripted the viewer's experience as exclusively male. Scottie, as we see in this opening scene and in the one immediately following in Midge's parlor, is already searching for identity, feeling emasculated by his vertigo and by the (woman's) corset that he wears. He speaks frequently of "wandering," as if he is searching for something to fill the emptiness of the self now that he has had to retire because of his vertigo. After Elster tells him the "ghost story," Madeleine quickly becomes the object of his desire, a purpose for his wandering. He appeases that desire in his surveillance of her in the first half of the film, gradually reaching the point when he proclaims to Madeleine, just prior to her apparent suicide, "No one possesses you. You're safe with me," while embracing her tightly. At the time of her apparent death, Scottie identifies with Madeleine totally, so the shock of that break drives him mad. What has he seen? And how does this shocking elimination of the object of identification affect him? (Recall also the shock felt when Marian Crane is murdered halfway through *Psycho*.) What happens when the (male?) desire for identification with the woman has been thwarted? In Wood's view, by the end of the film, the "total and unquestioning identification invited by the first part of the film is no longer possible. We are too aware at that point that the fantasy *is* fantasy, and too aware of it as an imposition on the woman" (35).

These are questions that vexed Laura Mulvey in the mid-1970s and then her commentators in the 1980s and later. To build her case, Mulvey explains: "In their traditional exhibitionist role women are simultaneously looked at and displayed, with their appearance coded for strong visual and erotic impact so that they can be said to connote *to-be-looked-at-ness*" (11). The woman is the image, and the man is the bearer of the look. Mulvey sees Hitchcock as rehearsing this visual relationship in predictable ways and only grudgingly admits the self-reflexiveness of this look:

> [Hitchcock] takes fascination with an image through the scopophilic [voyeuristic] eroticism as the subject of the film. [...] As a twist, a further manipulation of the normal viewing process which in some sense reveals it, Hitchcock uses the process of identification normally associated with ideological correctness and the recognition of established morality and shows up its perverted side. (15)

In Mulvey's view, Hitchcock forces the male perspective on the spectator, leaving little possibility for any other. "Hitchcock's skillful use of identification processes and liberal use of subjective camera from the point of view of the male protagonist draw the spectators deeply into his position, making them share his uneasy gaze" (15). There's no question that even in the opening credits, the woman is the object-image, the mystery to be solved (presumably) by the male. But there's more than one-way looking involved, and it is the viewer's capacity for multiple identifications, born of conflicting desires, that Hitchcock addresses. As Elkins notes in *The Object Stares Back*, even "just looking" is hardly passive or one-way:

> Looking is hoping, desiring, never just taking in light, never merely collecting patterns and data. Looking is possessing or the desire to possess—we eat food, we own objects, and we "possess" bodies—and there is not looking without thoughts of using, possessing, repossessing, owning, fixing, appropriating, keeping, remembering and commemorating, cherishing, borrowing, and stealing. I cannot look at *anything*—any object, any person—without the shadow of the thought of possessing that thing. Those appetites don't just accompany looking: they are looking itself. (22)

For Elkins, looking is the appetite functioning simultaneously with (or even guiding) the perceptual process. Simultaneously, objects stare back, scripted as they are (and as Mulvey suggests) to appeal to these ideological and physiological appetites. What seems clear but often remains underappreciated in Hitchcock criticism is that we—the spectators—are watching and being watched, spying on ourselves with the same degree of desire and intensity that we often see acted out in his films. How better to express that stare back than to open the film with a woman being watched, staring back at us? Although Mulvey admits that Hitchcock makes the gaze wielded in *Vertigo* "uneasy," she underemphasizes this reflexiveness in the film in the interest of reifying the ideology of identification that she believes is formulated in psychoanalytic theory and acted out through the phallocentric order of the Oedipal triangle. There is, in other words, an inevitability to the relationship of the bearer of the gaze and the image—an unequal distribution of power resulting from the patriarchal order. And yet we also have the object staring back, both in the opening credits and elsewhere in the film. The ease, uncomfortable or not, with which the spectator (male or female) can assume the gaze and receive it, suggests the underlying rhetorical motive at work in the act of seeing and being seen and that Hitchcock foregrounds more than Mulvey will admit.

In *The Women Who Knew Too Much*, Tania Modleski argues that Mulvey does not allow for this possibility of multiple identifications and that contrary to Mulvey's insistence on locating the spectatorial gaze in the male protagonist of films like *Vertigo* and *Rear Window*, Hitchcock allows that perspective to shift in unexpected but prominent ways and thus suggests the plasticity of identification. In *Vertigo*, for instance, although Madeleine is the object-image for much of the first half of the film, equal screen time is afforded Scottie. We are watching him as much as we are watching Madeleine through him, and we do not necessarily view him from the perspective of the male's gaze that has been established and rehearsed in Scottie's voyeuristic tracking of Madeleine. The best example of this comes fairly early in the film when Scottie follows Madeleine into the flower shop. He watches from behind a door as she picks out a floral bouquet that we later discover is similar to the one Carlotta Valdes holds in her portrait in the Palace of the Legion of Honor. For much of the scene, we see from Scottie's perspective with the use of the subjective camera. Hitchcock even uses an iris filter to suggest further that we / Scottie are scrutinizing Madeleine. But then suddenly Madeleine walks toward the camera, and Scottie, and there's the urgent feeling that Scottie might be noticed. The shot shows Madeleine reflected in the mirror on the door that Scottie hides behind (see Fig. 5.2).

As Madeleine approaches the camera, we might expect once again to observe Scottie watching her—as Modleski suggests—in visual possession of the woman (92). However, in this split frame, we see both Scottie and the reflection of Madeleine in the mirror, which is a distorted image of the "real" Madeleine. Modleski cites Donald Spoto's observation that Scottie and the viewers may be seen as Madeleine's reflection, and then notes that Spoto, however, "does not pause to note the extraordinary significance of this observation, which suggests that identification is 'disturbed, made problematic' [Robin Wood's terms] *at the very outset* of Scottie's investigation" (92). We see (reflected) what Scottie sees, and we see Scottie watching her. At the same time

FIG. 5.2.   The viewer watches Madeline and Scottie watching Madeleine simultaneously. Copyright © 1986 Universal City Studios, Inc. Restored Version © 1996 Leland H. Faust, Patricia Hitchcock O'Connell, and Kathleen O'Connell Fiala.

and if we break the filmic plane, Scottie is watching us also. And what of the reflection in the mirror? It is reflecting back a scene that we can only imagine, somewhere in the numinal space we also occupy in front of the screen. What of our reflection?

Indeed, it is this foregrounded process of identification that I think is the central theme of *Vertigo* and that I believe best illustrates the nature of filmic rhetoric. As Burke points out, there would be no need to identify with each other, no occasion for rhetoric, if we were absolutely divided (*A Rhetoric of Motives* 22). But identification and division are ambiguously contemporaneous such that there's the urge to either assert identity or to elaborate its potentiality. Whether the means are verbal or visual, the rhetorical act involves imagining that such identity is possible and that its effects are real. Furthermore, there is something strangely unsettling about this desire for identification that Hitchcock also makes us feel. The act of total identification requires abandoning thoughts of the self as a unique identity, and thus there is loss. When we're reminded of how eagerly we give ourselves over or how absentmindedly we take possession of the other through the look, we realize the danger of total abandonment. There is, as Woods argues, the "fear of spying" (*passim*). Finally and from a rhetorical perspective, we are compelled to identify verbally and visually as a matter of course in social life. As Burke notes, a doctrine of consubstantiality "may be necessary to any way of life" and "a way of life is an *acting-together*" (21). In acting-together, we "have common sensations, concepts, images, ideas, attitudes" that make us consubstantial (21).

Identification is inherently an acting-together of subject–object, with identity a constructed middle ground in the symbolic (visual and verbal) realm where individual identity can be played out, reformed, channeled, encoded, visualized, and even asserted as if it were a verbal and visual proposition. In *Visual Analogy: Consciousness as the Art of Connecting*, Barbara Maria Stafford suggests that this process is analogical. Analogy is "born of the human desire to achieve union with that which one does not possess" (2). She proposes also that "the proportional and participatory varieties of analogy are inherently visual. It requires perspicacity to see what kinds of adjustments need to be made between uneven cases to achieve a tentative harmony. It also presupposes discernment to discover the relevant likeness in unlike things" (3). Throughout *Vertigo*, Hitchcock stresses this desire to connect and control the other with the look, which travels in both directions between object–image and subject by, as I have already suggested, making the object of fascination into a portrait, which can serve as an empty repository for projections of identity. As we will see, when Scottie descends into madness, he has recapitulated Madeleine's dream, falling into the darkness of the grave, where there is no other and no self.

This process begins prior to his initial surveillance of Madeleine around San Francisco. Scottie goes to Ernie's Restaurant, where Elster and Madeleine will be dining, so that he can see the person he has been hired to follow. Already, there is some fascination with Madeleine's story of possession, which Elster related to Scottie earlier. Scottie sees Madeleine from behind as she dines but gets a closer look when she and Elster leave. As Madeleine nears Scottie, he turns away slightly so as not to be caught staring. She pauses right next to him, and the right side of her face is framed like a portrait. At the time, of course, we are not aware that Judy is deliberately staging this close encounter. What's striking about this shot is that it echoes the extreme close-up of the opening credits, but here the angle is oblique and the image of the woman only partial, suggesting that there is still a mystery here to untangle.

The next day, and after the close encounter in the flower shop, Scottie follows Madeleine to the Mission Dolores, where Carlotta Valdes is buried. As Madeleine leaves, there are two shots reminiscent of both the scene in the flower shop and the one at Ernie's (see Figs. 5.3 and Fig. 5.4). In the first shot, Madeleine once again pauses near Scottie, who then backs away slightly. The tension in the scene comes from both the fascination with the mysterious story of possession that we see unfolding, but also from, once again, the danger of the object staring back, that the one wielding the look will be seen. In the second shot, we see Scottie once again turn away slightly into the shadows where he won't be noticed.

Scottie next follows Madeleine to the Palace of the Legion of Honor, where he watches her as she sits before a painting that, he discovers, is called, "Portrait of Carlotta." Hitchcock stages the scene so that we observe Madeleine observing the painting in a point-of-view shot from Scottie's perspective (see Fig. 5.5).

Intercut with this scene are shots of Scottie standing before two paintings, both of which he takes some interest in. In this shot (Fig. 5.6), he is framed by Carle Vanloo's "Architecture" (1753), which depicts three small boys holding

FIG. 5.3. Madeleine at the Mission Dolores. Copyright © 1986 Universal City Studios, Inc. Restored Version © 1996 Leland H. Faust, Patricia Hitchcock O'Connell, and Kathleen O'Connell Fiala.

FIG. 5.4.   Scottie is nearly caught spying. Copyright © 1986 Universal City Studios, Inc. Restored Version © 1996 Leland H. Faust, Patricia Hitchcock O'Connell, and Kathleen O'Connell Fiala.

FIG. 5.5.   The Portrait of Carlotta. Copyright © 1986 Universal City Studios, Inc. Restored Version © 1996 Leland H. Faust, Patricia Hitchcock O'Connell, and Kathleen O'Connell Fiala.

blueprints, and Largilliere's "Portrait of a Gentleman" (1710). The dialectic between these alternating shots further suggests that both Madeleine (and Carlotta) as well as Scottie are on display, portraitures themselves. (There may also be some suggestion that Scottie is, in terms of his sexual maturity, still in a grey area between a child and a gentleman.)

This theme of watching and posing comes full circle a short time later in Midge's apartment when she shows Scottie her version of "Portrait of Carlotta"

FIG. 5.6.   We watch Scottie watching Madeleine in an art museum. Copyright ©
1986 Universal City Studios, Inc. Restored Version © 1996 Leland H. Faust, Patricia
Hitchcock O'Connell, and Kathleen O'Connell Fiala.

(see Fig. 5.7). Midge herself is posed next to the painting, setting Scottie in the
position of painter. Midge has painted her own head onto Carlotta's body (with
a prescient sense of the crisis to come in the challenge to photographic and representational realism). Scottie can hardly bear to look. At this point, he is unwill-
ing and perhaps unable to corrupt the perfection of the image he has begun to
paint of Madeleine.

The repetition of this pattern of surveillance and portraiture rehearses the
desire of the voyeur for observing and constructing the object-image without

FIG. 5.7.   Midge's "Portrait of Carlotta." Copyright © 1986 Universal City Studios,
Inc. Restored Version © 1996 Leland H. Faust, Patricia Hitchcock O'Connell, and
Kathleen O'Connell Fiala.

being seen but still in danger of being seen. What happens when the object stares back? Why is it so unsettling? (Midge's bespectacled Carlotta stares back at him and appears to make him ill.)

In *Vertigo*, we don't experience that break when the observer becomes the observed in as abrupt a fashion as we do in *Rear Window*, when Lars Thorwald catches L. B. Jefferies spying on him through his camera, or when Norman Bates stares back at us from his cell at the end of *Psycho*. The possibility for this to happen in *Vertigo* is there nevertheless, and it gives the narrative its edge for the first half of the film. When Scottie finally transgresses the observer–observed boundary in his rescue of Madeleine from San Francisco Bay, he literally takes possession of her, bringing her back to his own apartment, undressing her and putting her to bed, and then watching her with a desiring eye as they sit by the fire.

After Madeleine's death and the coroner's inquest that legally absolves Scottie but nevertheless makes him culpable for her "suicide," he visits Madeleine's grave. In the next scene, we witness the famous nightmare sequence, with its crude animation (by today's standards), showing, among other things, a point-of-view shot as we plunge into Carlotta's grave (again, repeating the imagery of Madeleine's dream), Carlotta's flower bouquet splitting apart, washes of color from shot to shot, and the image of Scottie's disembodied head (see Fig. 5.8).

The dream sequence closes with a matte shot of Scottie's falling body against a bright white background. He awakens with a terrified look on his face. The next scene takes place at the sanitarium, where Scottie is diagnosed as having acute melancholia. There is a Freudian basis for understanding melancholy in terms of subject–object identification that has some bearing on our understand-

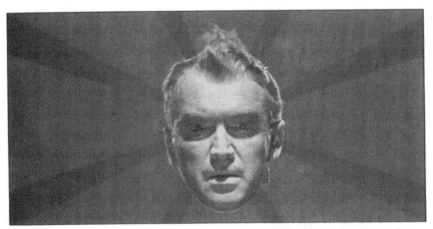

FIG. 5.8. Scottie's Dream. Copyright © 1986 Universal City Studios, Inc. Restored Version © 1996 Leland H. Faust, Patricia Hitchcock O'Connell, and Kathleen O'Connell Fiala.

ing of Scottie's "problem" at this stage in the film. As Modleski points out, Freud described melancholy as an extraordinary diminution of the self, "an *identification* of the ego with the abandoned object" (qtd. in Modleski 95–96). Scottie has identified with Madeleine so thoroughly that in her absence, there is no ego-identification or, as Freud would suggest, even self-reproach, because Scottie is made to feel responsible for her death and, symbolically, his own.

There is another explanation as well, one that brings us closer to understanding the motives for Scottie's total identification with Madeleine, and thus, to an explanation of his madness in terms other than those provided by the Freudian terministic screen. As Elaine Showalter points out in "Feminist Criticism in the Wilderness," Edwin Ardener suggests that "women constitute a *muted group*, the boundaries of whose culture and reality are not wholly contained by the *dominant (male)* group" (471). The region of experience beyond or inaccessible to the dominant group Ardener calls "the wild zone" (471). This wild zone is outside of male consciousness and unstructured by language. It is muted and entirely imaginary. It is the experience alluded to by Pop Liebl when he tells the story of the "mad Carlotta, sad Carlotta." In Helene Cixous's formulation, the wild zone is the Dark Continent where the laughing Medusa resides (Showalter 472). Scottie's descent into Carlotta's grave, down the dark tunnel that Madeleine sees as her destiny and her past, brings him ever closer to this imaginary wild zone. In his nightmare, the Medusa's head is his own, staring back and rendering him speechless, for nothing can be or need be spoken once identification with the other is total (and especially when the other is purely symbolic). This desire for consubstantiality, or oneness—being with, being as—is acted out in an imaginary realm of the symbolic that has been determined by the stories of Carlotta Valdes told by both Gavin Elster and Liebl, then acted out by Judy in her role as Madeleine. Elster and Judy have been acting out a drama written explicitly for Scottie and designed to appeal to his vanity and to take advantage of his weakness. Identification, here, becomes the expression of desire, an appeal grounded in the narrative of woman as other, as unexplainable. Scottie's madness results from his crossing over into the realm of the wild zone, the symbolic space inaccessible to the dominant male cultural narrative and also beyond language. This transgression is echoed later in the film in another form, when Judy's role is discovered because Scottie recognizes that she has taken the symbol of Carlotta—the necklace—as her own. "You shouldn't have been so sentimental," he tells her. It is this act that breaks the plane of the imaginary and the real and helps Scottie realize that he has been played the fool and that his descent into madness has been scripted from the start.

VISUAL RHETORIC AND IDENTIFICATION

As a predominantly visual medium, film makes identification even more inviting than it might otherwise be. We ease into novels and it normally takes a while before we begin to live the lives of the characters with them, to see ourselves in them, or to laugh at them as if we were laughing at ourselves. In film, however, identification is an insistent force, sometimes leaving the viewer no choice but to identify or at least to play out the drama of identification. When it works well, it induces submission, a relinquishing of power to the idea and image of the other. What makes identification so powerful is its pliability—the ease with which the viewer can shift identifications almost effortlessly, provided the film provides sufficient impetus to construct multiple identifications. The visual elements of film not only foster identification, but they appeal to the capacity of the mind to assert its vision of the world even as the active agency of this assertiveness remains hidden. The visual field seems readymade—arriving in consciousness as fully formed visual experience. As James Elkins, Richard L. Gregory, and many others note, however, the visual field is never innocent or untainted by ideology or desire.[7] What we see, even at the moment of perception, is a consequence of what we're looking for. As Hitchcock knows—and Burke theorizes—the desire to assert identifications on the visual world—the objects of sight—is not only necessary, it is insistent, powerful, and, because of the unconscious ease with which that visual field is shaped, always beguiling. Because the processes and compulsion of identification assert themselves so readily, any film—in its capacity as visual representation—will wield this power, will direct the attention to A rather than B, or make us believe that *framed* experience is *all* experience. A central proposition of film rhetoric is thus that film's visuality is not merely a language or a representation of the real (a simulation), or even simply a sign of value or belief. The visual functions as an appeal, an assertion that has been constructed and placed by pointing the camera in particular directions at objects that have been manipulated (staged), by developing, editing, and screening films in particular ways, and even by marketing them to particular audiences. There is, in other words, a rhetoric that elaborates and exploits visual ambiguity to foster identification, and that rhetoric will be operative whether a film's director self-consciously directs our attention to that process or not.

The concluding scene of *Vertigo* can help us see how complex these problems of identification can become. As Mulvey observes, we are compelled to identify with Scottie and to view everything from his perspective. And yet it is also clear that in foregrounding this process—in making us so compelled and aware—Hitchcock wants us to see that other identifications are possible, even if they are often repressed by ideological narratives or predispositions. Scottie is also the object of our scrutiny—and even derision—especially in the latter half of the film as he attempts to remake Judy into Madeleine. His authoring of the object of identification is so obvious and forceful that it is unsettling. By the end of the film, when Scottie stands on the precipice of the tower, Judy having fallen to her death, we are compelled to identify with him even as we may be ever conscious of Judy having fallen victim to his desire to reassert himself in his role as detective, as bringer of the law. We're not shown Judy's body sprawled on the rooftop, as we are Madeleine's, which would seem to suggest that we no longer identify with her. However, the last subjective, point-of-view shot of the film is through Judy's eyes as she is startled by the dark figure of the nun, so there is the sense also that we have fallen with her, that we share her guilt, or that Hitchcock wants us to feel guilty. Scottie's "possession" of Judy, reminiscent of Carlotta's presumed possession of Madeleine, is also so assertive that although we may have forgiven his first failure to protect her in her role as Madeleine (still believing perhaps other-worldly possession had something to do with it), this time, Scottie is indeed to blame, having just forcibly dragged her back to the scene of the crime. We have witnessed the processes of identification even as we have experienced them, and we have seen where the madness of *consubstantiality*—of total identification with the other—can lead. Rather than simply reasserting the ideology of dominant male (and visual) culture for its own sake, Hitchcock reasserts it to place it in full view, as risky as it is, and was, to do so. It is in the duplicity, or multiplicity, of identification that we can appreciate his accomplishment, and it is through the terministic screen of film rhetoric that we can see this scrutiny of identification as an expression of the human desire to connect, albeit symbolically and visually, with each other.

NOTES

1. Qtd. in *Vertigo: The Making of a Hitchcock Classic* by Dan Auiler, 180.
2. See, for instance, Christian Metz, *Film Language*, 1971, 1974, and *The Imaginary Signifier: Psychoanalysis and the Cinema*, 1977, 1982; Stephen Heath and Patricia Mellencamp, *Cinema and Language*, 1983; Vivian Sobchack, *The Address of the Eye: A Phenomenology of Film Experience*, 1992; and Stephen Prince, "The Discourse of Pictures: Iconicity and Film Studies," 1993, and *Movies and Meaning: An Introduction to Film*, 2000.
3. For a detailed critique of Metz's attempt to forge a rhetoric for film studies, see Ann Chisholm's "Rhetoric and the Early Work of Christian Metz: Augmenting Ideological Inquiry in Rhetorical Film Theory and Criticism."
4. See, for instance, Bill Nichols, *Ideology and the Image: Social Representation in the Cinema and Other Media*, 1981; Robert Stam, *Reflexivity in Film and Literature: From Don Quixote to Jean-Luc Godard*, 1985, and *Subversive Pleasures: Bakhtin, Cultural Criticism, and Film*, 1989; Barry Brummett, *Rhetorical Dimensions of Popular Culture*, 1991; and Thomas Benson, and Carolyn Anderson *Reality Fictions: The Films of Frederick Wiseman*, 1989.
5. See, for instance, J. Hendrix and J. A. Wood, "The Rhetoric of Film: Toward a Critical Methodology," 1973; David Bordwell, *Making Meaning: Inference and Rhetoric in the Interpretation of Cinema 1989; Seymour Chatman, Coming to*

132 BLAKESLEY

Terms: The Rhetoric of Narrative in Fiction and Film, 1990; and David Bordwell and Noel Carroll, *Post-Theory: Reconstructing Film Studies* 1996.

6. See, for instance, Laura Mulvey, "Visual Pleasure and Narrative Cinema," 1975; Kaja Silverman, *The Subject of Semiotics*, 1983; and Tania Modleski, *The Women Who Knew Too Much*, 1988.

7. See Richard L. Gregory's *Eye and Brain: The Psychology of Seeing*, 1997, for a detailed account of how the visual field is actively constructed.

WORKS CITED

Auiler, Dan. *Vertigo: The Making of a Hitchcock Classic*. New York: St. Martin's P, 1998.

Benson, Thomas W. "Rhetoric of Film." *Encyclopedia of Rhetoric and Composition: Communication from Ancient Times to the Information Age*. Ed. Theresa Enos. New York: Garland Publishing, 1996: 620–621.

—, and Carolyn Anderson. *Reality Fictions: The Films of Frederick Wiseman*. Carbondale: Southern Illinois UP, 1989.

Blakesley, David. "Introduction: The Rhetoric of Film and Film Studies." *The Terministic Screen: Rhetorical Perspectives on Film*. Ed. David Blakesley. Carbondale: Southern Illinois UP, 2003.

Bordwell, David. *Making Meaning: Inference and Rhetoric in the Interpretation of Cinema*. Cambridge: Harvard UP, 1989.

Bordwell, David, and Noël Carroll. *Post-Theory: Reconstructing Film Studies*. Wisconsin Studies in Film. Madison: U of Wisconsin P, 1996.

Brummett, Barry. *Rhetorical Dimensions of Popular Culture*. Tuscaloosa: University of Alabama P, 1991.

Burke, Kenneth. *Language as Symbolic Action: Essays on Life, Literature, and Method*. Berkeley: U of California P, 1966.

—. *Permanence and Change: An Anatomy of Purpose*. 1935. 3rd ed. Berkeley: U of California P, 1984.

—. *A Rhetoric of Motives*. 1950. Berkeley: U of California P, 1969.

Chatman, Seymour. *Coming to Terms: The Rhetoric of Narrative in Fiction and Film*. Ithaca: Cornell UP, 1990.

Chisholm, Ann. "Rhetoric and the Early Work of Christian Metz: Augmenting Ideological Inquiry in Rhetorical Film Theory and Criticism." *The Terministic Screen: Rhetorical Perspectives on Film*. Ed. David Blakesley. Carbondale: Southern Illinois UP, 2003.

Elkins, James. *The Object Stares Back: On the Nature of Seeing*. San Diego: Harvest/Harcourt, 1996.

Gregory, Richard L. *Eye and Brain: The Psychology of Seeing*. 5th ed. Princeton, NJ: Princeton UP, 1997.

Heath, Stephen, and Patricia Mellencamp, Eds. *Cinema and Language*. Frederick, MD: University Pub. of America, 1983.

Hendrix, J., and J. A. Wood. "The Rhetoric of Film: Toward a Critical Methodology." *Southern Speech Communication Journal* 39 (1973): 105–122.

Metz, Christian. *The Imaginary Signifier: Psychoanalysis and the Cinema*. 1977. Trans. Celia Britton, et al. Bloomington: Indiana UP, 1982.

—. *Film Language*. 1971. Trans. M. Taylor. New York: Oxford UP, 1974.

Mitchell, W. J. T. *Picture Theory: Essays on Verbal and Visual Representation.* Chicago: U of Chicago P, 1994.

Modleski, Tania. *The Women Who Knew Too Much: Hitchcock and Feminist Theory.* New York: Methuen, 1988.

Mulvey, Laura. "Visual Pleasure and Narrative Cinema." *Screen* 16.3 (1975): 6–18.

Nichols, Bill. *Ideology and the Image: Social Representation in the Cinema and Other Media.* Bloomington: Indiana UP, 1981.

Prince, Stephen. "The Discourse of Pictures: Iconicity and Film Studies." *Film Quarterly* 47.1 (Fall 1993): 16–28.

—. *Movies and Meaning: An Introduction to Film.* Boston: Allyn and Bacon, 2000.

Psycho. Dir. Alfred Hitchcock. Universal, 1960.

Rear Window. Dir. Alfred Hitchcock. Paramount, 1954.

Rorty, Richard. *Philosophy and the Mirror of Nature.* Princeton, NJ: Princeton UP, 1979.

Showalter, Elaine. "Feminist Criticism in the Wilderness." 1981. Rpt. *Contemporary Literary Criticism* 2nd ed. Ed. Robert Con Davis and Ronald Schleifer. New York: Longman, 1989. 457–478.

Silverman, Kaja. *The Subject of Semiotics.* New York: Oxford UP, 1983.

Sobchack, Vivian. *The Address of the Eye: A Phenomenology of Film Experience.* Princeton: Princeton UP, 1992.

Stafford, Barbara Maria. *Visual Analogy: Consciousness as the Art of Connecting.* Cambridge: MIT Press, 1999.

Stam, Robert. *Reflexivity in Film and Literature: From Don Quixote To Jean-Luc Godard.* Ann Arbor: UMI Research Press, 1985.

—. *Subversive Pleasures: Bakhtin, Cultural Criticism, and Film.* Baltimore: Johns Hopkins UP, 1989.

Vertigo. Dir. Alfred Hitchcock. Paramount, 1958.

Wood, Robin. "Fear of Spying." *American Film* 9.2 (November 1983): 28–35.

CHAPTER SIX

Political Candidates' Convention Films: Finding the Perfect Image— An Overview of Political Image Making

J. Cherie Strachan and Kathleen E. Kendall

American political candidates expend considerable effort to construct favorable images of themselves in order to accomplish particular goals or advance political agendas. Rather than a strictly *visual* impression or depiction, the term *political image* refers to a carefully constructed condensation of all the attributes a candidate wants to convey to the voters into easily recalled, visual and verbal symbols. Hence political images are symbolic devices, which can be constructed with both visual and verbal messages, that provide a shorthand cue to audiences for the identification and enhancement of specific character traits. Through symbolic representation, they simplify candidates' messages by offering "materials from which their observers supply interpretations and draw conclusions" (Melder 5).

Although discussions of political image making often center on the efforts of contemporary candidates and their media consultants, political image making has a long history in the United States. Candidates have always attempted to construct favorable images in their efforts to appeal to the electorate and attract supporters. Melder describes how political candidates at least as far back as the founding fathers of the nation developed images as the brave conquering hero, the ingenious military leader, the industrious yeoman farmer and the egalitarian frontiersman (5–11). Corcoran and Kendall found that the presidential candidates of 1912 presented themselves in ads and speeches as possessing much-admired image traits, especially the trait of the *fighter* (15–29). In the political arena, it is important to note that images are often intended to symbolize far more than candidates' most attractive personal traits. Instead, they have often been constructed to imbue candidates with mythical, larger-than-life qualities that stand for not only the candidate, but the nation itself. In these symbolic representations, the identity of the candidate and the nation are merged. Hence, images of conquering heroes and military leaders glorify not only the candidates' past military experience, but the military successes of the nation. Similarly, images of the yeoman farmer or the frontiersman stand not only as a cue for a candidate's socioeconomic status and values, but as a patriotic identity for the entire nation—where the concerns of average people are paramount and where even they, through individual merit, can rise to claim the mantle of leadership.

Politicians usually construct images that reflect core political values because embodying exalted American values—such as individualism, freedom or equality—enhances their status, legitimizes their claim to wield power and justifies their policy preferences. Moreover, such constructions increase their appeal to the electorate. Citizens who want to embrace and uphold these patriotic values can do so by accepting candidates' conclusions and voting for them.

Yet, even though political images typically correspond to widely held core values, it is important to note that they are not organic, but are constructed to advance a particular agenda. The emotional appeal of these images to patriotic values encourages unquestioned acceptance of candidates' images and candidates' patriotic definitions of the nation, as well as the stands on policy positions that flow from these definitions. A classic example can be found in the history of our nation's earliest years, when "the very foundation of national survival in the era of the Constitution rested on the image of authority and unity embodied in George Washington" (Melder 5). These images of authority and unity served as shorthand cues for Washington's character, but also provided an identity for an emerging nation state. If one accepted the definition of nationhood provided by Washingtonian images, one also rejected criticisms launched by Anti-Federalists, who had argued vehemently against the authority granted to the new national government.

Political rhetoric, or messages communicated with the intention of persuading the electorate, has included image construction since the beginning of American history. Yet changes in the electoral arena and in communication technology have moved such efforts to center stage. As other influences on vote choice, such as party preferences, have declined, the electorate has come to rely more heavily on candidate imagery. At the same time, candidates have embraced image construction because it can now be accomplished with a far greater variety of persuasive visual symbols.

Verbal or written rhetoric, which attempts to persuade with verbal symbols or words including the full array of assertions and arguments, has historically been the primary means of political persuasion simply because available means of communication did not allow candidates to convey messages visually to a vast electorate. Hence, in the past, candidates' linguistic construction of political images was supplemented by visual symbols, which were portrayed on campaign novelties and in campaign brochures. Yet with advances in communication technology, the use of visual rhetoric has expanded as visual symbols that construct meaning can be readily conveyed to a mass audience. In particular, as the medium of television matured, candidates have increasingly relied on visual symbolism to construct persuasive imagery. As a result, candidates are increasingly apt to use powerful visual symbols—including portrayals of icons, past political heroes, the flag or even idealized American landscapes—in their attempts to convey messages intended to persuade American voters.

To demonstrate the shift toward visual rhetoric and image construction, this analysis focuses on a relatively new genre of political rhetoric, the biographical candidate films aired at the major political parties' conventions. To gain insight into these persuasive efforts grounded in visual imagery, the 2000 convention films of the most recent presidential candidates, Al Gore and George W. Bush, are compared.

A NEW RHETORICAL GENRE EMERGES

As the influence of partisan identification waned after the 1950s, many citizens began turning to alternative cues—such as candidate images—when making voting decisions. At the same time as shifting electoral circumstances underscored the importance of political image construction, the invention of television dramatically enhanced the candidate's ability to accomplish this task. As Morreale notes,

> television is a particularly apt mediator of images in both the visual and psychological senses of the term. The medium creates the impression of live, immediate and transparent reproduction of the "real" and thus serves as a substitute for viewers' direct experience. (*The Presidential Campaign Film* 2)

Television, and the accompanying ability to construct images with visual symbols, has had such a pervasive influence in our political life that Smith and Nimmo claim we have entered a telepolitical age (xvi). In the major parties' nominating conventions, television coverage has expanded the audience size and spawned new genres of political rhetoric. In the past, party conventions reached primarily those in attendance. The party faithful from across the United States could meet, nominate a candidate, and resolve party differences in order to present a united front in the upcoming general election. Once live television coverage reached millions in 1952, however, the conventions were no longer a precursor of the general election campaign, but became the first event to kick off the campaign. Not only could conventions offer newly nominated presidential candidates the opportunity to reach the party faithful, but with television coverage, they could begin communicating campaign messages to the much broader public that constitutes the general electorate.

Hence party conventions play an important role in presidential campaigns, despite the fact that the presidential primaries have taken over the role of selecting the candidates. A convention unites the party members, and "converts the individual campaign themes of the winter and spring into the party discourse of the fall" (Smith 19). The nominee attempts to establish "thematic continuity" through the 4 days of convention events, "positioning ... the candidate in terms of the [fall] campaign" (Timmerman 365).

The desire to communicate such messages to a wider and less attentive audience led to the development of a new rhetorical genre—the biographical convention film. Morreale ("The Political Campaign Film" 188) traces the use of these films to as early as the 1952 campaign, when both Eisenhower and Stevenson incorporated documentary-style films in their campaigns. Although these films represent the origins of the genre, both candidates' efforts still relied heavily on words rather than visual cues to convey meaning. Eisenhower's film, entitled *Report to Ike*, began by conveying biographical material about the candidate. The visual cues presented included still photos of Eisenhower's parents, as well as newsreel footage of him as a general in Korea, in an appearance with Winston Churchill, and at the birth of his granddaughter. The film also presented interviews with people—including celebrities, politicians, and average Americans—testifying about why they supported Eisenhower (Morreale, *The Presidential Campaign Film* 49–52). Yet the visuals presented in Eisenhower's film did not evoke meaning independent from oral assertions. As Morreale concludes, "the images do not carry the argument," and "few images appear without narration to explain their significance" (*The Presidential Campaign Film* 52). In a slightly different style, Stevenson's film, *Campaigning with Stevenson*, portrayed the candidate in chronological order. It opened with shots of Stevenson at the Democratic National Convention, and established the candidate's background by showing him at home, at work, and on vacation. To emphasize the current campaign, he was also featured driving himself to campaign headquarters, boarding the campaign's plane and giving speeches at various locations across the country (Morreale, *The Presidential Campaign Film* 53–54). Some of the visuals provided seem intended to evoke an image of "the common man," including footage of the candidate chopping wood, taking his children camping, and reading the newspaper, but Morreale indicates these portrayals evoke "little positive symbolic resonance" (*The Presidential Campaign Film* 54).

Over the years, candidates and their consultants have honed the ability to move audiences with visual symbols. For example, Reagan's overwhelmingly successful film in 1984 reportedly brought tears to the eyes of his opponent's campaign staff. Ever since, such films have replaced speeches as introductions for newly nominated presidential candidates. Reagan's film, aptly labeled, *A New Beginning*, was the first to weave together both documentary and advertising film styles (Morreale, *The Presidential Campaign Film* 140). Throughout the film, footage of Reagan engaging in presidential activities—such as taking the oath of office, siting at a desk in the Oval office, enduring an assassination attempt and giving a speech to D-Day veterans at Normandy—are interspersed with a montage of patriotic visuals of an idealized, traditional America. In one scene, a farmer plowing his field fades into a picture of a quaint, white farm house. In another, children at a campground peer up at a flag. Another fast-moving series of vignettes includes the silhouette of a city, a happy couple on their wedding day, more children saluting the flag, the Statue of Liberty, a policeman with a flag, and a woman embracing a soldier. As the film progresses, this montage of visual stimuli is framed by either moving orchestral music or Lee Greenwood's country music song, "God Bless the U.S.A" (Morreale, *The Presidential Campaign Film* 140–144).

Throughout the Reagan film, the audience is drawn in by a cinema-verite style, as if the shots are framed "for the absent … witness—the American public"(Mackey-Kallis 310–11). Unlike initial efforts in candidate films, the visual cues in Reagan's film were integral in "constructing a unified American community of adherents to mythic Main Street America and the positive values of hope and optimism" (Morreale, *The Presidential Campaign Film* 143). Yet the film moves beyond simply linking Reagan's character to the patriotic values portrayed. In his total commitment to American values, he is a synecdoche for America, in Burkean terms. In his humility, and courage, and perseverance in overcoming hardship, he IS America. As Mackey-Kallis claims of the Reagan film: "If we believe in the American story, we must believe in the Reagan story as well" (311).

Presidential candidates' unanimous decision to shift from speeches to films is easy to explain. These films, as so dramatically illustrated by Reagan's 1984 effort, can incorporate elements of entertainment programming, which can both attract and hold an audience's attention. Films have assumed the function of lengthy campaign advertisements capable of introducing a candidate's image, theme and issues in an engaging format. Moreover, films can condense this wealth of information into a tight time frame. As Morreale notes, "an orator may require 15 minutes to argue a point; in 15 minutes of film, the candidate's ethos and message can be put forth and illustrated through the strategic display of words, music and pictures" (*The Political Campaign Film* 188). In addition, biographical films allow candidates to shape the visual and verbal message to perfection, controlling production and creating a story to move the emotions. Kern establishes that the political advertisement, a highly visual form of message, persuades mainly through emotional appeals. The convention film is also a televisual form of communication, which "serves to celebrate values rather than persuade by virtue of rational argument" (Morreale, *The Political Campaign Film* 188–189). As Morreale summarizes the convention film genre, it is "a way to define the character and qualifications of candidates and the broad themes that shape their campaigns" ("The Bush and Dukakis Convention Films" 141). Given their persuasive potential, it is little wonder candidates have seized the communication opportunities films provide and made their use an American campaign tradition (Timmerman 364–373).

COMMON PATTERNS IN CONVENTION FILMS

Examinations of the convention film genre have discovered a number of common strategies and patterns. The films typically adopt a narrative style, developing a plot with story lines and conflict. In addition, Morreale identifies three traits typical of most convention films. First, Morreale notes they present archetypal images of candidates as the ideal American male (*The Presidential Campaign Film* 7). As a result, they often emphasize candidates' participation in male-dominated institutions, such as politics, the military and sports. Women characters in the narrative are often relegated to the traditional female roles of "wives, mothers, and homemakers largely concerned with private rather than public matters" (Parry-Giles and Parry-Giles 338, 346). A second common trait Morreale identifies is the tendency to play on themes of the American dream by portraying candidates as rugged individualists with effective leadership skills, or as populists who empathize with the common people. While one of these two images is stressed, most candidates attempt to incorporate both (*The Presidential Campaign Film* 13). Similarly, Mackey-Kallis finds that the films often use the cultural mythology of the "West" or the "new frontier," with the "cowboy/hero, a rugged individual [who fights] to protect the values of community and civilization" (309). The third trait Morreale identifies is reserved for the most successful convention films. These introduce a candidate's vision for the future, emphasizing patriotic myths about the country and its people. Candidate visions are associated either with malaise, identifying a problem that must be overcome, or with resurgence, claiming the country need only persevere to achieve greatness (*The Presidential Campaign Film* 14). Finally, Morreale notes that Republicans, who typically stress optimistic messages, tend to use the televisual techniques with more skill than Democrats (*The Presidential Campaign Film* 178).

Bill Clinton's films represent a notable exception to this Republican advantage. Clinton's 1992 convention film was especially successful, moving audiences and winning acclaim for its skillful persuasive strategies. When taken at face value, Clinton's film, *The Man from Hope*, represents an attempt to recast the "Slick Willy" image linked to him during the primary season. To this end, the film eschews the glossier, high-production advertising style used so effectively by Reagan in 1984 for a less finished documentary style. The film, which develops three story lines about Clinton's early childhood, his days at Yale, and his experiences as a father and presidential candidate, is purposefully informal and sustains an "intimate and personal quality" from beginning to end (Timmerman 366).

The Man from Hope presents testimonials by Clinton and various members of his family. To reinforce their sincerity, the film incorporates soft lighting, tight facial close ups and slow music. Meanwhile, still photographs supplement the meanings of the ongoing narration. When Clinton opens the film by stating he was born in a small town called Hope, Arkansas, a photograph featuring a tiny train station and his grandfather's country store underscores his modest beginnings and small town background. When Clinton's mother describes how her son was affected by meeting John F. Kennedy, archival footage of the event portrays a young Clinton, in Washington DC representing Boys Nation, shaking the President's hand. When Clinton's brother describes how his older brother was inspired by Martin Luther King, Jr., footage of the civil rights leader delivering his "I Have a Dream" speech appears on screen. Clinton's recollection of the impact Robert Kennedy's assassination had on him is accompanied by still photographs of the Senator. This series of visual presentations allows Clinton, without explaining his positions, to link himself to past leaders and the unfinished issue agendas they represent. Finally, Clinton's character as a family man is reinforced by footage of him playing sports and dancing with his daughter Chelsea and of him relaxing with both Chelsea and Hillary in a hammock.

While the film emphasizes character over issues, it does merge Clinton's identity with a patriotic vision for America. Parallels drawn between Clinton as a unifying force in his own family and his agenda as a political candidate make it clear that his relationship to his family serves "as a metaphor for his relationship to his country" (Morreale, *The Presidential Campaign Film* 167). "Clinton's America is represented by his recollection's of growing up in Hope, Arkansas, where everyone was happy, safe and secure" (Morreale, *The Presidential Campaign Film* 168).

Perhaps the most striking thing about these films, however, is the way they conceal their political nature. There is little sign of conflict or disagreement, and no sense that the candidates are engaged in a struggle over scarce resources. Yet the political implicitly involves "the conscious, deliberate exercise of power among people for public ends" (Pitkin 213). Political rhetoric is symbolic and arbitrary, with contested and changing meanings. As Corcoran emphatically points out, in constructing political meaning, "something is always at issue" (75). Convention films, in part because of their persuasive visual appeals, downplay this conflict and encourage viewers to accept candidates' versions of America's future without critical analysis. Candidate films, which both include a vision for America and allow candidates to embody the patriotic values associated with that vision, accomplish this end more successfully than others. Comparing the Gore and Bush 2000 convention films clearly illustrates what a difference incorporating a patriotic vision for the future can make.

THE GORE FAMILY PHOTO ALBUM

As the 2000 general election neared, Vice President Al Gore was in dire need of image reconstruction, and he could have helped to reshape his image with a well-crafted biographical film. After a highly visible 8-year tenure as vice president, Gore was a familiar public figure. Unfortunately for Gore, however, the old adage "familiarity breeds contempt" tends to ring true for vice presidents. Americans often subject their elected officials—especially prominent, powerful ones—to critical commentary and sarcastic humor. Such attention reminds both them and the electorate that politicians serve at the pleasure of the people. For holding the second highest office in the executive branch, vice presidents are criticized and lampooned by everyone from average citizens to syndicated columnists and late night talk show hosts. Yet unlike presidents, they cannot deflect charges by wrapping themselves in the honor and prestige of the office of the presidency. Hence negative images created during a tenure as vice president tend to stick. Recall, for example, the way George Bush was labeled a "wimp" after serving as vice president in the Reagan White House.

Gore faced a similar dilemma, except he had been labeled a "stiff" who was incapable of displaying human warmth and spontaneity. During the election, both editorials and letters to the editor addressed how "Al Gore could ... erase our perception of him as a stiff who underestimates voters' intelligence" ("The Gore Method" A-30). Even with the baggage of a negative image, Gore's bid for the White House was by no means a lost cause—a point underscored by poll results throughout the fall contest, and by the number of votes he eventually received. Yet the convention represented the chance to reintroduce himself to the American electorate and to emerge from behind Bill Clinton's shadow. Gore had the opportunity to capitalize on the many successes of the Clinton–Gore administration, and to present his own vision for America's future. His convention film began to address these image problems and made a concerted effort to replace his stiff image with that of a spontaneous, fun-loving family man.

Yet, as anyone familiar with the most recent presidential race can attest, Gore's reintroduction at the convention did not solve the problem. The issue of his image kept recurring, despite his campaign's efforts to paint a more positive picture of Gore. Part of the problem seemed to be that Gore's image construction efforts became transparent. He adopted a different style of interaction during each of the debates, and he was even criticized for changing the type of clothes he wore. Both media pundits and his opponent's supporters repeatedly pointed out inconsistencies in Gore's behavior and accused him of trying to portray an appealing, electable image instead of his true character. For Gore, the campaign process highlighted "his search for both an identity and a message" (Seelye A-26). Such criticisms eventually led to the Republican mantra of "Who is the 'real' Al Gore?" Hence despite the persuasive opportunity presented initially by the convention film and later throughout his advertising efforts and speeches, Gore's attempt to reconstruct his image was problematic.

At first glance, the Gore film appears well crafted. The film is structured as a straightforward candidate biography. It is narrated by a credible figure, the candidate's wife, and her account of Gore's accomplishments and character are accompanied by persuasive visual proof. To introduce the film, Tipper Gore informs the audience that she wants to "share a little bit more about Al," and that she is going to do so by sharing family pictures taken across the years. She specifically refers to the film as their family photo album and then proceeds to share pictures from their lives together, beginning with high school dances, progressing through marriage, her husband's entry into political life and the births of their children and grandchild. Unlike many modern convention films, Tipper's account does not stray far from chronological order to achieve dramatic impact. Although some of the photos may be out of order, the narrative follows the true time line of Al Gore's life, from the time he met Tipper until his nomination.

This format may prohibit structuring the story of Al Gore's life to achieve the most dramatic impact. Yet the presentation flows out of the attempt to simulate a family photo album, which enhances the authenticity of Tipper's claims about her husband. More than 100 snapshots of Al Gore, taken throughout his lifetime, are presented throughout the film. The chronological order of their presentation makes it appear unplanned. Meanwhile, the sheer number of photos, and their candid quality, reinforce this appearance, creating the impression of an accurate portrayal of Gore's life. Yet the photographs presented throughout this film serve primarily as persuasive visual proof of Tipper's verbal claims. In this sense, the Gore film reverts back to the efforts of earlier candidate documentaries, when the potential to use visual cues to construct meanings independent of the film's narration were underutilized.

Throughout the chronological account, the Gore film incorporates two elements typically found in convention films. Gore is portrayed as the archetypal American male whose populist appeal justifies his election to office. Yet other important elements, such as a presenting the candidate's vision for America's future and responding to audience needs, are glaringly absent. Hence Gore commits, and perhaps even exaggerates, errors in crafting his convention film that, according to Morreale have been endemic to Democratic presidential candidates, with the exception of Bill Clinton (*The Presidential Campaign Film* 178).

First, as expected, Gore is portrayed as the archetypal American male by emphasizing his athletic abilities, connection to farming, dedication to country, and love of family. His life story even comes complete with heroic military service, as Gore served in Vietnam.

In addition to this portrayal of Gore as the archetypal American male, the film incorporates a second expected element in this genre by addressing why Gore is qualified to hold office. The film resolves the conflict between the desire for a man of the people and for a talented, heroic leader by portraying Gore as a populist who has learned to be an effective leader. It is not surprising that Gore, as a Democrat, chose to emphasize his populist roots. Yet accomplishing this portrayal is no small feat given Gore's privileged background as a U.S. senator's son. The film however, artfully presents Gore as a common man whose experiences mirror those of many middle-class Americans. It subtly downplays Gore's elite background, describing him as a man who married his high-school sweetheart after they went to high school dances and fell in love, and as a man who began his married life living in a trailer park. The family photographs exclude any visual cue that the Gores enjoyed any trappings of the upper class. Gore is also explicitly identified as a populist when Tipper describes his entry into politics. She avers that her husband's leadership style was formed in the "hundreds" of open meetings he has held over the years. Numerous snapshots of Gore actively interacting with groups testify to the authenticity of Tipper's interpretation of her husband's political career. Visual reminders of his last 8 years as a member of the current administration are not included.

Although the film successfully incorporates these two expected elements, the third is notably absent, as Gore fails to take a position on the nature of the country or on its people. This omission probably results from Gore's ambivalent feelings toward the Clinton administration. In different historical circumstances, Gore could have relied on a resume structure, more typically used by incumbents, in his campaign film (Morreale, *The Presidential Campaign Film 5*). This structure would have enabled him to claim the accomplishments of the Clinton White House and to portray himself as Clinton's torchbearer. He could have argued that the nation had experienced resurgence under Democratic leadership, and that he was the most logical choice to ensure that resurgence continued.

Yet Gore backs away from this strategy, perhaps to distance himself from the Monica Lewinsky scandal tarnishing Clinton's image. On the other hand, Gore clearly would not want to claim that the country is experiencing a crisis because he, after all, has been a high-level member of the administration for the past 8 years. Rather than presenting Gore's vision of America's future, his convention film adopts a much narrower agenda. Instead, it simply serves as an effort to redefine two aspects of Gore's image. First, to further distance himself from Clinton's sex scandals, the film emphasizes his relationship with Tipper and their children in order to portray a dedicated family man. Second, to overcome the negative label of "stiff" that he acquired as vice president, the film emphasizes the warmth and spontaneity of his interactions with these family members. With this narrow agenda, the film remains exclusively focused on the candidate himself. Hence Gore never embodies patriotic values important to the American electorate. He does not use powerful visual imagery to evoke an emotional response to patriotic values, and he fails to take full advantage of the medium of television. Gore's film reverts to the Democratic tendency to reflect "images of the candidates with little regard for the hopes and desires that fuel the American psyche" (Morreale, "American Self Images" 38).

As a result, the Gore film fails to live up to the full potential of its genre. Yet this failure does not explain why the film was not more successful in achieving its narrower agenda. Selecting Tipper as the narrator makes a great deal of sense, considering the film's goal. Who better to portray her husband as a family man who would not think of straying, let alone embarrassing the nation with a sex scandal? Because she has known Al Gore for 30 years, Tipper is also qualified to testify about the warmth of his true personality. Throughout the film, the emphasis on Gore's wife and family moves far beyond an attempt to appropriate the "family values" issue. Gore's dedication to family becomes the central message of the film, overshadowing any of his political accomplishments. This emphasis is reinforced by the visual proof provided. Of the more than 100 photographs of Al Gore presented throughout the entire film, only 15 depict the candidate in official roles as a representative, senator or vice president. Even more striking is the fact that only one of these photos features Bill Clinton. Instead, the bulk of the snapshots show Gore interacting with his family. The central message is apparent in Tipper's concluding remarks. She does not argue that Al Gore should be the next president because of his qualifications, experience or issue positions. Rather, she notes that Gore's father would be proud "not just of his son's sense of duty and love of country, but for his dedication as a father and grandfather."

Tipper's testimony about her husband's spontaneity and warmth is less overt than her description of his dedication to family. Yet numerous examples of these personality traits are woven throughout the film. She begins, for example, by describing an exciting courtship; she and Al rode on his motorcycle and went to rock concerts. The emphasis extends into their married life when she confesses that her husband enjoyed family vacations "as much as the kids did." One of the most lasting visual impressions of these character traits accompanies Tipper's description of Gore as the kind of person "who still makes time for Halloween." Gore appears dressed as Frankenstein, complete with green face paint. A second persuasive visual proof, appearing near the end of the film, features Gore holding his grandson on the beach. Gore has tousled wet hair, a bare chest and a huge grin on his face, presenting visual cues that defy the label "stiff." As the film ends, Al Gore makes a final effort to imprint his revised image on the public's mind. He takes the convention stage, kisses his wife and embraces her for a long moment. This famous kiss represents the "spontaneous" act of a loving and dedicated husband.

The kiss, in combination with the film, is intended to introduce a new and improved version of Al Gore to the American public. Although the film does not address the audience's patriotic values, and thus fails to evoke strong emotional reactions to the candidate, it does present a favorable account of Al Gore's character. One might expect that this film would have launched a successful effort to recast his image. Yet even this narrower agenda was not successfully achieved. The American electorate never seemed to fully accept the image of Al Gore as a fun-loving family man. Even at the end of the campaign, Gore was described in news reports as "stiffer than ever, smiling but robotic ... turning into a caricature of himself, as if he were mimicking Darrell Hammond's *Saturday Night Live* parody of him" (James A-29). The remaining question is why, and that question is best answered by understanding how people process political information.

IMPLICATIONS OF SCHEMA THEORY

Graber relies on schema theory, first developed by cognitive psychologists, to explain how people process political information and make decisions based on it. According to this theory, people abstract information from their personal or vicarious experiences to create mental constructs that organize information about situations and individuals. Each mental construct, or schema, includes a conception of a general pattern, as well as a limited number of illustrative examples. This cognitive structure is used to process new information or to retrieve existing information. According to Graber:

> Schemata include information about the main features of situations or individuals and about the relationships among these features. They also include information about the expected sequence of occurrences or behaviors under various contingencies (28).

One of these schemata's major functions is to help people solve problems and make decisions. By providing information about "likely scenarios and ways to cope with them," they are "an important element in deciding whether to act and how to act" (Graber 29). Hence, when people have a well-defined schema, they are able to develop a judgment about a person or a situation and to make decisions more quickly.

To provide a simple example, when people have a well-developed schema of "eating in a restaurant," they have learned that the sequence of events typically occurs in a particular scenario, as well as the roles they and other people play. They know they should wait to be seated by a hostess, and that a waiter or waitress will ask them to order items off the menu. They know they will have to linger over drinks and an appetizer or salad while the chef prepares their food. They know they are expected to leave a tip based on their satisfaction with the service provided, and that their experience will end by paying the tab—either to a member of the wait staff or to a cashier depending on the quality of the establishment. In addition to this set of expectations, people may also develop a normative judgment about whether eating out is an enjoyable experience or whether it is worth the expense.

Note, however, that the experiences used to develop these expectations and judgments are not treated equally. People can learn how to behave appropriately in a restaurant from several sources. They may learn through their own direct experiences, or they may learn by gathering information from secondary sources. A friend, for example, may have gone to dinner and described the experience in great detail. The learning opportunities provided by these two sources of information vary considerably. Direct experiences allow people to process rich details and cues from all of their senses. They can hear the sounds of dishes clashing and cash registers ringing, see tables being cleared and money being exchanged, feel the texture of the menu, and smell the aroma and taste the flavor of the food. These perceptual experiences have a more dramatic, lasting impact than being told even the most vivid story—which explains why people often conclude the stories they tell with the line, "I guess you just had to be there."

Hence firsthand, direct experiences have far more influence on schema development than secondhand, vicarious ones (Graber 90–91). Yet the invention of television provided a new and far more persuasive way to learn from vicarious experiences. The medium, with its appeal to visual and auditory senses, comes closer to recreating the perceptual cues of real-life experiences. These qualities help to explain why television is such a persuasive medium, especially in the process of developing new schema. Timmerman touches on this process when he describes the dramatic difference between merely hearing Bill Clinton describe meeting President Kennedy as a youth, and actually seeing a black and white photograph of the same event. He notes, "now we have seen the event and we have interpreted it .... In the telepolitical age, pictures do not lie" (364). Television's ability to dramatically enhance the impact of vicarious experiences supports the old adage, "seeing is believing."

Yet the same pattern of information processing that makes people susceptible to such influence also protects them. Once a schema has been developed and a judgment put into place, it is particularly difficult to change because people engage in selective perception. To return to the example of restaurants, people who have repeatedly received poor service or bad food when they have gone out to eat will probably develop a schema for the experience that includes a strong negative judgment. It is not likely that they will easily abandon this judgment, even if they see a televison advertisement for a new café or hear their friends testify about how great the café's food is. In short, when people are exposed to information that contradicts existing judgments, they often reject it, either by ignoring it or by finding a reason to disregard it (Graber 186).

This practice of selective perception helps to explain why the Gore film was not more successful. First, most Americans have a well-developed judgment about politicians in general. Socialization in American political culture repeatedly warns them to be wary of political actors' motivations and to be suspicious of political messages (Graber 202). So, even though the scores of photographs presented in the Gore film painted an attractive picture, both they and "the kiss" were automatically subjected to skeptical examination. Gore opponents fed this existing cynicism by describing the efforts as a blatant attempt to convince people that Al Gore was someone he was not.

Second, as previously noted, many Americans had existing judgments about who Al Gore was. They thought he was a stiff man incapable of conveying spontaneity and warmth. Altering such judgments is a difficult, although not impossible, task. Past vice presidents, most recently former President George Bush, have managed to alter negative images acquired during their time in the limelight. The key to success in such a task is consistency. A convention film represents a powerful opportunity to convey a candidate image that will help win an election. Yet a campaign consists of a series of messages communicated over a longer period of time. And in order to be effective, the messages communicated during this time span must be consistent. Hence it is important that a convention film introduces an image that the candidate will be capable of conveying throughout the duration of the campaign. The best way to ensure this level of consistency is to carefully evaluate the candidate's strengths and weaknesses. Good campaign professionals develop images of a candidate's characters that are inherently true and that the candidate will not have difficulty portraying. Perhaps the current era of advanced communication technology has increased this need for accuracy because it is more difficult for candidates to control all of the cues provided to voters about them. Now, candidates not only need to have internally consistent campaign messages, but they need to promote an image that will not be contradicted by the mass media or by their opponents. Shea notes that sometimes campaigns attempt to shape candidate images solely based on polling data, but he warns that "the hard truth is that this strategy too often fails because the [actual] qualifications and capabilities ... are not given enough heed" (40).

Here it seems the Gore campaign made its fatal mistake. Al Gore may very well be a warm, spontaneous man in the privacy of his own home. Yet he has consistently had difficulty portraying this side of his personality when he is in the limelight. His convention film emphasized aspects of his character that he was unable to live up to as the campaign progressed. This failure made him vulnerable to opponents' criticism of his efforts to construct a new image. Moreover, this criticism was easy for the American public to accept because it fits with the existing judgment that political messages should be treated with skepticism. Gore's convention film was unsuccessful first because it failed to construct a patriotic vision for America's future, and second because the image he attempted to construct did not correspond to the one he conveyed throughout the remainder of the campaign.

BUSH'S PAEAN TO AMERICA

As he approached the Republican Party Convention, Texas Governor George W. Bush faced a somewhat easier task than Gore. Despite Bush's status as the son of a former president and the sitting governor of a large state, many voters in the general electorate were still unfamiliar with his personality and political agenda. The convention presented his first opportunity to introduce himself to the broader American public and to launch the themes of his campaign. The result was an 8-minute convention film, entitled *The Sky's the Limit*, that incorporated the important traits of the genre more effectively than his opponent. Although Bush's effort placed less emphasis than most films on portraying an archetypical American male, it incorporated a value-laden patriotic image, providing an identity for both himself and the nation.

Bush narrates much of this optimistic film himself. His effort is reminiscent of Reagan's *A New Beginning* in a number of ways. The film's high-production values evoke patriotism, as Bush's narrative and others' testimonials are interspersed with surging music and emotional visual cues. American icons such as the flag, the Statue of Liberty, and the Lincoln Monument, as well as American heroes such as Teddy Roosevelt, President John F. Kennedy, and Reverend Martin Luther King, Jr., all make appearances. In addition, the televisual techniques draw in the audience. For example, the film makes transitions between scenes by portraying Bush, in the role of a casual rancher, driving an open Jeep across his Texas land with his dog—descended from his father's famous dog Millie—at his side. As Bush drives, he turns to speak to the audience, creating the feeling that each viewer is part of the scene. The Bush film also seems inspired by the success of Clinton's efforts in *The Man from Hope*, as it makes heavy use of extreme close-ups of Bush speaking while he drives around his ranch. The tactic is effective because facial closeups are "exceptionally powerful in attracting and holding the viewers' attention." They also stir emotions and produce "feelings of positive or negative identification with the people shown on the screen" (Graber 168).

In a pattern uncharacteristic of most convention films, Bush's effort downplays the importance of male-dominated institutions. It is true that most of the women in the film hold traditional female roles, including Bush's mother, Barbara, his wife, Laura, and his twin daughters, who are shown as babies. The one exception to this pattern is Phyllis Hunter, of READ for Texas, who testifies that George W. gave the schools of Houston whatever they needed. Yet the film includes only fleeting visual references to the military or sports, including a baseball player and the flag raising at Bataan. Bush's father, with all of his experience in governing institutions, makes only a brief appearance,

whereas Laura Bush and Barbara Bush are featured prominently. Most conspicuously, George W. Bush does not capitalize on his role as Governor of
Texas. He never appears at the State House, and only once refers to running
for Governor of Texas; only Phyllis Hunter calls him "Governor," and shortly
afterward refers to him as George. Throughout the film he is George. This
film's effort to distance Bush from stereotypical masculine institutions and activities may be a result of the Republican Party's recent efforts to address the
gender gap by appealing to women voters. Similarly the emphasis on women
of the Bush family instead of on George Senior may have reflected the desire
to distance "W" from his father, making it clear that he was his own man.

In addressing why Bush is qualified to hold office, the film also emphasizes
that Bush is his own man. Like most Republicans, Bush's film resolves the conflict between the desire for a man of the people and for a talented, heroic leader
by portraying him as a leader with middle-class roots. The film plays on the cultural mythology of the West with Bush fulfilling the role of a cowboy and rugged individualist. Because the film is largely self-narrated, and Bush cannot
make boastful claims about himself, this image is conveyed with visual cues.
Bush embraces his southwestern roots, appearing in an open-necked blue
denim shirt, jeans, and in some scenes, a cowboy hat. He is filmed casually driving around his ranch with a loyal dog, passing the crepe myrtles and cattle and
ranch buildings, narrating the film in his Texas accent. The entire film appears to
have been shot in Texas, further linking Bush to the traditional values of that region of the country. Yet, quite cleverly, the film's references to Midland, Texas
are used to connect Bush to the middle class, even though he comes from a
wealthy family. Still photos of the community are portrayed as Bush and others
describe his life, growing up in Midland, going to public schools (though Bush
attended high school at an elite Massachusetts' boarding school) and meeting
and marrying his wife, the school librarian. As Bush stresses the sense of community surrounding his upbringing, pictures of casually dressed people going
to barbecues or attending football games after church convey Bush's identification with average people despite his status as a leader.

Hope for maintaining (or re-establishing) such communities in America
pervades the film. Bush and others who speak exude optimism in both speech
and manner. They smile and laugh, recalling heartwarming stories of the past.
The emphasis is most conspicuous when the source of the film's title is revealed. While a still photo of a Midland sign on the outskirts of town is displayed, Bush indicates that the slogan of Midland—the small Texas town that
has been used as a metaphor for his image and is about to become a metaphor
for America's idealized future—is "The Sky's the Limit." It's "such an optimistic slogan," he says; it's "how I feel about America." Yet throughout the film, it
becomes clear that this optimism is reserved for an America that exalts the
core value of a Texas cowboy, of a rugged individualist—the value of individual responsibility tempered with compassion. In one particularly powerful

scene, for example, footage of gushing oil wells establishes an impression of boundless wealth as Bush praises Midland for being a home to "entrepreneurial pioneers." The unspoken inference is that America can enjoy the same boundless wealth if its people embrace Midland's values.

The theme of responsibility to family and children re-occurs again and again. As photographs of Bush's early years are highlighted, the film makes it clear that his parents put their children's welfare above all else. Bush himself is portrayed tenderly holding his newborn twin daughters in his arms—visual proof of his claims that they brought a sense of responsibility to his life. He goes on to claim that the great challenge of his generation is to "assume responsibility and lead." The happy tale of the Bush family is contrasted with the sad story of a little boy named Jimmy Dean, who Bush took a "took a shining to" and accompanied home. Ominous black-and-white pictures of slum housing appear on the screen to illustrate the tragic results of irresponsibility. Bush explains that Jimmy's mother was "on drugs," and there were "hanger on-ers" in the house; several years later, Jimmy was shot and killed. There is a dramatic difference in the care for children portrayed in these two versions of responsibility, between Bush, the responsible parent and governor, and Jimmy Dean's mother, the irresponsible parent.

The emphasis on personal responsibility that permeates the film is tempered by highlighting a second Bush trait, compassion. Barbara Bush, for example, describes how her young son attempted to console his grieving parents when his little sister died. Later in the film, when Bush tells the story of Jimmy Dean, his facial expressions and demeanor clearly convey concern. A third scene intended to convey Bush's compassionate nature focuses on his desire to help children by improving the quality of education. Visual proof of this commitment is provided by footage of Bush reading to children and by the testimony of Hispanic leaders, who describe Bush's deep concern for the quality of the Texas schools. This emphasis on compassion for children and concern for education may have been incorporated to address the Republican Party's need to attract women. Bush was positioning himself for a campaign in which the majority of female voters supported his Democratic opponent. He needed to make inroads in this important group of voters, particularly to win in the suburbs.

The emphasis on constructing an image that embraces the value of personal responsibility in this film suggests that herein lies the contested world view, the main political issue of the film. The contested nature of this concept lies in the question of how much support a society should give to needy individuals, and how much self-reliance should be expected of them. In the Jimmy Dean story, Bush shows his personal compassion for the child, and his shock at finding such an irresponsible mother. Although he and his family have been responsible, loving their children through thick and thin, Jimmy Dean's home is a place of drugs and alcohol and deprivation. Yet if one accepts Bush's definition of such problems, which some would argue require better social programs and more government intervention, the appropriate answer is to call for more personal responsibility.

In most respects, *The Sky's The Limit* conforms to the constraints of the convention film genre. It celebrates values through emotional appeals, using pictures not only to document verbal assertions, but to construct independent meaning. Through a strategic presentation of narration and testimony, surging music and value laden visual cues, the film becomes a paean to America with George W. Bush and his heroic image of rugged individualism standing for America.

Unlike the Gore film, Bush's effort to construct his political image is less hindered by the public's information-processing patterns. First, fewer members of the general public had established strong judgments about Bush before the convention, so he had more opportunity to begin shaping opinions about his personality and policy agenda. This is an easier persuasive task than changing pre-existing opinions. Information provided as the campaign season progressed contradicted some of the characteristics stressed in the Bush film. Yet Bush's campaign team used the film as an opportunity to prepare people for one of his most apparent character flaws—his tendency to mispronounce words—instead of trying to contradict or conceal it. At one point in the film, for example, Bush stumbles over his words. Yet he and his wife laugh at his mistake; their relaxed demeanor reassures viewers that they can laugh at his malapropisms as well. Second, Bush's emphasis on individual responsibility is a traditional Republican position. Hence it met the public's existing expectations for a Republican candidate, which enhanced Bush's credibility. Finally, Bush's embodiment of a broadly held American value—individual responsibility—also played on existing schema patterns about America and its people. The image he presented could be easily integrated into the public's existing beliefs, making it easy to accept and difficult to criticize.

CONCLUSION

Convention films provide candidates with the opportunity construct or reconstruct their images, to introduce their public policy agendas, and to link their visions with deeply held patriotic values. Films incorporate emotion-laden visual cues that simulate firsthand experiences—which enhances their ability to persuade. Yet, as clearly demonstrated here, the messages conveyed in a convention film are not automatically accepted by the audiences who view them. Success depends on evoking a favorable reaction from a cynical electorate suspicious of politicians' motives. Persuasion is enhanced when a convention film is consistent with messages conveyed throughout the remainder of the campaign. Moreover, critical reactions are less apt to result when convention films encourage an emotional response by evoking and reinforcing the public's existing judgments and values.

Some may be troubled by this process whereby politicians strategically construct images in order to pursue controversial political ends, fearing that such manipulation undermines democracy. Yet there is a large reality check to this process. Both the public and the media bring their expectations and prior experiences to any political message. The political leader who is exposed for gross distortion or a pattern of lying risks losing the positive reputation so central to a successful political image. In addition, political image construction fulfills an important, if not essential, function in American democracy. The use of symbolic imagery to unify the country behind a common vision may be necessary to overcome the fragmentation inherent in such a large and diverse republic.

WORKS CITED

Bush, George W. *The Sky's The Limit*. Republican Convention Film, 2000.

Corcoran, Paul E. "Language and Politics." *New Directions in Political Communication: A Resource Book*. Eds. David L. Swanson and Dan Nimmo. Newbury Park, CA: Sage Pub., 2000.

Corcoran, Paul E., and Kathleen E. Kendall. "Communication in the First Primaries: 'The Voice of the People' in 1912." *Presidential Studies Quarterly* 22 (1992): 15–29.

Graber, Doris A. *Processing the News: How People Tame The Information Tide*, 2d ed. New York: Longman, 1988.

Gore, Albert. Democratic Convention Film, 2000.

"The Gore Method." *New York Times*, 2 November 2000: A-30.

James, Caryn. "The 43rd President: On Television – Critic's Notebook." *New York Times* 14 December 2000: A-29.

Kern, Montague. *30-Second Politics: Political Advertising in the Eighties*. Westport, CT: Praeger, 1989.

Mackey-Kallis, Susan. "Spectator Desire and Narrative Closure: The Reagan 18-Minute Political Film." *Southern Communication Journal* 56 (1991): 308–314.

Melder, Keith. "Creating Candidate Imagery: The Man on Horseback." *Campaigns and Elections, A Reader in Modern American Politics*. Ed. Larry J. Sabato. Boston: Scott, Foresman and Company, 1989: 5–11.

Morreale, Joanne. *A New Beginning: A Textual Frame Analysis of the Political Campaign*. Albany, NY: State University of New York P, 1991.

—. "American Self Images and the Presidential Campaign Film, 1964 1992." *Presidential Campaigns and American Self Images*. Ed. A. H. Miller and Bruce E. Gronbeck. Boulder, CO: Westview Press, 1994: 19–39.

—. "The Bush and Dukakis Convention Campaign Films." *Journal of Popular Culture* 27 (1994): 141.

—. "The Political Campaign Film: Epideictic Rhetoric in a Documentary Frame." *Television and Political Advertising, Vol. 2*. Ed. Frank Biocca. Hillsdale, NJ: Lawrence Erlbaum Associates, 1991: 187–201.

—. *The Presidential Campaign Film: A Critical History*. Westport, CT: Praeger, 1993.

Parry-Giles, Shawn J., and Trevor Parry-Giles. "Gendered Politics and Presidential Image Construction: A Reassessment of the 'Feminine Style.'" *Communication Monographs* 63 (1996): 337–353.

Pitkin, Hannah. *Wittgenstein and Justice: On the Significance of Ludwig Wittgenstein for Social and Political Thought.* Berkeley: U of California P, 1972.

Seelye, Katharine Q. "The 2000 Campaign: On the Stump—The Speech." *The New York Times,* 24 October 2000: A-26.

Shea, Daniel M. *Campaign Craft: The Strategies, Tactics and Art of Political Campaign Management.* Westport, CT: Praeger, 1996.

Smith, Larry David. "The Nominating Convention as Purveyor of Political Medicine: An Anecdotal Analysis of the Democrats and Republicans of 1984." *Central States Speech Journal* 38 (1987): 252–261.

Smith, Larry David, and Dan Nimmo. *Cordial Concurrence: Orchestrating National Party Conventions in the Telepolitical Age.* Westport, CT: Praeger, 1991.

Timmerman, David M. "1992 Presidential Candidate Films: The Contrasting Narratives of George Bush and Bill Clinton." *Presidential Studies Quarterly* 26 (1996): 364–373.

CHAPTER SEVEN

Gendered Environments: Gender and the Natural World in the Rhetoric of Advertising

Diane S. Hope

Image-based advertising is the omnipresent signature of corporate commodity culture. Advertising endorses and legitimates consumerism by saturating the culture with images intended to position commodity purchase at the center of identity. In spite of international recognition of worldwide environmental degradation, financial institutions, corporations and their advertisers continue to promote overconsumption as the path to economic security and individual liberty. As such, advertising constitutes a dominant genre of visual rhetoric whose power is integral to the continuance of consumer based economies—and the consequential risks to the environment. The *visual rhetoric of advertising* rests in the cumulative effect of ubiquitous images—separate promotions that collectively celebrate the righteousness of the consumer ethic. Like verbal rhetoric, visual rhetoric depends on strategies of identification; advertising's rhetoric is dominated by appeals to gender as the primary marker of consumer identity. Constructs of masculinity or femininity contexualize fantasies of social role, power, status, and security as well as sexual attractiveness. Strategic to advertising's rhetoric of gender identification is iconography appropriated from a complex of cultural, religious, and historic sources; central among these floating signifiers are images of nature. Attached to commodities for purchase and reassigned in an infinite array of associations for gendered definitions of self, images of nature in advertising are a significant figure in advertising's justification of consumerism as a prevailing ethic (Hope).

Whenever advertising chooses to elaborate its rhetoric with images of nature, the relationship between consumer identity and the environment is implicated. In an era when serious environmental problems are evident, the rhetorical task of consumer advertising is especially demanding: Advertising must mask the ecological impact of overconsumption. This chapter develops the term *gendered environments* to explore one strategy in advertising's visual rhetoric. I argue that when image based advertising complicates images of nature with gender narratives, a rhetoric of gendered environments works to obscure the connections between environmental degradation and consumption. Advertisments that combine images of nature with narratives of gender offer consumers visualizations that cloak the impact of consumption on the environment with essentialist fantasies of masculinity or femininity. The rhetoric of gendered environments is particularly compelling in an age when gender is problematized and natural environments are under threat. Offering facile resolutions to consumer tensions, a rhetoric of gendered environments affirms two traditional ideologies at once: belief in distinct gender attributes as essential to sexual identity, and belief in an infinite, unchanging natural world. Essentialist mythologies of feminine passivity and masculine conquest are transferred to the earth, promoting an ethic of irresponsible consumerism that endangers the very environments exploited in advertising images.

Advertising's promotion of overconsumption—most frequently through constructs of gender identity—is a major link between overproduction and environmental degradation. A wealth of scholarship investigating the effects of the commodity culture on the environment exists in tandem with separate research on the exploitation of gender in advertising images, yet scant research focuses directly on advertising's rhetoric of gender in relation to environmental issues. If one of the functions of rhetorical criticism is to unmask the power of cultural mythologies (Barthes; Burke), then the study of advertising's visual rhetoric of gendered environments seems a pressing critical undertaking. Absent the rhetorical powers of music, narration, dialogue and motion common to television, radio, and Internet commercials, print ads provide the "purest" source of advertising's visual rhetoric and will be used to examine three critical questions: (1) What are the identifying characteristics of advertising's rhetoric of gendered environments? (2) What visual strategies are evident in the rhetoric of gendered environments? (3) How has advertising's history influenced the depiction of gendered environments?

DEFINING CHARACTERISTICS

The power of a rhetoric of gendered environments is evident in the enduring use of such images as promotional devices. Persuasive use of the iconography of gendered environments was in place at the turn of the 20th century on advertising cards, posters, and brochures and remains, nearly unchanged, a century later. Promotions for the Buffalo Pan American Exposition of 1901 and the San Francisco Panama Pacific International Exposition in 1915 provide especially strong contrasts and contain the visual prototypes typical of advertising's portrayal of feminized and masculinized environments. "Niagara," personifies the great falls as a slim young woman (see Fig. 7.1). She stands under a rainbow—still and posed, the fertile shape of breasts and legs revealed by her diaphanous gown as it is transformed into cascades of water that fall from her outstretched arms to the encircling river. She does not harness the falls; she *is* the falls. Depicted as a voluptuous woman, the waterfall is a sign of nature's unending fertility; she stands passively, a figure of seduction. In contrast, the poster created for the 1915 Panama-Pacific International Exposition Brochure, titled "The Thirteenth Labor of Hercules" (see Fig. 7.2) shows a male nude forcing apart North and South America to create the Panama Canal. The muscular giant is braced between the continents. He uses his arms, hands, elbow, back, legs, knees and feet to physically push the two land masses apart, allowing the waters of the canal to pass under his massive body. "Niagara" is painted in greens, whites and touches of yellow, the illustration of the titan is executed in reds, browns, deep golds and bold lines. The masculine figure acts upon an awesome environment—literally shaping it to his control, while nature feminized is a seductive object of our gaze (Berger; Butler). The visual and rhetorical differences

in these two presentations of nature reemerge in countless advertisements throughout advertising history, but are especially dominant in the later 20th century and into the 21st.

Scores of modern advertisements repeat the visual patterns of gendered environments. Described in broad strokes, the dominant story of advertising's feminized environment is the ancient story of nature as passive–seductive woman, woman as fertile nature. In these advertisements, nature *is* the essential feminine—images are exotic and lush with icons of fertility and female sexuality. Advertising's feminized environments use nature as background for romance, eroticism or nurturance to advertise products that promise to increase a woman's femininity. Further, as in "Niagara," many advertising images

FIG. 7.1. "Niagara." Courtesy of the Wolfsonian Museum, Florida International University.

FIG. 7.2. "The Thirteenth Labor of Hercules." Courtesy of
the Kansas State Historical Society.

merge natural scenes with a female form or body part, creating a visual metaphor of woman as nature, nature as woman. Examples abound.

Advertisements produced over the last half of the 20th century promoting
products to increase a woman's femininity offer remarkably similar images of
nature as background to erotic fantasies. The ads use visual symbols of fertility, notably water and plants. All the ads target women and typically focus on a
female model: An 1945 advertisement for Woodbury soap pictures a (heterosexual) couple on a beach, a beautiful woman is prone and passive on the sand
with her eyes closed as a man kisses her (Reproduced in Hill 233). A 1957 Veto
deodorant ad pictures a (heterosexual) couple on the grass, the beautiful
woman is prone and passive with her eyes closed as a man caresses her (Reproduced in Hill 233). In both ads, sand, sky, grass or ocean frame the scene. The
faces and bodies of both men are turned away from the camera to focus

viewer attention on the sensuality of the female model. A 1963 ad for Sego diet drink alters the pattern somewhat and pictures a young (heterosexual) couple in a rowboat moored near rocks on a large body of water. The man is standing and has picked up the woman whose legs extend in the air; he holds her "playfully" as if to throw her overboard. The text line reads, "How slender you were on that wonderful vacation ... *Would he think so now?*" (Reproduced in Hill 127). Other ads do not picture women in the ads, but present nature as a place for romance, glamour or nurturing. A long-running campaign for tourism to Puerto Rico presents images of a tropical rainforest, a beach, the ocean or palm trees as places for romantic interludes ("Puerto Rico"). A inside front cover campaign for Parliament cigarettes displays tropical scenes in the moonlight—social gatherings are depicted on a beach hut ("Parliament," *Time*) or inside a large grass ("Parliament," *Newsweek*). An ad for Massachusetts vacations features a weathered, shingled, beachfront home that fills the left side of the frame. Potted flowering plants poke from window boxes and line the deck and porch. On the right is a fading sunset illuminating the ocean and beach where two small figures are barely visible. The whole scene is permeated with a pinkish hue except for an inset of three black and white photographs of a blond child who extends her arms appealingly. "You are here to share 1,500 miles of cherished coastline.... To see how many shells one little girl can fit into a pail," reads the text in part ("Massachusetts Vacations"). Ads like these promise social exchange, family nurturing or romance and promote travel to natural sites as settings for relationship narratives. In these ads, nature is feminized as background for the erotic, social or familial, traditionally associated with the essential feminine.

Some ads go further and explicitly merge images of nature with the female body or body part to claim that woman and nature are one. An advertisement for Naturally Blonde hair color circulated in 1971 is a full-page photograph of a pale sand dune with blowing grasses and a distant sea. The textline, "The 18 colors of Naturally Blonde are the blonde colors found in nature," crosses the center of the image. An inset photograph of a pretty women's face slightly turned to show off her shining blond hair is captioned *"I'm sand."* (Reproduced in Hill 103). As in the "I'm sand" ad for hair color, signs of femininity and signs of exotic nature are frequently fused. An ad for Fidji perfume pictures a woman's face and a tropical island merged in a single image. Greatly enlarged, the woman's dark eyes hover over an island that appears to be floating in mist. The sea hides the bottom half of the woman's face in an appropriation of a veil, a sign of exotic female "otherness". The text reads: "Woman is an island. Fidji is her perfume" (Reproduced in Williamson 107). A Hermes scarf advertisement appearing as a two page spread in the *New York Times Magazine* in 2001 merges woman with nature in a different strategy ("Hermes"). The close-up image titled "Encounters with the Earth's beauty," features a photograph of a beautiful woman's face and head wrapped in a scarf; monarch butterflies "from the Americas" crawl off the pattern on the scarf to merge with the model. One butterfly sits on her face, several rest in her hair, another adorns her ear and neck. She has become home for the insects, is one with them, is, in fact the "image of earth". A final example is an ad for Mikimoto Tahitian cultured pearls from 2001 that vividly demonstrates the symbolic merging of passivity, eroticism and nature common to advertising's visual rhetoric of at the turn of the 21st century. The Mikimoto design is similar to many ads in its symbolization of fertile sexuality with wetness and water. The display features a beautiful blond woman, even more sultry than "Niagara," kneeling in the ocean surf, posing passively for the camera. Nearly nude, her legs are spread as the surf swirls around her knees and thighs, her lips are parted in a posture of seduction and submission. The sea and sky frame her sexual invitation ("Mikimoto"). As these examples demonstrate, the identifying characteristics of a feminized environment are beauty, fertility and passivity. Wetness (rainfall, waterfalls, small streams, mist and ocean surf); bowers and canopies of trees, vines, flowers; fruits, birds, butterflies, sunsets and moonlight signal the feminized environment. Although not necessary, a seductive image of a woman is often present, frequently merged with aspects of the natural world. Woman and nature are sites for erotic play or nurture of men and children. Color palettes reflect the shades of the tropics, emphasizing multihued greens of plants and water, golds, yellows and whites of diluted sunshine, and muted pastels with small spots of bright reds, blues and purples. Image focus is often soft.

In sharp contrast to feminized environments, advertising's story of a masculinized environment presents images of nature as a vast "pristine" wilderness, frequently dry, rocky and barren, evoking the western landscapes of North America. As in the 1915 poster for the opening of the Panama Canal, the essential masculine environment is a place of action, risk, individualism and challenge for male prowess. At the turn of the 21st century, ads for a number of products but especially cars, sports utility vehicles, pick-up trucks and tobacco present countless images of red rocks, canyons, deserts and sky. Advertisements for Marlboro cigarettes provide the classic examples of masculinized environments in advertising rhetoric, persisting for over 35 years.[1] The Marlboro man advertises his death-defying habit as an endless machismo adventure against scenes of natural beauty from the western landscape. A 1997 ad from the long-running campaign is a two-page spread of steep red canyon walls that fill the pages. Two cowboys are riding herd on wild horses in the bottom 1/8 of the frame. The invitation to "Come to Marlboro Country" highlights the attractiveness of the mystical west for "real" men, and promises an identity far away from urban routine and responsibility. In another ad, a bold blue sky is background to the working cowboy who fills the frame. He walks in a desert canyon with his saddle slung over his back, sunlight gleams off his belt buckle emblazoned with a bucking horse. His hat, chaps and gloves indicate the work of a horseman.

Muscles bulge through his shirt and jeans. He is lean, sinewy and serious ("Marlboro"). Not unlike the image of Hercules, the 21st-century cowboy has work to do, and as in numerous images of "Marlboro Country" the male figure acts upon his environment, exerting control through his physical prowess. The "big country" defines advertising's masculinized environment and excepting the occasional cowboy or Indian, the space is there for urban man to play at adventure. Ads using the imagery of mountains, deserts, cowboys and Indians are scattered throughout the 20th century. A 1950's ad for Schweppes Tonic Water uses the European styled corporate icon, Captain Whitehead as a contrast to the Native-American Indian: Pictured in the ad is a spacious plain, framed by a western mountain range, and Native American Indians on horseback drink a tonic water prepared by the Captain (Sivulka 281). The horse, essential to the frontier myth, is replaced by gasoline-powered vehicles in a variety of similarly constructed advertisements. A 1982 ad for a Buick sedan typifies a common approach by picturing the car on a western road, with mountains as background (Reproduced at Adflip.com). But the dominance of masculinized environments especially in ads for vehicles reached a peak in the late 1990s and early years of the 21st century.

Pick-up trucks, sports utility vehicles, and cars sit atop mountains, ride through desolate deserts, and descend into rocky valleys in countless advertisements. Unlike the social environments of feminized ads, these ads frequently feature environments with few humans or signs of habitation—typically the vehicle is the focus of the ad, often even the driver is invisible. Images of vehicles in pristine environments make no pretense of nostalgia. No one is seen working. Leisure, isolation and adventure mark the masculinized environment: An ad for a Acura MDX pictures the car parked on a dirt road in front of foothills and a distant mountain range. Emphasizing the achievement of isolation, a photograph inset shows a cell-phone reading "no service" ("Acura"). Often activity is restricted to driving or to forms of adventure that carry some risk to the environment. An ad for Chevy Trailblazer pictures the SUV up to its fenders in mud and rocks against a rocky mountain and stormy sky ("Trailblazer"). In a 2002 Nissan ad campaign "Not that you would. But You Could," Nissan vehicles are boldly pictured in fragile environments. One two-page ad for Nissan Pathfinder, positions two cars side by side on a vast stretch of desert and dunes. Two men occupy each car. The driver of a muddied Nissan hands a relay baton to the driver of another. The text promises that "an all-powerful, 240-horsepower 3.5 V6 engine instantly tames the most unruly terrain, "Perfect for when you encounter those pesky Himalayas" ("Pathfinder"). Another displays the car parked in a trout stream while one man fishes from the window ("Pathfinder Two"). While such texts and images can claim tongue-in-cheek humor, the features of these advertisements emphasize a mythic world where men play at heroics and a vast environmental wilderness promises control and adventure. Nature is the object of conquest or background for demonstrations of power. Iconic representations feature rocks, hard edges, deserts, mountain ranges, canyons, snowy peaks, bright sunshine and wide skies. Colors are typically high contrast and dramatic and frequently reflect the reds, browns, blues and whites of the west. Image focus is sharp. There are no environmental problems in this space or in the fertile seas of feminized lands, there is only opportunity to consume.

STRATEGIES: APPROPRIATED ICONOGRAPHY
AND CULTURAL UBIQUITY

Advertising's rhetoric performs one of the great rhetorical achievements of the commodity culture by rendering invisible the basic production processes of resource use and depletion, toxic omissions, and disposal of waste necessary for the continuous production and consumption of goods. The rhetoric of gendered environments uses strategies common to image-based advertising but presents a particularly troublesome mythology. Advertisements that portray an unspoiled natural world as feminized picture a fertile passive earth ready for erotic seduction, available for pleasure, and infinite in bounty. In contrast, masculinized environments present the earth as a vast wilderness created for conquest, adventure and challenge. Together, the gendered images work to justify consumer resignation to environmental degradation as "natural," unavoidable and ahistorical—an aspect of human progress. To achieve its rhetorical goals, advertising appropriates powerful visual icons and makes them ubiquitous signs of commodification throughout the culture.

Appropriated iconography is the basic strategy of pictorial advertising. Appropriation of familiar symbolic icons provides consumers the illusion of permanence and stability in a culture charged with the tensions of change. Especially reassuring are images of gender and nature as immutable touchstones of human experience. Iconic representations from religious traditions, historical and political events, fine art, celebrity lives, film, television and drama are lifted from their original context, rearranged, and attached to commodities. Images of nature are powerful symbols, traditionally associated with life, growth, goodness, power, fertility, homeland and conquest. Visual history is replete with images of woman as nature that resonate as archetypes in diverse cultural settings and provide central motifs in fine art, religious icons, and decorative and commercial art throughout the world. Whether represented as mother, virgin, or dangerous seductress (Dijkstra), nature has been personified as female since the earliest visual expression, and a variety of representative images are available for appropriation. Carolyn Merchant reviews the pervasiveness of female signs of fertility in early western representations of nature and concludes that as mechanization became central to the economic structure of western cultures, images of a powerful "mother earth" began to give way to images of a passive seductress. Citing examples of the Arcadia theme in poetry and paining, Merchant describes the virginal, seductive passivity of woman that came to dominate nature imagery. For example, a 16th century painting cited in her text is Lucas Cranach's, *The Nymph of the Spring*. The painting features a nude young woman asleep on a grassy bank of a stream. She is surrounded by birds and flowers while deer calmly graze nearby. Merchant writes: "This pastoral representation of a nymph of the woods and meadows implies the passive role of nature: her quiver of arrows, borrowed from the ancient huntress-goddess Diana, is laid aside, and she herself reclines invitingly on the ground" (9). Thousands of nymphs, bathers and goddesses (including multitudes of Venuses and Dianas) from the ancient and the modern world populate visual culture with images of woman as nature. Icons of the passive–seductive female figure, surrounded by symbols of "natural" fertility in water, plants and animals are a staple of advertising's rhetoric of a feminized environment.

Discussing the "logic of appropriation," Goldman and Papson write, "Producing marketable commodity signs depends on how effectively advertisers are able to colonize and appropriate referent systems" (9). The Marxist critic, Judith Williamson, also discusses appropriation in terms of colonization. Her analysis of the Fidji perfume ad previously described emphasizes the double effect:

> Woman and colony become completely confused here. Fiji is an island but has been appropriated as nothing but a perfume; while the wearer of perfume, Woman, has been turned into an island, generalized, non-specific, but reeking of exoticism .... Woman is an island because she is mysterious, distant, a place to take a holiday. (107)

As a rhetorical strategy, appropriation of woman as nature iconography allows for the confusion of a consumption ethic with values earlier associated with reproduction, religious experience and aesthetics. A 1973 ad for Moon Drops perfume features a photograph that fills ¾ of the page. A slender nude woman's body is silhouetted against a large full moon, the grace of her curves illuminated in silver light (Reproduced in Hill 126). The image and the photographic style evoke Edward Weston's black and white photographs of the sculptured female form (Weston). Appropriation of fine art and religious images is augmented by stock images available through commercial sources that further complicate visual meanings.

Goldman and Papson speak to the commercial duplications of imagery available through image banks that "deal in stock photos of mountain tops, sunsets, farm scenes, sea birds, and so on—that have been severed from meaningful contexts" (14). Advertisements of feminized environments frequently appropriate the same stock images used by environmental organizations. Even in the rare case where the photographer of promotional images is known, the images are indistinguishable from hundreds of stock images available in the marketplace of iconography. For example, a photograph by Harold E. Malde used to promote the Nature Conservancy's Last Great Places fundraising campaign in 2001, features an ocean, beach, dune and grasses and might have served as the background shot for many of the ads just described (28–29). When nature images move back and forth between advertisements for commodities, promotions for environmental conservation, and fine art and religious artifacts, meanings about nature become particularly vulnerable to commodification. Emptied of particulars, appropriated iconic representations of woman and nature transform the rhetorical power of the ancient and mysterious into familiar and accessible visualizations of consumption.

Depictions of advertising's masculinized environment appropriate visual icons from a more recent past. The exploitation of environmental images as an exercise in masculine identity became an artistic, economic, and cultural reality in the United States through images of "The American Sublime,"[2] especially as represented in 19th century painting and photography of the American west: Awesome pristine views and open spaces with little or no visible vegetation dominate the visual mythology. Thomas Moran's "Grand Canyon of the Colorado," painted in 1892 is only one example of the genre that became immediately popular with corporate America as promotional material: "The power of these images of an almost unimaginably distant and strange landscape to promote travel, exploration and tourism was quickly understood by the new railway barons, who commissioned from Moran pictures that they could use in advertising their services" (Wilton and Barringer 250). Images from the era serve as prototypes for advertising that constructs masculinized environments by appropriating the icons of western mythologies. Philip Stokes examines the expeditionary photography of the American West in the work of Eadweard Muybridge, Timothy O'Sullivan, William Jackson and others and remarks on the implications of a masculinized apprehension of nature:

> Moreover if, as has been intimated, the exploration of America was a working out of the Manifest Destiny to pastoralize the wilderness, then those who recorded this exploration were not insensate mercenaries of expansionism, but worked in the context of a system in which Nature was a manifestation of God, perceived as immanent in its sublimity, and where the life and structure of every part, great or small, symbolized the operation of divine law. It was a ready convenience that the gentle, harmonious qualities held to constitute beauty were thought of as feminine, and that within the nineteenth-century pantheon, Nature was enthroned in the feminine gender: already infused by God, awaiting the penetration of Man, which would bring her to a state of submissive, wifely fertility. If there was to be a little rape along the way, then that was more a necessary part of Nature's schooling than a sign of philosophical confusion. (69)

As realized in North America, the *sublime* is the genesis of a particularly American mythology of land, power and masculinity. Transported to the vastness of the North American continent, wilderness, space and masculinity became significant elements of the sublime aesthetic. The vastness of the land, explored, colonized, and imaged, was inseparable from capital and power, and those were inseparable from the status of men. Clive Bush argues that in the United States, that combination assumed fateful significance:

> The spirit of original title claims on the grounds of "discovery" and settlement was maintained. Since land was also the basis of the male suffrage, Native Americans lost political rights along with their lands. Uniquely, however, in the early Republican era, and perhaps uniquely in history, land was seen *as money* and became a primary agent of economic development.

Thus the landscapes of North America came early to symbolize mysticism, conquest, power *and* male privilege:

> The Sublime is ... a strongly gendered aesthetic through its rugged, primitive, patriarchal associations. Its antithesis, in Burke's account, is a model of beauty that is recognized by the sense as having a fragile delicacy, an alluring smoothness of contour, and a submissiveness—all of which are exemplified in the female form and in the cultural expectations of what is "properly" feminine. (Andrews 133)

Advertising's gendered environments thus oppose powerful and enduring icons of femininity, masculinity, and nature that have been culturally significant symbols in art, literature and religion for hundreds of years. In addition to the appropriation of iconography as a rhetorical strategy, the power of advertising's narratives of gendered environments resides in the collective impact of such images.

Especially strategic to the rhetoric of gendered environments is advertising's *cultural ubiquity*. Coupled with the appropriations of familiar iconography, the ubiquitous presence of advertising defines the commodity culture. A view from Times Square (see Fig. 7.3) captures the dominant presence of advertising in urban life. Although the excessive commercialization of space in Manhattan, Los Angles, Tokyo and other centers of cultural production is not typical of smaller cities and towns, advertising images enter every home—everywhere. Goldman and Papson attribute an increasingly competitive production of visual symbols to the "cluttered landscape" of advertising and explore some of the "cultural consequences" of such rapid mass production of images: "We titled this book *Sign Wars* to emphasize the theme that corporate competition in selling consumer commodities has become centered on the image, the look, the sign. Over the years the cycle of this sign competition

FIG. 7.3.   A view from Times Square.

has begun to race along, while its density and intensity has escalated" (5). Images of unspoiled nature in association with gender are used to promote the
consumption of automobiles, vacations, computers, cigarettes, cosmetics,
pharmaceuticals, perfumes, financial services, jewelry, housewares, clothing
and other commodities. Although ads focusing on nature images are fewer in
number than those featuring images of people or products,[3] advertising's rhetoric of gendered environments is dominant in some of the most aggressive
campaigns in print. As we have seen, of particular significance are campaigns
to advertise automobiles, cigarettes, tourism, perfumes and cosmetics. For
these commodities, images of the natural world are frequent features of identity fantasies constructed through stories of masculinity and femininity.

Although advertising images presented in high-end magazines may differ in style from those on highway billboards, every ad presumes and is granted legitimate authority to fill visual space with identity fantasies associated with commodity purchase. In addition to the traditional placement of ads in magazines, newspapers, television and radio, media usually consumed at home, "place-based" advertising occurs in venues of entertainment, retail, travel, health, and education (McAllister 63–92). Even traditional environmental organizations allow advertisers the use of visual space to promote the commodity culture. As Kevin DeLuca points out, glossy magazines from mainstream environmental organizations are "littered with car and oil company advertisements" (71). For example, the Summer 2002 issue of *Nature Conservancy* features advertisements for Johnson and Johnson, General Motors, and the American Electronic Power corporation, as "sponsors" of the Conservancy, all using images of unspoiled nature.

The strategic placement of countless numbers of ads in multiple venues dominates public space and intrudes on private space as well. But the sheer numbers of commercial images do not alone explain the influence of advertising's gendered environments. Although individual advertisements are frequently notable for their effectiveness or aesthetic value, study of individual ads rarely moves beyond identification of singular attention-gaining displays that may shock, inspire, amuse, delight, or titillate. It is in their aggregate impact that advertising's rhetorical force is experienced. Marshall McLuhan's 1951 treatise, *The Mechanical Bride*, helped to establish the significance of popular visual artifacts and a way to think about the impact of advertising's cultural ubiquity. Writing that the visual displays produced "from the laboratory, the studio and the advertising agencies," are "unfolded ... as a single landscape," McLuhan considered the images to be "the folklore of industrial man" (v). In the aggregate, the folklore of advertising's gendered environments provides a fable of the natural world constrained only by essentialist gender identities. Merchant argues that changes in "controlling imagery" in the 16th century was directly related to changes in "human attitudes and behavior toward the earth"(2). Although it is impossible to isolate the influence of advertising images from other cultural artifacts, when nature is pictured as essentially masculine or essentially feminine in thousands of images, consumer fantasies of the environment are sanctioned by gender expectations and stereotypes. It can be argued that at the turn of the 21st century, the source of controlling images is found not in artistic or religious origin but in advertising's commercial appropriations of their iconography. As attitudes and behaviors of consumption are influenced by advertising images, it is probable that consumer attitudes towards the environment are likewise influenced by the rhetoric of visual persuasion. The collective impact of multiple advertisements, in which images of nature are conflated with essentialist mythologies of masculinity and femininity, presents a repetitive surround of symbolic forms attaching nature to gender and detaching consumption from environmental abuse. Shared by all who consume the visions, regardless of class, sex, race, ethnicity or age, such typecasting of nature as essentially masculine or feminine sanction beliefs that nature's fertility is limitless and exists for male conquest.

Advertising's strategies of appropriated iconography and cultural ubiquity together create a mythology of gendered environments. Emptied of history, politics and experience, mythologies present themselves as timeless and eternal (Barthes 109–159). Myths of gender and myths of nature are especially powerful and enduring and lend themselves to static ideologies of power hierarchies and status—necessary for an ethic of consumption to prevail. Transferring essentialist myths of gender to a mythologized natural world, the visual rhetoric of advertising provides an "alibi" for the obvious connections between commodity consumption and environmental degradation by pretending that the natural environment, *like gender*, is immune to human agency. In a rather blatant appeal to fantasies of timelessness and fortune, an advertisement for an affluent real estate development community in Utah pictures mountain ranges and wide-open vistas: "NOT SUBJECT TO CHANGE. NOT NOW. NOT EVER. Wolf Creek Ranch. "Where Father Time Can't Change Mother Nature." The ad text promises 45 buyers "spacious lots" of "160–1600 acres," each with a view of mountain ranges, and secluded wilderness. "A conservation easement will protect 95% of the land from further development. Forever" ("Wolf Creek Ranch"). Advertising's strategy of visual rhetoric works to obliterate the consequences of overconsumption by presenting countless images of an immutable and mythical natural world, unassaulted by the realities of environmental degradation and available to affluent consumers as status markers of success (Hope). When such images are gendered, the rhetoric reveals advertising's continued reliance on static constructs of masculinity and femininity to promote consumerism.

ADVERTISING HISTORY AND GENDERED ENVIRONMENTS

The strategies of advertising's rhetoric of gendered environments are rooted in the early decades of the 20th century. The press toward modernity and the growth of advertising were intertwined as the United States completed the transformation from a rural to an urban culture of mass production. Advertising struggled to portray the benefits of a world in which the traditional values of thrift and the production of hand-crafted goods were replaced by credit buying and consumption of mass produced goods (Ewen). During this transition, displays of gender and of rural nature were especially important. To establish the desirability of the emerging ideology of consumerism, advertising developed a rhetoric that visualized nostalgic images of rural life along with modernistic dreams of progress. As the actual culture was transformed by mass production and urbanization, advertising increasingly relied on gender to personalize its contradictory narrative claims.

Although advertising would eventually perfect a "fetishism" of commodity consumption (Jhally, McAllister 61) early 20th-century advertising did not hide the production process nor its effects on nature. Advertising's paradoxical images extolled the benefits of modernity and mass production while insisting that commodity purchases reaffirmed traditional values. Such images often coupled displays of production with lessons for appropriate gender behavior in the modern era. Describing an advertising parable he calls "Civilization Redeemed," Marchand writes, "It confirmed Americans in one of their treasured common beliefs—the belief in unequivocal progress, in the compatibility of technology with the most desirable qualities of Nature" (227). Common to many ads, the "natural" environment of the rural past signified purity and (female) nurturing whereas polluted urban cityscapes signified (male) modern power. Advertising displays frequently positioned rural and urban signs together as testimony to the happy coexistence of health, the women's sphere, and progress, the responsibility of men. In advertisements selling a variety of items including cereal, newspapers, gum, and automobiles as antidotes for headache, stomachache, and "nervousness" brought on by the move away from nature, mothers were urged to buy products that enabled city children to grow up with natural health. Signs of industrialization were presented as background to images of children enjoying the benefits of fresh air and grassy fields. For example, in an ad for Scripps-Howard Newspapers, background smokestacks darkly pollute urban skies behind a pastoral family picnic; in the foreground a happy pair of children provide a visual pronouncement that the effects of mass production can be kept distant from healthy family life by the right purchases (Marchand 227, f. 7.10). Such conflicted images reflect the "disjunctive" experience of the transition to modernity (Meikle 143).

Social anxiety reached a peak between World War I and World War II and visions of modernity needed to be "domesticated" by governments and corporations seeking stability:

> They had to persuade ambivalent populations that new modes of living retained or promoted traditional values .... As social and economic chaos overtook both Europe and the U.S.A., it became necessary to construct reassuring narratives and iconographies—in other words, to insist on the paradox that a self-conscious machine age retained stability even as it celebrated technological change. (Meikle 143)

One of the ways modernity was "domesticated" was through the development of new advertising strategies, a major source of cultural narratives and icons. Advertising's primary response was to design ads that exploited the increasing separation between men's roles and women's roles promoted by industrialization and urbanization. "American advertisements can be said to have become 'modern' precisely to the extent to which they transcended or denied their essential economic nature as mass communications and achieved subjective qualities and a personal tone," writes Roland Marchand (9). The "personal tone" of modern advertising focuses sharply on gender.

In the 1920s and 1930s, advertising increasingly associated masculinity and femininity with production and consumption respectively. Nature was controlled by men who were smart enough to exploit its resources for production, whereas women were privileged as the primary consumers responsible for the health of families and the maintenance of new standards of beauty and glamour (Frederick, Naether, Wolf). Hill points out that neither suffrage nor feminist movements of the 20th century influenced advertisers' conviction that woman's identity was primarily that of consumer. In his words, "… the demands of home and family were a daily concern; infrequent elections and politics could not compete with that" (8). Male entitlement was bolstered with scenes associating the industrialization of nature with successful modern masculinity. Icons of mass industry included factories, assembly lines, smokestacks, and smoke as desirable signs of progress and were linked to the male role of modern work. Ads picturing a male executive sitting at a desk contemplating the view from a large office window became "visual clichés" for identification of the "master of all he surveys" (Marchand 239). A 1934 Gulf Oil ad is typical. The man is identified as "a scientist of the Gulf refining Company." He stands with his hand on a phone, reflectively gazing at a framed view of the sky above and a river below; smoke clouds billow from numerous factory stacks; the river carries a ship (with its own black smoke) past an ultramodern cityscape. An airplane flies overhead to further illustrate the text: "Men who live for tomorrow" (243). As Marchand points out, these innumerable window-view scenes rarely included depictions of women. When the exceptional ad featured a woman posed in front of a window, her view was most likely to be the nature in her own back yard, as typified by a Association of American Soap and Glycerin Producers ad in which a woman appears guilty under the scornful glance of her husband, as she watches her "grimy"-faced children at play (246). Consumption, in this case, of soap, was the primary female task, necessary for the efficient performance of her domestic chores.

A 1931 trade advertisement for J. Walter Thompson Company heralds the beginning of the end of advertising that pictured the production process and its polluting presence, instead the agency ad exhorted advertisers to recognize gender divisions in the modern world of consumption (Hill 12). In the ad the top frame is divided into two photographic portraits labeled Maker and User. On the viewer's left is the "maker," a dignified authoritative man in suit and tie who unsmilingly faces the camera, hands clasped. The "user" is a woman, pretty and competent, dressed in the modest floral print of a homemaker. She too gazes steadily out at the viewer. Her clasped hands reveal a wedding ring (Hill 12). The ad promoted J. Walter Thompson's market research technique of polling women as the primary consumers to test what the male producers had wrought. As advertising began to focus on consumption rather than the production of products, and as urban pollution increased, advertising appealed increasingly to the identification of a strongly gendered self contextualized by scenes of nature. Images of production and pollution soon disappeared altogether from the mythological environments of modern advertising to be replaced with images of an unspoiled nature, increasingly gilded with gender displays.

By the end of World War II, the commodity culture was fully entrenched. Commodity advertising favored images of a natural world unaffected by mass production. Advertising rhetoric continued to rely on constructions of gender as the basis for consumer myths but with important changes in image making. No longer did constructions of masculinity rely on signs of production and no longer was woman the only sex designated as consumer. Indeed, all identity stories including those of gender, status, work and citizenship were stories of consumption, and in sophisticated commodity advertising, nature and consumption were disconnected.

As "meaning-based models" of advertising theory emerged as an alternative to information-based theories (McCracken) and market researchers acknowledged advertising "as an omnipresent communication arena in which human reality is mediated" (Mick and Buhl 317) visual theory and art criticism were promoted as underused tools for understanding and generating meaning in market research on gender and consumerism (Schroeder and Borgerson). To this end, advertising images are increasingly sophisticated visualizations of fantasies identified by market researchers as the fuel for commodity purchases. Alan Durning echoes myriad scholars when he writes, "advertising increasingly resembles dreams" (119). But unlike the individual dreams of the unconscious, the dreams of advertising are professionally produced, visual messages are circulated throughout the mass media with the specific intention of increasing market share. Dreams of an unspoiled natural world are prevalent in advertising's rhetoric of consumerism. As Goldman and Papson point out, "As noncommodified natural spaces become scarcer, the sign of nature has been made a fundamental sign of the authentic" (156). Through the images produced by creative teams, consumer advertising celebrates an ethic of "self-indulgence, frivolous wastefulness and decadent extravagance" as it has since the early 20th century (Marchand 158). The environmental scenes presented in advertising's pervasive images mediate experience of nature: Advertising's natural world is in turn erotic or challenging, nurturing or wild, and has no connection to consumer ethics.

James Swain insists that modern culture "guides us to avoid contact with nature," and reports that the average American spends 84% of the time indoors (26). For many urban dwellers, advertising's visual depictions of a mythical natural are more prevalent than any lived experience of the natural environment. For such consumers, representations of gender and nature remain static in constructions of reality negotiated in long-ago eras of human relationship to each other and to the land. Largely composed of photographic images, contemporary advertisements appear to depict "real people" and "real" places. Thus do mediated images of the natural environment, gendered through essentialist constructions of masculinity and femininity, hide the obvious consequences of consumption: "As long as commodity signs are the raw material for identity construction (i.e., authenticity), excessive production and consumption practices are probable. By stimulating the high levels of consumption necessary to support the logic of capital in the endless pursuit of increased profits, advertising aggravates tendencies toward environmental crisis" (Goldman and Papson 187). Because commodity consumption is necessary for the maintenance of gender identity in advertising's stories, advertising must create mythic natural environments immune to the consequences of consumerism, although the consumption and waste necessary to the maintenance of the commodity culture is in direct conflict with environmental health. William A. Shutkin states the consequences of over consumption simply and directly:

> Consumption produces pollution and waste and eats up land and natural resources. For over three hundred years, Americans have consumed nature at unprecedented rates. Such consumption, fueled by the forces of the market and mass production, has over time eroded American's connection to nature and sense of reciprocity. By consuming more and more, it seems, we are left with fewer places and ecosystems with which to connect. (59)

There are, of course, exceptions to the general pattern of gendered environments in advertising. *Audubon* magazine features a two-page advertising spread for the Chevy Suburban without obvious gender appeals. The car is parked in a large spacious meadow, the horizon behind the car features rolling hills. The ad is created in sepia, mirroring a photographic inset of a 1935 Suburban: "That was THEN. This is WOW" ("Chevy Suburban"). An ad for *away.com*, an Internet travel service, appearing in *Archaeology* magazine features a photograph by Skip Brown of a woman alone at the bow of a rowboat facing a high mountain range. We see her only from the back and neither beauty nor seduction is emphasized. The body of water is identified as Lake Pokhara, Nepal ("*away.com*"). But exceptions like this are offbeat, appearing in magazines of specialized interest. In high-circulation magazines, hundreds of nature images appropriate existent icons of masculinity and femininity.

Although androgynous images are present and occasionally trendy, the story of essential femininity and the story of essential masculinity dominate advertising's rhetoric. The characteristic features of gender advertising were well documented by Erving Goffman and a host of other scholars and market researchers have continued to reveal the same patterns (Goffman; Hirschman; Schroeder and Borgerson). Despite decades of challenge from feminists, "femininity" in advertising's symbolic world continues to signify above all else, beauty and passivity (Barthel; Bristor and Fischer; Butler; Douglas; Weems; Wolf). Nurturing, domesticity, seductiveness, and eroticism further embellish the essential woman. The essential masculine in advertising signals action and strength, material success, power and adventure (LaFrance). In a press report on an advertising trend away from the use of male models in favor of using professional sportsmen, executives, and other real men in male fashion layouts, gender differentiation in advertising is bluntly described by Simon Doonan, the creative director of the fashion store, Barney's New York: "Male models don't communicate to the customer at all. People think they are funny and goofy. The basic premise is absurd. Men are supposed to embody power and decision-making, and what could embody passivity more than modeling?" (Bellafante 20). Essentialist visions of a gendered nature mirror the contrasting gender stereotypes evoked by Mr. Doonan and depict a particularly troubling vision of consumer relationship to the environment.

IN SUMMARY

Social, civic and environmental consequences of a commodity culture have been and continue to be central subjects of scholarship and concern in a wide variety of disciplines (Calder; Ewen; Galbraith; Grieder; Manning; Shutkin). Scholars of environmental issues have long decried consumer economics for the promotion of needless (and frequently toxic) waste, (Carson; Berry; McKibben; Roszak) and grassroots movements for "democratic globalization,"[4] environmental justice, simpler lives, organic farming, and others have isolated consumerism as a powerful propagator of environmental degradation (Brandt; DeLuca; Durning; Freeman; Lilienfeld and Rathje). Yet with few exceptions, scholars of rhetoric, advertising, mass media and popular culture have not yet focused substantial research on advertising's ideological connection to environmental degradation.

In this chapter we have examined a rhetoric of gendered environments, a dominant strategy of image based advertising. In images, sublime or beautiful, serious or playful, advertising appropriates a rich visual history of nature images as sites of femininity and masculinity in order to sell commodities. Examination of advertising through a double lens of gender and nature reveals that, in the main, performances of essential masculinity and essential femininity promote authenticity through different visual experiences of nature, preserving myths of spacious wilderness for masculine adventure, and fertile tropical seas for female eroticism. Because overconsumption must inherently generate environmental degradation, environmentally aware audiences present a particular challenge to advertising practitioners. Cultural ubiquity and appropriated iconography are powerful strategies used to overcome viewer resistance to advertising's appeals. In hundreds of thousands of images, stories of femininity and stories of masculinity appropriate images of nature to establish commodity purchases at the center of gender identity. Ancient iconography provides images of idealized women and nature, creating narratives of nature as female, fertile and seductive. Using iconography appropriated from images of the western frontier, stories of a masculine environment evoke attitudes of the American sublime. These twin concepts of a feminine environment and a masculine environment contain ideological references that structure meanings of nature as well as gender; associations between female seduction and exotic locations feminize nature as eternally fertile, eternally nurturing, vulnerable (and welcoming) of rapacious acts. Masculinized environments present a natural world made for conquest and control, vastly immune to ecological distress. Together, the rhetorics of gendered environments presents a bold denial of connection between consumption and environment and imply that worries of overconsumption are but picayune and sterile concerns; rendered invisible, environmental degradation is reduced to minor and solvable sets of technological problems. Advertising's rhetorical use of nature images insinuates overconsumption into the center of gender identity beyond the reach of human control, intent or responsibility. Wendell Berry offers a different view of consumer responsibility: "The responsible consumer slips out of the consumer category altogether. He is a responsible consumer incidentally, almost inadvertently; he is a responsible consumer because he lives a responsible life" (25). Gendered environments of advertising provide a cynical rationalization for over consumption. Although it is unrealistic to expect advertisers to disengage from the promotion of product purchase and brand loyalty, as the environmental crisis deepens, critical research identifying additional strategies in advertising's visual rhetoric is necessary to reconnect the link between consumption and the environment for responsible consumers.

NOTES

1. For an informative research project on Marlboro, see <http://www.courses.rochester.edu/foster/ANT226/Spring01/index.html>.
2. The term is from the Tate Gallery exhibit, "American Sublime, Landscape Painting in the United States 1820–1880" on tour at the Pennsylvania Academy of Fine Arts, June 17–August 25, 2002.
3. For 4 consecutive years, student researchers counted the central image in print advertisements in six categories of magazines. Each year, ads focusing on nature constituted less than 1/3 of ads focusing on images of people or manufactured objects.
4. I have borrowed the term from K. M. DeLuca and J. Peeples, "From Public Sphere to Public Screen; Democracy, Activism, and 'Violence' of Seattle,"

who reject the media label of *anti-globalization* as the "first step in dismissing the protesters ...." (147). I agree.

WORKS CITED

"Acura" Advertisement. *New York Times Magazine* (June 16, 2002): back cover.

Adflip.com <http://www.adflip.com>. 9 September 2003.

Andrews, Malcolm. *Landscape and Western Art*. Oxford and New York: Oxford UP, 1999.

away.com. Advertisement. *Archaeology* (March/April 2001).

Barthel, Diane. *Putting on Appearances: Gender and Advertising*. Philadelphia: Temple UP, 1988.

Barthes, Roland. *Mythologies*. Trans. Annette Lavers. New York: Hill and Wang, 1972.

Bellafante, Gina. "Want to be a Male Model? Wear a Real Face." *New York Times* 21 May 2002. A 20.

Berger, John. *Ways of Seeing*. New York: Viking, 1973.

Berry, Wendell. *The Unsettling of America: Culture and Agriculture*. San Francisco: Sierra Club Books, 1977.

Brandt, Deborah. "On the Move for Food." *Women's Studies Quarterly* 29.1-2 (2001): 131-43.

Bristor, Julia and Eileen Fischer. "Feminist Thought: Implications for Consumer Research." *Journal of Consumer Research* 19 (1993): 518-36.

Burke, Kenneth. *Language as Symbolic Action*. Berkeley: U of California P, 1968.

Bush, Clive. " 'Gilded Backgrounds': Reflections on the Perception of Space and Landscape in America." *Views of American Landscapes*. Eds. Mark Gidley and Robert Lawson-Peebles. Cambridge and New York: Cambridge UP, 1989. 13-30.

Butler, Judith. *Bodies that Matter*. London and New York: Routledge, 1993.

Calder, Lendol. *Financing the American Dream: A Cultural History of Consumer Credit*. Princeton, NJ: Princeton UP, 1999.

Carson, Rachel. *Silent Spring*. Boston: Houghton Mifflin, 1962.

"Chevy Suburban" Advertisement. *Audobon* (March/April 2002): inside front cover.

DeLuca, Kevin. *Image Politics: The New Rhetoric of Environmental Activism*. New York: Guilford, 1999.

DeLuca, Kevin and Jennifer Peeples. "From Public Sphere to Public Screen: Democracy, Activism, and the 'Violence' of Seattle." *Critical Studies in Mass Communication* 19.2 (June 2002): 125-51.

Dijkstra, Bram. *Evil Sisters: The Threat of Female Sexuality and the Cult of Manhood*. New York: Knopf, 1996.

Douglas, Susan J. "Narcissism as Liberation." *The Gender and Consumer Culture Reader*. Ed. Jennifer Scanlon. New York: New York UP, 2000. 267-82.

Durning, Alan Thein. *How Much is Enough?: The Consumer Society and the Future of the Earth*. New York: Norton, 1992.

Ewen, Stuart. *Captains of Consciousness: Advertising and the Social Roots of the Consumer Culture* New York: Basic Books, 2001.

Frederick, Christine. *Selling Mrs. Consumer*. New York: Business Course, 1929.

Freeman, Carla. "Is Local:Global as Feminine:Masculine? Rethinking the Gender of Globalization." *Signs: Journal of Women in Culture and Society* 26.4 (2001): 1007-37.

Galbraith, John Kenneth. *The Affluent Society*. 4th ed. Boston: Houghton Mifflin, 1984.

Goffman, Erving. *Gender Advertisements*. New York: Harper, 1976.

Goldman, Robert and Stephen Papson. *Sign Wars: The Cluttered Landscape of Advertising.* New York: Guilford, 1996.

Grieder, William. *One World, Ready or Not: The Manic Logic of Global Capitalism.* New York: Simon & Schuster, 1997.

"Hermes" Advertisement. *New York Times Magazine.* (November 11, 2001): inside front cover.

Hill, Daniel Delis. *Advertising to the American Woman, 1900-1999.* Columbus: Ohio State UP, 2002.

Hirschman, Elizabeth C. "Ideology in Consumer Research, 1980 and 1990: A Marxist and Feminist Critique." *Journal of Consumer Research* 19 (March 1993): 537-55.

Hope, Diane S. "Environment as Consumer Icon in Advertising Fantasy." *Enviropop: Studies in Environmental Rhetoric and Popular Culture.* Ed. Mark Meister and Phyliss Japp. Westport, CT: Praeger, 2002. 161-74.

Jhally, Sut. *The Codes of Advertising: Fetishism and the Political Economy of Meaning in the Consumer Society.* New York: St. Martin's P, 1987.

LaFrance, Edward. *Men, Media and Masculinity.* Dubuque, IA: Kendall/Hunt, 1995.

Lilienfeld, Robert and William Rathje. *Use Less Stuff: Environmentalism for Who We Really Are.* New York: Ballantine, 1998.

Malde, Harold E. Photograph. *Nature Conservancy* (May/June 2001): 28-29.

Manning, Robert. *Credit Card Nation: The Consequences of America's Addiction to Credit.* New York: Basic, 2000.

Marchand, Roland. *Advertising the American Dream: Making Way for Modernity, 1920-1940.* Berkeley: U of California P, 1985.

"Marlboro." Advertisement. *Harper's* (August 2001): inside cover.

"Massachusetts Vacations." Advertisement. *New York Times Magazine* (June 2, 2002): 12.

McAllister, Matthew P. *The Commercialization of American Culture.* Thousand Oaks, CA: Sage, 1996.

McCracken, Grant. "Advertising: Meaning or Information?" *Advances in Consumer Research* 14 (1988): 121-24.

McKibben, Bill. *The End of Nature.* New York: Random House, 1989.

McLuhan, Marshall. *The Mechanical Bride: Folklore of Industrial Man.* New York, Vanguard Press, 1951.

Meikle, Jeffrey L. "Domesticating Modernity: Ambivalence and Appropriation, 1920-40." *Designing Modernity: The Arts of Reform and Persuasion, 1885-1945.* Ed. Wendy Kaplan. New York: Thames and Hudson, 1995. 143-67.

Merchant, Carolyn. *The Death of Nature: Women, Ecology, and the Scientific Revolution.* New York: Harper, 1980.

Mick, David Glen and Claus Buhl. "A Meaning_Based Model of Advertising Experiences." *Journal of Consumer Research* 19 (December 1992): 317-37.

"Mikimoto Tahitian Cultured Pearls." Advertisement. *New York Times Magazine* (November 11, 2002): 4.

Naether, Carl. *Advertising to Women.* New York: Prentice-Hall, 1928.

"Parliament Cigarettes." Advertisement. *Time* (May 20, 2002): inside front cover.

"Parliament Cigarettes." Advertisement. *Newsweek* (July 8, 2002): inside front cover.

"Pathfinder." Advertisement. *New York Times Magazine* (June 2, 2002): inside front cover.

"Pathfinder." Advertisement. *New York Times Magazine* (November 11, 2002).

"Puerto Rico." Advertisement. *Smithsonian* January 1996: 11.

Roszak, Theodore. *Where the Wasteland Ends: Politics and Transcendence in Postindustrial Society.* New York: Doubleday, 1972.

Schroeder, Jonathan E. and Janet L. Borgerson. "Marketing Images of Gender: A Visual Analysis." *Consumption Markets and Culture* 2.2 (1998): 161-201.

Shutkin, William A. *The Land that Could Be: Environmentalism and Democracy in the Twenty-First Century.* Cambridge, MA: MIT P, 2002.

Sivulka, Julianna. *Soap, Sex, and Cigarettes: A Cultural History of American Advertising.* New York: Wadsworth, 1998.

Stokes, Philip. "Trails of Photographic Notions: Expeditionary Photography in the American West." *Views of American Landscapes.* Ed. Mark Gidley and Robert Lawson-Peebles. Cambridge and New York: Cambridge UP, 1989. 64-77.

Swain, James. "Lessons from Ring Mountain." *Earth Keepers: A Sourcebook for Environmental Issues and Action.* Ed. Leslie Baer-Brown and Bob Rhein. San Francisco: Mercury House, 1995. 21-30.

"Trailblazer." Advertisement. *Time* (May 13, 2002): back cover.

Weems, Robert E., Jr. "Consumerism and the Construction of Black Female Identity in Twentieth-Century America." *The Gender and Consumer Culture Reader.* Ed. Jennifer Scanlon. New York: New York UP, 2000. 166-78.

Weston, Edward. *Nudes.* New York: Aperture, 1977.

Williamson, Judith. "Woman is an Island: Femininity and Colonization." *Studies in Entertainment: Critical Approaches to Mass Culture.* Ed. Tania Modleski. Bloomington: Indiana UP, 1986. 99-118.

Wilton, Andrew and Tim Barringer. *American Sublime: Landscape Painting in the United States, 1820-1880.* Princeton: Princeton UP, 2002.

"Wolf Creek Ranch." Advertisement. *New York Times* (June 21, 2002): F9.

Wolf, Naomi. *The Beauty Myth: How Images of Beauty are Used Against Women.* New York: Perennial, 2002.

CHAPTER EIGHT

Echoes of Camelot: How Images Construct Cultural Memory Through Rhetorical Framing

Janis L. Edwards

Since the development of mass media, images disseminated in connection with newsworthy events become attached to the event in the form of cultural remembering. Whether through print or television, some images are routinely re-presented long past the time when they are actually "happening," creating through visual equivalence a new experience that calls forth the reminder of the depicted event. Such images are regarded as encapsulating a critical moment in history, the social imaginary of a persona, a critical historical condition, or the social values and effects that attend the moment. Even people who did not witness history engage in a replay of experience through the simulation of iconic photographs and other well-known images. Photographs such as Dorothea Lange's *Migrant Mother*, Joe Rosenthal's shot of a flag raising at the battle of Iwo Jima, and Nick Ut's poignant image of anguished children and adults fleeing their napalmed village in Viet Nam are repeatedly presented in the media as representative of the historical moment and shared perceptions about the enduring meanings of such moments. Their power is in a perceived ability to frame an event and to suggest more universal values that attach to the event in the public imagination.

It is not unusual for iconic images to be appropriated to new contexts, creating analogies that recall past moments and suggest future possibilities. In this sense, visual images express particulars to evoke the universal. Very specific images such as news and documentary photographs echo in the public consciousness due to their subject matter, their unique composition, or their resemblance to other remembered images. The resonance of a news photo showing fire fighters raising a flag over the ruins of the World Trade Center in 2002 is due, at least in part, to a thematic resemblance to the image of a flag being raised over the scene of a protracted and difficult battle in the war with Japan. Both photographs evoke values of collective effort and victory over threat, with the 2002 photo obviously building on the established rhetorical framework of its 1945 predecessor. An editorial cartoonist's substitution of the flag in the Iwo Jima image with a baseball bat to comment on a different subject also exploits the existing framework of effort and victory, although ironically. The alteration of elements in the cartoon does not alter the obvious reference of Rosenthal's Iwo Jima photograph because the compositional elements are both unique and familiar. Remembered and re-presented images transcend their positions in relation to specific events and create larger rhetorical frameworks that revive and reimagine the narratives that constitute cultural myths.

Traditional rhetorical studies emanate from discursive texts; a more contemporary view allows for a range of textual possibilities ranging from Presidential speeches to a constellation of "image events" staged by antiglobalization activists.[1] Although a single photograph or drawing may seemingly fail to offer the discursive complexity of a speech or a series of enacted visuals, rhetorical theory identifies modes of rhetorical presentation that are as condensed as pictorial images. Constructs such as culture types (Osborn) and ideographs (McGee) promote specific vocabularies of terms that function rhetorically as conditioning agents that guide human behavior and belief (McGee 426). Similarly, specific visual images fit Osborn's definition of "depictive rhetoric" that dominates contemporary discourse as "strategic pictures, verbal or nonverbal visualizations that linger in the collective memory of audiences as representative of their subjects" (79). Although pictoral images seemingly capture a single moment, in the same way that an ideograph such as *liberty* or *freedom of speech* denotes a particular concept, we might say of pictures that, like the example of the ideograph, they "are more pregnant than propositions could ever be" (McGee 428) in their reference to old events and ideas and their adaptability to new contexts.

Not only do iconic photographs "represent their subjects" but they expand representation. Lange's portrait of a worried mother stranded among other migrant workers and their families in a frozen pea field successfully represented the subject; donations of food and blankets gave the families temporary relief. Seen in subsequent presentations, the photo represents the collective experience of the Great Depression, and has been appropriated in visualizations referencing late 20th century social movements. A news photo serves as a reminder of the event it captures, but also potentially serves as a template that (like an ideograph) "guides, warrants, reasons, or excuses" an orientation, summed up in a single term (for the ideograph) or image (for the photograph).[2] The template may be used by others, such as editorial cartoonists, as visual source material that links past and present in narratives that explicate values and ideals. To illustrate the point, this chapter investigates the use and re-use of a familiar photographic image from the news story of the assassination of a President to reconstitute national narratives on celebrity, mourning, and regret.

CAMELOT REVISITED

One of the most enduring images from the days following the assassination in 1963 of John Fitzgerald Kennedy, then President of the United States, was a photograph of his 3-year-old son, dressed in short pants and formal coat, saluting in the November sun as his father's funeral cortege went by. Although John Kennedy, Jr. would later remark that he remembered little from that time, and corresponding news film of the scene suggests the salute was neither spontaneous nor meaningful to the little boy, the public knowledge of the photographed act imbued it with special poignancy. The loss of a father's presence in the life of a little boy served as emotional analogy to a nation's loss, not only of a leader, but of a certain hope and innocence, as many writers were to recount. This particular picture of the Kennedy child was only the latest in a parade of media images portraying the young, attractive, and vital Kennedy family, and all combined to produce a *parasocial relationship* with members of the First Family. Theoretically, parasocial relationships are "defined as one-sided relationships with media personae" (Newton 152) that gain adherence through repeated presentation. Because the many published photographs of the Kennedy children are reminiscent of familiar family scenes, and because photographs simulate reality—the visual equivalent of "being there"—the public feels as though they know the children as in a real relationship. The power of parasocial relationships is the increased sense of identification and empathy we feel for public figures.

The famous photograph of JFK, Jr.'s childish salute is probably remembered by everyone who witnessed media coverage of November, 1963, and even some who do not, due to its status as one of several visual icons of the Kennedy era. The image depicts a moment of remembrance and passage, as the presidential hearse passes by, and a child's salute stands for a national gesture of farewell. Its uses transcend the historical context of JFK's funeral cortege. At least two editorial cartoonists, J.D. Crowe and Joel Pett, recalled the image in their artistic tributes to Jacqueline Kennedy's passing years after 1963.

The salute photograph/film was replayed in the media in the summer of 1999 with the news that JFK, Jr., along with his wife and sister-in-law, had met with an untimely, accidental death. The image of the 1963 salute became part of a flood of images of the deceased as child and man that wallpapered television news for a week. But no single image seemed so everpresent as the salute, particularly in print. It graced the cover of a commemorative edition of *LOOK* magazine, was reproduced on the cover of *TIME* two weeks in a row, and was appropriated by at least 25 American and Canadian cartoonists within the space of a few days. The photograph also became part of the visual newstream when an anonymous mourner left a copy on the mounting flower altar outside Kennedy's New York residence. The memorial copy of the photograph was captured in close-up in an Associate Press photograph and printed in countless newspapers. The image was not just reprinted, but assumed to be remembered, as references to it were made in verbal reminiscences. Kennedy images such as the funeral salute, wrote journalist Richard Reeves, are "as familiar as family snapshots, most famously the Oval Office photograph of him at the age of 2 ... and on his third birthday, saluting the American flag draped over his father's coffin" (21). Garrison Keillor, writing in *TIME*, referred to "the aching sadness of ... the little boy's salute" (102). Editorials in such newspapers as the *San Francisco Chronicle* (see "Camelot Buried at Sea") and the *New York Times* (see Morganthan) remarked on the memorability of the picture: "As a nation, we remember John-John, a three-year-old in short pants saluting his father's coffin, a memorable image of a terrible day" (A24), wrote one *Chronicle* editor. An acquaintance of the young Kennedy's, Robert M. Morgenthau, considered the picture of the 3-year-old's salute a "shadow" image that the grown JFK, Jr. always lived in. News accounts referred to the poignant picture from the past. Actress Cicely Tyson recalled seeing the salute at the funeral and the power of the resulting image; not only its visual reappearance in print form, but also its use in calling forth a recollection of a chronologically remote national tragedy, the salute became a touchstone for the media's intense coverage of the plane crash (see Zelizer *Covering*).

Along with the grief evident at mourning sites and implied in the relentless coverage of every available aspect of the lives of the lost and of other members of Kennedy's extended family, there were concerns over the nature and motivation for a perceived "national grief" for one who had no direct connection to the lives of most Americans, who was largely unknown except as fodder for celebrity magazines (and whose own magazine was not immune to celebrity coverage). In this context, the "national grief" was declared inauthentic, even objectionable.

The media attention to JFK, Jr.'s plane crash was driven by a number of factors, including the celebrity appeal of the accident victims, the emotional engagement in a story of untimely and sudden, inexplicable death (following similar stories of the death of Princess Diana 2 years earlier and the victim's father in 1963), and the necessity to fill 24-hour news venues with interesting stories. The availability of images from the Kennedy presidency and assassination aftermath, especially images featuring the young Kennedy scion, provided news film where little was available from the crash itself, and served to define the story of the plane crash and implicitly justify the extensive coverage. In utilizing the familiar and poignant image of a fatherless boy saluting his father's funeral cortege, news outlets and editorial cartoonists linked the tragic and premature deaths of father and son and established the grounds for mourning as a continuation of a narrative of national regret over unrealized potential, and national ambivalences over social change and deeply experienced events in the past 36 years. In their use of the "salute" picture as a touchstone and lens through which to interpret July, 1999, the media also reified and framed the larger historical narratives and the mythic story of the Kennedy family.

PHOTOGRAPHS AS ICONS

Consideration of how the "salute" image functions rhetorically involves the tension between its truth value and its symbolism. The appropriation and re-presentation of the "salute" image plays on the verisimilitude of a remembered event (the 1963 funeral of an assassinated leader) and one of its associated subjects (the son of the fallen leader) combined with the symbolic aspects of the national tragedy that were transferred to a personal family tragedy from which no defining image can emerge. Unlike the assassination of JFK, which is replete with specific images of the scene in Dallas, the assassin, the schoolbook depository, the victim before and after death, the bullet's effects, the immediate aftermath of the shooting, the First Lady's panicked response, the blood on her dress, the faces of witnesses, a public funeral, and the murder of the assassin, there was no photographic footage that could document the crash of a plane at sea at night. There were no bodies to survey, there was no public witness, there was no public ceremony. There was no son. There was only an imaginary connection between the feelings evoked in a 36-year-old photograph and the parasocial relationship it prompted in the public, and the presumed feelings of family, friends, and acquaintances of the plane crash victims. In using the "salute" photograph to frame events, the media, and particularly editorial cartoonists, appropriated and transferred these feelings to the nation.

As the story of the plane crash unfolded with no defining visuals, the "salute" photograph functioned as a media tool of negotiated meaning which depended on and revitalized collective memory. Guy Debord suggests the rhetorical dynamics of the negotiation in his observation that "the spectacle is not a collection of images, but a social relation among people, mediated by images" (95). Thus, while viewers were treated to hours of camera footage depicting the scene of the plane crash, the mourning scenes in New York City, and simulations of the presumed scene inside the plane, images from the Kennedy family's history, including the "salute" photograph, became a connecting thread that provided visual and symbolic context, justifying the extensive news coverage as part of a larger narrative that was not just about the extended Kennedy family, but about the nation, as well. As Zelizer has noted the role of photographs in framing momentous events that evolve into sustained cultural narratives, "the compelling weight of the photograph is determined by a linkage between its material and discursive dimensions, and the power created by that linkage draws us to a photograph's many meanings, both now and then" (*Remembering* 8). In using the 1963 photograph, as well as other images, the news media poses a situation that requires a distinction between how a photograph was understood at the time and how it might be understood in the current day.

I propose that the "salute" photograph exhibited two different functions between 1963 and 1999, although elements of both exist across time. In 1963, the "salute" photograph, as noted before, was one of many memorable and repeated images stemming from the assassination and subsequent related events, what Zelizer has termed "assassination lore" (*Covering* 166). Pictures of Jackie's blood-stained skirt at the swearing in of Kennedy's successor, witnesses pointing up at the schoolbook depository, from where gunshots were heard, Zapruder's film footage of the bullet's impact on the President's brain, Jack Ruby's gunshot fatally hitting Lee Harvey Oswald—these are just a few of the images frequently re-presented and readily recalled, although, arguably, the picture of John-John saluting his father's casket was one of the most significant. As an example, *Time-Life* chose the image as one of two most appropriate with which to conclude the end of a memorial volume titled, *Life in Camelot*. (The other photograph pictured the President walking on the beach.) (Kunhardt) In this way, unlike the images of horror, the "salute" photograph also links us in content to a happier recollection of Camelot, and the antics of a small boy reacting to his living father. The "salute" image also belongs to a group of images that contradict the horror of the assassination. Some of these images were also replayed in 1999: JFK, Jr., peeks out from under his father's desk or dances with his sister in the Oval Office. The small boy runs to greet his father on the tarmac,[3] and so on. These images did not horrify us so much as they comforted us with a memory, however poignant, of a good man living a good life. Of course, the dissonance between the happy family scenes and the assassination invoke outrage, but the symbolic aspects of the "salute" photograph spoke to us in 1963 about the enduring nature of life and hope for the future as much as sadness for the present. Even the innocence of the boy's prompted gesture speaks to the idea that future generations will not feel the pain of the moment, and that they will have the capacity to restore hope and optimism to the country. In her noted study of media coverage of the 1963 assassination, Zelizer cites a number of revealing instances that indicate the "salute" photograph played a special role in remembering the narrative that contrasts innocent idealism with violent reality.[4]

The pathos and remorse prompted by the "salute" picture readily transfer to the apolitical tragedy of the 1999 plane crash, and translate to a national regret over promise denied. This narrative is accomplished through the media's linkage of the 1999 plane crash to the 1963 political assassination, as well as to other premature deaths suffered within the Kennedy family. No rational argument ties the events together. The deaths are random and unconnected. Even when they are similar in the details—two murders, three deaths in a plane crash—there is no link between them in shared modes of dying. Instead, the "salute" photograph functions to engender outrage—not simply the outrage that accompanies a premature and (apparently) avoidable accident, but the outrage that "this can be happening again"—to the Kennedys, to us. The "salute" photograph connects the past and the present through its symbolic twin expressions of outrage and regret.

Perlmutter's examination of photographs of outrage—photos that depicted horrifying international news events and are presumed to have had an effect on public opinion that altered events—is useful in establishing the rhetorical act of fitting the 1999 plane crash into the narrative of outrage about the 1963 assassination. Although Perlmutter disputes the commonplace of photographic *determinism*—that photographs can drive public policy—he observes that certain photographic images that capture news events can evoke strong reactions and become a vortex for political and cultural discourse. Perlmutter's work is applicable to the sympathy function (itself, a form of "outrage" against fate) performed by the 1963 "salute" photograph in more current contexts, especially the death of JFK, Jr. In asking how certain photographs achieve iconic status, Perlmutter identifies eleven characteristics of outrage-provoking photographs, at least ten of which are applicable to this image of sorrow:

(1) *Celebrity.* This criterion refers to the fame of the photograph. There is an underlying suggestion that such a photograph has been widely published or viewed, as familiarity is a condition of its resonance apart from the depicted event. "The celebrity status of a picture is often signaled by the fact people assume others must know of it" (12). In the case of the "salute" photograph, not only had it been widely seen in 1963, but it was arguably the most prominent still image used to mark and memorialize the 1999 air tragedy. The image was featured as the cover of a *LIFE* special issue published immediately after the crash, while *TIME* magazine ran it 2 weeks in a row, first in a grainy, sepia-toned close-up of JFK, Jr.'s face and arm, his head obscuring the *TIME* cover logo (August 2, 1999), and the following week as an inset—again obscuring part of the *TIME* logo—on a cover featuring a contemporary portrait of the deceased subject.

(2) *Prominence.* The positioning of the "salute" photograph on *TIME* and *LIFE* covers illustrates this criteria of iconic photographs, "one of the least ambiguous qualities of the icon" (12). Perlmutter argues that prominent news placement results in a greater likelihood of featuring in our collective memory. Although no study was done by this author to determine the extent to which the "salute" photograph was accorded special prominence in 1963, its prominent display in 1999 fulfills another aspect of iconic status through prominence. Perlmutter notes that initial prominent display makes it more

likely that the same image will be repeatedly featured in subsequent publications, such as history books, "because they are thought to sum up a great event" (13). While JFK, Jr.'s death was unconnected to his father's assassination, the use of the "salute" photograph in the context of 1999 appears to draw a connecting thread between the two events.

(3) *Frequency.* Frequency of publication or appearance, argues Perlmutter, contributes to an impression of power regarding an iconic image. In the public mind, repeated observations of a picture become equated with a picture's deserving quality. In the 1999 plane crash aftermath, not only was the "salute" image the most widely published and recalled image of JFK. Jr.'s boyhood, it was the image most frequently appropriated by editorial cartoonists to mark the occasion of his death. This utilitarian aspect to the "salute" image, that it provides a means by which commentators can frame the occasion and articulate a response, adds particular dimension to the picture's status as an icon.

(4) *Profit.* Perlmutter notes that in the business aspect of journalism, an oft-published image generates profit for the image's producers. No study has been made of the profit potential of the "salute" image, either in its original context or in recent usages and appropriations. But more relevant to the "salute" photograph is Perlmutter's amplification of the profit criteria to consider the cost to the subject in terms of disregard for suffering. The 3-year-old boy in the photograph cannot fully comprehend the enormity of the ritual he witnesses, but the public memory of that event, and of the saluting child, fixed JFK, Jr. in the nation's imagination as the child of Camelot, an image the grown man could not share.

(5) *Instantaneousness* and (6) *Fame of Subjects.* Perlmutter marks two seemingly contradictory characteristics of photographic icons, those that catapult relative unknowns into celebrity status through the rapid dissemination of the image in the media, and those that are famous because their subjects are famous. The "salute" photograph clearly embodies the second category, yet there is something in it, and in the cultural prescriptions of inheritance, that endorses the persona of the fatherless boy in a way not matched by his sister's persona.

(7) *Transposability.* Again, we see in the "salute" image a clear example of transposability in its replication across media. This quality is so effective in the "salute" photograph that, not only was it the most commonly appropriated image used by editorial cartoonists to mark the death of JFK, Jr., but some cartoonists used it to respond to Jacqueline Kennedy Onassis's death in 1994.

(8) *Importance of Events.* The assassination of the President in 1963 was regarded as an end to an era of innocence and hope among the American people. Few momentous events in the 20th century have been similarly associated with an image, or a set of images, as profoundly regarded as those that marked the Kennedy assassination. The transference of the 1963 image of a child's salute to his death as a man in 1999 carries with it the memory of the earlier event and imbues the plane crash with a significance and poignancy far be-

yond its actuality. A young, handsome, wealthy man from a well-known family perishes in an unremarkable plane crash, along with his wife and his wife's sister. But the visual analogy to his father—a handsome, wealthy, and powerful man, cut down before his full life expectancy by an event that causes calamity in the nation—creates a resonance and a reliving (for those old enough) of what was lost in 1963.

(9) *Metonymy*. Perlmutter observes that iconic images act metonymically, summing up a situation so as to represent a larger idea. "The inclination to present a picture as an explicit or implicit metonym is almost overwhelming, for journalists, scholars, and politicians. Yet, in truth, no picture ever says it all" (17). The media seemed to employ the "salute" photo in 1999 to contextualize a tragic event that would have been unremarkable except for the enduring fame of the subjects. The visual references to a 36-year-old photograph provided justification for extensive news coverage by linking the contemporary with historical significance. The "salute" photograph bears no direct relationship to a current news event; its relationship to a past event is obscured by the lack of signifying detail. However, the presumption of familiarity with, not just a funeral procession, but an entire process of grieving, dreams lost, and changes in history's course is assumed. Those of us old enough remember "where we were when we heard Kennedy was shot," are likely to remember the *national* feeling (expressed through the media's interpretive lens) better than our own.

(10) *Primordiality and/or Cultural Resonance*. Although the "salute" image may not reflect a classical historical scene that Perlmutter references, the salute to a military superior or a fallen hero is sufficiently ingrained in the public consciousness that it lends its own symbolic overtone to JFK. Jr.'s salute to his father. The situation is made all the more poignant by the boy's childish obliviousness to the import of events, not just the loss of a father, but the nation's loss of a dynamic leader, of whom much was expected. In making some allusions to the similarity in format of some iconic news photos to classic paintings, Perlmutter notes that every icon adds to the total cultural expression of its familiar incarnations. Edwards and Winkler have argued elsewhere that visual images function as ideographs in this same sense; each application of an image repeats, intensifies, and reifies its meanings. Although the "salute" photo does not bear a similar relationship to a past image, it recreates itself in every appropriation and re-presentation over time.

(11) *Striking Composition*. Perlmutter argues that one important feature linking visual icons is that they express "the decisive moment" when elements such as lighting, expression, and position coincide to make a memorable composition (18). The "salute" photograph is an interesting case; because of its origins as film footage (as a number of stilled image icons are), it can be presented in a number of ways. Not only has there been variance in the angle of the shot, but there is particular variance in range. The close-up that graced the covers of

Time and *Look* in the summer of 1999 highlighted the figure of the boy standing in his short coat, almost awkward, yet precise, in displaying the salute. Although the background can be darkened (especially in cartoon renditions), the
photograph accentuates his vulnerability by the juxtaposition of adult legs
and hands that contrast with the boy's small size. As the photograph's range
expands, we see the figures of his sister, his uncle, and his veiled mother, but
this father's caisson remains out of view. Perlmutter notes that almost all icons
have a quality of spareness and simplicity. The boy's light-colored winter coat
against the dark morning attire of the adults, the brightness of the sun falling
toward his face, are elements that allow the image to speak its pathos in cropped close-up as well as more medium-range shots. Even in visual renditions
that include the other family figures, JFK, Jr.'s salute is so unique, even incon-
gruous, that along with his size and light clothing (visual presentations shared
by his sister, as well) he remains the focal point for each rendition of the image.
It is not the scene of the family that is remembered in the verbal accounts of
this photograph, it is the image of the boy and his salute. His face and the action are directed at the unseen President, forever linking the two in our imagination and memory. In its repeated use of the picture in 1999, the media links
the President and his son symbolically, engendering a narrative continuity between two disparate events.

EDITORIAL CARTOON APPROPRIATION

The mutable nature of the image's symbolism as an image of hope, regret,
and outrage is even more clearly revealed when we look at the recent history
of its appropriation by editorial cartoonists.[5] In advancing propositions about
political and social events, cartoonists act rhetorically. Although research fails
to prove that cartoons change reader opinion, the visual presentations in cartoons create images and define social realities. Familiar imagery is often employed to create metaphors or analogies that guide interpretation. They are
rhetorical in the sense that social values and effects are expressed when symbolic forms are put into public play (Edwards 7). The use of visual parodies on
iconic imagery is a potentially potent form of rhetoric, often corresponding to
McGee's concept of the ideograph as a "one-term sum of an orientation" that
prompts and reformulates understanding when it is repeatedly invoked (Edwards and Winkler). Even in cases where there exists no appropriation, where
the cartoonist has chosen caricature or situational picturing as a visual strategy, cartoons operate as narratives. "In this sense, the 'still' image is seen as
something which does not eternalize an instant, but, rather, encompasses a situation" (Edwards 56). Because cartoon imagery, especially appropriated imagery, refers back to its earlier contexts and suggests future action, it activates
narratives regarding the depicted events. When the framework for the narrative is provided by an iconic image such as John-John's salute to his slain

father, the narrative inevitably takes on mythic dimensions. Even more than the cable news networks' constant replays of film related to the assassination of a President to fill an implicit demand for visual content related to an unfolding story that was relatively devoid of eventfulness, cartoonists adopted the imagery of a presidential assassination as an explanatory strategy for understanding the unexplainable.

John Kennedy's plane crash was not the first event where cartoonists recognized and exploited the potential for visual continuity between the myth of Camelot and its more contemporary translations. Five years prior to the accident that killed JFK, Jr., at least two cartoonists used the "salute" image to frame memorials of Jacqueline Kennedy Onassis. The image supercedes the logic of its content. In 1994, JFK, Jr. was an adult, not a 3-year-old child, his sister mourned their mother's death as well, there was no public funeral procession, and Mrs. Onassis was well beyond the relative youth of her slain husband when she died. In appropriating the image, these cartoonists invoked collective memory to express, not outrage, but regret. Although noting a point of passage in a national narrative, Mrs. Onassis's death could hardly be seen as a final moment. The presence of the boy, now a man, militated against narrative closure even as it alluded to the narrative of Camelot and the Kennedy legacy.

The events of 1999 would suggest closure (in spite of the survival of Caroline Kennedy) as well as outrage over the repetition of the narrative kernel. Some cartoonists accentuated the media-constructed linkage between 1963 and 1999, not only by using the 1963 image as a touchstone, but by visually linking the boy and father in heaven. Others assisted in the framing of the plane crash as a national tragedy, rather than a family tragedy, by incorporating the image of Uncle Sam in the salute image.

The reproducibility of (news) photographs facilitates their reappearance in new journalistic contexts, however distanced from the events that prompted their original appearance. In recontextualizing images, the media provides a symbolic association between phenomena by metaphor or allegory. The parodic appropriation of existing images by cartoonists reconfigures the parodied subject from an object of ridicule to an object of veneration. That is, the parodied original is held up as an implied ideal to which other situations are compared. Similarly, cartoonists who employed images such as the "salute" invoke the idealism inherent in the 1963 image of regret (which, nevertheless, implies a sense of optimism) to provoke the outrage against fate in 1999. Although the use of the "salute" image differs from other similar examples of visual appropriation in cartoons in that it is self-referencing (back to JFK, Jr. and his familial history) rather than other-referencing, the cartoonists' appropriation still articulates an ideal that frames current events against historical memory.

Cartoon appropriations of famous photographs carry the symbolic and connotative associations of the photograph into new territories. While MSNBC and CNN news directors juxtaposed the unique image of 1963 with

the vaguer images of 1999 (e.g., the site of the crash and contemporary pictures of the victims), cartoonists were able to reinvent contexts by translating
and transforming the present through the lens of the past. A logical reversal
takes place as a grown man is returned to his form as a child in order to provide
commentary about his death. The attitudes displayed by cartoonists exhibited
various perspectives on the rhetorical implications of the image as a framing
device. For some cartoonists, the singular recognizability of the boy's short
coat and salute gesture served to visually denote and memorialize JFK, Jr. Typical examples of denotative cartoons show the saluting child in a bare landscape with his name enscribed below, or standing on a foundation of clouds, or
wearing angel's wings. The image of JFK, Jr. as a child is more recognizable
than he is as a man. In spite of significant media coverage of his adult life, he is
known to us primarily in the parasocial relationship established through his
childhood photographs. Were his father not a president of mythic proportion,
his death would not invite extensive commentary. This idea is advanced in cartoons that depict a heavenly reunion of father and son. (At least two cartoonists employed the image of John-John running to greet his father on the
tarmac to suggest reunion in the afterlife.) The continuity of time is disrupted
in these examples. The departed President is pictured much as he was at the
time of his death, but the son morphs backward to his childhood (see Fig. 8.1),
reframing the 1999 tragedy in the terms of 1963. It is not the deaths of John
Kennedy, his wife, or his sister-in-law that are noteworthy, it is only the long-
ago assassination that continues to define collective acknowledgment of the
Kennedy family. In the hands of cartoonists such as Locher, John, Jr.'s death
becomes a rhetorical device that visually returns us to history and the mythic
narrative of promise cut short. The horrific assassination is erased and a new
narrative is inserted where the child is reunited with his father. ("I'm coming,
Daddy," the child promises in a cartoon by Steve Benson. "Dad ... wait on
me," the child says in a cartoon by Marshall Ramsey.) And time moves forward
in a new way, as the President now returns his son's salute.

     Other cartoons refer to the "salute" image as remembrance of things past,
rather than a reconciliation and renovation of the past. For Horsey, the "salute" image is a photograph in a scrapbook about the tragic drama of the Kennedy family. Similarly, Breen depicts the country, in the incarnation of Uncle
Sam, reviewing a scrapbook where the salute photo appears. Brice McKinnon,
a Canadian cartoonist, presents the salute image as a photograph washed
ashore. Wright is most suggestive in referring to the place of the salute image
in the collective memory (see Fig. 8.2). In his cartoon, the image floats within
the mind of the people—again, incarnated in the image of Uncle Sam, who al-
ludes to the lasting power of the images: "Some memories just won't go
away," he ponders.

     In the most potent reference to collectivity, the image of the saluting child is
presented as an image of America. In these cartoons, JFK, Jr. is not the subject

FIG. 8.1. Locher's father-child reunion recalls the narrative of 1963.

FIG. 8.2. Wright's cartoon testifies to the lasting power of images in the national consciousness.

of reflection, but the means, in much the same way as embodiments of the child going to heaven return us to the past. Three cartoonists employ different visual strategies for this transference. While Plante labels his boy "JFK Jr." the boy wears swim trunks and looks out to sea. The reader is positioned behind the boy, a positioning that invites us to step into the experience of the salute and look toward the tragic scene of 1999 rather than survey the saluting boy on that November day long ago. Rogers blends the stance and character of the saluting boy with the image of Uncle Sam (see Fig. 8.3). In both cartoons, JFK, Jr. ceases to exist as "other" (the distance invoked by celebrity) and we subsume or are subsumed by the stories the boy represents.

More dramatically, Darrin Bell depicts the entire scene surrounding the saluting boy, labeling him "America" as the salute is directed toward the coffin of John F. Kennedy. Cartoonists and news producers use the image of the salute as a rhetorical device to recall and restructure the narrative of two family tragedies and a national tragedy that are remembered through iconic images.

CONCLUSION

Questions about media practice in the age of celebrity spectacle often revolve around the pack mentality and the relentless push to define events as significant. In the case of the death of JFK, Jr., such questions are germane, considering the monumental coverage of the story. But my purpose has been to examine the vi-

FIG. 8.3.   Cartoonists condense images of the past with national symbols in current contexts. (ROB ROGERS reprinted by permission of United Feature Syndicate, Inc.)

sual rhetorics inherent in that coverage. The frequent invoking of the "salute" photograph as well as other historical images of Kennedy and his family members served to justify coverage by positioning the plane crash as part of a larger narrative that involved a nation, as well as a family. Critics may be right in lamenting that our grief was false because we did not know John F. Kennedy, Jr. and he played no critical role in public life. But, in the end, grief was not directed toward the victims of a plane crash as sea. Rather, the invocation of the mythic narrative of the Kennedy promise and end of that promise prompted a mourning that was directed inward. As a nation, we mourned our own destiny, remembered through media images that returned us to that earlier time. In a sense, we mourned the symbolism inherent in the "salute" picture, guided by the media's use of that picture as a framing mechanism.

Shortly after the plane crash off Martha's Vineyard, Richard Reeves speculated on the future of history, suggesting that what will count as history in the future are those events that leave a trail of visual record in their wake. "Mass or popular history will be based on the images preserved on film, video, or new technologies ... How we see ourselves will depend not on what we are formally taught or made to read, but on what we see or what we can be shown" (21). Reeves's comment overlooks one part of the dynamic, and that is, in the showing, the media constructs history as an interpretation of events. When visual images from history are replayed, no matter how connected to events they appear to be on the surface (as with a childhood image of a downed pilot), the use of such images connects two messages, from now and then, linking together the "truth value" of a photograph and its symbolic value in harmonious resonance.

NOTES

1. For an extended explanation of image events as rhetorical acts see DeLuca, *Image Politics: The New Rhetoric of Environmental Activism.*
2. See McGee, pp. 428–429, for a definition of the ideograph.
3. Seemingly, he runs to greet his father, although the President quipped that the boy's exuberance could be attributed to the presence of flying machines.
4. Just as in 1999, the "salute" image was not only printed in subsequent rememberings of the assassination and the Kennedy presidency, but it was recalled in verbal references by political figures such as John Connally and journalists such as Lance Morrow (for *TIME*) as an artifact of pathos and remorse in public memory.
5. The cartoons discussed in this chapter appeared as reprints in two periodical collections, *The National Forum's Best Editorial Cartoons* and *Comic Relief,* published in August and September of 1999, respectively, and on the website www.cagle.com.

WORKS CITED

"Camelot Buried at Sea." *San Francisco Chronicle*. 23 July 1999: A24.

DeBord, Guy. "Separation Perfected." *Visual Culture: The Reader*. Ed. Jessica Evans and Stuart Hall. Thousand Oaks, CA: Corwin Press, 1999: 95–98.

DeLuca, Kevin Michael. *Image Politics: The New Rhetoric of Environmental Activism*. New York: Guilford Press, 1999.

Edwards, Janis L. *Political Cartoons in the 1988 Presidential Campaign: Image, Metaphor, and Narrative*. New York: Garland Publishing, 1997.

Edwards, Janis L. and Carol K. Winkler. "Representative Form and the Visual Ideograph: The Iwo Jima Image in Editorial Cartoons." *Quarterly Journal of Speech* 83 (1997): 289–310.

"John F. Kennedy, Jr. An Album of Unseen and Unforgettable Pictures." *Life* (special issue) 1999: cover.

Keillor, Garrison. "Goodbye to Our Boy." *TIME* 2 August 1999, 102.

Kunhardt, Philip B. Jr., (Ed.). *Life in Camelot: The Kennedy Years*. New York: Time-Life Books, 1988.

McGee, Michael C. "The 'Ideograph': A Link Between Rhetoric and Ideology." *Quarterly Journal of Speech* 66 (1980): 1–6.

Morgenthau, Robert M. "As an Assistant D.A., JFK, Jr. Wanted to Be Just a Member of the Staff." The *Sacramento Bee* 21 July 1999: B9.

Newton, Julianne H. *The Burden of Visual Truth: The Role of Photojournalism in Mediating Reality*. Mahwah, NJ: Lawrence Erlbaum Associates, 2001.

Osborn, Michael M. "Rhetorical Depiction." *Form, Genre, and the Study of Political Discourse*. Ed. Herbert W. Simons and Aram Aghazarian. Columbia, SC: U of South Carolina P, 1986: 79–107.

Perlmutter, David D. *Photojournalism and Foreign Policy: Icons of Outrage in International Crisis*. Westport, CT: Praeger, 1998.

Reeves, Richard. "The Images of History." *The Washington Post Weekly Edition* 2, August 1999, 21.

Time. July 26, 1999: cover.

Time. August 2, 1999: cover.

Zelizer, Barbie. *Covering the Body: The Kennedy Assassination, the Media, and the Shaping of Collective Memory*. Chicago: The U of Chicago P, 1992.

—. *Remembering to Forget: Holocaust Memory Through the Camera's Eye*. Chicago: U of Chicago P, 1998.

CHAPTER NINE

Doing Rhetorical History of the Visual: The Photograph and the Archive

Cara A. Finnegan

DEFINING VISUAL RHETORICS: PRODUCT OR PROCESS?

Consider two rhetorical documents, both appearing at approximately the same moment in history. The first, President Franklin D. Roosevelt's second inaugural address, is a text memorable not only for its association with the era's most towering rhetorical figure, but also for its unique use of visual language. Roosevelt's famous "one third of a nation" incantation comes at the end of a series of paragraphs in which Roosevelt outlines the ways in which conditions have improved since he first took the oath of office in 1933. On that day, Roosevelt reminds the audience, "We dedicated ourselves to the fulfillment of a vision—to speed the time when there would be for all the people that security and peace essential to the pursuit of happiness" (127). Now, in 1937, Roosevelt outlines the accomplishments of his first administration, then poses a pressing question: "Let us ask again: Have we reached the goal of our vision of that fourth day of March 1933? Have we found our happy valley?" Speaking as an omniscient narrator with all the available facts before him, Roosevelt literally tells us what he sees: "I see a great nation, upon a great continent, blessed with a great wealth of natural resources. Its hundred and thirty million people are at peace among themselves; they are making their country a good neighbor among the nations" (130). But the President also sees something more troubling:

> But here is the challenge to our democracy: In this nation I see tens of millions of its citizens—a substantial part of its whole population—who at this very moment are denied the greater part of what the very lowest standards of today call the necessities of life. I see millions of families trying to live on incomes so meager that the pall of family disaster hangs over them day by

day. I see millions whose daily lives in city and on farm continue under conditions labeled indecent by a so-called polite society half a century ago. I see millions denied education, recreation, and the opportunity to better their lot and the lot of their children. I see millions lacking the means to buy the products of farm and factory and by their poverty denying work and productiveness to many other millions. I see one-third of a nation ill-housed, ill-clad, ill-nourished. (130–131)

This vivid litany fresh in his listeners' minds, the eternally optimistic Roosevelt hastens to add, "It is not in despair that I paint you that picture. I paint it for you in hope—because the Nation, seeing and understanding the injustice in it, proposes to paint it out" (131). In describing the conditions of the present and defining a plan for the future, Roosevelt speaks with a visual rhetoric, relying on the trope of *ekphrasis* to describe the scene, to literally make the audience see through his eyes.[1]

Now let us consider another document from early 1937 that also visualizes conditions of poverty for its audience (see Fig. 9.1). In March 1937 *LOOK*, the new and popular picture magazine, published a two-page feature on conditions for sharecroppers in the American south ("Children of the Forgotten Man!"). The feature used six images made by government photographers working for the Historical Section of the Farm Security Administration (FSA), an agency charged with managing and alleviating chronic rural poverty in the United States. As framed in the *LOOK* feature, the FSA photographers' images visualize to a great extent that which Roosevelt's second inaugural address paints in words. Using the trope of the "forgotten man," *LOOK* vividly visualizes Roosevelt's anxiety about current conditions of chronic poverty.

Both Roosevelt's speech and the *LOOK* layout are explicitly rhetorical documents in that they are products of what Thomas Farrell calls "the collaborative art of addressing and guiding decision and judgment" (1)—though we could certainly argue about what specific judgments or decisions each would guide us to make. Both constitute *visual* rhetorics as well, Roosevelt relying upon *ekphrasis* in the context of a Western linguistic tradition steeped in ocularcentrism, *LOOK* deploying techniques of graphic design alongside the products of photographic practice.[2] Yet, apart from these similarities, we probably would not consider these documents to be very similar; indeed, the differences might matter for a rhetorician interested in constructing a critical account. From the point of view of methodology, we may feel more comfortable engaging Roosevelt's textual picture drawn in the second inaugural than we are engaging the FSA's pictorial text in *LOOK* magazine.[3] In the case of the *LOOK* feature, it may simply be less clear as to how we should proceed.

In the early 1990s, when I began work on the rhetorical aspects of visual culture, library searches of relevant databases turned up few responses to the search term, *visual rhetoric*. Today, however, a similar search suggests that vi-

FIG. 9.1. "Children of the Forgotten Man!" *LOOK*, March 1937, pp. 18–19. Image courtesy of the Library of Congress.

197

sual rhetoric has gained currency in a range of scholarly contexts, including that of rhetorical studies.[4] Yet, as the editors of this volume note in their introduction, increased use of a term does not necessarily constitute a universally accepted meaning; thus, the search for definitions, even broad ones, is useful. The first, and perhaps most obvious, way is to define visual rhetoric as a *product*—a proper noun, if you will—that names a category of rhetorical discourse that relies on something other than words or text for the construction of its meaning. Thus a photograph would constitute visual rhetoric insofar as it consists of non-textual or non-discursive features. But there are at least two problems with defining visual rhetoric as product. First, such a definition implies that there are substantial differences between "word" and "not-word." Jacques Derrida's discussions of the visual nature of writing as *grapheme* have reminded us that such distinctions are theoretically tenuous at best, not to mention pragmatically difficult to sort out in the context of real-life rhetorical activity. In addition, the construction of a category or genre of visual rhetoric has the perhaps unintended consequence of reinforcing the subordinate status of visuality in the contexts of rhetorical culture. That is, visual rhetoric is destined always to be *visual* rhetoric, whereas verbal rhetoric, or textuality, gets to be just *rhetoric*. Although it is understandable why some would want to privilege the oft-neglected visual in rhetorical studies, such distinctions may in the end reproduce the hierarchies that have discouraged analysis of the visual all along. Rather than focus on what makes the visual distinct, then, we might question instead why the two need to be separated in the first place. Following W. J. T. Mitchell's contention that "all media are mixed media" (95), David Blakesley and Collin Brooke observe that we might instead start "seeing visuality and textuality not as isolated phenomena, but as sharing at a deeper level some common roots in perceptual and linguistic processes" (2).

In order to make this move, however, we need to define visual rhetoric as something more than merely a genre category or product. I offer that we conceptualize visual rhetoric as a mode of inquiry, defined as a critical and theoretical orientation that makes issues of visuality relevant to rhetorical theory. As a mode of inquiry, the visual rhetoric project would urge us to explore our understandings of visual culture in light of the questions of rhetorical theory, and at the same time encourage us to (re)consider aspects of rhetorical theory in light of the persistent problem of the image. As I have noted elsewhere (following W. J. T. Mitchell and others), such work "relies upon critiques of vision and visuality to illuminate the complex dynamics of power and knowledge at play in and around images ... embraces the complexities of the relationships between images and texts and argues that visual images should not be artificially separated from texts for analysis" (Finnegan, "Documentary as Art" 39).

One goal (though not the only goal) of such inquiry might be the construction of a rhetorical history that accounts systematically for the ways in which images become inventional resources in the public sphere. This chapter argues for a method of doing rhetorical history of visual images that accounts for *images as history* as well as *images in history*. In doing so, it poses the question, "What is the place of rhetorical history in visual rhetoric?" Although others have proposed schema for the rhetorical study of images, this account is different in that it seeks explicitly to demonstrate how the rhetorical *historian* might engage the visual.[5] In what follows, I model a way of doing rhetorical history of the visual by turning to the example of FSA photography as it was mobilized in *LOOK*. Through that analysis, I argue that those interested in visual culture may benefit if they mobilize the tools of rhetorical history to sort out three moments in the life of an image for which a critic must account: production, reproduction, and circulation. Using the example of the *LOOK* layout, I demonstrate how the rhetorical historian of images might make just such an accounting and how that accounting may deepen our understanding of the history in and around this body of photographs.

RHETORICAL HISTORY MEETS THE ARTIFACTS OF VISUAL CULTURE

Although public address studies in the discipline of Speech Communication are decades-old, the practice of rhetorical history (often framed in the guise of "American Public Address") has a conflicted past.[6] While Kathleen J. Turner argues that the past 30 years or so produced theory-driven criticism that de-emphasized historical work as "mere history" (1), David Zarefsky argues such a reading smacks of "strange defensiveness." The practice of rhetorical history, Zarefsky contends, is alive and well in a thriving culture of public address studies: "Even a casual inspection of journals and books will suggest that good historical scholarship in rhetoric does get published and that it attracts a healthy audience" (19). For Zarefsky, the danger is not the absence of historical work, but the undue attention paid to "distinctions that do not matter." For example, Zarefsky argues that traditional distinctions between criticism and history are unimportant, for if historical scholarship is sophisticated enough it will produce "critical judgment" that renders distinctions between history and criticism "superfluous" (22). Similarly, distinctions between history and theory are equally problematic because they erroneously imply that historical scholarship should be "noninterpretive and self-contained" rather than address the pertinent "so what?" questions of a given field (25).

Distinctions that *do* matter, for Zarefsky, are those that enable us to sort out the different senses of the term, *rhetorical history*. Understanding these senses is important, he observes, "useful not only for boundary drawing but for understanding the richness of our field" (26). Zarefsky goes on to outline four senses of rhetorical history: the history of rhetoric, the rhetoric of history, the historical study of rhetorical events, and the rhetorical study of historical events. I will set aside the first two in the list, for only Zarefsky's third and fourth senses are relevant to my argument in this chapter. In the *historical study of rhetorical events* (sense #3), discourse is studied "as a force in history," as a part of the history of a culture, or as a microcosm for history itself (30). Using such an approach, a critic might study the history of terms relevant to particular instances of rhetorical discourse, attempt to uncover the history of the production of a text, or look for patterns in discourse that "suggest a rhetorical trajectory" (29). To return to an example with which this chapter began, the rhetorical historian might study the rhetorical event of Roosevelt's second inaugural address from an historical perspective by engaging the text in light of Roosevelt's general speech practices and looking for common themes, key terms, or arguments. One can imagine using the speech to construct a rhetorical portrait of Roosevelt himself, attempting to understand the rhetorical practices of the most dominant figure of the era by studying this speech as a microcosm of them. One might even tease out the process of composition of the text itself, utilizing archival materials to demonstrate the origins of particular phrases or ideas.

The fourth sense of rhetorical history takes something of the opposite approach and is one Zarefsky clearly prefers, for it is both the "most elusive" but "also the most rewarding"—the *rhetorical study of historical events* (30). Here, one uses the critical tools cultivated by one's rhetorical sensibility to understand history itself, conceiving of people, events, and situations as *rhetorical problems* for which responses must continually be formulated, reformulated, and negotiated (30). If one were to study the second inaugural address in this sense, such an approach would entail investigation of the world around Roosevelt's text with a sensibility cultivated to view the speech as a response to rhetorical problems operative at that historical moment: the continuing trauma of the Depression, the controversial status of New Deal reforms, prevailing beliefs and attitudes about poverty, and the like. Thus, rather than using history to understand the speech (sense #3), one would use the speech to understand history.

What I argue in the remaining portion of this chapter is that one may approach the *LOOK* feature in a similar fashion, with the caveat that doing rhetorical history of the visual must entail *both* the third and fourth senses of rhetorical history; neither is sufficient alone. Taken together, they enable the rhetorical historian to pay attention to each of three distinct but equally important moments in the life of photographs—production, reproduction, and circulation. Production must be accounted for if we are to know where images come from (literally) and why they appear in the spaces where we find them. Reproduction acknowledges that images are hybrid entities, that we do not encounter them in isolation, and that their arrangement (at least in the spaces of print culture) is always the result of particular editorial choices and framing of ideas. Circulation must be accounted for as well, for—as Walter Benjamin reminded us long ago—it is the fundamental property of photography.[7] Analysis of these three moments is possible when one utilizes the methods of investigation implied in both the third and the fourth senses of rhetorical history. Thus in what follows I study the history of the sharecropper feature as a rhetorical event (Zarefsky's sense #3) by accounting for the origins of *LOOK* magazine, tracing the story of the production and reproduction of the FSA photographs, and tracking the key terms invoked in this particular arrangement of images and text. I also engage in the rhetorical study of the feature as an historical event (Zarefsky's sense #4) by exploring the *LOOK* feature as one response to the complex problems of Depression-era poverty, both practical (how shall we care for the poorest of the poor?) and representational (how shall we attempt to make people care about the poor?). In doing so, I situate *LOOK* as it circulated in the context of Depression-era discourses about poverty, provide insight into public attitudes about poverty during the Depression, and illustrate the unique way visual images contributed to the rhetorical politics of the age.

THE HISTORICAL STUDY OF RHETORICAL EVENTS: PRODUCTION AND REPRODUCTION OF THE FSA PHOTOGRAPHS IN LOOK

Production

"Keep Informed!" the March 1937 cover of *LOOK* trumpeted (see Fig. 9.2). Inside, on pages 18 and 19, six FSA photographs appeared in a feature titled, "Children of the Forgotten Man! *LOOK* Visits the Sharecropper" (Fig. 9.1). Although, as I elaborate, the picture magazines made possible mass circulation of the FSA photographs, the picture magazines themselves were made possible by rapidly changing technologies of photographic production and reproduction after World War I. Although photographs had for years been reproducible in magazines and newspapers, it was not until the mid-1930s that photographs could be reprinted in magazines with the quality and in the quantity that came to be associated with *Life*, or, to a lesser extent, *LOOK*.[8] In addition, the kinds of photographs reproduced in *LOOK* and *Life* and other picture magazines were different from images previously available. Beginning in the 1920s in Germany, changes in photographic technology created a revolution of sorts in photographic production and reproduction. The new technology of the "miniature" 35-mm camera made it possible for photographers to make large numbers of images quickly and relatively unobtrusively. The camera's fast shutter speed, small size, and use of roll film (rather than cumbersome plates) made it easy to, as one *Fortune* magazine article put it, "shoot from the hip and get your man" ("U.S. Minicam Boom" 160). Furthermore, the development of 35-mm photography coincided with the introduction of the flash bulb, making it even more possible for photographers to make good quality images in less-than-ideal conditions (Carlebach 160–165).

The profusion of images provided much-needed fodder for the picture magazines. *Life* debuted in late 1936, *LOOK* just a few months later in early

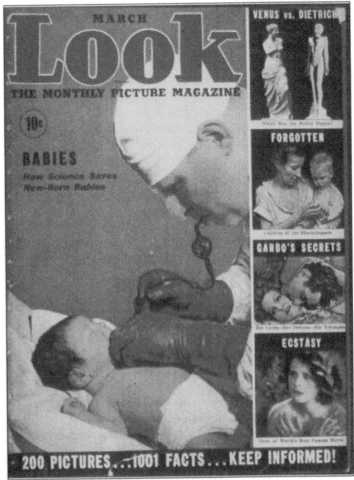

FIG. 9.2.   Cover of *LOOK* magazine, March 1937. Image courtesy of the
Library of Congress.

1937. By 1938, it was reported that there were 13 picture magazines being published in the United States. In addition to *Life* and *LOOK*, these included *Focus*,
Picture, *Click*, and *See* (Edwards 102). *LOOK*, in particular, was nearly as popular
as *Life*, but considered *Life's* working-class cousin because of its poorer technical quality; it was published on lower quality paper of the type used in newspaper Sunday rotogravure sections. In addition, early on the magazine became
known for having "salacious" content; after its debut, *The New Republic* ridi-
culed *LOOK* as "a combination morgue and dime museum, on paper" ("Picture Papers" 197). Editorially, the magazine lived up to its demand that readers
"LOOK," providing a steady diet of celebrity gossip, self-help articles, and fea-

tures that emphasized the odd and/or salacious ("Auto Kills Woman Right Before Your Eyes!"). But despite the magazine's early taste for curiosities, LOOK nevertheless reflected the new ideology of the picture magazine in that it sought to use photographs to tell narratives about real people in specific situations, but always in ways that cultivated universal interest.[9]

In some ways, LOOK would appear to be an odd outlet for the FSA photographs. From 1935 to 1943, the Historical Section, a division of the FSA, conducted a photography project designed to document American life during the Depression and chronicle New Deal efforts to relieve rural poverty. Photographs by the likes of Dorothea Lange, Walker Evans, Ben Shahn, Arthur Rothstein and Russell Lee were used not only to demonstrate that profound rural poverty existed, but also to illustrate potential solutions. Such images were circulated widely to government and media outlets, their goal to educate and influence public opinion on issues related to rural poverty. In early 1937, the new picture magazines offered the possibility of mass circulation for the images, making it possible to expose hundreds of thousands, perhaps even a million, readers to the issues facing the rural poor. Until the picture magazines appeared on the scene, the Historical Section's photographs had not appeared in periodicals with circulations much over 25,000; thus although it was an unlikely marriage, Historical Section chief Roy Stryker pursued with interest publication of the photographs in magazines like LOOK.

Before the first issue of LOOK had even hit the newsstands, LOOK founder Gardner "Mike" Cowles, Jr. contacted Roy Stryker for pictures: "I should much appreciate it if you would mail me a fairly large number of pictures which show the worst conditions in the south, pictures which might run under the caption 'Can such conditions possibly exist in the United States?' " (23 Nov. 1936). Stryker replied promptly, providing Cowles with a set of photographs and offering even more: "At the present time we have a photographer working in Iowa and Illinois on material concerning farm tenancy. As soon as his pictures begin to come in, I will see that you receive some of this material as I am sure that it would be useful" (2 Dec. 1936). Although we have no way of knowing what pictures Stryker sent to Cowles, we do have the March 1937 sharecropper feature as LOOK published it (Fig. 9.1).

At this point, it may be useful to point out several moves I am making in my attempt to account for the ways the FSA photographs were used in the LOOK feature. First, in keeping with the third sense of rhetorical history (the historical study of rhetorical events), I have attempted to account, albeit very briefly, for the forces that made magazines such as LOOK possible in the first place, the history and goals of the FSA's project, and LOOK's interest in the Historical Section's photographs specifically. In doing so I have turned to secondary material that has enabled me to reconstruct the technological developments that made LOOK and other publications feasible, primary source material discussing the origins of and reactions to the picture magazines, and the archival material of the Historical Section (Stryker's letters back and forth with Cowles). In short, I have sketched an account of *production* that seeks to answer the question, "How did these photographs end up in this magazine at this particular moment in time?" Though there is clearly more that may be said, what I have outlined thus far should at least suggest a few ways that tools of rhetorical history (such as the archive) may be used to make an account of the production of images.

Reproduction

In addition to production, another equally important moment in the life of images is reproduction. We need to understand, not only where images "come from," but also what they are made to do in the contexts in which we discover them. In doing so, we investigate what Barthes called the "rhetoric of the image"—the ways that the arrangement of image, text and caption work to create meaning in the contexts of particular rhetorical events like the reproduction of the FSA photographs in the *LOOK* feature.[10]

The feature is made up of six FSA photographs accompanied by textual material in the form of headlines and captions (Fig. 9.1). Visually, the feature reflects *LOOK*'s early editorial and graphical fits and starts, pitting the magazine's purported interest in "facts" against its desire to increase readership through the use of dramatic photographs and vivid captions. We might begin by noting the feature's placement within the rest of the issue of the magazine. Readers encountering the sharecropper feature would find it sandwiched between a 2-page illustrated feature on marriage in Zululand, titled "A Savage Buys a Wife," and a two-page centerfold of actress, Myrna Loy, posed provocatively in a bathtub filled with flower petals (the caption announcing that Miss Loy "wears only tailored underwear" ("Myrna Loy" 21). Although this arrangement of materials may appear jarring (to say the least), within *LOOK*'s vision of the picture magazine there is no cognitive dissonance here. The "savage," the sharecropper, and the sexy starlet all merit equal representation and treatment in the genre of the picture story; as we shall see, however, such treatment does have implications in terms of the rhetorics of poverty made available in the magazine. Analysis of the feature reveals several themes reproduced in this particular arrangement of text and image: the use of candid, often crude images, a layout encouraging surveillance on the part of the reader / viewer, an emphasis on children that encourages an infantilized view of the poor, and dramatic captions and headlines that narrativize the experiences of the poor at the expense of offering a context for understanding that poverty as real, material, and pressing.

The sharecropper feature offers a crude layout, cropping the FSA photographs into odd shapes and cutouts. The dominant visual element is a large cutout of a small child crying. Dressed in ragged clothing, the child has a face

distorted in pain or tears; he is clearly in distress. Each image in the feature is accompanied by a caption; this one states in part, "Alone and Hungry: This is no
child of destitute European peasants. He is an American whose parents work all
day in the fields of our 'Sunny South.' He is the son of a cotton sharecropper.
America has eight million like his parents" ("Children" 18). The shocking image,
combined with this caption, makes the child a visual synecdoche, encouraging
the reader/viewer to see him not as an individual child, but as representative of
literally millions of others living in similar destitution.

There is strong shock value to this photograph, thanks not only to its content but to *LOOK*'s distortion of photographic scale in the layout. The image
appears crude and not particularly respectful of its subject; yet Roy Stryker
wrote approvingly to *LOOK*'s Mike Cowles of the layout of photographs in
the sharecropper feature and mentioned this image specifically: "I think the
placing of that little boy in the burlap clothes in a prominent position as you
did was extremely effective" (6 Feb. 1937). Stryker's reply is disconcerting, but
as I will note later, not surprising given the institutional constraints that
Stryker faced in attempting to keep the FSA's photography project alive.

All of the images in this feature reject the formal pose of the photographic
portrait in favor of more "candid" subject matter. A search of the negative
numbers of the images reveals that most of the photographs were made with
the relatively new 35-mm technology, which produced visual effects different
from those of larger format cameras.[11] One of the primary effects of the use of
candid, somewhat crude imagery is that the feature constructs for the
reader/viewer a stance of surveillance. We are positioned to look in on the giant image of the crying child dressed in the burlap sack or to surveil the pregnant mother and her children in the doorway. Cropping also encourages
surveillance through the use of odd, cookie-cutter shapes. The images of the
African-American children, in particular, demonstrate the strange rhetorical
impact of such cropping. In the top left corner, an African American girl is isolated in a circular cutout frame. The cropping of the photograph, coupled
with the layout of the image in a circular shape, isolates the girl and makes her
appear as though she is under surveillance—seen as if through the camera's
circular lens.

Another theme of the feature is a focus on children. Few images in the feature show children with adults. The dominant figure is a crying child, with no
adult anywhere present. The irony of the title "Children of the *Forgotten Man!*"
is clear, because the sharecropper himself, the "forgotten man," is utterly absent in the photographs. The mothers, while present, appear passive and anxious. An Arthur Rothstein photograph of a pregnant mother leaning in the
doorway, with three children of various ages gathered near her, is captioned,
"More Children Indoors: Sharecropper children are often hungry. Under-
sized, scrawny, with large heads, misshapen bodies, they are easy prey of disease" ("Children" 19). Using vivid and crude language, the caption implies

that the mother, though present, cannot care for her brood. The hint of "more children indoors" suggests slyly that the place is literally overrun with children, that the perhaps excessively fertile mother cannot care for her "scrawny" and "misshapen" offspring. In fact, a check of the Historical Section file in the Library of Congress reveals that there are several images made by Rothstein of this family; they show only one additional child not featured among the group of three here, not the unspecified large brood implied by the caption. As a result of the feature's emphasis on children, the reader/viewer's *direct* visual encounters with the poor happen with the children, not the adults. The impulse on the part of editors is obvious: Use children to create pity in the viewer, and sympathy for the plight of the poor, by showing those most innocent and helpless in the face of poverty. Yet, at the same time, the emphasis on children in both features has the effect of infantilizing (and thus disempowering) the poor, particularly the non-White poor.

The two images of African-American children demonstrate this point most vividly, and suggest another aspect of this feature's rhetorical stance: its reliance on dramatic captions to accompany the images. LOOK uses both images and captions to point out that although tenancy impacts both Black and White, the "news" is that Whites are suffering. We can see this most vividly in the photograph of the three boys at the water pump. The barefoot children stare at the camera from inside of an oddly cropped image that, like the image of the African-American girl, frankly invites surveillance. The caption below the image reads:

Many Sharecroppers are Negroes

But not as many in proportion to whites as there used to be. Fifteen years ago 65 out of 100 croppers were Negroes. The tables are turned now and there are 60 whites and only 40 Negroes in every 100 sharecroppers. ("Children" 19)

Here the images of Black children are deployed to reference the shift toward greater White tenancy, erasing the children's experience at the same time that it is presented visually. Although White adults do appear in the guise of the passive mother, no African-American adults appear in the feature; they may be the truly "forgotten men" and women LOOK so dramatically announces. The feature's reliance on images of Black children not only functions to erase the Black experience of tenancy from consideration, but it does something more insidious by erasing the African-American *adult* experience entirely. Thus LOOK not only infantilizes the poor, but particularly the African-American poor, reinforcing plantation-era stereotypes about dependence and the "child-like" nature of the Black laborer.

The text not only infantilizes the poor and reinforces an interest in White sharecroppers, but it does so with often vivid crudeness. Indeed, the "factual"

nature of many of the captions is undercut by their tendency to dramatize the
conditions the captions are describing. So, for example, the sharecropper feature
declares, "Humanity Hits Bottom ... In the Deep South." In describing the dangers of unionizing, *LOOK* observes, "Black terror stalks the cotton fields." Head-
ings such as "black and white," "alone and hungry," "homeless," and "sharecroppers declare war" function to capture reader attention. At the same time,
the captions reinforce a narrow treatment of the issues facing the sharecroppers; the reader/viewer is given no context for understanding how the sharecroppers depicted came to be in this dire situation. The captions do offer some
information about sharecropping, explaining for example the "furnishing" system in which tenants buy food on high-interest credit from plantation owners
(18). But the "factual" information offered in the captions is not credited to any
kind of expert who might testify as to the accuracy of the facts. The feature does
suggest possibilities for change in the future, but here, too, little context is present. "Sharecroppers Declare War," announces the heading of one caption:

> Sharecroppers have organized a union. The plantation owners are fighting
> it. Floggings, kidnappings, and lynchings by night riders have resulted.
> Black terror stalks the cotton fields. But the union is growing and sticks to
> its demands for better pay (it asked $1.00 for a 10-hour day last spring). (19)

The caption here refers obliquely to the Southern Tenant Farmers Union
(STFU), actively organizing in the South (particularly in Arkansas) at the time.
Another caption goes on to suggest that the STFU has also "meant eviction for
hundreds of sharecroppers. They wander the rutted roads, no shelter, no relief, no food. Some are living in tents and old autos" (19). But unionization, one
potential solution readers might infer for themselves, is immediately dismissed by *LOOK* as a hopeless and downright dangerous option.

Although the photographs published in *LOOK* had great potential to expose
viewers to the FSA's plans, the picture story itself suggests that, really, there is
nothing to do but look. The magazine positions the reader/viewer to be a passive spectator, to see and consume images and text in a vacuum devoid of context or history. The cumulative impact of the feature, then, is that there is no
difference between the American sharecroppers and the "savage" taking a
wife in Zululand. Sharecroppers are just as much a "curiosity" to be looked at,
a "them" to be surveyed, as are the "savages" of Zululand or the celebrity centerfold in the bathtub. Although *LOOK*'s picture stories were ostensibly meant
to educate readers and generate sympathy for the poor, the content and layout
of the feature largely undermine such goals. By constructing the picture story
as a closed, relatively ahistorical narrative, *LOOK* constructs a rhetoric of poverty that keeps the reader on the outside "LOOK"ing in.

Yet again, at this point let us break away from my sketch in order to determine where we are in the construction of a rhetorical history of the *LOOK*

feature. In the last several pages, I have moved beyond issues of *production* to consider issues of *reproduction*, attempting to understand the feature's placement within the magazine itself and the themes raised by its peculiar arrangement of images and text. Yet we cannot stop here, for we have yet to take account of circulation. In moving to the realm of circulation, we attend to the feature in terms of the way it fits into broader social, political, and institutional discourses about poverty circulating during the Depression. The move to circulation, as we shall see, allows us to tap into the "elusive" yet vital realm of Zarefsky's fourth sense of rhetorical history: the rhetorical study of historical events.

THE RHETORICAL STUDY OF HISTORICAL EVENTS: VISUAL RHETORICS OF POVERTY AND LOOK

Circulation

LOOK's marriage of the FSA photographs with vivid, largely ahistorical captions produces a rhetoric of poverty that makes certain narratives about the poor available while curtailing the availability of others. As I have just briefly sketched, the sharecropper feature says little, if at all, about the causes of the poverty depicted in the images, nor does it suggest much in the way of solutions to the problems so vividly visualized. *LOOK's* failure to do so is partly the result of the generic constraints of the picture magazine. *LOOK* was never meant to be a "news" magazine. Bookended by picture stories that reflect *LOOK's* primary investment in human interest stories—celebrity entertainment and "curiosities"—the sharecropper feature stands in isolation from the current events of the day. Each picture story, even the sharecropper story, is presented as a hermetically sealed narrative. The reader is not encouraged to go beyond the narrative for further investigation of the issues, for this is not the function of the magazine. *LOOK's* primary interest is in showing—in encouraging (indeed, commanding) the viewer to LOOK. Realization of these limitations of the genre of the picture magazine is vital if we are to understand how the *LOOK* feature operates within broader public attitudes about rural poverty as well as in terms of the institutional goals of the FSA.

The *LOOK* feature needs to be understood in terms of how it participates in a complex web of discourses about poverty during the Depression. Neil Betten argues that discourses about poverty in the United States have historically operated along a continuum between the "hostile view" and the "environmental view." What Betten calls "the hostile view" treated poverty as a moral flaw, "a sickness freely chosen through laziness, drinking, extravagance and sexual vices" (3). These rhetorics of poverty resounded with echoes of what William Ryan has called "blaming the victim"—if one were poor, one had somehow caused that poverty. A second view, the "environmental" view, argued that poverty was not always the result of an individual's failings, but of structural inequities in the socioeconomic system. By the early 20th century, for example, progressive-era social reformers were coming to define rural poverty in terms of the oppressive nature of the socioeconomic structure of the farm tenancy system that left sharecroppers at the bottom of the economic ladder.

It might be tempting, then, to suggest that the *LOOK* feature simply communicates a "hostile view" of poverty that blames the victim and suggests moral failings are the cause of the sharecroppers' poverty. Although, as I have shown, there is evidence for such a reading, such a conclusion would not reflect the complexities of Depression-era rhetorics of poverty. As many scholars of poverty discourse have shown, an era's conception of poverty is not "either/or." Robert Asen argues that a range of views about the poor appear and reappear throughout American history, "subjected to alternative inflections, recombinations, and reversals as advocates have deployed the discourses of poverty in a shifting and conflicted terrain" (25). For example, just as the *LOOK* essay seems to invite a hostile reading of the sharecroppers' plight through its use of vivid images and dramatic text, it also suggests a more environmental view through its deployment of the powerful trope of the "forgotten man." Revived by Roosevelt during his 1932 presidential campaign, by 1937 the forgotten man was a powerful symbol of both the promise of American capitalism and its apparent failure; the forgotten man is not to blame for his poverty, but rather is someone swept up by forces largely beyond his control. The trope of the forgotten man was rhetorically available not only in political discourse, but in art and popular culture, too; by the late 1930s, references to the "forgotten man" were quite frequent in the visual arts, movies, and popular songs.

Such ambiguous blending of the hostile and environmental views persisted in government, as well, often influenced by the paternalism for which Roosevelt was so legendary. Though Roosevelt championed the right to economic security for all citizens, Roosevelt and his New Deal appointees agonized over "the dole." In his second inaugural address, Roosevelt described "the need to find through government the instrument of our united purpose to solve for the individual the ever-rising problems of a complex civilization"—thus seemingly invoking an environmental view of poverty. Yet Roosevelt also consistently spoke of his preference for work relief over "cash" relief because he feared creating a population of dependent individuals (127). Often, such conflicting views of poverty were articulated by members of the public as well, with bizarre inconsistencies. In 1938, the FSA participated in a photography exhibit in New York City. Many of the agency's most powerful images of the poor were hung, and visitors were provided comment cards on which to write their reactions. One visitor wrote, "Wonderful pictures! Pitiful sights! They need help sooner than many worthless W.P.A. [Works Progress Administration] workers" ("FSA Picture Comments" 18–29 Apr. 1938). In one sentence, the viewer managed both to praise and pity the individuals in the exhibit, who were apparently the blameless and deserving poor, and caricature WPA workers who, apparently, were not.

Despite recognizing these complex rhetorics of poverty circulating during the Depression, we might still wonder why Roy Stryker would have pursued publication of the FSA photographs in the pages of a magazine such as *LOOK*. I noted previously that Stryker approved of the ways in which the images were arranged in the sharecropper feature. In addition, he even praised the use of crude and vivid captions. He wrote to Mike Cowles, "May I compliment you on the frank captions which you attached to these pictures. You certainly 'shot the works' on your captions here" (6 Feb. 1937). Why would Stryker endorse such representations of the poor? The question may be addressed by turning to what we know about the agencies for which the photographs were made and the institutional constraints facing Stryker as he struggled to keep his photography project afloat.

The FSA, and its predecessor the Resettlement Administration (or RA), was founded on the assumption that the very structure of American agriculture needed to be radically changed if rural poverty were to be conquered. A 1935 government pamphlet introducing the Resettlement Administration observed, "American agriculture is undergoing fundamental changes." These changes were changes to the very socioeconomic foundations of agriculture: "Rapidity of communication and transportation, mechanization, scientific advances, the decreased growth of population, spoilation of land resources have developed a new set of national economic concepts and problems" (Resettlement Administration 1). Part of the Historical Section photographers' job was to account for these changes by visualizing their effects on individuals. The Historical Section's goals, however, were often not shared by those in power in Washington. The Historical Section was consistently threatened with extinction, its goals questioned by those in Congress in charge of the budgets of the FSA. Why, many in Congress wondered, did the FSA need to spend so much time, energy, and money on making "mere photographs"? Surely there were other ways to spend money. Given such institutional constraints, Stryker's apparent appreciation of the images in *LOOK* must be understood at least in part as his desire to protect the Historical Section by demonstrating the relevance of the work to the largest number of people possible.

Another reason why Stryker might not have found the representation of the poor in *LOOK* to be particularly objectionable is that the FSA photographs circulated in a number of different contexts, so the images themselves would not necessarily be tied in the minds of the public to a single rhetoric of poverty. The images were used to illustrate government publications and exhibits, displayed in the art contexts of museums and galleries, and published in numerous periodicals. For example, the social welfare journal *Survey Graphic* circulated the FSA photographs to support a social science rhetoric of poverty that sought to demonstrate the importance of federal, bureaucratic solutions designed to manage rural poverty "scientifically" (Finnegan "Social Engineering"). In attempting to understand the rhetorics of poverty made available in *LOOK*, then, it is important to recognize the fluidity of the circulation of the FSA photographs. Because the FSA images circulated in a range of contexts and tapped into the complex variety of discourses about poverty during the Depression, they need to be understood as both *products* of that history of poverty discourse as well as a *process* by which poverty itself was visualized.

CONCLUSION

In this essay I have proposed and modeled a way of doing rhetorical history of the visual that accounts for three key moments in the life of photographs: production, reproduction, and circulation. Although it may be easier to envision how one might do a rhetorical history of a more traditional text such as Roosevelt's second inaugural address, the path one should take when engaging visual culture may seem less obvious. Yet perhaps the differences are not so great after all if we utilize the tools of rhetorical history itself. I have suggested a way that we might invigorate our study of visual culture with a methodology that accounts for both the history of images as rhetorical events and the rhetoric of images as historical events. For those of us interested in "defining visual rhetorics," the issue of methodology would seem to be particularly important. A definition of visual rhetoric(s) alone cannot be useful unless it simultaneously suggests a way of seeing that combines an understanding of the unique qualities of visual discourse with a rhetorical sensibility that can account for how visual discourse comes to mean something in the public sphere. It is my hope that I have at least gestured toward one productive possibility here.

ACKNOWLEDGMENTS

The author wishes to thank Michèle Koven, Charles Hill, and Marguerite Helmers for their helpful feedback on earlier drafts of this chapter. Earlier versions of these ideas were presented at a roundtable discussion, "Visual Rhetoric and Rhetorical History: Exploring the Connections," at the National Communication Association convention in Atlanta, Georgia in November 2001, and at the Rhetoric Society of America meeting in Las Vegas, Nevada in May 2002. A more detailed analysis of FSA photography in *LOOK* magazine may be found in Cara A. Finnegan, *Picturing Poverty* 168–219.

NOTES

1. Richard Lanham defines *ekphrasis* (or, alternatively, *ecphrasis*), as "a self-contained description" that can be "inserted into a fitting place in a discourse."

It is a subcategory of *enargia*, a "vivid description which recreates something or someone, as several theorists say, 'before your very eyes'." In Latin, *ekphrasis* would be translated as *descriptio* or description, one of the techniques of rhetorical amplification. See Lanham 62, 64; see also Thomas O. Sloane 220–221.

2. On the implications of ocularcentrism for philosophy and visual culture, see Jay; Levin; Snyder; Jenks; and Crary.

3. The terms, *pictorial text* and *textual picture* are W. J. T. Mitchell's; see Mitchell.

4. A search of Humanities Abstracts, Dissertation Abstracts, and MLA International Bibliography in July 2002 produced, respectively, 15, 14, and 23 matches to the search phrase "visual rhetoric" for the years 1995–2002.

5. The most explicit attempt at method is Sonja K. Foss, "A Rhetorical Schema for the Evaluation of Visual Imagery."

6. This history has been traced by, among others, Medhurst and Benson.

7. See Walter Benjamin's "The Work of Art in the Age of Mechanical Reproduction" and "A Small History of Photography."

8. The invention of the halftone process in the late 19th century made such reproduction possible; see Taft 436–446; Mott 3–10. On the technical aspects of producing *Life* in the mid-1930s, see Spencer; Wainwright; Baughman.

9. For a detailed account of the assumptions grounding the picture magazines' approach to narrative, especially *LOOK*'s, see Mich and Eberman.

10. I would argue that much of what passes for "rhetorical analysis" of visual images operates at this level by invoking (either explicitly or implicitly) Barthes' notions of "coded" and "non-coded" messages to get at the semiotics of meaning in a given context. Thomas Farrell has called this approach "the study of images as little visual speeches" and suggests that it only takes us so far in understanding the broader role of visual culture in the public sphere; I agree. See Barthes; Farrell, personal communication with the author.

11. The Historical Section photographs are catalogued and numbered in the FSA-OWI Collection in the Prints and Photographs division of the Library of Congress. Each Library of Congress negative number contains a letter designating the format in which the image was made; the letter "M" indicates a 35-mm photograph.

WORKS CITED

Asen, Robert. *Visions of Poverty: Welfare Policy and Political Imagination.* East Lansing: Michigan State UP, 2002.

"Auto Kills Woman Before Your Eyes!" *LOOK* Feb. 1937: 14.

Barthes, Roland. "The Rhetoric of the Image." *Image—Music—Text.* New York: Hill and Wang, 1977: 32–51.

Baughman, James L. *Henry R. Luce and the Rise of the American News Media.* Boston: Twayne, 1987.

Benjamin, Walter. "A Small History of Photography." *One Way Street and Other Writings.* London: Verso, 1985: 240–257.

—. "The Work of Art in the Age of Mechanical Reproduction." *Illuminations: Essays and Reflections.* Ed. Hannah Arendt. New York: Schocken Books, 1968: 217–251.

Benson, Thomas W. "History, Criticism, and Theory in the Study of American Rhetoric." *American Rhetoric: Context and Criticism.* Ed. Thomas W. Benson. Carbondale, IL: Southern Illinois UP, 1989: 1–18.

Betten, Neil. "American Attitudes Toward the Poor: A Historical Overview." *Current History* 65 (July 1973): 1–5.

Blakesley, David, and Collin Brooke. "Introduction: Notes on Visual Rhetoric." *Enculturation* 3 (Fall 2001) <http://enculturation.gmu.edu/3_2/introduction.html> 12 May 2003.

Carlebach, Michael. *American Photojournalism Comes of Age.* Washington, DC: Smithsonian Institution P, 1997.

"Children of the Forgotten Man! LOOK Visits the Sharecropper." *Look* Mar. 1937: 18–19.

Cowles, Gardner, Jr. Letter to Roy Stryker. 23 Nov. 1936. Roy Emerson Stryker Papers, series 1, microfilm reel 1. Photographic Archive, University of Louisville, Louisville, KY.

Crary, Jonathan. *Techniques of the Observer: On Vision and Modernity in the Nineteenth Century.* Cambridge: MIT P, 1990.

Derrida, Jacques. *Of Grammatology.* Trans. Gayatri Chakravorty Spivak. Baltimore: Johns Hopkins Press, 1974.

Edwards, Jackson. "One Every Minute: The Picture Magazine." *Scribner's* May 1938: 17–23; 102–103.

Farrell, Thomas B. *Norms of Rhetorical Culture.* New Haven: Yale UP, 1993.

Finnegan, Cara A. "Documentary as Art in *U.S. Camera.*" *Rhetoric Society Quarterly* 31 (Spring 2001): 37–67.

—*Picturing Poverty: Print Culture and FSA Photographs.* Washington, DC: Smithsonian Books, 2003.

—. "Social Engineering, Visual Politics and the New Deal: FSA Photography in *Survey Graphic.*" *Rhetoric and Public Affairs* 3 (Fall 2000): 333–362.

Foss, Sonja K. "A Rhetorical Schema for the Evaluation of Visual Imagery." *Communication Studies* 45 (1994): 213–224.

"FSA Picture Comments." 18–29 Apr. 1938. Roy Emerson Stryker Papers, series 2, microfilm reel 6. Photographic Archive, University of Louisville, Louisville, KY.

Jay, Martin. *Downcast Eyes: The Denigration of Vision in Twentieth-Century French Thought.* Berkeley: U of California P, 1993.

Jenks, Chris. "The Centrality of the Eye in Western Culture: An Introduction." *Visual Culture.* Ed. Chris Jenks. New York: Routledge, 1995. 1–25.

Lanham, Richard. *A Handlist of Rhetorical Terms,* 2nd ed. Berkeley: U of California P, 1991.

Levin, David M. (Ed.). *Modernity and the Hegemony of Vision.* Berkeley: U of California P, 1993.

Medhurst, Martin. "The Academic Study of Public Address: A Tradition in Transition." *Landmark Essays on American Public Address.* Ed. Martin Medhurst. Davis, CA: Hermagoras Press, 1993. xi–xliii.

Mich, Daniel D., and Edwin Eberman. *The Technique of the Picture Story: A Practical Guide to the Production of Visual Articles.* New York: McGraw-Hill, 1945.

Mitchell, W. J. T. *Picture Theory: Essays on Verbal and Visual Representation.* Chicago: U of Chicago P, 1994.

Mott, Frank Luther. *A History of American Magazines, Vol. IV: 1885–1905.* Cambridge: Harvard UP, 1957.

"Myrna Loy: Dream Wife of a Million Men." *LOOK* Mar. 1937: 20–21.

"Picture Papers." *The New Republic* 24 Mar. 1937: 197.

The Resettlement Administration. Washington, DC: Resettlement Administration, 1935.

Roosevelt, Franklin D. "Second Inaugural Address." *The Essential Franklin Delano Roosevelt.* Ed. John G. Hunt. New York: Gramercy Books, 1995: 127–132.

Ryan, William. *Blaming the Victim.* New York: Vintage Books, 1976.

Sloane, Thomas O. *Encyclopedia of Rhetoric.* New York: Oxford UP, 2001.

Snyder, Joel. "Picturing Vision." *Critical Inquiry* 6 (Spring 1980): 499–526.

Spencer, Otha Cleo. "Twenty Years of 'Life': A Study of Time, Inc.'s Picture Magazine and Its Contributions to Photojournalism." Diss., U of Missouri, 1958.

Stryker, Roy. Letter to Gardner Cowles, Jr. 2 Dec. 1936. Roy Emerson Stryker Papers, series 1, microfilm reel 1. Photographic Archive, University of Louisville, Louisville, KY.

—. Letter to Gardner Cowles, Jr. 6 Feb. 1937. Roy Emerson Stryker Papers, series 1, microfilm reel 1. Photographic Archive, University of Louisville, Louisville, KY.

Taft, Robert. *Photography and the American Scene.* New York: Dover, 1938.

Turner, Kathleen J. "Rhetorical History as Social Construction: The Challenge and the Promise." *Doing Rhetorical History: Concepts and Cases.* Ed. Kathleen J. Turner. Tuscaloosa, AL: U of Alabama P, 1998: 1–15.

"The U.S. Minicam Boom." *Fortune* Oct. 1936: 125–129+.

Wainwright, Loudon. *The Great American Magazine: An Inside History of Life.* New York: Alfred A. Knopf, 1986.

Zarefsky, David. "Four Senses of Rhetorical History." *Doing Rhetorical History: Concepts and Cases.* Ed. Kathleen J. Turner. Tuscaloosa, AL: U of Alabama P, 1998: 19–32.

CHAPTER TEN

Melting-Pot Ideology, Modernist Aesthetics, and the Emergence of Graphical Conventions: The Statistical Atlases of the United States, 1874–1925

Charles Kostelnick

Visual rhetoric in technical, business, and professional communication spans a wide array of forms, ranging from text and screen design, to pictures and illustrations, to the display of quantitative information. These forms constitute a visual language that, like verbal language, rhetors adapt to a specific audience, purpose, and context. In a given rhetorical situation, for example, a document designer can choose a certain type style and size, arrange text on a page, and insert graphical elements to make the page or screen more accessible to readers, to emphasize information, and to create an inviting tone. Similarly, the designer can rhetorically tailor pictures to a given situation by selecting certain information to represent, using an appropriate style, and deploying drawing conventions (textures, color-coding). Likewise, the designer can shape quantitative information by organizing and articulating it within a generic structure (pie chart, bar chart, line graph; see Kostelnick, "Conflicting"; Kostelnick and Roberts 263–308). All of these rhetorical strategies are easier to implement than in the past because of the contemporary technology of design software, laser printers, and computer networking.

Although visual rhetoric always begins with a designer shaping visual language for a specific audience and purpose and culminates with a reader interpreting that language in a specific situation—e.g., interpreting a diagram to set up a VCR in a living room—that specific rhetorical act is embedded in a much larger and more social set of rhetorical circumstances. Visual language develops within discourse communities that enculturate its members in its conventional codes, and those codes embody cultural values and norms, including aesthetics. These social factors are inherently rhetorical because they profoundly influence how, at a given historical moment, communities use visual language to achieve certain ends.

One such historical moment occurs in 19th-century America with the emergence of data displays to represent statistical information. Beginning with the 1870 census, collections of data displays called "statistical atlases" were created to visualize the progress of the nation. Statistical atlases were published for six consecutive censuses (1870 to 1920), five of them by the U.S. government. Before the atlases, census data were published as uninviting tables, which hindered comparisons and limited the public's access to the information. The U.S. statistical atlases represented an emerging trend, which began earlier in Europe, to display data about nation states; atlases strengthened the national identities of the countries that issued them; the first U.S. atlas (1874) also symbolized the scientific progress of the nation (Monmonier 1, 4). A landmark in information design, the U.S. statistical atlases collectively stand as one of the most public acts of visual rhetoric in the nation's history. They played a pivotal role in the development of conventional forms to represent data, forms that we now largely take for granted. By visualizing a rapidly changing nation transformed by westward expansion and the assimilation of immigrants, the designers of the atlases shaped attitudes about public policy. They enhanced their visual arguments by imbuing their designs with the aesthetic values of the era, initially deploying a decorative Victorian style and then shifting to modernism, which fostered universal forms and aimed to objectify representations of cultural diversity by making them appear economical and perceptually transparent.

In this chapter, then, I will explore how the statistical atlases for the 1870 to 1920 censuses reveal the rhetorical nature of data displays in a larger social context. I will provide historical background that sets the stage for the design of the atlases, then examine how the atlases developed and certified data design conventions by teaching Americans how to interpret a wide variety of graphical forms. I will examine how those forms created visual arguments about the progress of the nation, particularly the assimilation of immigrants, and how they embodied the aesthetic values of the era, initially projecting a Victorian sensibility and later modernism and its ideology of cultural homogeneity.

BACKGROUND FOR DATA DISPLAY OF THE STATISTICAL ATLASES

The graphical display of economic and demographic data was a relatively new phenomenon in the 19th century, having earlier been applied primarily in science, mathematics, and engineering. Publications like the *Philosophical Transactions of the Royal Society* included line graphs as early as the late 17th century to display weather data, and later inventor James Watt used indicator diagrams to measure steam power (Funkhouser 289; Biderman 15). In the late

18th century William Playfair applied graphing techniques to economic data—trade, national debt, revenues—an innovation that greatly expanded their audiences. In the 19th century, techniques for displaying data continued to develop and proliferate, particularly in disciplines such as engineering, medicine, and the natural and social sciences.

Beginning with the 1850 census, the U.S. government started collecting a variety of economic and social data, which formed detailed factual profiles of the nation that organized its citizens into what Daniel Boorstin calls "statistical communities" (165–173). The statistical atlases were designed to make this wealth of census data more accessible to the public, thereby fostering civic participation. According to the U.S. Secretary of the Interior, the first atlas (1874) was intended:

> ... for distribution to public libraries, learned societies, colleges and academies, with a view to promote that higher kind of political education which has hitherto been so greatly neglected in this country, but toward which the attention of the general public, as well as of instructors and students, is now being turned, with the most lively interest. (Walker, Preface 1)

Because many of these readers were unfamiliar with the visual language of data displays, the atlases had immense instructional value, educating citizens not only in the progress of the nation but also in visual literacy.

The atlases completely transformed the design and reception of census data, making them more compelling and comprehensible to the public. The first three atlases (for the 1870, 1880, and 1890 censuses) were published as folios and included a wide array of maps, charts, and graphs, many of them in full color (Walker; Hewes and Gannet; Gannett, *Statistical, Eleventh*). The second set of three atlases (for the 1900, 1910, and 1920 censuses) were published as smaller quarto-sized volumes, the last two rendered chiefly in black and white (Gannett, *Statistical, Twelfth*; Sloane, *Statistical, Thirteenth and Fourteenth*).[1] The primary transformation in statistical display occurred in the three folio atlases, heroic acts of visual rhetoric that were produced during the founding era of statistical graphics (when "statistics" still largely meant data about "states"). The first atlas (for the 1870 census), the folio with the fewest pages, included over 50 plates, many of which contained numerous displays that together comprised a total of 1,200 figures (Walker, Preface 1). The first atlas contained a wide variety of "illustrations," which were classified into two types: "Geographical" and "Geometrical." The former consisted of maps with various systems for coding data, both physical and demographic, and the latter were constructed of "lines and plane figures" (Walker, Preface 1–2). The Geometrical illustrations included an array of configurations, including population distribution charts (males on one side, females on the other), area charts, line graphs, pie charts, percent charts, and several novel displays. Maps accounted for about 2 / 3 of the plates, a proportion that shifted in subsequent atlases as other forms were introduced, including rank charts and wind roses (circular charts showing monthly distributions of deaths and diseases).

The graphical displays in the initial 1874 atlas visualized the distribution of people across the country, their religious affiliations, occupations, literacy, mortality rates, and health (including charts for blindness, deafness, idiocy, and insanity). The 1883 atlas, published by Charles Scribner's, included a more comprehensive design of the census data, although it contained a smaller range of display types, mainly maps, line graphs, and horizontal bar charts, the latter of which often appeared in close proximity on the same plate. The 1883 atlas also visualized more economic data—about occupations, agricultural production, manufacturing, finance, and other business activities (Hewes and Gannett). The 1898 atlas contained probably the richest variety of designs, introducing some new forms (e.g., wind roses) as well as displaying variations of existing forms, with increased emphasis on visualizing data about the burgeoning foreign population (Gannett, *Statistical, Eleventh*). The quarto-sized 1903 atlas refined and consolidated existing forms, which were then further winnowed down in the 1914 and 1925 black-and-white editions (Gannett, *Statistical, Twelfth*; Sloane, *Statistical, Thirteenth and Fourteenth*).

Over the half century that the U.S. atlases appeared before the public, they profoundly shaped visual discourse about statistical data. Before the 1874 atlas appeared, graphical display in the United States lagged behind practices in Europe, which developed rapidly during the nineteenth century (see Funkhouser). Some of the U.S. atlases' designers—civil servants, academics, and members of professional organizations, including the American Statistical Association—were undoubtedly familiar with European developments in data display (see Dahmann 2). International statistical congresses that were held in Europe provided a forum for deliberating about graphical methods, but a consensus about conventional practices was not reached (Funkhouser 311–322). Having considerable leeway to visualize census data, the designers of the U.S. atlases both modeled contemporary forms and invented their own, in the process sanctioning a variety of genres, teaching American readers how to interpret them, and building reader expectations.

THE EMERGENCE OF DATA DISPLAY CONVENTIONS

Design is inherently rhetorical because its forms are largely negotiated and shared by groups of users, or visual discourse communities (see Kostelnick and Hassett 24–30). By socially constructing design forms, visual discourse communities create, codify, and perpetuate conventional practices, which engender expectations among its members. Those processes occur with all forms of visual language—from architecture (houses, banks, campus buildings) to consumer products (furniture, cars, stereos) to information design, including typography (left justification, boldface for emphasis), screen design (icons, pull-down menus), pictures (perspective, cross-sectional views), and data displays (pie charts, line graphs). Conventions also vary in their flexibility and in the size of their currencies (the numbers of users who deploy and interpret them), and they evolve differently: Some have a long history (paragraphing, left-to-right lineation), others are relatively new (screen design, hypertext), and others have virtually become extinct (handwriting styles for business). Regardless of their profiles, all conventions share one crucial element—a supporting visual discourse community, which can be large and amorphous (a culture) or small and well defined (a corporation, a discipline; see Kostelnick and Hassett 36–39, 58–66, 83–96).

The atlases played a key role in shaping conventional data display practices, supplying a hinge between the inchoate, experimental forms of the 19th century, which were largely the domain of specialized disciplinary communities, and the emerging conventions of the 20th century, which served a much larger and increasingly multi-ethnic audience of U.S. citizens. The atlases were a laboratory for visually representing census data, encompassing a rich variety of graphical displays, several of which are recreated conceptually in Fig. 10.1. Forms like the data density map (a, b), pie chart (g), bar chart (j), and line graph (k) developed strong conventional status over the past century and today claim enormously large currencies. Other forms like the population distribution chart (c), percent chart (f), rank chart (i), and wind rose (l; also known as a polar chart) still have conventional status, though they claim smaller currencies. The currencies of other forms like the rectilinear area chart (m) and the circle chart (h) were short-lived and have long since evaporated. For example, the circle chart (h) was used in the 1874 atlas to compare the size of the blind population in each state with that of the previous census, with the inner circle displaying the 1860 population, the outer circle the 1870 population, and the shaded area the difference between them—i.e., the thicker the filled area the greater the increase in that state's blind population (Walker, Plate LI).

Other forms were entirely novel: The chart shown in Fig. 10.1d, which appeared in the 1874 atlas (Walker, Plate XXXVa), displays the evolution of the national debt from the founding of the nation through the high-debt bulge of the Civil War. Fig. 10.1n, which appeared in the 1898 atlas (Gannett, *Statistical, Eleventh*, Plate 22), displays the evolution of the U.S. population since the first census (at the top), with native Whites shown in the middle, Blacks on the right, immigrants on the left, and a summary below in the form of a rectilinear area chart. Numerous bi-polar population distribution charts also appeared in the 1874 atlas, showing males on one side and females on the other according to age groups, with the gender having the larger population shaded on its side. The compiler of the 1874 atlas, Francis Walker, considered these charts "to be a novelty in the graphic illustration of Statistics" (Walker, Preface 2; see, for example, Plates XLVII-L). Figure 10.2 shows a small segment of a plate contain-

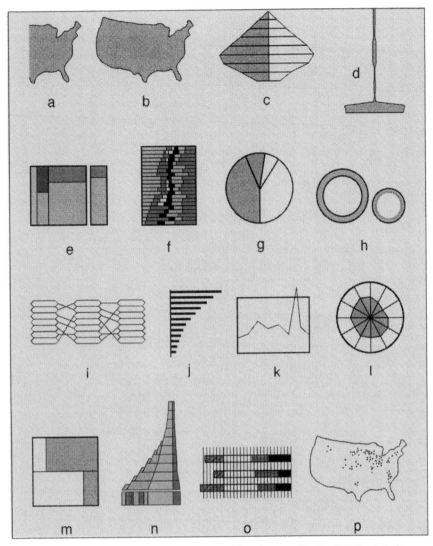

FIG. 10.1.   Sampling of Data Design Forms That Appeared in the U.S. Statistical
Atlases.

ing numerous such charts, with males outnumbering females in each of them,
particularly in western states like Nebraska and Nevada. Bi-polar charts appeared again in 1898 and succeeding atlases to represent population data divis-
ible into two distinct but relatively equal groups. To many early readers of the
folio atlases, most of these forms were initially novel and supplied fresh, inviting, and even challenging interpretive experiences: Those readers had little

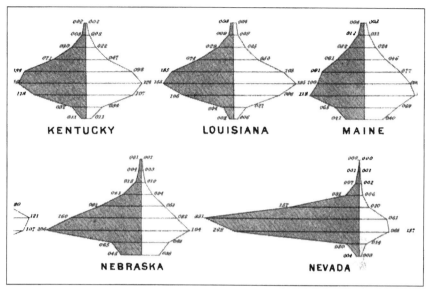

FIG. 10.2. Bi-Polar Charts from the 1874 Statistical Atlas Showing the Distribution by Sex of the Foreign-Born Population of States (Walker, Plate XXXIX).

sense of what was, or would become, conventional; to them, a pie chart may have looked as exotic as the debt or bi-polar chart.

Many graphical displays in the atlases underwent novel adaptations because their conventional boundaries had not yet been established and data display genres themselves still lacked stability. For example, early bar and line graphs with values that exceeded the plot frame were typically adapted to accommodate the data. In the 1883 atlas, the designer of the bar graph in Fig. 10.3 represents two variables (Agricultural Laborers and Farmers and Planters) that vastly exceed the horizontal baseline by snaking their bars back and forth until they accumulate their total values. Dozens of bar graphs in the 1883 atlas use this novel and ingenious technique (see, for example, Hewes and Gannett, Plates 34 and 35). A similar adaptation is used for line graphs with anomalous values (Fig. 10.1k), which by extending or exceeding the plot frame (Fig. 10.1k), climb up the plate like wild, unpruned branches (see Hewes and Gannett, Plates 108 and 123). Although today's readers might find these practices curious or bizarre, they were not uncommon in the past (for examples, see Tufte, *Envisioning* 106–7). In the 19th century, conventions for displaying statistical data remained unsettled, and because the displays were executed by hand, designers had both the opportunity and the exigency to improvise. The large public audiences of the early atlases were no doubt receptive to these practices because they were still largely unenculterated in emerging genres like bi-polar, pie, and area charts.

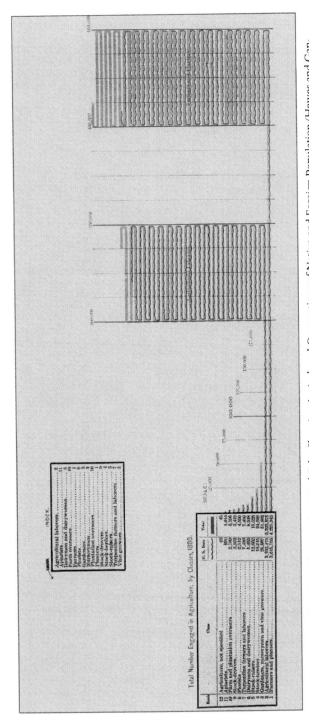

FIG. 10.3. Bar Chart from the 1883 Statistical Atlas Showing Agricultural Occupations of Native and Foreign Population (Hewes and Gannet, Plate 64). Courtesy of the Rare Book and Special Collections Department of the Northern Illinois University Libraries, Northern Illinois University, DeKalb, Illinois.

However, design novelty combined with conventional naiveté placed interpretive demands on readers. To compensate, the folio atlases (particularly the 1874 and 1898 atlases) provide ample instruction in visual literacy. Although maps and line graphs were presumed to be less challenging to readers and therefore receive little, if any, textual explanation, many charts in the 1874 atlas are explained at length in the Preface and Introduction and on the notes on the plates, leaving little to the interpretive hunches of readers.[2] Readers are taught, for example, how to read bi-polar population distribution charts (Figs. 10.1c and 10.2), which isn't surprising because they are identified as an original genre (Walker, Preface 2). However, readers also receive extensive instruction in reading pie charts, a genre that William Playfair experimented with 70 to 80 years earlier in England but with which U.S. readers may have had little prior experience. Specifically, readers are taught how to interpret a pie chart that shows four groups of blind people in the United States—males and females, native and foreign—as shown in Fig. 10.1g, with the males in the shaded segments and foreigners (males and females) in the two smaller segments (Walker, Plate LI). These divisions of the pie chart are compared to hands on a clock:

> If we may compare the radii of the circle to the hands of a clock (supposing these to be, instead of two, four, all of equal length), one hand, in these figures, always stands at six o'clock, and the others are moved around at various angles to it and to each other, to represent the distribution indicated above. (Walker, Preface 2)

The Preface and Introduction then tell readers how to interpret each of the four segments of the pie chart, instruction that would likely strike contemporary readers, fully enculturated in the genre of the pie chart, as both gratuitous and condescending.

Extensive explanations also accompanied area charts, novel forms that, unlike bi-polar charts and pie charts, no longer claim conventional status. For example, a plate in the 1874 atlas uses square area charts to represent "Church Accommodation" by religious groups and states (see Fig. 10.4). Each square contains five colored bars, four representing each state's major denominations (e.g., Methodists, Baptists, Presbyterians, Roman Catholics, etc.) and the fifth showing all others combined. The note at the top of the plate explains this system of representation:

> The interior squares represent the proportion of the population which is provided for by the aggregate sittings in the churches of all denominations. The shaded interval between the inner and out squares represents the population for which no church accommodation is provided. Where the aggregate church accommodation equals or exceeds the population over 10 years of age the shaded interval disappears. (Walker, Plate XXXI)

FIG. 10.4.   Field of Square Area Charts from the 1874 Statistical Atlas Showing
Church Accommodation by State (Walker, Plate XXXI).

So, for example, the square for Ohio (fifth row, second from the right) has no "shaded interval" and therefore has room in its churches to accommodate virtually everyone; on the other hand, Nebraska (directly above it) has a large "shaded interval" and therefore has far fewer spaces in its churches than its population. Fig. 10.1e shows another variation on the area chart that appears on a field of like charts (Walker, Plate XX), each of which shows the relative size and composition of a given state's present population (the square on the left) as well as of the native population that emigrated from the state (the rectangle on the right). Other than intuitively correlating area with population size, readers must rely on explanations in the text (Walker, Preface 3) and at the top of plate to interpret this complex system of representation.

Such explanations were far less frequent in the 1883 atlas, which used primarily maps and horizontal bar graphs. The superiority of "simple *linear*" diagrams (vii), which included bar and line graphs, was noted by Hewes and Gannet in their Preface: "Of the many kinds of diagrams hitherto used in the illustration of statistical facts, this form is at once the simplest and the most effective" (vii). Empirical research has largely since corroborated Hewes and Gannett's choice of horizontal bar graphs by finding that readers can more accurately compare data plotted along a scale extending from a baseline (Cleveland and McGill; see also Cochran, Albrecht, and Green). The 1898 atlas includes a larger variety of displays, and hence more explanations, although the explanations diminish markedly in subsequent atlases as the visual literary of readers increased and as the atlas designers shunned novelty in favor of conventional genres. In the later atlases (1914 and 1925) the variety of genres diminished, some genres (like the wind rose) disappeared, and other genres underwent additional refinements—for example, maps signified density with patterns and dots (Fig. 10.1p) rather than colors.

The atlases demonstrate a key principle of visual rhetoric—that information design is socialized by discourse communities that construct, adapt, and refine conventional practices and that enculturate users in those practices. As decade-by-decade snapshots in the evolution of data displays, the atlases modeled the process of convention building, as readers gradually became enculturated into genres that they came to understand and expect. Today, many of these forms—bar graphs, pie charts, bi-polar diagrams—have become so familiar that we don't question their conventional status as genres. This process of enculturation creates rhetorical efficiency as well as poses an interpretive problem because readers come to regard conventional forms as natural, direct representations of fact unmediated by the artificial lens of design (see Barton and Barton "Ideology"). For example, a designer might select a divided bar graph (similar to Fig. 10.1o), a conventional form with high currency, to show subdivisions among several quantities—for example, the relative health risks to consumers of various types of prescription drugs. Although deploying a divided bar graph may be more visually efficient than deploying pie charts or separate bars for each variable, the design may undermine the readers' ability to compare data because some bar segments won't share the same baseline, an interpretive problem that in this situation could have serious consequences for readers. Nonetheless, readers will likely accept this representation because it meets their expectations as a conventional genre.

As socially constructed forms of representation, data displays, like other forms of visual language, attain conventional status within the discourse communities in which they are deployed. Through the atlases, the U.S. government sanctioned data display genres that were widely disseminated among the American public, fostering both their currency and credibility. That process was rhetorically significant because it cultivated readers' expectations over half a century, a long process compared to convention building in other domains (corporations, universities), which through new management or visual identity programs can more rapidly transform their conventional languages.

DATA DISPLAYS AS VISUAL ARGUMENTS

Visual language is also rhetorically charged because designers deploy it in specific situations to achieve certain ends. In a given situation the designer can deploy visual language to foreground or embed information, help readers organize it, speak with a certain tone, foster credibility, and perform other functions that influence readers' interpretations. Even when various forms of visual language—typefaces, illustrations, icons, screen designs—are deployed to represent the most mundane information, they can embody elements that direct attention, persuade, and shape attitudes. An entirely artificial form like a data display can be particularly tendentious because designers have a great deal of leeway to visualize data within the universe of conventional genres. That flexibility also allows designers to manipulate data, which has generated widespread concern about the ethical abuses of data design.

In the late 19th century, however, such concerns did not yet pervade public discourse about statistical data generated by the U.S. Census Office. Those who authorized and produced the atlases pursued the admirable civic goal of educating citizens about the status of the nation so that they might participate in its development, a purpose Hewes and Gannett articulated in their Preface to the 1883 atlas:

> Let these facts be expressed not alone in figures, but graphically, by means of maps and diagrams, appealing to a quick sense of form and color ... and their study becomes a delight rather than a task. The density of settlement, the illiteracy of the people, the wealth or poverty of different sections, and many other features of great importance, hitherto but vaguely comprehended, are made to appear at a glance, and are so vividly impressed as not to be easily forgotten. By such aids not only the statistician and political

economist, but the masses of the people, who make public sentiment and shape public policy, may acquire that knowledge of the country and its resources which is essential to intelligent and successful government. (vii)

To achieve that civic end, then, images "so vividly impressed as not to be easily forgotten" (Hewes and Gannett vii) would serve as mnemonic devices that enabled readers to process and retain information. Nearly a century earlier, William Playfair made a similar claim in his *Commercial and Political Atlas*, arguing that with the aid of his charts "as much information may be *obtained in five minutes as would require whole days to imprint on the memory, in a lasting manner, by a table of figures*" (xii). Making information accessible and memorable to readers was the paramount goal of visualizing it in maps and charts; as a reviewer of the 1874 atlas put it, "the very reason of their being is because words and numbers cannot or will not tell the whole truth" (Brewer 85). Utilitarian, rather than argumentative, benefits justified designing data, as they continue to today.

However, designing information so that readers can comprehend and retain it is scarcely an objective, neutral process. In the statistical atlases, data are *designed* in thousands of artificial constructs that project a reading of the nation at a specific historical moment, and in that sense those constructs are highly rhetorical, even argumentative. The visual arguments that the atlases posed to the public address issues of nation building, dynamic migration, and the rapid assimilation of foreigners. Nineteenth-century graphical displays were often used to argue for public policy issues, with some of these displays envisioning epic narratives of meteorology, natural history, economics, and health (and combinations of these). They typically appeared in books and journals as foldout plates, displaying several variables on the same plot frame, including annotations about the data and historical events. These displays were exemplified by Charles Joseph Minard's chart of Napoleon's Russian campaign, which represents the army's march eastward over 400,000 strong and its retreat as it dwindled to barely 10,000 (Tufte, *Visual Display* 40–41). Minard's chart, lauded by Tufte as perhaps "the best statistical graphic ever drawn" (*Visual Display* 40), brilliantly expresses the consequences of expansionism and implicitly argues to keep French resources at home rather than squandering them on schemes abroad. Another compelling visualization of a public policy issue was articulated by Florence Nightingale's charts, in which she used a circular time pattern (akin to a wind rose) to display the death rates in hospitals during the Crimean War (Funkhouser 343–345; see also Biderman 17–18).

How were public policy issues advanced by data displays in the statistical atlases? First, the displays visualize the concept of manifest destiny by charting the deterministic narrative of westward expansion across the midwest, plains, and west. In doing so, the atlases both narrate and advocate dynamic change by envisioning a nation that is geographically mobile. All of the atlases included physical maps of the entire country, coast to coast, and the vast regions awaiting settlement. Although population maps in the 1874 atlas displayed primarily the eastern half of the country (Fig. 10.1a), the 1883 atlas and its successors included the whole country (Fig. 10.1b). To document manifest destiny, each atlas included a map tracing the population center of the country as it progressed west, beginning in 1790 near Baltimore and moving through West Virginia, Ohio, and Indiana. In the 1883 and 1898 atlases these vast, dynamic shifts in population were documented on maps showing the migration of population across states, and they were further dramatized in rank charts (Fig. 10.1i), as some of the original states lost their places to those more recently settled (see Hewes and Gannett, Plate 18; Gannett, *Statistical, Eleventh*, Plate 2).

Visualizing westward migration argued that vast regions of the nation still awaited settlement, which required additional sources of population. The atlases used several design strategies to track the movement of immigrants as they were geographically assimilated. One strategy was to show, primarily through maps, that foreigners were in fact migrating across the country and were not merely concentrated on the coast. In the 1874 atlas, maps of the eastern half of the country show the distribution of foreigners, including specific ethnic groups (e.g., Germans, Irish; Walker, Plate XXVII), and as we've seen in Fig. 10.2, bi-polar population charts for each state show the distribution of foreigners by gender and age. In the 1883 atlas, bar charts were also used extensively to locate immigrants, displaying the foreign population by state, its percentage of the state's population, and the percentages of each main ethnic group (e.g, Irish, Scotch) by state as well as some large cities (e.g., New York, Philadelphia). Virtually all of these charts displayed bars in ranked order so readers could easily compare the size of each ethnic group. The migration charts in the 1898 atlas emphatically visualize immigrants as the black segment on right of each bar (Fig. 10.1o; Gannett, *Statistical, Eleventh* 24). Collectively, these displays argued that foreigners were being assimilated geographically and playing a key role in westward expansion.

Visualizing the national assimilation of foreigners is epitomized in Fig. 10.5, a plate from the 1898 atlas showing a field of pie charts representing the relative mix of foreign immigrants by state and territory. Fourteen ethnic groups (in addition to a combined "Other Countries" group) are represented, with most of the pie charts showing at least half of them. The field of pie charts serves several rhetorical ends, principally by arguing that the foreign population is both highly diversified and well distributed geographically. Because the equally sized charts show only the *relative* concentrations of foreigners within a given state, they obscure the fact that some states had very high concentrations of certain ethnic groups—e.g., Irish in New York, Germans in Wisconsin, Scandinavians in Minnesota—and others far lower concentrations. Southern states like South Carolina and Georgia, which experienced a relatively small influx of foreigners, appear to have the same diversification as

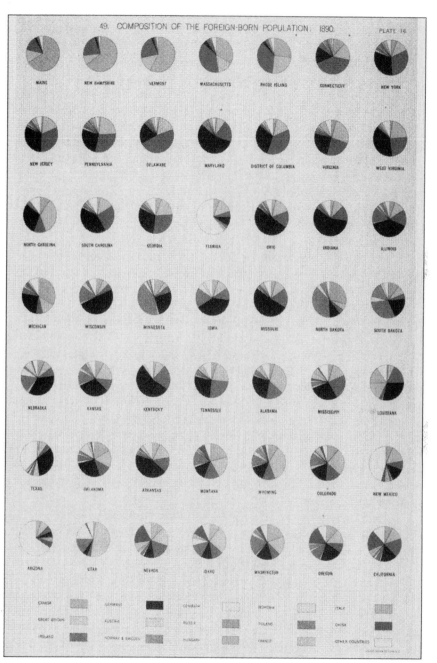

FIG. 10.5. Field of Pie Charts from the 1898 Statistical Atlas Showing the Nationalities of the Foreign-Born Population by State (Gannett, *Statistical, Eleventh,* Plate 16).

states like New York and Illinois. Because the field of pie charts prevents readers from comparing absolute values from one state to another, it makes a compelling argument for broad diversification and assimilation.

The atlases envisioned how foreigners were being assimilated not only geographically but also economically and vocationally. Although arguing visually
for geographical assimilation may have partly reduced the threat of foreigners
to native inhabitants, the social and economic effects of assimilation were
complicated by historical circumstances. In the 1890s the western frontier was
closing, and Americans were increasingly wary of foreigners, especially those
from southern and eastern Europe. Anti-immigrant sentiment ran particularly high in the 1890s because jobs were scarcer during the financial down-
turn. "Nativist" groups opposed to immigration began to form, including the
Immigration Restriction League initiated by several Harvard graduates
(Daniels, *Not Like Us* 39–45; "Two Cheers" 14).

Amid these changing conditions, several visual strategies were deployed in
the atlases to represent the occupations of immigrants. The presence of foreigners in the occupational displays of the 1883 atlas was so subtle that readers
had to look closely to discern it. Occupations were displayed in bar graphs,
with natives signified by a wavy line inside the bars that distinguished them
from foreigners, a graphical technique illustrated in Fig. 10.3. In the 1898 atlas,
native and foreign workers were distinguished much more emphatically, both
in the form of separate bar charts displaying occupations of individual ethnic
groups (e.g., Italians, Russians) and of a percent bar chart categorizing the occupations of foreigners in relation to those of other groups (Gannett, *Statistical, Eleventh* 48–49, Plate 43). The shift to a more explicit form of display places
the immigrant issue squarely before the public and begs the question: By
showing economic assimilation during hard times, were the designers trying
to reduce the threat of foreigners, or were they fueling anti-immigrant sentiment? Depending on readers' interpretive frameworks, they might be receptive to either argument.

The 1903 atlas strikes a rhetorical compromise by combining natives and
foreigners in the same display, shown in Fig. 10.6. The chart represents over 40
occupations, which are itemized in the legend below, coded numerically
within the rectilinear areas on the chart, and grouped into five color-coded categories, from Agricultural Pursuits to Manufacturing and Mechanical Pursuits. The population is divided into four groups: native Whites of native
parents at the top of the chart, followed by native Whites of foreign-born parents, foreign Whites, and Blacks at the bottom. This design enables even the
most casual reader to see that immigrants and their children are fully integrated into a wide range of occupations that broadly mirror the patterns of
native Whites and Blacks, though foreigners are less active in Agricultural Pursuits and more active in Manufacturing and Mechanical Pursuits. By juxtaposing the four population groups, the chart argues for broad assimilation but

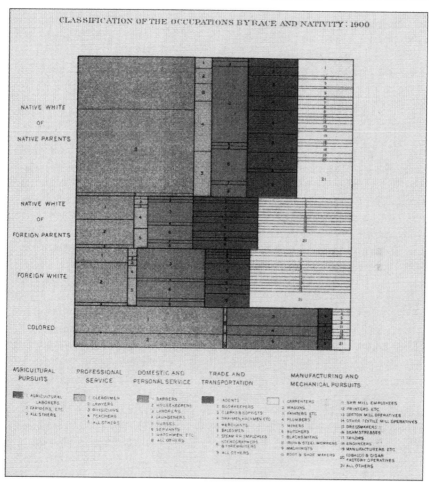

FIG. 10.6.   Area Chart from the 1903 Statistical Atlas Showing the Occupations of Population Groups (Gannett, *Statistical, Twelfth*, Plate 87).

also enables readers to identify micro-level differences—e.g., the relative activity of any of the four population groups in each occupation. The intense focus on the occupations of foreigners, however, was only short-lived; data design in subsequent atlases shifted to another public policy issue—the occupational activities of children and adolescents.

Data designs, then, generally argued for the geographical and occupational assimilation of foreigners, though perhaps those designs produced mixed results with native Whites threatened by mass immigration. Visual arguments can also be advanced on the basis of how much, if at all, data are actually visualized. Designers control what is and what is *not* visualized, and that control has rhetorical consequences, which Ben Barton and Marthalee Barton refer to as the "rules of inclusion" and "rules of exclusion" ("Ideology" 53–62). In the atlases, that control is clearly apparent in charts that downplayed, if not excluded, the foreign population. In a massive chart from the 1898 atlas showing the growth in U.S. population from the first census in 1790 (Fig. 10.1n; Gannett, *Statistical, Eleventh*, Plate 22), native Whites occupy the central core of the display, swelling with each census from top to bottom. To the right, a thin dark strip represents the Black population. On the left, however, foreigners appear only incrementally, a design strategy that marginalizes them in relation to the total population, shown beneath in an area chart that subdivides them by nationality. Graphical techniques also assuaged the impact of foreigners on public health. In the 1874 atlas, a line graph shows the incidence of diseases in both the native and foreign populations (adult and children) so that readers can compare the data (Walker, Plate XLIV). However, the line graph genre minimizes variations because the lines connecting data from one disease to another rise and fall at approximately the same angles. Subsequent atlases simply dodged the issue, as little information about diseases was designed to compare foreign and native populations.

For some issues, like occupations, including or excluding information in the atlases reflected the tenor of public discourse. The literacy of the foreign population, for example, figured importantly beginning in the 1890s with attempts to legislate literacy tests that would curb immigration, an effort that finally succeeded in 1917 (Daniels, *Not Like Us* 43–44; "Two Cheers" 14). The atlases reflected the increasing public attention to literacy and the ability to speak English. In the 1874 atlas, general illiteracy and adult White male illiteracy are plotted on maps (Walker, Plates XXIX and XXX), but in the 1883 atlas, the ability to write is mapped for foreigners as well as visualized in a bar graph (Hewes and Gannett, Plate 50). Subsequent atlases also charted illiteracy rates, including a population distribution chart in the 1914 atlas comparing data from the last and present censuses about foreigners' ability to speak English (see Fig. 10.7). Overall, the language charts argue that foreigners as a group are being assimilated linguistically into mainstream culture, though these displays selectively reveal the data—including only the aggregate numbers and excluding the rates of individual ethnic groups. As a result, readers are not invited to compare the relative literacy or English-speaking skills of Italians, Germans, Russians, or other groups.

Although data about some public policy issues appear prominently in the atlases, other data appear less frequently, if at all. In the climate of the post-Civil War Reconstruction, displays of the Black population, for example, appear consistently but sparsely and seem to reveal the nation's ambivalence about their status. Data about Blacks appear in close proximity to data about native Whites and foreigners, a gesture towards assimilation, but Blacks are stereotypically represented graphically by darker shades (Figs. 10.1e and

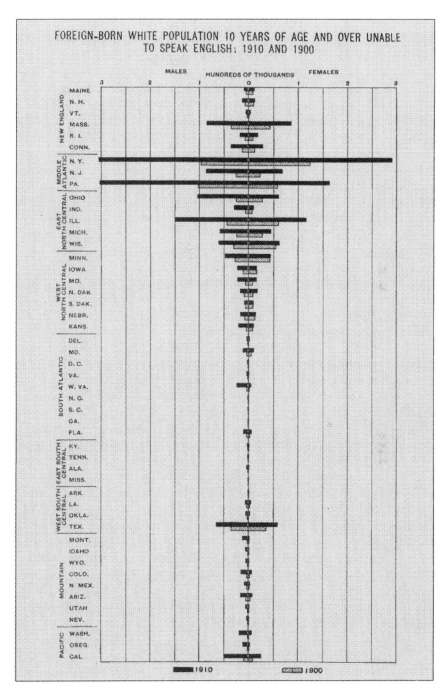

FIG. 10.7.   Bi-Polar Chart from the 1914 Statistical Atlas Showing Foreigners by Sex Unable to Speak English (Sloane, *Statistical*, Thirteenth, Plate 226).

10.1n) or they are visually marginalized, illustrated by their placement on the right side of the massive population chart (Fig. 10.1n) and at the bottom of the occupational chart (Fig. 10.6). In the 1874 atlas the distribution of the Black population is charted on maps similar to those used for foreign groups. In the 1898 atlas, the Black population (relative to the White population) is visualized in rectilinear area charts for southern states (Gannett, *Statistical, Eleventh* 18), charts that reappear almost verbatim in the next two atlases. Overall, Blacks are represented relatively constantly, but minimally compared to the increasing attention given to foreigners.

Although the design of data about Blacks is limited and ambiguous, scant information about Indians is visualized, beyond an occasional map displaying reservations (see Walker, Plates XVIII and XIX). No maps chart Indian migrations and displacement, which remains one of the most compelling stories of 19th-century America. One rationale for this exclusion may be that little census data had been collected about such migrations; another may be that Indian migration directly conflicted with the mainstream narrative of westward expansion and immigrant assimilation. Whatever the practical or political reasons for not charting this story—and undoubtedly there were many—it has to be one of the most glaring rhetorical exclusions in 19th-century statistical graphics.

Today, civic discourse continues to be shaped by data design, though design is typically characterized pejoratively by caveats about how it's misused to manipulate data. Edward Tufte, one in a long line of critics, developed what he calls the "Lie Factor," which quantifies perceptual distortions that deceive readers and jeopardize the "graphical integrity" of the design (Tufte, *Visual Display* 53–77), undermining its ethos.[3] Skepticism about designed data continues to permeate public discourse in which charts and graphs appear, especially when they are embellished with "chartjunk" (Tufte, *Visual Display* 107–21).[4] Because contemporary readers are wary of deceptive charts and graphs and because computers make these forms so malleable, arguing with data displays has become a highly contested form of visual rhetoric. Rhetors who deploy charts and graphs in civic discourse, therefore, must proceed with extreme caution. Readers of the atlases a century ago, less savvy about the power of charts and graphs to construct a nation, could scarcely have imagined the rhetorical processes that the production and interpretation of those displays initiated.

DATA DISPLAYS AS CULTURAL ARTIFACTS

Visual language embodies cultural knowledge about the world and about its values, as we have already seen in the representation of public policy issues. Visual language also embodies another form of cultural knowledge—aesthetics (Kostelnick "Cultural"). However, the role of aesthetics may seem invisible because both readers and designers may be so entrenched in a given design style that they become oblivious to its influence over them. However, aesthetics permeates all areas of functional design, leaving a trail of cultural tracks. For example, a technical illustration from the Renaissance will reveal the cultural influence of the period (in the viewing angles, human figures, and other contextual details), just as a high-contrast page of sans serif text with geometrical forms will evoke early modernism. By projecting the aesthetic sensibility of a given historical moment, visual language creates rhetorical energy by cultivating and meeting readers' expectations.

In the half century in which the atlases appeared, a sea change in aesthetics occurred—from the decorative Victorian sensibility visible in the folio atlases to the machine-age functionalism of the later ones. The folio atlases reflect a late 19th-century aesthetic that fostered complexity, subtle variation, and natural forms. Although readers may not have recognized the data display genres that first appeared in the atlases, they most likely experienced an affinity with their aesthetic composition and texture. The displays are colorful, detailed, and sometimes multi-layered (e.g., the wavy line in the bar in Fig. 10.3). Shades of the same color are typically employed in the maps to create subtle gradations of population density, which invite the reader's careful study. The complex variety of the forms and their richness of detail, linework, and color predate the functional economy of modernism. Moreover, the displays rely on textual explanations for their interpretation, creating an interdependence between word and image. Notes and labels on the plates are primarily set in a serif typeface and often italicized; display text is often rendered in handwritten capitals; and decorative arrows direct readers from text to charts (see Fig. 10.3). Overall, the folio atlases reveal their historical and cultural origins by embodying an aesthetic that the designers shared with their readers and that gave the atlases a credible, authentic voice.

Although the folios embrace a delicate and highly ornamented aesthetic of the late 19th century, the latter three atlases exemplify the transition to functional modernism with its emphasis on economy and perceptual directness. Modernism fostered cultural assimilation in two key ways: Its international aesthetic visually dissolved cultural differences, and its emphasis on perceptual immediacy made data accessible to all readers, regardless of cultural background. Modernism sought to erase the stylistic conventions that separated cultures by developing an "international" style that transcended national borders and unified cultures. Clean, geometric forms supplied a basic design vocabulary for implementing the modernist program, engendering an aesthetic of cultural homogeneity that dovetailed with the melting-pot ideology of early 20th-century America.

Several design elements were deployed in the later atlases to visualize that ideology. In the 1914 and 1925 atlases, color is largely superseded by black-and-white patterns, or simply white space, virtually eliminating issues associated with interpreting color across cultures (see Horton 165–166). The segments of pie charts, for example, are no longer distinguished by color and legends but only by blank spaces, which are directly labeled with a sans serif font, the modernist standard. This clean, objectified aesthetic is exemplified by the visual language of population maps. Figure 10.8 shows a U.S. map from the 1914 atlas showing the state-by-state percent of German immigrants. The textured patterns reveal the distribution of German immigrants: heavy in the upper Midwest and virtually nonexistent in the Southeast. No subtle or suggestive cultural tracks infiltrate this map or others like it displaying immigrant groups. Cleansed by the minimalist language of modernism, the data are visualized as hard, objective facts devoid of any cultural associations.

The minimalist, international style of modernism well served the readers of the later atlases, who were increasingly part of the melting pot, either as immigrants themselves or children of immigrants. The data not only *visualized* a burgeoning multi-ethnic society; that society was also its audience—highly diversified, representing virtually every European language and nationality (and others from around the world) as well as native Whites, some of whom may have harbored ill feelings toward immigration. This culturally and linguistically mixed audience was well matched with the international design program of modernism, which aimed to democratize design by making it accessible to all. An advocate of this philosophy, Otto Neurath attempted to democratize statistics in the early 20th century through his Isotype system of pictographic display. Neurath's Isotype used pictures (e.g., of humans, cars) in small, high-contrast, and equally sized increments, rather than as relative ar-

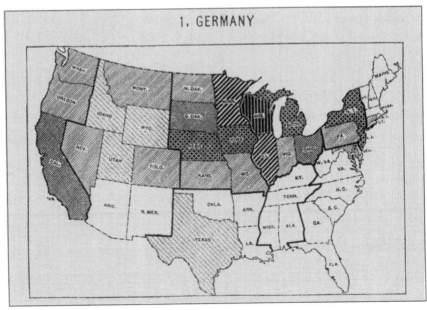

FIG. 10.8.   Map from the 1914 Statistical Atlas Showing the Distribution of German Immigrants by State (Sloane, *Statistical,* Thirteenth, Plate 217).

eas as had been done previously, so that readers could accurately compare data. An extension of logical positivism, Isotype exploited visual perception so that readers could directly apprehend facts about the economic and social conditions of modern society (Lupton).[5]

The German immigration map (Fig. 10.8) illustrates several of these modernist tenets. Like most displays in the 1914 and 1925 atlases, the map stands largely on its own, perceptually linking reader and data with little textual mediation. Although a single legend keys the data patterns for the six immigrant maps that appear on the same page, readers can perceive the main themes in the data without even referencing the legend. Using black-and-white patterns to represent relative population density exploits the gestalt principle of figure–ground contrast (darker equals denser), and it flattens and economizes the maps compared to the color-coding systems used in previous atlases. The flat black-and-white patterns, however, have their drawbacks: They limit both the designer's and the reader's ability to differentiate them, and the repetitive patterns (e.g., stripes) create what Tufte calls "moiré effects" (*Visual Display* 107–11). But within the cultural framework of functional modernism, these liabilities are offset by the aesthetic and practical economies of black-and-white print.

Modernism, of course, did not have sole claim to perceptual accessibility. From the start, the designers of the atlases intended their displays to be readily perceptible to their readers—as Hewes and Gannett put it, to enable readers to see data "at a glance" (Preface vii). In the Preface and Introduction to the 1874 atlas, Francis Walker explains the perceptual qualities of its displays and their effects on the eye, both in terms of a "general impression" of the data as well as closer readings of details (Walker, Preface 2). Tufte describes these two modes—on the one hand, the big picture and on the other hand, the smaller local view—as the "macro" and "micro" levels of interpretation (*Envisioning* 37–51; see also Barton and Barton, "Modes" 150–155). All of the atlases give readers access to data on both levels, though the emphasis gradually shifts away from the micro-level access in the folios to the more perceptually immediate macro-level, a shift that generally mirrors the modernist emphasis on perceptual efficiency.

In the early atlases, especially the 1874 and 1898 atlases, graphical displays were often spread across folio pages—as in Fig. 10.5, the field of pie charts—which added another level of complexity by variegating their perceptual context. Although the segments of the pie charts (e.g., British, Austrian, or Polish immigrants) are consistently color-coded across the displays in the visual field, the larger narrative is visually fragmented into the individual profiles of each pie chart, one state at a time. The same applies to folio plates of population distribution charts: Readers can readily identify the anomalies (in asymmetrical states like Nevada in Fig. 10.2), but the profiles of other states are rendered more subtly in individual charts, as they are in the field of square area charts for church accommodations (Fig. 10.4). In these instances, the micro-level reveals more compelling information than a *glance* at the whole plate.

The rectilinear area chart of occupations from the 1903 atlas (Fig. 10.6) strikes a balance between the macro- and micro-levels. The color and grouping of elements enable readers to see the big picture and to compare variables— e.g., to see that the foreign population has a larger share of workers in Manufacturing and Mechanical Pursuits than the other population categories, and fewer in Agricultural Pursuits. On the micro-level, readers can explore the sub-plots embedded in the larger narratives. For example, they can discover that the foreign population includes few lawyers and virtually no barbers, housekeepers, or masons. Readers are empowered to access information on both levels and to shuttle freely between the two.

In the later atlases, the emphasis shifts decidedly to the more perceptually accessible macro-level. The design of the German immigration map (Fig. 10.8) emphasizes the macro-level through the visual immediacy of its high-contrast design. The bi-polar chart in Fig. 10.7 (also from the 1914 atlas) similarly foregrounds the macro-level with a linear, minimalist design. Readers can readily see the dominant patterns—heavy concentrations of non-English speaking immigrants in the Middle Atlantic states and a few other local areas—but no horizontal gridlines encourage the eye to explore micro-level data for individual states. The dot density map (Fig. 10.1p), which appeared initially in the 1883 atlas (Hewes and Gannett lix) but was refined and expanded in the 1914 atlas, exemplified this shift to the macro-level by visualizing data as tiny uniform dots. Most readers wouldn't try to count the individual dots in a given region (unlike the folio maps where readers could often, if they wished, scrutinize the data county by county). Densely concentrating in some regions and lightly dusting others, the dots on the maps provide an unmediated macro-view, a gestalt that links data and eye through direct perception. By emphasizing "seeing" over close "reading," the macro-view over the micro-view, modernist design presumed to tap directly into the perceptual faculties of readers—*any* readers, *anywhere*, regardless of their ethnicity—and therefore required minimal learning or enculturation (see Bertin 179–181; Lupton).

The shift toward a modernist aesthetic for the data displays, then, reinforced the melting-pot ideology by representing changes in population in a seemingly objective design accessible to a multi-ethnic audience. As Robin Kinross points out, however, the rhetorical "neutrality" of modernism embodied its own ideology. An aesthetic program that aimed to erase cultural difference by creating an "international" style was hardly neutral. Historical perspective further clarifies its ideological bent. Today the forms of early modernism—the rectilinear grid of steel-and-glass buildings, the sleek lines of furniture, the sans serif page of text, as well as the high-contrast displays of the last two atlases—appear starkly, even gratuitously, functional. The cultural framework of modernism has long since yielded to the nuanced, pluralistic aesthetic of postmodernism with its punctured facades, multilayered surfaces, and emphasis on contextual fit.

The cultural knowledge of aesthetics embeds the visual rhetoric of any design: Typography, screen designs, pictures, and data displays all leave their cultural tracks by embodying an aesthetic element that both meets and engenders reader expectations. The early atlases met reader expectations by projecting a delicate, decorative aesthetic, and the later atlases redefined those expectations by adopting a machine-age aesthetic that embraced an ideology of cultural neutrality. Staying in step with the shifting tides in taste enhanced the ethos and usability of the atlases. It also addressed the more specific rhetorical problem of representing immigrants to a multi-ethnic audience with forms that were ostensibly objective.

CONCLUSION

During the half century in which they appeared, the statistical atlases played a key role in defining the visual language of data displays in the United States. By experimenting with a variety of forms, imitating them in successive atlases, and educating readers in how to interpret them, the designers of the atlases developed and modeled a conventional visual language for displaying data. By envisioning the progress of the nation, the atlases also shaped civic discourse about public policy issues, particularly regarding the influx of immigrants and their assimilation geographically, vocationally, and linguistically. In doing so, the atlases also projected the prevailing tides in taste, from an aesthetic that valued ornament and close reading to one that valued economy and perceptual immediacy. In several ways, then, the atlases built a rhetorical bridge to contemporary information design.

This bridge-building process reveals a good deal about the nature of visual rhetoric in practical communication. Visual rhetoric is an intensely social process that entails convention building within discourse communities and a process of enculturation that fosters visual literacy among group members. Information design also embodies the shared cultural knowledge—values, ideologies, and aesthetic tastes—of its designers and readers at a given historical moment. Although these social elements provide a foundation for information design, visual rhetoric is scarcely deterministic. Rather it turns on readers' interpretations in specific situational contexts, one reader at a time. That some readers of the statistical atlases, however, may have initially found the data displays novel, clever, or incomprehensible testifies to the powerful social forces that drove the visual rhetoric of these images. By constructing a coherent visual narrative from a wealth census data, over a half century the atlases progressively enabled a diverse, multi-ethnic audience to envision together the nation's rapid growth.

ACKNOWLEDGMENT

I wish to thank the editors of this collection, Charles Hill and Marguerite Helmers, for their helpful suggestions on an earlier draft of this chapter.

NOTES

1. The statistical atlases were published from three to eight years after the actual census year. Copies of the 1874, 1883, and 1898 atlases appear on the Library of Congress Web Site (http://memory.loc.gov/ammem/gmdhtml/census.html), which also contains additional background information (see Dahmann).
2. According to the 1874 statistical atlas, "The Geographical illustrations, in general, require no verbal description and explanation, beyond what is given on their face" (Walker, Preface 3); a line graph is described as a "more familiar mode of illustration" (Walker, Preface 2).
3. Tufte's predecessors include Willard Brinton, whose *Graphic Methods for Presenting Facts* (1914) analyses distortions caused by areas and volumes (20–40). Several decades of empirical research have clarified and authenticated these concerns (see Cleveland and McGill; Macdonald-Ross; Cochran, Albrecht, and Green).
4. In the political arena, for example, Ross Perot was lampooned for using charts and graphs in his 1992 presidential campaign.
5. Although Neurath's Isotype system was infused with the democratic ideals of early modernism, Clive Chizlett argues that Neurath may have used his design skills in the Soviet Union in the 1930s to misrepresent mass deaths resulting from famine.

WORKS CITED

Barton, Ben F., and Marthalee S. Barton. "Ideology and the Map: Toward a Postmodern Visual Design Practice." *Professional Communication: The Social Perspective.* Ed. Nancy Roundy Blyler and Charlotte Thralls. Newbury Park, CA: Sage, 1993: 49–78.

—. "Modes of Power in Technical and Professional Visuals." *Journal of Business and Technical Communication* 7 (1993): 138–162.

Bertin, Jacques. *Graphics and Graphic-Information-Processing.* Trans. William J. Berg and Paul Scott. New York: Walter de Gruyter, 1981.

Biderman, Albert D. "The Playfair Enigma: The Development of the Schematic Representation of Statistics." *Information Design Journal* 6.1 (1990): 3–25.

Boorstin, Daniel J. *The Americans: The Democratic Experience.* New York: Random House, 1973.

Brewer, W. H. "Walker's Statistical Atlas of the United States." *The American Journal of Science and Arts* (Third Series) 10 (1875): 83–88.

Brinton, Willard C. *Graphic Methods for Presenting Facts.* New York: Engineering Magazine Company, 1914.

Chizlett, Clive. "Damned Lies. And Statistics. Otto Neurath and Soviet Propaganda in the 1930s." Special Issue on Diagrams as Tools for Worldmaking. Ed. Sharon Helmer Poggenpohl and Dietmar R. Winkler. *Visible Language* 26.3/4 (1992): 298–321.

Cleveland, William S. and Robert McGill. "Graphical Perception: Theory, Experimentation, and Application to the Development of Graphical Methods." *Journal of the American Statistical Association* 79.387 (1984): 531–554.

Cochran, Jeffrey K., Sheri A. Albrecht, and Yvonne A. Green. "Guidelines for Evaluating Graphical Designs: A Framework Based on Human Perception Skills." *Technical Communication* 36 (1989): 25–32.

Dahmann, Donald C. "Presenting the Nation's Cultural Geography: 1790–1920." Lib. of Congress, Washington. June 2003. <http://memory.loc.gov/ammem/gmdhtml/census2.html>.

Daniels, Roger. *Not Like Us: Immigrants and Minorities in America, 1890–1924.* Chicago: Ivan R. Dee, 1997.

—. "Two Cheers for Immigration." *Debating American Immigration, 1882–Present.* Ed. Roger Daniels and Otis L. Graham. Lanham, Md.: Rowman & Littlefield, 2001: 5–69.

Funkhouser, H. G. "Historical Development of the Graphical Representation of Statistical Data." *Osiris* 3 (1937): 269–404.

Gannett, Henry. *Statistical Atlas of the United States, Based upon Results of the Eleventh Census.* U.S. Census Office. Washington: GPO, 1898.

—, comp. *Statistical Atlas: Twelfth Census of the United States, Taken in the Year 1900.* U.S. Census Office. Washington: U.S. Census Office, 1903.

Hewes, Fletcher W., and Henry Gannett. *Scribner's Statistical Atlas of the United States, Showing by Graphic Methods Their Present Condition and Their Political, Social and Industrial Development.* New York: Charles Scribner's Sons, 1883.

Horton, William. "Overcoming Chromophobia: A Guide to the Confident and Appropriate Use of Color." *IEEE Transactions on Professional Communication* 34.3 (1991): 160–173.

Kinross, Robin. "The Rhetoric of Neutrality." *Design Issues* 2.2 (1985): 18–30. Rpt. in *Design Discourse: History, Theory, Criticism.* Ed. Victor Margolin. Chicago: U of Chicago P, 1989: 131–143.

Kostelnick, Charles. "Conflicting Standards for Designing Data Displays: Following, Flouting, and Reconciling Them." Special Issue on Visualizing Information. Ed. William M. Gribbons and Arthur G. Elser. *Technical Communication* 45 (1998): 473–482.

—. "Cultural Adaptation and Information Design: Two Contrasting Views." *IEEE Transactions on Professional Communication* 38 (1995): 182–196.

Kostelnick, Charles, and Michael Hassett. *Shaping Information: The Rhetoric of Visual Conventions.* Carbondale, IL: Southern Illinois UP, 2003.

Kostelnick, Charles, and David D. Roberts. *Designing Visual Language: Strategies for Professional Communicators.* Needham Hts., MA: Allyn and Bacon, 1998.

Lupton, Ellen. "Reading Isotype." *Design Issues* 3.2 (1986): 47–58. Rpt. in *Design Discourse: History, Theory, Criticism.* Ed. Victor Margolin. Chicago: U of Chicago P, 1989: 145–156.

Macdonald-Ross, Michael. "How Numbers Are Shown: A Review of Research on the Presentation of Quantitative Data in Texts." *Audio-Visual Communication Review* 25 (1977): 359–409.

Monmonier, Mark. "The Rise of the National Atlas." *Cartographica* 31.1 (1994): 1–15.

Neurath, Otto. *International Picture Language: The First Rules of Isotype.* London: Kegan Paul, Trench, Trubner & Co., Ltd., 1936.

Nightingale, Florence. *Notes on Matters Affecting the Health, Efficiency and Hospital Administration of the British Army.* London: Harrison, 1858.

Playfair, William. *The Commercial and Political Atlas, Representing, by Means of Stained Copper-Plate Charts, the Progress of the Commerce, Revenues, Expenditure, and Debts of England, during the Whole of the Eighteenth Century.* 3rd ed. London, 1801.

Sloane, Charles S., comp. *Statistical Atlas of the United States.* Thirteenth (1910) Census. U.S. Bureau of the Census. Washington: GPO, 1914.

Sloane, Charles S., comp. *Statistical Atlas of the United States:* Fourteenth (1920) Census. U.S. Bureau of the Census. Washington: GPO, 1925.

Tufte, Edward R. *Envisioning Information.* Cheshire, CT: Graphics P, 1990.

—. *The Visual Display of Quantitative Information.* Cheshire, CT: Graphics P, 1983.

Walker, Francis A., comp. *Statistical Atlas of the United States Based on the Results of the Ninth Census 1870.* U.S. Census Office. New York: Julius Bien, 1874.

CHAPTER ELEVEN

The Rhetoric of Irritation: Inappropriateness as Visual/ Literate Practice

Craig Stroupe

Given the popularity of technologies that enable writers to combine prose, graphics, sound and video online, many English and composition departments now offer classes in the production and interpretation of Web sites and other New Media texts.[1] Department faculty, therefore, increasingly pursue tenure by publishing scholarly work and instructional materials about, and in, these hybrid media. Such articles, textbooks and Web sites typically use phrases like "media literacy" and "visual rhetoric" as if they were stable concepts, although they are in fact metaphors or tropes that attempt synthetically to describe one mode of communication in terms of another: to understand electronic communication (media) as a kind of writing (literacy), for instance, or iconographic discourse (visual images) as a kind of speech (rhetoric).

Such tropes enable us to impose the conceptual categories of print culture, such as "literacy" and "authorship," onto the practices of HTML coding, WYSIWYG editing, and image manipulation, combining the traditional cultural capital of verbal literacy and even literary accomplishment with the contemporary commercial value that digital skills carry in the employment marketplace.[2] In this way, "visual rhetoric" and "media literacy" offer faculty a conveniently slippery political reversibility. That is, we can provide students with the *instrumental*, bread-and-butter skills of communicating effectively in the employment marketplace, corporate workplace or commercial media, while simultaneously leading them, we hope, to a more critical awareness of the *constitutive* processes by which languages (including what we oxymoronically call "visual languages") function to produce and reproduce culture and identity. Indeed, most university faculty in the humanities would agree with the idea that education is more than equipping students with instrumental literacy for employment, and that teaching the practices of a constitutive literacy encourages a desirable critical consciousness that helps enable students to understand, and even act to expose and change, the usually unspoken ideologies that inform their cultures.

In teaching New Media Writing at the university, however, the necessity of using, and therefore teaching and learning, various information technologies foregrounds the instrumental mechanics of producing satisfactory texts. Lacking a well-established method of visual/verbal composition, a tradition of online *belle-lettres*, or a prevailing theory of digital cultural studies, the potential for constitutive literacy in the use and end-products of Dreamweaver or Photoshop can seem a mere abstraction, something that rhetorically ennobles our educational enterprise in scholarly analysis, but that is difficult to show students and to help them emulate in practice. Yoking together "media" and "literacy" or "visual" and "rhetoric," therefore, presents imaginary, linguistic resolutions in scholarly writing which elide the broad differences between the purposes of corporate training and liberal-arts curricula.

Saying that these tropic resolutions are metaphorical or imaginary doesn't mean they are not both conventional and useful in scholarly discourse. These critical metaphors or oxymoronic neologisms produce what Wolfgang Iser calls "gaps," interpretive dilemmas that both negate the norms represented by the opposed elements—in the case of "visual rhetoric," the conventional assumptions we make about how images work as opposed to how words do—as well as suggest positive alternatives at some "virtual point of convergence" (34, 49). In a phrase, such dilemmas represent a creative irritant, the grain of sand that ideally instigates a pearl.

The challenge of teaching visual rhetoric lies in transplanting our "virtual" critical resolutions between visual and literate cultures (our scholarly pearls) into the practical work of digital production. We need to show students specific examples and techniques of genuinely converged literate and iconographic authorships in New Media environments, to provide them with a critical language for understanding and imitating these models in a variety of situations, and thus to establish a new pedagogical method and institutional practice appropriate both to the humanities and to the needs of students. In essence, we must decide whether Dreamweaver and Photoshop can be used for "literate" purposes and, if so, whether such purposes can and should be taught.

Before answering *yes* to all of these questions, we must recognize that the competition between visual design and verbal rhetoric long predates the advent of digital culture. W. J. T. Mitchell has characterized and critiqued the customary attitudes of bibliocentric disciplines like English and composition as combining an iconoclastic "contempt" for graphic images as uncritical "idolatry, fetishism, and iconophilia," a "fear" toward visual discourse as a "racial, social and sexual other," and a tendency to see any genre that combines the two discourses, such as the theater, as a "battleground between the values associated with verbal and visual codes" (151, 157–158). Those who feel the need to defend print culture against a supposed obsolescence draw a similar line in the sand between traditionally linear, sustained print discourse and digital hypertexts that "chunk" content and bedevil the act of reading with interminable clicks and choices. As George Landow among others has observed, hypertext realizes the long-theorized "death" of the author—the idea of a unified and discreet authorship being fundamental to most literature and composition curricula—and a shift of authority to readers, viewers or, most recently, "users," who cannot as readily be canonized or studied textually.

Just as the *idea* of "visual rhetoric" is made intellectually imaginable in the very act of combining these categorically opposed terms in a single trope, I will argue that the *practice* of visual rhetoric is made methodologically imaginable in the principle of juxtaposing "inappropriately" opposed categories into a constitutive whole. In what follows, I only half facetiously call this method of inappropriate juxtapositions a "rhetoric of irritation," and I will examine two specific visual texts, a Web page and a photocomposite, to show how these "irritating" juxtapositions represent a ideologically expressive dialogue—what Mikhail Bahktin calls "dialogism." In Greg Ulmer's Web essay, "Metaphoric Rocks" and George E. Mahlberg's Photoshopped image, "Oswald in a Jam," I will show that this dialogism, this dialogue among normally unrelated voices and contexts, produces both an irritation in the *text* as a kind of discursive friction between these perspectives—whether expressed visually, verbally or in some hybrid form like a Web page—as well as a social irritation in the *audience* who registers this friction as a kind of disruption of "normal" discourse. Like Iser's "gaps," this sense of disruption calls attention to interpretive dilemmas and cultural instabilities that exist socially beneath the veneer of appropriate assumptions (that is, ideology) at any moment in history, and which these dialogues echo and enact explicitly in the visual/verbal texts.

The rhetoric of irritation can be a *visual* rhetoric, as we'll see in Mahlberg's photocomposite, because it is not exclusive to the verbal medium. In the case of "Metaphoric Rocks" as I shall discuss in more detail below, Ulmer combines images and words by enacting a dialogue between academic and promotional intentions, a dialogue made possible by his blithely ignoring the appropriate distinctions between their purposes and contexts. Ulmer's words and images are thus able to speak to one another because neither illustrates the other. Instead, both verbal and visual elements illustrate and enact the dialogical tug-and-pull between these cultural tensions and identities, words and images essentially riffing off the same theme. The lack of an instrumental, illustrative word/image relation thus suggests a *constitutive* relation in the spirit of the dialogism that Mikhail Bakhtin describes among languages in the novel, and which I am arguing represents the basis for a "literate" practice in digital or visual discourse. Bakhtin writes:

> [T]he novelistic hybrid is an artistically organized system for bringing dif-
> ferent languages in contact with one another, a system having as its goal the
> illumination of one language by means of another, the carving-out of a liv-
> ing image of another language. (361)

Notice here that the emphasis of Bahktin's concept of dialogism is neither on
the languages themselves, nor the technical details of their contact, nor the artistic organization of parts, which enables that contact, but on the *mutual illumination* of the languages inside the system of the text.

For Bahktin, a "language" is more than a representational system—be it
verbal, visual, written, spoken, edited or Photoshopped—but a worldview:

> All words [or images] have the "taste" of a profession, a genre, a tendency, a
> party, a particular work, a particular person, a general, an age group, the
> day and hour. Each word tastes of the context and contexts in which it has
> lived its socially charged life; all words and forms are populated by inten-
> tions. (293)

Bahktin's choice of the word "taste" here is worth noting because it underscores what he does and doesn't mean by *languages* and their "mutual illumination." That is, the "literate" effect of a dialogical text (what he calls
"novelistic discourse") depends not on the cultivated taste developed in the
classroom or the art gallery, but the taste acquired by the word from its use in
the street, the field, or the office—from the life that the word (*bad, eclectic,
gnarly, convergence*) has lived, and *is* living, socially. The "artistic organization" of the text doesn't itself illuminate notational systems, but reflects the
light and energy of living words rubbing up against other words, languages,
lives, contexts, tastes and intentions.

Greg Ulmer's "Metaphoric Rocks: A Psychogeography of Tourism and
Monumentality," demonstrates how such dialogical, cultural energies can in-
tegrate words and images by combining tastes and contexts into meaningful,
if not entirely stable, hybrid compositions. In essence, rather than a page made
monological (as opposed to *dialogical*) by the dominance of either alphabetic
or iconographic language, both verbal and visual elements are located within
a dialogically animated field of contrasting (in this case, comically resonating)
intentions.[3] Conventional, formal word/image relations are disrupted by the
unconventional, cultural play of voices and purposes.

The verbal text of Ulmer's essay is ostensibly addressed to the Florida Tourism Commission, on behalf of the "Florida Research Ensemble [or FRE] ... a
faculty group at the University of Florida that practices an experimental approach to arts and letters." Ulmer's narrator takes exception to the fact that the
Commission has paid $250,000 to the New York consulting firm, Penn and
Schoem, to advise the state on its role in promoting tourism:

If there is an agricultural problem the Institute for Food and Agricultural Sciences at the University of Florida is called on for advice. But when there is a cultural problem, why does no one ask the experts in culture at the University for advice? ... This question is addressed as much to the professors as to the state agency, of course ... FRE is not "competing" with Penn and Schoem for the PR job; we offer a different expertise, which until now has not been applied to tourism except in the negative mode of critique.

From this not-unreasonable premise, Ulmer's modest proposal blossoms into an unlikely vision of a "Florida Rushmore" constructed in a sinkhole outside of Gainesville. Ulmer imagines a kind of underground, holographic drive-in movie theater where tourists take advantage of techniques of composite photography ("used by the FBI to update photographs of missing children, and by PEOPLE magazine to project the effect of age on celebrities") to construct mythic, national images out of the faces not of dead presidents, but of "figures with whom ... [the tourists] identify—figures that represent their 'personalized' or internal Rushmores."

Ulmer's mingling of words and images is made possible by his very deliberate misunderstanding of the conventional, cultural distinctions between academic–critical and state-promotional discourses, which creates in "Metaphoric Rocks" a dialogical tension between these usually divergent languages and intentions. Despite the theoretical content of much of the essay's verbal text, the academic language never entirely subsumes or incorporates the public-relations discourse as it might in singly intended rhetoric. Nor does the essay obey the convention of the tall tale to give itself away.

Under the businesslike heading, "Project Pleasure-Dome," for instance, Ulmer describes the 18th-century travels of William Bartram through an area south of Gainesville now known as Payne's Prairie, "part" he hastens to add, "of the local formation in Alachua County that includes the Devil's Millhopper." Modulating then from the language of state historical promotion to that of literary scholarship—or, perhaps, parodies of these—Ulmer observes:

It is said that Samuel Taylor Coleridge's reading of Bartram's *Travels* (one of the most popular books of its day) influenced the dream that led to the writing of the poem, "Kubla Kahn," about the place "Xanadu," in which "did Kubla Khan / A stately pleasure-dome decree: Where Alph, the sacred river, ran / Through caverns measureless to man / Down to a sunless sea / So twice five miles of fertile ground / with walls and towers were girdled round." (Coleridge)

Ulmer then associates Coleridge's Xanadu with Ted Nelson's model of an electronic, literary metatext, Project Xanadu—an early hypertextual experiment—that he in turn compares to the "network of underground rivers of

Florida Karst," (*karst* being the soluble limestone topology of northern Florida which features caverns and sinkholes like the Devil's Millhopper, site of Ulmer's proposed "school of monumentality"). The languages of scholarly transhistorical synthesis and touristic promotion remain mutually opened and dialogical because it is never made explicit whether Ulmer's satire is aimed at the over-reaching pedant or the over-reaching salesman, or indeed if the proposal is satire at all.

What is most relevant about "Metaphoric Rocks," for the present purpose, is not the verbal text itself, of course, but its relation to the 21 visual graphics interspersed throughout. The capacity or trope of verbal/visual hybridity is made possible on the page by the very slipperiness of determining *which* of the verbal intentions the images might be illustrating. The verbal text here is, in Bakhtinian terms, highly double-voiced and stratified, and that internal dialogism among the words allows for a sense of independent play among the collective body of accompanying visual texts—all existing within what Bakhtin would call a disputed zone between languages/intentions in which the images, not just individually but in combination, objectify and "italicize" these dialogical tensions. These images, therefore, comprise an alternative, parallel text that doesn't simply follow the verbal text, but rises and falls independently on these same dialogical waves of discursive contention.

The first and second JPEG images, for example (Fig. 11.1 and Fig. 11.2), are obviously linked by their captions: the old and new Atlantis. They are connected spatially and intellectually by a paragraph in the essay arguing that "travel was an essential element of archaic theoria," and that the first tourists were, in fact, Greek philosophers and "theorists."

At this point in the written text, scholarly language and intentions seem to dominate, methodically and univocally asserting the authority of modern theorists (that is, the academically affiliated Florida Research Ensemble's "New Consultancy") "to apply our knowledge to the design of an improved tourism." The image of "Plato's Plan of Atlantis" illustrates what the text defines as "Plato's effort to understand how to put into practice the principles of a just state outlined in the Republic." The legend of Atlantis, writes Ulmer, came to Plato from Solon, the first theorist/tourist, who had learned of the lost civilization on a visit to Egypt. In this sense, the image titled "Plato's Plan of Atlantis" is simply presented illustratively: a map of the ideal state, as well as a tourist's (or "Solonist's") souvenir.

The second image, "The New Atlantis," visually repeats the first image's symmetrical design, with right and left sides facing one another to create the effect of insularity and unity. Like the first image, it is both a map and a souvenir. What may first appear an artistic arrangement of different advertisements proves on closer examination to be a happy accident of the processes of mechanical reproduction and mass marketing: a trifold pamphlet advertising the Kennedy Space Center, spread out flat to show one complete side of the printed

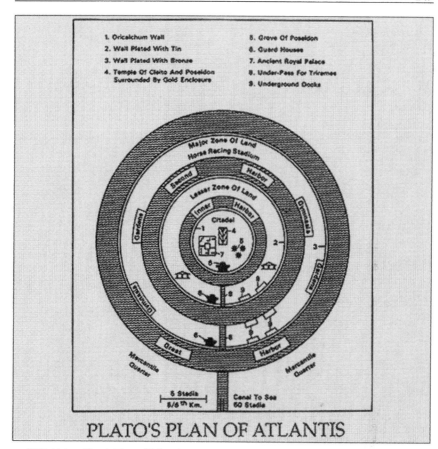

1. Oricalchum Wall
2. Wall Plated With Tin
3. Wall Plated With Bronze
4. Temple Of Cleito And Poseidon Surrounded By Gold Enclosure
5. Grove Of Poseidon
6. Guard Houses
7. Ancient Royal Palace
8. Under-Pass For Triremes
9. Underground Docks

PLATO'S PLAN OF ATLANTIS

FIG. 11.1.   Plato's Plan of Atlantis

sheet. But does the suggested comparison work completely? Does the pamphlet also represent—perhaps in its proclamation of "FREE ADMISSION AND PARKING!"—a visualization of the principles of a just society? The pairing and captioning of the images, as well as the academic argument of the verbal text, insists on this possibility. However, the "everyday," contextual distinction between the intentions of Platonic philosophy toward Atlantis in the *Timaeus* ("to understand ... the just state") and the intentions of the promotional ad ("Florida's Best Visitor Value ...") exemplify and "italicize" strains among these differing languages that the verbal argument at this point would suppress.

Ulmer's "Metaphoric Rocks," then, represents a larger, dynamic structure in which both the verbal text *and* the string of images are dialogical. The role played by the images, however, is not simply illustrative because the zigzagging lines of dialogical development—the explicit shifts and juxtapositions be-

FIG. 11.2.   The New "Atlantis"

tween these languages/intentions in verbal and visual terms—is roughly parallel but not precisely synchronous. At just the point when the verbal essay deploys its most monoglossic, academic language (and the loftiest and most sustained appeal to Classical learning), the images "spoil things" by presenting a jarring, playful contrast of the intellectual/philosophical and touristic/commercial. This is the very same contrast, however, that the verbal text makes manifest elsewhere: in the New Consultancy's feigned begrudging of the state's $250,000 payment to Penn & Schoen, or in the deliberate absurdity of its proposing a "Tourist Hall of Fame commemorating tourist sacrifices to chance" in a state now internationally famous for out-of-state visitors falling prey to random highway shootings and public robberies. In essence, the visuals zig where the verbal text zags.

So, the literate, hybrid discourse of Ulmer's "Metaphoric Rocks" is realized not simply with haphazardly inappropriate juxtapositions of word and image, but through a more coherent inappropriateness—a rhetoric of irritation—that underlies the entire Web essay as a culturally situated act of communication. It is not Ulmer's "art" that redeems the inappropriateness, but the consistency and deliberateness of his misunderstanding and violation of common-sense distinctions that enable the literate effect. George E. Mahlberg uses this rhetoric of irritation in more strictly visual terms in his photocomposite "Oswald in a Jam" (Fig. 11.3). Unlike many Photoshopped images that instrumentally juxtapose images from different pictures seamlessly into a new scene—the surfer riding the desert dune and casting a brown shadow on the beige sand, for instance—Mahlberg's literate practice here lies in the highlighting of cultural fault lines evident beneath (and beyond) the smooth, technically accomplished surface of manipulated pixels. As with Ulmer's satire on (or protest against) the cloistered insularity of academic work, "Oswald in a Jam" presents a dissonance that isn't simply inappropriate or surprising, but that echoes categorical instabilities or cultural conflicts that already inform an audience's historical situation and moment.

FIG. 11.3. "Oswald in a Jam," George E. Mahlberg, <http://www.doctorcosmo.com/oswald/oswaldillustration.html>. Photo Permission, Bob Jackson, Copyright 1963; Illustration, George E. Mahlberg, Copyright 1996.

To create his composite, Mahlberg used Photoshop to rework Bob Jackson's famous news photo of Jack Ruby assassinating Lee Harvey Oswald in the garage of the Dallas police station on Sunday, November 24, 1963. In Mahlberg's revision, the scene of violence is recast into a rock-and-roll venue, with Jack Ruby lunging forward grasping an electric guitar, Oswald's face contorted into a microphone, and the wide-eyed officer, Jim Leavelle, playing an electric keyboard. The relationships among the three—the assassin's stealthy aggression, the victim's surprise and anguish, the guard's shocked recognition—is rendered by Mahlberg's introduction of the instruments into the intensely coordinated performance of a garage band at a perfect musical moment. "One afternoon, I was eating lunch and surfin' the Web," Mahlberg writes,

> when I came across the historic picture by photographer Bob Jackson of Jack Ruby shooting Lee Harvey Oswald. Jackson's camera certainly caught that rare moment in time; the gray area between certainty and unreality. Jack Ruby was in a posture that spoke of conviction and drive and there was something in Oswald's face;[sic] a look of passion that's hard to duplicate. It struck me that he was certainly screamin' the blues, in fact, he looked to me like a young rock and roller beltin' out a serious tune. Uh, oh ... the Photoshop bug bit me and, 40 minutes later, the picture below was born.

Mahlberg's words (*conviction, drive, passion, blues, beltin', serious*) verbally express the surprising relationship, made visually apparent in the picture itself, between political violence and music, or terrorism and performance. These words specify the photocomposite's provocative juxtapositions between the institutional tumult of the 1960s—represented by the Vietnam War, antiwar protests in the streets, and the assassinations of John and Robert Kennedy and Martin Luther King—and the decade's promise of freedom and cultural revolution as embodied in the idealism of the rock-and-roll generation. The appropriate inappropriateness of the juxtaposition offers a glimpse beyond romanticizations of transcendent '60's rebellion and even of tragic '60s violence. More fundamentally, the interpretive tensions called out by the image bring into consciousness the normalizing ideological categories that we customarily use to separate ideas of social chaos and cultural progress, and that suppress the realization that political violence and terrorism are varieties of theatrical spectacle.

On his previous website, where "Oswald In a Jam" appeared for years under the title "In-A-Gadda-Da-Oswald," Mahlberg's commentary suggested the dialogical nature of the images conception and execution. In addition to being an obvious reference to Iron Butterfly's 1968 song, "In-A-Gadda-Da-Vida," the original title also recalls, wrote Mahlberg,

> a semi-regular feature on my weekly radio program, *Nocturnal Transmissions*. It is a live music mix featuring three simultaneous (and slightly out of

sync) recordings of Iron Butterfly's immortal garage-rock anthem (especially the drum solo!) plus recordings of police radio announcements and press reporters during and immediately following JFK's assassination, techno tracks by Baby Ford, numerous poems written about JFK and his death read by the poets, and a couple of tracks from Brian Eno's Nerve Net release. You can almost taste the Dallas air ...

In the context of Mahlberg's work across media, the original title of the photo thus provides a key to how the image was conceived creatively, and how it must be interpreted aesthetically and culturally. Indeed, the photo is a visual corollary to the aural performance Mahlberg describes here, a densely layered radio experience that combines '60s-era rock, live journalistic texts, ruminative oral poetry, and contemporary electronica in an intentionally disorienting, suggestive and provocative way. The deliberate anachronism of combining the political events of 1962 and 1963 with a hit song of 1968 in a single, dramatic sequence serves to bracket the years between, to explicitly set off "the '60s" as a subject of the piece. The invocation of Brian Eno recalls that artist/producer's trademark, avant-garde techniques of layering and repeating variable tape loops, which he developed in the 1970s.[4]

Although Mahlberg refers to neither the radio feature nor to Brian Eno in the image itself, the image "Oswald in a Jam" is a "cover"—in both music industry senses of the word as an imitation of or *homage* to the original radio work, as well as a visual correlative of its aural performance. Both these sources serve as discursive models (of radical juxtaposition and deferred meaning) for Mahlberg's production and our interpretation of the image, placing the viewer among apparently conflicting or competing layers of context, where the image's unresolved dialogical tensions resist easy settlement.

Tellingly, the suggestiveness of this image is *not* an automatic result of combining surprising visual elements in the same scene, as evidenced by comparing Mahlberg's image to the relatively mild and conventional effects achieved by the run-of-the-mill "Photoshopped" images (essentially photographic single-frame cartoons) that circulate on the Internet by e-mail, or featured on such sites as <http://www.worth1000.com>. Like distinctions between academic and commercial cultures that Ulmer invokes (by blithely transgressing) in "Metaphoric Rocks," the dialogical tensions in "Oswald in a Jam" draw their energy and meaning from corresponding cultural and ideological tensions called out from among the viewers' own cultural norms and assumptions. Because the viewer is implicated in the instabilities and interpretive dilemmas presented by the image's juxtapositions, meaning is not immediate but deferred, everywhere and yet nowhere, contained not in one element or in the meeting of the elements, but in the irritating, Iserian gaps between the familiar, historical scene of terrorism (a society in crisis) and Mahlberg's insinuation of rock-and-roll transcendence.

A suggestion of Mahlberg's aesthetic intentions and approach lies in one of the image's only alphabetic interventions, an example of what Edward Tufte calls "direct labels" (13). On a brick wall of the Dallas police station which stands behind Oswald, Mahlberg projects a shadowy outline of a stylized "DK" design that some viewers will recognize as the logo of an American punk band called the Dead Kennedys (1978—circa 1986). In songs like "Welcome to Cambodia," this band assailed what they saw as the self-satisfied and self-serving complacency of Reagan-era America, particularly of the young generation:

So you been to schools

For a year or two

And you know you've seen it all

In daddy's car

Thinkin' you'll go far

Back east your type don't crawl

Play ethnic jazz

To parade your snazz

On your five grand stereo

Braggin' that you know

How the niggers feel cold

And the slums got so much soul (Biagra)

Mahlberg—who introduces his own image Hitchcock-like into the scene as a floor-staring bystander, missing the critical moment of history entirely!—uses the distinctive, stylized "DK" not simply as a visual pun on the band's name, but to declare his own similarly oppositional style, visually and rhetorically. He challenges the viewer's easy, nostalgic notions of the '60s (as emblematized by phrases like the "birth of rock," or the "Summer of Love") by bringing those cultural developments back into contact with the realities of political and societal turmoil, which are the music's material and historical milieu. More fundamental than a comment on attitudes toward the '60s, however, Mahlberg's "In-A-Gadda-Da-Oswald" challenges the neat categorical distinctions that our culture conventionally maintains—all the more insistently after September 11—between art and terrorism, entertainment and violence, us and them.

I began this chapter by asking whether composition via Dreamweaver and Photoshop could be constitutive and literate, and, if so, how such a method could be imitable, thus making unstable, critical terms like *visual rhetoric* bases for teachable, creative practices. The examples of Ulmer's "Metaphoric Rocks" and Mahlberg's "Oswald in a Jam" show one means to this literary and rhetorical ideal: a compositional method that highlights the convergent, Bahktinian "tastes" of words and visual forms in mutually illuminating dialogue. Ironically, this rhetoric of creative irritation depends on the convention-bound sense of appropriateness, the necessarily social barometer of common-sense thinking that circumscribes what is variously known as normal life, ideology, or "false consciousness." For this reason, inappropriateness, as a method, must begin not with eternal principles of formal design or internal arrangement of parts (whether visual or verbal) but with a living dialogue of divergent voices, languages, perspectives and intentions that already circulate in and among a particular audience at a particular moment. Writing, design, and "art" follows from them.

Starting as it must with the audience, then, this rhetoric of irritation shares a point of departure with the most current and dominant explanation of Web design and popular visual rhetoric, the principles of "usability," promulgated most famously by software engineer Jakob Nielsen in books like *Designing Web Usability*. Where the science of usability and the rhetoric of irritation diverge, however, is in the distinction between a "user" and an "audience." Usability takes as its central tenet the "practice of simplicity," as the subtitle of Nielsen's book puts it, or, in the words of another usability guide's title, "Don't Make Me Think!" (Krug). The unspoken assumption of much usability instruction is that documents are made of "content" or "information" that should be laid out as unambiguously and conventionally as airports. Users are travelers whose destinations and desires are simple: to understand on the most cognitive level how to get themselves to Dallas and not Dulles.

On the other hand, most of us working in the humanities tradition, as I said at the beginning, see discourse as more often constitutive, intentionally or not, because the experience of the text—its design, context, rhetoric, and interpretive alternatives—contributes to its meaning. From a humanities perspective, texts *should* make you think, all the more so when they attempt to erase all trace of their cultural work under the pretext of simplicity, transparency, or universalism. Years ago, a feminist group pasted stickers on the slick advertising posters in London's Tube stations which asked, "Who Does This Ad Think You Are?" The provocative question does not raise issues of a cognitive user, but of a socially situated audience and of the media's role in defining subjectivity. Similarly, the institutional role of the humanities is not to contribute to the transparency of culture, but, like those disruptive and revealing stickers, to call attention to its material surfaces, its underlying mechanisms, its historical antecedents, and its ultimate social effects. Simplicity is a fiction that elides the implication of form and context in content—or, more accurately, in "meaning."

Authorities in usability and interface design might respond that pages like Ulmer's "Metaphoric Rocks" are anomalies on the Web, which is increasingly corporate and civic in use and must speak to the lowest common denominator to successfully provide as many users as possible with the content. They might point out that Mahlberg's image is more notable as a novelty than a true example of visual culture as seen across media. "Oswald in a Jam" is thus a rarified highjacking of the iconic language that, like images of the burning Twin Towers, more often serves in popular discourses to represent already understood ideas. Since meaning in Ulmer and Mahlberg is deferred, reflective and implicit—rather than direct, immediate and explicit—the chronically impatient user posited by usability studies might take *anything* from these texts, or nothing. Who's to say?

Yes, *who's to say?* That is the question. These differences raised here between *users* versus *audiences*, these assertions of what the Web or visual culture is or isn't, remind us that describing, theorizing, and instructing are ways of talking—abstract and figurative, whether arrived at empirically or intuitively—and never the thing itself. A Web page or an image might really *be* simple until someone, literally or figuratively, pastes a sticker on its surface asking an irritating question that reminds us that culture happens—always. A class in New Media Writing or other digital production is a class largely concerned with how to *talk* about reading and creating digital texts. In English or composition, such a class uses words that emerge from their critical traditions, words that have, in Bakhtin terms, lived their "socially charged lives" in the disciplines and are "populated by [their] intentions" (293). This chapter has been an exercise in one such way of talking, of applying the adjective, "literate," and the noun, "rhetoric," to the business of reading and composing digital or visual texts.

In concluding, then, I must reconsider this chapter's opening dichotomy between teaching the *instrumental* and *constitutive* senses of "literacy," between the mechanical, bread-and-butter skills of digital production and the critical awareness of the cultural work of words and images. Insisting on such an opposition is useful for those in the humanities tradition teaching Dreamweaver and Photoshop because these faculty feel a necessity to resist the class's natural undertow toward a focus on software instruction, computer science, graphic design, or usability, which follow the tug of students' expectations and novices' needs. In practice, what distinguishes the two kinds of literacy is not the action of the classroom or the means of production, but the words we use, just as a visitor might not distinguish a typing classroom from computer-assisted writing classroom until hearing what is said, the kinds of words being used. In this way, use of the oxymoron, "visual rhetoric," is not just a critical trope, but also a key to a practice, because practice follows seeing, and seeing follows talking. Who's to say? The visual is always rhetorical when rhetoricians are doing the looking, and especially when they are talking about the visual with the taste of rhetoric in their mouths.

NOTES

1. Portions of this chapter previously appeared in my article "Visualizing English." This essay extends and elaborates the previous work.
2. HTML is the mark-up language used to encode Web pages. WYSIWYG is an acronym—"What You See Is What You Get"—for an editing program that enables someone to compose a Web page without knowing or even seeing HTML code.
3. While both my examples, Ulmer and Mahlberg, are arguably comic in effect, the dialogical rhetoric of irritation is not restricted to humor. Bakhtin identifies dialogism as an essential feature of much literary discourse, which he terms "a novelistic hybrid" (361). I use the word "irritation" to suggest the positive effect of such dialogical or novelistic discourse when it is encountered outside typically literary genres and contexts.
4. In Eno's work, these tape loops were sometimes recordings of "found" sounds, such as archival Folkways recordings of a radio preacher or an exorcism used on *My Life in the Bush of Ghosts*, which Eno repeated and blended into a rhythm track to create something like a traditional song. Often, though, as on *Ambient 1: Music for Airports*, Eno's work operates not in traditional musical genres, but essentially as sound sculptures or aural room furnishing, which frustrate and elude conventional "listening." Such works of what Eno calls "Discreet Music" (the title of a 1975 album) are dialogical and ironic on the most fundamental level because they subvert the modernist assumption that artistic or "serious" music can be distinguished from popular music by the degree of close attention and study it rewards. In essence, Eno enlisted the most self-effacing and culturally pervasive of musical forms, Muzak, to make an artistic statement and offer an alternative to the loud, middle-brow pretensions of much '70s "progressive" rock. Eno's example provides a suggestive, aural model for examining Mahlberg's visual rhetoric and method.

WORKS CITED

Bakhtin, Mikhail. *The Dialogic Imagination*. Trans. Caryl Emerson and Michael Holquist. Austin: U of Texas P, 1981.

Biagra, Jello. "Holiday in Cambodia." *Fresh Fruit for Rotting Vegetables*. Dead Kennedys. Alternative Tentacle, 1980.

Eno, Brian. *Ambient 1: Music for Airports*. Eeg, 1978.

Iser, Wolfgang. *Implied Reader: Patterns of Communication in Prose Fiction from Bunyon to Beckett*. Baltimore: Johns Hopkins UP, 1978.

Krug, Steve. *Don't Make Me Think: A Common Sense Approach to Web Usability*. Indianapolis: New Riders, 2000.

Landow, George P. *Hypertext: The Convergence of Contemporary Critical Theory and Technology*. Baltimore: Johns Hopkins UP, 1992.

Mahlberg, George. "Oswald in a Jam." Online image. 26 May 2003. <http://doctorcosmo.com/oswald/oswaldillustration>.

Mitchell, W. J. T. *Iconology: Image, Text, Ideology.* Chicago: U of Chicago P, 1986.

Nielsen, Jakob. *Designing Web Usability: The Practice of Simplicity.* Indianapolis: New Riders Publishing, 2000.

Stroupe, Craig. "Visualizing English: Recognizing the Hybrid Literacy of Visual and Verbal Authorship on the Web." *College English* 62.5 (May 2000): 607–632.

Tufte, Edward. *Visual Explanations: Images, Quantities, Evidence and Narrative.* Cheshire, CT: Graphics P, 1997.

Ulmer, Greg. "Metaphoric Rocks: A Psychogeography of Tourism and Monumentality." *Rewired.* 1 Feb 1998. <http://www.clas.ufl.edu/CLAS/Departments/Rewired/ulmer.html>.

CHAPTER TWELVE

Placing Visual Rhetoric: Finding Material Comfort in Wild Oats Market

Greg Dickinson
Casey Malone Maugh

What is more banal, more everyday, and more routinized, than shopping for groceries? Yet, the little choices and daily decisions made about where to shop for food and what to buy are constitutive elements of living in the contemporary world. Grocery stores, supermarkets, super-shopping centers, health-food stores, whole-food markets, and co-ops provide more than food, they materialize consumer culture in tidy, colorful packages. Further, they are material and visual sites in which individuals directly negotiate their relations with globalized consumer culture. Here, in the grocery store, the forces of global capitalism, the contemporary transformation of transportation, production and packaging technologies and the discourses of postmodern consumer marketing intersect with the lived bodies of individuals. Located at the intersections of these elements of the contemporary condition, the grocery store—as banal as it may be—is a crucial place for understanding everyday, visual rhetoric in a postmodern world.

It is only within particular stores, within specific material locations, that these global transformations intersect with the particularities of bodies and subjects. We turn our attention, then, to the Wild Oats Market in Fort Collins, Colorado. Although this Wild Oats—one store in an international chain of upscale, organic food stores—is not exactly analogous to the big-box supermarket in which a huge portion of all groceries are sold, it provides a particularly felicitous place for thinking about the relations between global and local that are fundamental to postmodernity.[1] Wild Oats is a powerful rhetorical site because for many of its visitors, it serves as one hub in their daily lives, sliding, as many daily habits do, under the critical consciousness, and working within the comforts of habit and routine. We will argue that Wild Oats responds to the abstractions and discomforts of globalized postmodern consumer culture with a rhetoric of connection that draws on images of locality and nature, and asserts a particular form of community.

But, we turn our attention to Wild Oats not simply because of the ways it condenses particular problems of postmodernity, but also because of the ways it helps us think about the functions of visual rhetoric. As the chapters in this book demonstrate, studies in visual rhetoric often focus on what might best be called visual images. In this volume alone, we see investigations of film, advertising, photography, editorial cartoons, travel guides and statistical tables. These are obvious texts for both theoretical and critical reflection on visual rhetoric because these texts clearly do their work through visual means. As Martin Jay argues, scholars thinking about visuality across the disciplines, and over the scope of Western philosophy have consistently focused on precisely these kinds of images.

In this chapter we want to extend the analysis of visual rhetoric from the visual arts of photography, television, film and print to place.[2] Clearly the visual arts fill our vision on a daily basis. At the same time, the daily visuality of our lives consists of that which fills our everyday spaces. The places in which we live and work, the rooms in which we teach, drink coffee, and sleep, are always apprehended, understood, and constructed visually. In the everyday, then, visual rhetoric includes the visual suasion of images, but must also include the visuality of the spaces in which we live. Yet these places are not simply or primarily visual, they are always material and concrete and they are the sites of our embodied realizations of our selves. A well-rounded understanding of visual rhetoric needs to address the *embodiment* of visual rhetoric.

But how a definition or a theory of visual rhetoric should address materiality is a complex problem, a problem for which we have, at best, partially constructed solutions. As will be clear from our analysis of Wild Oats, buildings, and the institutions they house do not simply respond to the contemporary through visuality, instead they draw in the fully embodied subject. Indeed, although Wild Oats provides visual comforts, it also embeds the consumer in its rhetoric through taste, touch, smell and hearing. Wild Oats's appeal to the fully embodied subject became apparent in our investigation of the visual persuasion of Wild Oats. As we wrote, we kept finding ourselves sidetracked into writing about tasting and touching and smelling and hearing. This suggested to us that visual rhetoric in the built environment seldom if ever functions alone.

In the first section of the chapter, we will proffer one definition of the functions of visual rhetoric in postmodern spaces. This definition will lead us to a consideration of the ways everyday spaces serve as sites for negotiating the contours of postmodernity. In the second part of the chapter, we will turn to Wild Oats to ground this understanding of visual rhetoric in a particular site. In the final section, we reflect on what the analysis might tell us about the rhetorical power of at least some postmodern spaces and, more broadly, about the potentialities for a conceptualization of a fully embodied visual rhetoric.

VISUALITY AND THE EVERYDAY SPACES OF POSTMODERNITY

We want to suggest that one of the functions of postmodern visual rhetoric in the everyday built environment is to negotiate the contours of dislocation characteristic of postmodernity.[3] Although there is no singular experience that marks the postmodern, it seems clear that one of the constitutive elements of postmodernity is the way it challenges our ability to settle or locate our identities in either time or space (Collins 31–32; Soja, 25–27; Harvey vii). For example, our ability to locate ourselves in time—in history, memory or tradition—is fundamentally disrupted in the contemporary moment (Nora 7). Our histories are told and retold across a range of media and from widely divergent points of view. At the same time, we have nearly immediate access to an overwhelming number of texts and images from our pasts. All of this (which is an outgrowth of both information technologies and professionalization of history [Hutton 1–26]) undercuts the establishment of a single compelling narrative arc in which we can comfortably place ourselves and with which we can secure our identities. In short, our ability to locate ourselves in a history is undermined.

Similarly, our ability to clearly locate ourselves in space has been disrupted. Where once we might have gained identity based on long-established, geographically bound communities, we are now in a situation characterized by urbanization, migration, and immigration, and the fragmentation of locally coherent culture. Combined with the globalization of capital and media, it is increasingly difficult to distinguish one place from another. For example, Los Angeles is home to millions of people from across the globe, creating neighborhoods and enclaves that are neither characteristic of an older Los Angeles, nor exactly the same as the towns and cities from which the émigrés come (Soja, "Postmodern Urbanization" 130–131). At the exact same time, Tokyo and Seoul, Hamburg and Pretoria come to look more and more like Los Angeles (Iyer 45–49). Nearly everywhere you go you can be assured of McDonalds and Disney, Starbucks and the Gap (Iyer 99–103). As the distinctions between places disappear behind postmodern economic and cultural forces, personal identity cannot be founded on locality.

The problem of locating oneself is not just a visual or mental difficulty, but involves the body as well. Cybersex; reproductive technologies; psychotropic drugs; plastic surgery; liposuction; along with crucial debates about sex and sexuality, gender, race and ethnicity all put the "natural" body under strain. Recent theorists and critics from across a range of disciplines point to the constructed or performed nature of the body, posing profound critiques of the idea of the body as an ontological founding for identity (Butler 25; Haraway

1–3; Braidotti 41–56; Squier 113–132; Zita 76–79). In short, the identity crisis of postmodernity is one that challenges subjectivity, and does so in part by challenging the notions of the body itself.

Within this context of dislocation, postmodern visual rhetoric can be particularly useful as individuals seek to create coherent and comfortable identities. Many postmodern texts negotiate the problems of postmodernity in one of two ways. On one hand, many rely on a relentless quoting and referencing of a large range of other cultural texts. Jim Collins, writing about film, works through the ways many contemporary films combine visual conventions from two or more genres. Movies like *Shanghai Noon* or *Scream* refuse insertion in any one genre (western or horror, in these cases) but are constructed almost exclusively through quotations of and comment on the generic constraints that once made films predictable. These films revel in and rely on semiotic excess for their visual and narrative resources and in so doing, help audiences negotiate an image-saturated landscape (Collins 127). Some texts, however, utilize a very different strategy. These popular texts nostalgically recall simpler times or offer stories and images that seem more coherent. Collins calls films using this reactive rhetorical strategy *new sincerity* films. New sincerity films offer audiences simple and seemingly authentic identities and powerfully real connections with others. *Dances With Wolves* is a kind of touchstone in this postmodern genre. In this film, the generic constraints of the classic western are rewritten. Native American values and ways of life are portrayed as modes of salvation against the greed and avarice of White, Christian capitalism. What is crucial here is Collins's argument that the shifts of postmodernity have not left audiences completely adrift. It is not as though, Collins argues, culture is in a post-enlightenment moment while subjectivity remains foundered in enlightenment possibilities. Instead, these new texts and their audiences, working together, are creating new strategies through which individuals are able to more or less successfully negotiate the postmodern terrain.

Although films and other popular culture texts provide important resources as subjects traverse the dislocations of postmodernity, surely the everyday spaces in which these subjects enact themselves are at least as important. If postmodernity is characterized by dislocations within both time and space, and if these dislocations have their bodily effects, then the everyday spaces in which we enact our embodied selves become crucial to thinking through rhetorical responses to postmodernity. Architecture negotiates the postmodern visual landscape with strategies similar to those used in films and popular music (Jencks, "Hetero-Architecture" 60–63). On one hand, postmodern architecture (especially in the relatively narrow definition offered by Charles Jencks, *Language* 6) poaches from a range of historical styles to construct buildings that are not wholly new, but which create meaning through intertextual weavings of images. These buildings acknowledge the loss of concrete historical and geographical connectedness in modern place-making strategies while also suggesting the impossibility of returning to a moment in which singular architectural narratives are uncritically accepted. At the same time, much built space, rather than reveling in a freedom to quote from and critically comment on historical styles, draw much more carefully on single historical styles thereby creating buildings and landscapes that have an image of the old. This image is designed not to question by juxtaposition, but to offer comfort through unified statements that can be located in both time and geography. For example, gentrified, redeveloped old towns draw on this nostalgic rhetoric as they offer a vision of a time and place gone by (Zukin 187–195; Dickinson, "Memories" 101). Although the two strategies are different, both serve as ways of thinking about locality in both time and space. Both modes draw on traditional forms—the first through pastiche and hybridization, the second through reverential quoting—as a means of creating a sense of "place-in-time." In so doing, both modes work to create a sense of geographical place by trying to assert a particular or unique sense of belonging in a particular location.

Although Wild Oats is not historicist in the way an old town or gentrified neighborhood is, its visual rhetoric is very much of the some tenor: It responds to postmodernity not through a self-conscious poaching of styles, but rather with a more unified rhetoric of locality, nature and community. Wild Oats helps negotiate the terrors arising out of contemporary life by providing a comforting sense of place (Grossberg 209). Discussing the fears of postmodernism as it relates to architectural practices, Nan Ellin writes that,

> the virtual eclipse of the public realm, the growing encroachment of the marketplace and the state in the private realm, the shift to flexible accumulation, the growing gap between rich and poor, increased access to information technologies and influence of intelligent machines, the consequent obscuring of power, and the resultant challenge to dominance of the modern world view all contribute to a peculiar postmodern insecurity. (26)

Ellin argues that postmodern building has responded to these insecurities with a range of strategies including a nostalgia that, more than simply reaching to the past, looks for a past of "abundant simplicity" (31). It is not unusual to find postmodern spaces that proffer a simple past as an escape from the complexity what Ellin calls "real life" (32). Gated communities and shopping and leisure spaces that carefully control the types of people that visit while also controlling the visual and spatial design to maintain the coherent images the body and subject desire are prime examples of these kind of postmodern spaces (Dickinson, "Movies" 101–102). Wild Oats's rhetoric is precisely this rhetoric of abundant simplicity as it proffers the full range of products contemporary consumer culture makes possible within the comforts of a connected place.

SOWING WILD OATS

If Fort Collins, a town of just over 125,000 people, has an urban core, it is in what many refer to as "old town." Straddling College Avenue, old town has the oldest commercial buildings, a growing collection of civic buildings and, not surprisingly, houses the most visible difficulties of contemporary life including the homeless mission and the groups of homeless and aimless wandering the streets.[4] The city has grown south, leaving behind these conditions as it builds large houses in new developments and constructs shopping complexes filled with middle-class stores and restaurants. Across from the city's increasingly upscale mall, behind the Cadillac dealer, north of the BMW lot, south of the Porsche and Audi sellers, and within blocks of Fort Collins's more expensive established neighborhoods, Wild Oats is part of the new and prosperous Fort Collins. Shoppers arrive at Wild Oats only after passing through these staunchly bourgeois neighborhoods and retail districts. Already clued into the aesthetic and class concerns of the area, Wild Oats patrons parking in the store's lot are well prepared for the shopping experience Wild Oats proffers.

Our analysis begins here, in this parking lot. Like the range of stores surrounding Wild Oats and typical of suburbs and newer urban developments, Wild Oats in Fort Collins is a box building fronted by a parking lot. In this form—box floating in a sea of pavement and parked cars—Wild Oats in no way resists late modern and postmodern strip shopping complexes. At the same time, a number of exterior design features immediately distinguish the Wild Oats box from other boxes in parking lots. The building is not nearly as large as local supermarkets, and it is much smaller than a Super Wal-Mart. This smaller size gives the building a more human scale. It feels more personal and more local simply because it is smaller than its competitors. This personalized feel is reinforced by the planters with trees that line a table filled patio on the east, while liberal use of tile in the siding begins to pull the building outside of the prefabricated abstractions and the bigger-is-better ways of contemporary consumer culture. This relatively small store utilizing living trees as design elements resists the fast food, "biggie-meal" model of food consumption.

The name of the store—Wild Oats Market—announces the store's particular response to contemporary culture in two ways. First, the name emphasizes the store's connection to nature and food. Wild Oats could refer to a life in the wilds of nature (with convenient parking out front). Further, it suggests resistance to the rules as the shopper can sow wild oats in the store. And of course it connects to a grain—oats—that is particularly nutritious.[5] So the first two words work to connect us to natural, liberating food products.[6] Just as interesting, however, is the name, "Market."[7] Sharon Zukin, thinking both about the built environment and the troubles of market and place writes, "[i]n theory, a postmodern culture suggests the possibility of reconciling landscape and vernacular, and market and place; but the more visible it becomes, the more it takes on the decontextualized, market-oriented look of franchise culture" (27). Traditionally, market and place have been interconnected such that "market was both a literal place and a symbolic threshold" (Zukin 6). However, the globalization of the market results in the division of market and place, thereby diminishing local distinctions (Zukin 12). Pico Iyer writes in his provocative way that the postmodern individual's most familiar place may be "in airports that [look] more and more like transnational cities, in cities that [look] more and more like transnational airports" (19). For Iyer, these transnational sites of consumption have replaced the centering force of home. "Yet in the modern world," he writes, "which I take to be an International Empire, the sense of home is not just divided, but scattered across the planet, and in the absence of any center at all, people find themselves at sea" (18). The feeling of being "at sea" is a response to the loss of a clearly defined market that is situated in a particular place, tied to a community. But in name, at least, Wild Oats Market wishes to resist this late capitalist move by reconnecting market and place.

This reconnection is not just spatial or geographical, it is also historical; the word "market" references ancient modes of urban dwelling and economic life. As Zukin argues, market has long held a central and centralizing function in civic and communal life. The market was a place not just of buying and selling, but of communion with others both like and unlike oneself, a site of interactions that created and bound the community. Wild Oats Market clearly wants to assert itself into this historical lineage, thereby embedding consumers into a set of comforting historical structures. In this process, Wild Oats works hard to distinguish itself from its down-market competitors. Rather than the seeming ahistoricity and placelessness of Safeway, Albertsons, Piggly Wiggly, or Publix, Wild Oats asserts its connection to the earth and to particular geographical and historical structures. That this market—with all of its spatial and historical resonances—sells food, heightens the force of this rhetoric, for food can seem deeply connected to the earth from which it comes.[8]

As important as the name is, though, we do not think the name carries most of Wild Oats's rhetorical force. More important is the way the name combines with the small building and trees, tables and umbrellas to begin to remind the visitor that this will be a place to reconnect with nature and with other human beings. The transition from the abstractions of the world outside the store to the particularities inside is eased by the displays under the store's awning but outside the actual doors. Just as the sculptures in the portals of a gothic cathedral remind the visitor of the cathedral's purpose, the space under the awning with its live plants or autumnal displays begins to sew the visitor into the fabric of Wild Oats's rhetoric. Of course these displays extend the selling space outside the walls of the store but just as importantly they make an otherwise sterile site alive with organic produce or with potted plants for home gardens. Even before selecting a shopping cart or moving through the automatic glass doors, the visitor is greeted by the sight of Wild Oats's particular vision of marketplace in postmodernity.

Producing Locality

It is no mistake that on entering the store, the first vision shoppers see is that of organically grown fruits or vegetables piled high in wooden crates. Colorful and fresh, the produce proclaims Wild Oats's commitment to carefully grown food. But the food is not just displayed for vision; as the shopper moves to the display, other senses are engaged as well. Perhaps they pick up a peach feeling it for freshness; the shoppers smell it, hoping to catch the scent of a peach orchard. On many days, the display includes samples of produce encouraging the shopper to taste and literally consume and incorporate the produce. At this site then, the entire body is woven into the Wild Oats's rhetoric of nature. The fruit of the earth is seen and felt, its taste and scent available to the consumer.

This moment may present the store's most powerful rhetoric. Engaging a full range of embodied senses immediately draws the visitor into Wild Oats's attempt to overcome the complex abstractions of postmodernity. Tasting, smelling, touching, and looking lead to choices that involve the whole person in the complex systems by which produce moves from farm to table. In short, the forces of globalism bring produce from around the world to this store, to this consumer, to this body, finding in the body its final and its absolutely localized resting place.

This initial display is part of a larger display of fresh produce that takes up the entire right front of the store. Like the first display, the rest of the produce is artfully presented. You will not find the grapes pre-packaged or the cherries pre-selected, instead the produce is available to be touched and handled. Signs naming the produce also name the country or state that grew the produce and whether the produce is organic. The signs indicate that some of the produce is grown locally; however, most of it comes from places like Chile, Mexico and California. At first, this appears problematic for a store resisting globalization, but rhetorically it is presented to be just the opposite. Knowing the origin of the produce allows the store to tell the customer that they support organic produce regardless of where it was grown. Just as importantly, although the produce comes to Wild Oats from across the global, in naming its country of origin, Wild Oats works to demystify the systems that bring food to our tables. Fresh tomatoes do not appear magically in January, but are, as the signs proclaim, shipped from organic farms in Mexico. The produce section at Wild Oats is caught between resisting globalization and providing the full range of goods made possible by globalization. If our Wild Oats on the front range of the Rocky Mountains limited itself to produce grown locally, its selection would be slim even in summer. This problem is not as great in, say, Southern California, but even there, it is impossible to get all the produce desired all year long.

In the produce section, then, Wild Oats is not outside of globalization but negotiates our relationship to globalized structures through a rhetoric of locality rather than through a rhetoric of the local. This rhetoric of locality seeks not to reinforce the local versus the global, but rather to negotiate the range of possibilities offered by globally dispersed localities. Embedding the individual in one particular and well-known local site is less crucial then giving the subject the means by which they can locate themselves in the web of global systems, places and processes. Unlike the colonizing force of corporations like McDonalds, Wild Oats asserts a more progressive vision of globalization. In Wild Oats, global capitalism can work to encourage organic farming and a range of agricultural practices that sustain traditional, healthier modes of living not only for shoppers at Wild Oats, but for workers around the globe. In this way, Wild Oats fits into practices like Body Shop's use of "exotic" products from underdeveloped nations and produced by natives and Starbucks claims of support for fair trade practices (Kaplan 61; Mathieu 123). In both cases, the institutions claim that rather than colonizing native others, their practices enhance the lives and communities of workers. In Wild Oats's produce department, then, consumers are invited into an economic and cultural globalism in which buying tomatoes in January is a way of making better a world that is otherwise overly challenging.[9]

Nature in Bulk

Of course, the produce section, in keeping with our argument so far, is also deeply connected to nature. This connection to nature reinforces the rhetoric of locality because particular forms of earth and climate result in particular produce. But in connecting locality to nature, Wild Oats tries to reconnect individuals with the earth and its bounty. The wide variety of produce available is, of course, part of this rhetoric of nature. But so too is the wide range of goods available in the bulk section. The sheer number of bins, displaying a wide range of colors and shapes, works to insert the visitor into the abundance of natural goods the earth produces. Standing outside of the abstract systems that support agri-businesses and supermarkets, the bins pronounce nature's gifts that, for many shoppers, are unavailable in other supermarkets. The shopper, looking from one bin the next, reading the cards that explain the product or its use, choosing to fill a bag with flax seed flour or Brazil nuts, becomes intimately intertwined with the materials themselves. In these practices as in the practices enacted in the produce section, the shopper becomes part of the nature offered and seen. In a sense, the consumer becomes embedded in the labor that moves food from field to table. The consumer selects the product, packages and labels it. The shopper is not separated from the food by sealed packages that hide rather than reveal the status of the material bought. Instead the bulk section reconnects shoppers to nature, overcoming the separation from our "natural condition by instruments of [our] own making" (Burke 13).

This connection to nature fostered in the produce and bulk sections of the market, is reinforced throughout the store through broader design elements. A primary element at work in this feel is the use of wood around the store. The ends of the shelves are trimmed in wood. Wood display cases stand at each of the checkout stands, while fresh baked artisanal breads and pastries are held in blond wood cases. Add fresh-cut flowers throughout the store (even in the bathrooms) and a fireplace in the café and you have a store that consistently draws on visions of nature.

The packages in these wood cases also proclaim their naturalness. On the shelves in the middle of the store we find the packaged foods, from bags of chips to cans of tomatoes. Yet, nearly every package, in some way or another, proclaims the naturalness of the product inside. Of course, the labels *nature* and *natural* are in constant use, but also crucial are a whole host of other descriptors including *organic, pure* and *no preservatives*. Harvey Levenstein argues that consumers consistently believe that these key words denote foods that are "healthier, safer and better for them" (199). It is crucial, of course, for the packaging to declare the naturalness of the contents. Without this maneuver, the bag of chips at Wild Oats would seem to be more or less the same as a bag of Doritos. This would begin to undercut Wild Oats's rhetorical claim to connectedness within globalization. What the chip aisle and all the other aisles of processed, packaged foods in Wild Oats provide are the comforts of mass produced, processed foods, but with a "natural" difference.

Like the rhetoric of locality just discussed, the rhetoric of the natural is not so much opposed to global consumer culture, but rather is a particular position within that culture. Rather than a rejection of postmodern systems, "all natural" cups of soup exploit the very means of processing the language seems to resist. As postmodern consumer culture raises the desire for a more natural, less plastic life—in short, a simpler yet abundant life—natural foods companies and stores provide carefully processed and packaged food that consistently claims its own naturalness. By displaying these packaged products in wooden cases, bringing the consumer to packaged products after leading them through the produce and bulk sections that highlight the natural, the consumer is ready to believe the claims on the package label.

A Slice of Community

Wild Oats strives to create connection not just through a rhetoric of locality or nature, but also through the establishment of ethical, socially conscious community. Wild Oats produces community connections through a range of full service mini-markets located around the periphery of the store, through modes of inclusion of a wide range of shoppers, and through donation programs. Of these, perhaps the full-service areas around the store are the most important. Along the back wall, and circling around the wall on the south are a series of stations in which operate a fishmonger, a butcher, a cheese monger, a full service deli, and a bakery. This collection draws on a memory of a past in which the local butcher prepared the meat and the local baker baked the bread. In this warmly remembered past, the butcher would remember your name and preferences and have particular commitments to the needs of the neighborhood. The rise of the supermarket along with the development of massive meat packing plants and of corporate bakers that delivered hamburgers and buns for startlingly low prices, however, undermined the viability of these local establishments (Mayo). By providing full-service shops, Wild Oats takes on the image of this older mode of consumption. Watching the butcher weigh out the meat, or the fish-monger slice a pound of wild Alaskan salmon, or the cheese seller offer a sample of the Manchego fresh in from Spain provides a vision of this neighborhood and neighborly connection.

Of course this form of community connects to both the rhetoric of locality and of nature. It reinforces the rhetoric of locality in part by naming where the meats and fish come from and by providing foods baked in the store's bakery and kitchen. In watching the meat cut, or hearing the grinding of the beef, the customer is sutured into the final process of getting the food from the farm and the ocean to the table. But it also connects with the rhetoric of nature, as the products—outside of plastic wrap—seem more natural and wholesome. In seeing the large salmon steak from which our dinner is cut, we are led to believe that this fish is fresher and more natural than the precut, shrink-wrapped flesh we find in the standard supermarket. In these nostalgic shops, Wild Oats once again provides a response to the abstractions of globalized consumerism. It provides the convenience of one-stop shopping, but with the nostalgic vision of communal and neighborly forms of buying. Even more important, the store provides a neighborhood within its four walls. The shopper can become embedded into a neighborhood of consumption without the risks or responsibilities associated with the older, pre-suburban neighborhoods to which the store refers. Wild Oats provides the "image" and thus at least parts of the comforts of the neighborhood butcher while in no way undermining the anonymity of the housing developments from which many of the shoppers come.

This kind of neighborhood connection is reinforced by a series of adaptations of the store to particular visitors. Children are welcomed with miniature shopping carts and coloring books; customers wanting to buy just a few items but who do not want to carry a basket can use small carts on which their basket fits. The store is filled with workers whose apparent job it is to wander the aisles and provide help and advice, especially in the large section devoted to supplements and alternative health remedies. The store includes a large bulle-

tin board on which community groups can post announcements and advertisements. The magazine racks hold alternative magazines; *Organic Gardner*
replaces *Better Homes and Gardens, Yoga Journal* replaces *Sports Illustrated*. Taken
together, these differences between Wild Oats and the "mainstream" supermarket connect the store with a particular kind of consumer who is fully involved in consumer culture, but a consumer culture predicated on its status as
alternative. Wild Oats provides a site where individuals resisting the
one-size-fits-all, better living through chemistry model of consumption can
find a home, a place of comfort and connection.

Finally, a sense of belonging to a community outside the store's walls is reinforced at the "donation station." Wild Oats offers a bulletin board near the
front of the store where customers may pick up information about donating
money to various causes. A similar bulletin board is located in the back of the
store where customers can drop off their donations as they shop. In Wild Oats'
south parking lot, there is a permanently stationed Good Will donation trailer
where, each day during business hours, patrons can contribute household
items and clothing. Wild Oats strives to convince customers that it cares about
the community and they reinforce this value in their customers, as they invite
them to donate. The combination of the customer donations and the store's
donations allow the consumer to give back to the community in which they
live. Even if the customer does not directly give to a charity, Wild Oats does.
By simply shopping at Wild Oats, anyone can be a donor.

The mini-markets, inclusiveness and donation programs, combine with
rhetorics of locality and nature in inviting shoppers to feel part of a larger, organic community. This community, as proffered by Wild Oats, supports sus-
tainable farming and progressive economic development, it offers holistic
modes of eating and healing. In short, the community connections available
in Wild Oats seem to directly address the alienation and anomie that is characteristic of postmodern consumer culture. And yet the store does not directly
resist consumerism, it does not argue for a radical remaking of the economies
of globalization, it does not suggest a decentering of dominant social or cultural formations. Instead, drawing on a full range of consumer goods and
globalized markets, Wild Oats offers an image of home and community that is
comforting but not transformative, familiar but not radically new.

MATERIALIZING COMFORT, SEEING CONNECTION

We have been arguing that Wild Oats provides a particular way of negotiating the discomforts alienating tendencies of postmodern, globalized consumer culture. At first glance, Wild Oats appears to be offering a space of
action outside of the postmodernity to which it responds. In fact, this is not
the case. Instead, through its rhetoric of locality, nature, and community,

Wild Oats repackages the possibilities of globalization to at once supply the postmodern adventures of buying Spanish cheese and Italian olives while embedding these adventures within the comfort of connections. Each of these rhetorics—of locality, nature, and community—is not figured outside of or in direct opposition to contemporary culture, but rather is an alternative use of the resources available in the contemporary world. Take the rhetoric of locality, for example. Rather than resisting globalized systems that make fresh produce available in Colorado year around, Wild Oats takes the time to localize the produce, giving it a provenance. This locality remakes the rhetoric of nature, as well. The organic tomato sold in January is, on one hand, natural, but made available in Fort Collins only by way of sophisticated technologies of transportation and communication. All of which remakes the notion of community, such that the community site is one in which our identities as alternative are founded in, justified through, and exhibited by the insertion of ourselves in this particular chain of consumptive practices. The diversity we confront in the neighborhood marketplace is not the diversity of peoples but a diversity of products available for purchase. We are reminded here of Karen Kaplan's argument about Body Shop advertising. She contends that Body Shop marketing

> signals a desire for a dissolution of boundaries to facilitate personal freedom and ease of trade even as it articulates national and cultural characteristics as distinct, innate markers of difference. Enabled by transnational capital flows, these representations are heavily invested in signs of traditional, non-metropolitan industries (marked as "native," "tribal," or "underdeveloped"). (49)

Wild Oats, although not appealing directly to images of the native, the tribal, or the underdeveloped engages in a related rhetoric of connection creating transnational, postmodern bonds that leave open personal freedom to consume while providing enough details of time and place about the products consumed to provide comfort. But even in this specificity, even in these rhetorics of locality, nature, and community, the deep social injustices on which transnational consumers depend are constantly and always hidden and mystified (Kaplan 61).

This mystification in Wild Oats is particularly powerful because of the ways it works on the whole person. Wild Oats's rhetoric is of course visual. The sight of the produce, the bins of natural grains and beans, the vision of the butcher cutting our steak and the baker slicing our daily bread visually draw us into this rhetoric of connection. However, we do not just see the produce or the bread, the meat or the cheese—we taste and touch and smell. We do not just consume with our eyes but with our whole selves. The connections proffered by Wild Oats are materialized in an instant, in the sound and the smell, the taste and the touch, and the sight. As the individual searches for a locality in which to feel secure, as the body seeks a way toward its lost naturalness, as the subject desires the interconnections of community, visual rhetoric provides some of the hoped-for resources. But as this analysis of Wild Oats suggests, these connections can be even more powerfully made when we understand that the eye is embodied and rhetoric is material.

How then does this analysis enrich our initial definition of visual rhetoric in everyday built spaces? Earlier we suggested that postmodern visual rhetoric in everyday built environments serves as one way for customers to negotiate the dislocations characteristic of postmodernity. We went on to argue that postmodernity undermines our ability to locate ourselves in time or space or, for that matter, in our own bodies. Our discussion of Wild Oats intersects directly with both this definition and this naming of the difficulties of postmodernity. As our subjectivities and our bodies are fragmented and dispersed, we desire more than just a vision or a *sight* of comfort, we desire a *site* in which our whole bodies might find comfort. Visual rhetoric in space becomes most compelling not simply when the vision is compelling, but when the rhetoric appeals to the intersections among the five senses. The sight of the peach is made more powerful by the smell and touch and taste.

Visual rhetoric in space is *part* of the way a site like Wild Oats helps customers negotiate the postmodern terrain. But we negotiate that terrain with all of our selves, with all of our bodies. The rhetoric of locality helps us locate our bodies in relation with other bodies in the world. The rhetoric of nature helps assure us that some part of our bodies—as extended as they may be by postmodern technologies and cultures—are or can be also natural. And the rhetoric of community connects our individual values with those of others close to us in both time and space. As Elizabeth Grosz argues, locatedness in place is fundamental to both subjectivity and coherent understandings of bodies (93). Vision, along with hearing, touch and smell, become fundamental to the body in locating itself in the world and, thus, fundamental to the functioning of both the body and the subject. The body and the subject turn not so much to extraordinary spaces—museums, cathedrals, civic buildings, monuments—for comfort and coherence, but to places of everyday life. In grocery stores and offices, homes and coffee shops, the body and the subject search for places that, in very literal ways, help shape the contours of the everyday. Particularly powerful, we suggest, are those places like grocery stores, restaurants, kitchens, and coffee shops that can most thoroughly and explicitly address the seeing, tasting, hearing, touching, and smelling person into the rhetorics of space. The visual rhetorics of place, then, function most profoundly within these interconnections among bodies, subjects and vision.

NOTES

1. Wild Oats stores began in 1987 in Boulder, Colorado. Wild Oats Markets, Inc., with over 107 stores across the United States and Canada, not only specializes in natural, organic, and gourmet food, but also contain large sections devoted to natural health and beauty products including supplements, homeopathic remedies, essential oils and the like. In its marketing on the Web and, to some extent, in its in-store marketing, Wild Oats supports a liberal form of consumer capitalism that we will take up later in the chapter (WildOats.com).

2. A number of rhetorical critics have taken up space and architecture as important sites for analysis. See, Armada; Blair, "Contemporary"; Blair, Jeppeson, Pucci; Blair and Michel; Dickinson, "Joe's"; Dickinson, "Memories"; Gallagher, "Memory"; Gallagher, "Remembering"; Katriel.

3. We use the term, *everyday built environment* for at least two reasons. First, our interest lies more in the kinds of banal spaces most of us use most of the time rather than in high or "important" architecture. Second, we are signaling our intention to focus not just on the building or even the interior design, but on the wide range of visual and material elements that are part of the banal spaces, including the products for sale, the people in the building and the like (de Certeau xx-xxvi; Lefebvre, *Critique* 92).

4. Like many gentrifying old towns, Fort Collins's old town has both the appeal of centrality and the demerits of relative poverty and density. As a center, it contains fancy stores devoted to chocolate, kitchen goods, housewares and fine (for Fort Collins) restaurants. But as the dense center of the city with a range of civic and non-profit services for the poor and the homeless, it also is the most visible site/sight of the contradictions of postmodern consumer culture. As middle-class patrons sip $3 lattés, the poor and the homeless congregate at the bus stop. For a fuller discussion of these contradictions see, Zukin.

5. It is more than a bit ironic that wild oats are weeds of which the farmer tries to rid the field. Perhaps it is within a world in which most consumers are fully separated from the farming that produces the food that Wild Oats is a reasonable name for a grocery store.

6. It should be noted that Wild Oats's major competitor, Whole Foods, uses a similar strategy in naming. Although there is not quite the connection to resistance in the play on the old saying "sowing wild oats," or "feeling her/his oats," there is the distinction from the over-packaged, over-processed food sold at traditional supermarkets. The similarities do not end there. Indeed, although customers may be fiercely loyal to either Wild Oats or Whole Foods, our sense is that much of the visual and material rhetoric of the two stores is more similar than different. We base this claim on our visits and regular use of Wild Oats and Whole Foods stores in Fort Collins and

Boulder, Colorado and in Pasadena, Glendale, and San Diego, California, over the last 10 years.
7. The official name used in marketing literature is *marketplace*, reinforcing the argument we are making.
8. It seems to us that the appeal of a whole range of foods and food practices rely precisely on this connection. The rapid growth of farmers markets is an obvious form of this, but so too is the intense interest in fine wines, varietal coffees and teas, handmade cheeses and the like. The quality of many of these foods depends on the earth from which they are produced. The French call this a concern with *terrior*, or earth. We will return to this as we enter the store.
9. This sort of "progressive globalization" has received a variety of terms, perhaps most important is that of the "third way" that linked Tony Blair's and Bill Clinton's "progressive" politics (Callinicos 1–43). The arguments about globalism are vast and multivocal. See, for example, Hardt and Negri; Gunn 3–50; Dallymayr 17–34.

WORKS CITED

Armada, Bernard J. "Memorial Agon: An Interpretive Tour of the National Civil Rights Museum." *Southern Communication Journal* (1998): 235–243.

Blair, Carole. "Contemporary U.S. Memorial Sites as Exemplars of Rhetoric's Materiality." *Rhetorical Bodies*. Ed. Jack Selzer and Sharon Crowley. Madison: U of Wisconsin P, 1999: 16–57.

—, Marsha Jeppeson, and Enrico Pucci. "Public Memorializing in Postmodernity: The Vietnam Veterans Memorial as Prototype." *Quarterly Journal of Speech* 77 (1991): 263–288.

—, and Neil Michel. "Reproducing Civil Rights Tactics: The Rhetorical Performances of the Civil Rights Memorial." *Rhetoric Society Quarterly* 30 (2000): 31–55.

Braidotti, Rosi. *Nomadic Subjects: Embodiment and Sexual Difference in Contemporary Feminist Theory*. New York: Columbia UP, 1994.

Burke, Kenneth. *Language as Symbolic Action: Essays on Life, Literature, and Method*. Berkeley: U of California P, 1966.

Butler, Judith. *Gender Trouble: Feminism and the Subversion of Identity*. New York: Routledge, 1990.

Callinicos, Alex. *Against the Third Way: An Anti-Capitalist Critique*. Cambridge, UK: Polity, 2001.

Collins, Jim. *Architectures of Excess: Cultural Life in the Information Age*. New York: Routledge, 1995.

Cyphert, Dale. "Ideology, Knowledge and Text: Pulling at the Knot in Ariadne's Thread." *Quarterly Journal of Speech* 87 (2001): 378–395.

Dallmayr, Fred. *Achieving Our World: Toward a Global and Plural Democracy*. Lanham, MD: Rowman and Littelfield, 2001.

De Certeau, Michel. *The Practice of Everyday Life*. Berkeley, CA: U of California P, 1984.

Dickinson, Greg. "Joe's Rhetoric: Starbucks and the Spatial Rhetoric of Authenticity." *Rhetoric Society Quarterly* 32 (2002):5–27.

—. "Memories for Sale: Nostalgia and the Construction of Identity in Old Pasadena." *Quarterly Journal of Speech* 83 (1997): 1–27.

—. "Movies, Memories and Merriment: Making Postmodern Spaces in Los Angeles." *Philologia Hispalensis* 13 (1999): 99–103.

Ellin, Nan. "Shelter from the Storm or Form Follows Fear and Vice Versa." *Architecture of Fear*. Ed., Nan Ellin. New York: Princeton Architectural Press, 1997: 13–45.

Gallagher, Victoria J. "Memory and Reconciliation in the Birmingham Civil Rights Institute." *Rhetoric and Public Affairs* 2 (1999): 303–320.

—. "Remembering Together: Rhetorical Integration and the Case of the Martin Luther King, Jr. Memorial." *Southern Communication Journal* 60 (1995): 109–119.

Grossberg, Lawrence. *We Gotta Get Out of This Place: Popular Conservatism and Postmodern Culture*. New York: Routledge, 1992.

Grosz, Elizabeth. *Volatile Bodies: Toward a Corporeal Feminism*. Bloomington: U of Indiana P, 1994.

Gunn, Giles. *Beyond Solidarity: Pragmatism and Difference in a Globalized World*. Chicago: U of Chicago P, 2001.

Haraway, Donna J. *Modest_Witness@Second_Millennium. FemaleMan'_Meets_OncoMouse™: Feminism and Technoscience*. New York: Routledge, 1997.

Hardt, Michael, and Antonio Negri. *Empire*. Cambridge, MA: Harvard UP, 2000.

Harvey, David. *The Condition of Postmodernity*. Cambridge, MA: Blackwell, 1989.

Hutton, Patrick H. *History as an Art of Memory*. Hanover: U of Vermont P, 1993.

Iyer, Pico. *The Global Soul: Jet Lag, Shopping Malls, and the Search for Home*. New York: Alfred A. Knopf, 2000.

Jay, Martin. *Downcast Eyes: The Denigration of Vision in Twentieth-Century French Thought*. Berkeley: U of California P, 1993.

Jencks, Charles. "Hetero-Architecture and the L.A. School." *The City: Los Angeles and Urban Theory at the End of the Twentieth Century*. Eds. Allen J. Scott and Edward W. Soja. Berkeley: University of California P, 1996.

—. *The Language of Postmodern Architecture*. 5th ed. New York: Rizzoli, 1987.

Kaplan, Karen. "A World Without Boundaries: The Body Shop's Trans/National Geographies." *Social Text* (1995): 45–66.

Katriel, Tamar. "Sites of Memory: Discourses of the Past in Israeli Pioneering Settlement Museums." *Quarterly Journal of Speech* 80 (1994): 1–20.

Lefebvre, Henri. *Critique of Everyday Life*. N. Vol. 1. Trans. John Moore. London: Verso, 1991.

—. *The Production of Space*. Trans. Donald Nicholson-Smith. Oxford: Blackwell Publishers, 1991.

Levenstein, Harvey. *The Paradox of Plenty: A Social History of Eating in Modern America*. New York: Oxford U P, 1993.

Mathieu, Paula. "Economic Citizenship and the Rhetoric of Gourmet Coffee." *Rhetoric Review* 18 (1999): 112–127.

Mayo, James M. *The American Grocery Store: The Business Evolution of an Architectural Space*. Westport, CT: Greenwood Press, 1993.

Nora, Pierre. "Between Memory and History: Les Lieux de Memorie." *Representations* 26 (1989): 7–25.

Soja, Edward W. *Postmodern Geographies: The Reassertion of Space in Critical Social Theory*. New York: Verso, 1989.

—. "Postmodern Urbanization: The Six Restructurings of Los Angeles." *Postmodern Cities and Spaces.* Ed. Sophie Watson and Katherine Gibson. Oxford, UK: Blackwell, 1995: 125–137.

Squier, Susan M. "Reproducing the Posthuman Body: Ectogenetic Fetus, Surrogate Mother, Pregnant Man." *Posthuman Bodies.* Ed. Judith Halberstam and Ira Livingston. Bloomington: Indiana U P, 1995: 113–134.

Zita, Jacquelyn N. *Body Talk: Philosophical Reflections on Sex and Gender.* New York: Columbia U P, 1998.

Zukin, Sharon. *Landscapes of Power: From Detroit to Disney World.* Berkeley, CA: U of California P, 1991.

CHAPTER THIRTEEN

Envisioning Domesticity, Locating Identity: Constructing the Victorian Middle Class Through Images of Home

Andrea Kaston Tange

For the middle class in Victorian England, the concept of *home* was of paramount importance. A particular home confirmed a specific family's place in the social order, and, in ideological terms, reiterated middle-class standards through a concrete visual example that conformed to certain norms. Because middle-class identity was defined in large part through the imaginative value of domesticity, the physical images presented by actual homes were complemented with print images in texts that participated in creating domestic ideology. The cultural meaning of home thus depended heavily on the visual as both a tangible image and a metaphor. As I will argue, Victorian domesticity was importantly disseminated as a visual rhetoric that combined ideological significance—the intangible, ideal image of the respectable family—with physical images of homemaking in textual illustrations that reproduced this ideology in a consumable format.

Texts that illustrate how to achieve a proper home—and thereby establish and continually confirm one's middle-class identity—proliferated in Victorian culture. At mid-century, the available images of home ranged from paintings and literature that depicted domestic scenes to architectural treatises and housekeeping guides that offered multiple visions of how to build a house and live in it.[1] This wide range of genres, circulating around a common set of issues, defined the vital link between domesticity and identity: displays of good taste in decorating, brilliance at entertaining, and thorough competence at the daily management of a household full of children and servants were the surest markers of middle-class respectability. In her study on Victorian domesticity, Elizabeth Langland notes that, "appearances are productive of substantial effects, and those who know how to manage the social signifiers are individuals

277

to be reckoned with" (142). Indeed, the Victorian middle-class home functioned to maintain crucial boundaries of class and gender identities primarily because it provided a stable location in which to "manage the social signifiers" of one's position.

Creating domestic spaces that properly signified, however, was a delicate task because home was expected to maintain its integrity as a "private" place, despite the fact that establishing one's middle-class status required providing publicly consumable, constantly reiterated spectacles of domesticity. The notion of separate spheres idealized the domestic realm as a private, feminized place constructed against the public, masculine world of work and commerce.[2] Consolidating this notion was Coventry Patmore's four-volume poem, *The Angel in the House*, which traced the courtship, marriage, and domestic life of a woman whose name and individual story were almost immediately forgotten, replaced in the public imagination by the moniker Patmore created in his poem's title.[3] The ideal of the angel in the house became a cultural shorthand for the ways in which home and middle-class woman were reciprocal concepts: A respectable middle-class home by definition had a good woman at its center, just as a good middle-class woman defined herself largely through her capacity to manage her home. Homes and women had parallel functions; relying on their "natural" moral sense and capacity to nurture, they were to create a haven in which children would learn manners and values, and men could seek refuge from the anxieties produced by public life.[4]

Yet it is important to recognize that despite rhetorical efforts to gender domesticity feminine, it was as vital culturally to ensure that the home maintained the boundaries of middle-class identity. In fact, the concept of the angel in the house implies that domestic ideology relied as much on class position as on gender difference, for a woman whose primary duties were moral, spiritual, and management-based must necessarily be located in a home in which the hard, physical labor of cooking and cleaning was carried out by servants. Indeed, to be *middle class* was commonly defined as having the means to keep at least one domestic servant and an occupation that did not require physical labor or the handling of money on a regular basis.

The difficulty of this definition lay in complications created by a booming economy; a small-scale tradesman, for example, might slowly expand his business into foreign trade and make a fortune through the advantages of empire. His sons, then, would inherit a thriving mercantile company and never have to work in a shop, and yet having perhaps grown up "over the shop," they would have none of the experience necessary to understand how to build a house and live in it. The need for instructions in such matters, then, becomes clear in the context of the tremendous increase in wealth that industrialization and empire fostered in the middle decades of the century: The great quantity of people who were newly middle class in financial terms could not reasonably be expected to know precisely what was required in a middle-class home. And yet the idea of middle-class respectability required an unassailable image of home that would ensure the pre-eminence of middle-class standards and thereby guarantee the primacy of the bourgeoisie. Indeed, as Lenore Davidoff and Catherine Hall point out, by the 1840s, the home had come to represent a "repository of stability and firm values" in the face of the rapidly changing economic (and consequently social) landscape (180ff).[5] From this point onward, I would argue, the image of home served to consolidate the middle class around a stable ideological position, despite the great instability that in fact characterized a class whose rapid expansion was based on the vagaries of a capitalist marketplace.

In response to this complex desire to maintain home as a moral place but also to use it to define a class position that many people would be trying to create for the first time in their family's experience, countless texts appeared between 1835 and 1870 explicating for readers how to create that ideal home. Although housekeeping guides written for women have been the most common scholarly referent for information about Victorian domestic ideals and practices, images of home available to the Victorian reader include articles about home building in periodicals, dictionaries of architectural concepts written for young architects, detailed books on house design and building written for prospective home owners, and books on furniture and decorative principles. Providing multiple, intertextual visions of domesticity, such media also reveal the role of men, servants, and guests in creating the domestic universe and thus help locate domesticity in the context of identity categories beyond that of the middle-class woman. Variously emphasizing the moral qualities of home and the practical details of decoration, entertaining, and household management, these texts were often packed with illustrations. Floor plans, pictures of furniture, drawings of window treatments, diagrams of how to lay a table at a party, charts of servants' wages, and tables of what furniture to purchase given one's household budget were some of the many available images of domesticity that readers encountered in print. Offering a textual complement to the displays available in shop windows, at the Great Exhibition of 1851, or in other three-dimensional public forums, these print images envision the middle-class home in minute detail in order to ensure that the vision would be properly recreated by the newly middle-class reader. Written by unimpeachable representatives of the middle class—men whose names were followed by F.R.C.S. or R.I.BA., women whose positions as wives and mothers sanctioned their advice—these texts try to uphold the exclusivity of middle-class identity by rhetorically figuring their images as suggestions for how to achieve the home a reader desires.[6] In fact, however, these images were more likely to *create* the proper middle-class domestic desires in a reader who may have no experience with how to live in a middle-class house. Implicitly, they function to ensure through two-dimensional images that readers' three-dimensional domestic spaces conform to the cultural values signified by domesticity.

Cultural emphasis on the power of the visual image to disseminate proper domesticity and on the power of home to create a class-based cultural morality resulted in a storm of controversy over William Holman Hunt's "The Awakening Conscience," exhibited at the Royal Academy in 1854 (see Fig. 13.1).

Strident public objections identified the painting as immoral for depicting a "fallen woman" at the point of moral crisis when she becomes painfully aware that proper femininity abhors the position of mistress. (She is marked as "fallen" by her jewelry; although she has showy earrings and several rings on her hands, her wedding-ring finger is conspicuously bare.) Although scholarly discussion of this painting typically focuses on its religiously based social commentary because Hunt painted a motto from Proverbs onto the frame and in-

FIG. 13.1. "The Awakening Conscience" (1853) by William Holman Hunt (1827–1910). Copyright Tate Gallery, London, Great Britain. Reproduced by permission through Art Resource, NY.

cluded scriptural extracts in the exhibition catalogue entry, I would argue that the narrative implied by this image is that the highly detailed domestic interior has played a significant role in awakening the woman's conscience.[7] For a knowledgeable Victorian reader, this domestic space would serve as an indictment of the woman because the piano, the fashionable decorations, and the neglected embroidery wools on the floor are all guilty reminders of what her position at the center of this drawing-room ought to be. The seemingly endless proliferation of domestic detail in this painting was praised by John Ruskin, a well-known commentator on art and architecture, and a man whose public lectures, books, and articles often discussed aesthetic issues in terms of their relationship to identity. In his letter to *The Times* of May 25, 1854, he wrote, defending Hunt's painting:

> Nothing is more notable than the way in which even the most trivial objects force themselves upon the attention of a mind which has been fevered by violent and distressful excitement .... Even to the mere spectator a strange interest exalts the accessories of a scene in which he bears witness to human sorrow. There is not a single object in all that room, common, modern, vulgar ... but it becomes tragical, if rightly read. That furniture, so carefully painted, even to the last vein of the rosewood—is there nothing to be learnt from that terrible lustre of it, from its fatal newness; nothing there that has the old thoughts of home upon it, or that is ever to become a part of home? (7)

Ruskin argues that Hunt's careful painting of domestic detail, "even to the last vein of rosewood," is a purposeful means of conjuring tragedy and pity in the viewer who "rightly" reads the scene. Attributing the power of the painting to the way it ties the girl's moral failings to the failure of this fashionable decor "to become a part of home," Ruskin notes the reciprocity between the domestic space and the woman it contains. Her disgrace has prevented her from creating a home out of these domestic objects, just as the objects themselves have failed to impress her into moral action. Moreover, he collapses the woman herself with the viewer of the painting in his observation that "nothing is more notable than the way in which even the most trivial objects force themselves upon the attention of a mind which has been fevered by violent and distressful excitement"—it is both her mind and the spectator's that is forced to see the "distressful" significance of these "trivial objects."

It is additionally important that Ruskin reads this interior as "modern, vulgar" and terribly, fatally new, for these loaded terms would have immediately signaled to his readers that this domestic space has been created by people whose money is new and whose middle-class sensibilities might therefore be suspect. He implies that this image reveals one of the primary dangers that household advice texts tacitly address: the *nouveau riche* will have the money to buy middle-class goods but will not have the moral fiber or sense of taste to enable them to "do" domesticity properly. Hence, I would argue that one reason this painting caused such public discomfort is that it provides an inversion of the cultural value of middle-class domesticity by focusing too-detailed attention on how domestic identity might go wrong. Hunt's painting draws on the accepted notion that a respectable home with a good woman at its center might coincide to produce a moral culture, but it offers a picture of the obverse: a middle-class home occupied by those who are disreputable will ultimately be a failure as a space, unable to exercise the proper moral influence on its inhabitants. His picture was a scandalous image, then, not because it showed a fallen woman but because it revealed that domesticity might fail to produce respectable citizens.

Hunt's image is an important one to consider because it both reveals and challenges the cultural ideals of domesticity and the power of images to enforce those ideals. However, in terms of sheer quantity, Hunt's image was more than counterbalanced by the multitudes that elided this negative potential of domesticity by focusing on the positive power of home to influence behavior and consolidate class position. Works on architecture and housekeeping from the 1830s and 1840s owed a clear debt to the conduct manuals that had been important to defining identity since the 18th century. Following the conduct manuals' focus on character as paramount, these early homemaking texts relied on conceptual models of home based on intangible qualities such as personal taste, moral character, feminine influence, and the notion of domesticity as a haven from the public world of commerce and competition.[8] Minimally illustrated, these texts tended to show either generic domestic scenes, like a mother reading to a child, or historical models of aesthetic architectural principles. In the 1850s, however, texts on homemaking began to move toward the more practical concerns of contemporary households. These later works give directions on how to design, build, and decorate a healthy and convenient house; hire, manage, and fire servants; cook food, tend the sick, and clean every household item that might get dirty. Not surprisingly, these texts are more visually oriented, and the illustrations they provide contain informative images rather than classical models. Significantly, the movement from questions of the character of home and its occupants to practical directions for managing a household did not imply that character ceased to be a central component of domesticity. Rather, it rhetorically connects the value of character with the tangible facts of home creation to indicate that middle-class identity requires not just the sterling character described in conduct manuals but also the visible marker of having achieved that identity, the ideal home space in which to display that character.

Significantly, these advice texts occupy a paradoxical position, defining middle-class homes while simultaneously endorsing the assumption that such homes are the exclusive province of those who have "naturally" reached this class position. For home to serve as a relevant marker of class position—and thus social worth—it was ideologically necessary to maintain that "truly" middle-class people "naturally" wanted certain kinds of homes. The concept of *taste* was a convenient means of preserving this exclusivity, for if good household management could *only* be signified by impeccable taste in home decor and entertaining, and taste was the inherent, visible marker of one's birth and breeding, then a tasteful home would be the signifying marker of one's rightful class position.[9] That a *nouveau riche* home would likely be terribly "vulgar" in its ostentatious decoration was a cultural commonplace, as Ruskin's use of the term in discussing Hunt's painting suggests. Thus, even texts that offer detailed directions for proper etiquette when making social calls (something the newly wealthy might not know) at the same time do not define "taste," on the assumption that truly middle-class taste cannot be learned. The letterpress of these texts delimit the boundary of middle-class identity by implying at certain moments that tasteful readers will have mental images derived from experience to accompany the principles the text articulates. Yet these texts tacitly admit that middle-class identity is constructed rather than natural by offering visual images and explicit directions for the benefit of new housekeepers. Ultimately, they demonstrate that visual elaboration is an essential component of consolidating the rhetoric of domesticity for those who are new to the middle-class image.

As we have seen, the Victorian home space contained conflicting desires to create a space for privacy that would simultaneously publicize middle-class status. For the middle-class home owner, negotiating this tension required carefully dividing private from public spaces within the home. Marking their class privilege, middle-class families had private spaces (feminine boudoirs, masculine studies, sitting rooms interconnected with private bedrooms) to which guests were rarely admitted and servants entered only when summoned; and they had spaces for public entertaining (drawing rooms, large dining rooms, smoking rooms) that were decorated to display their class position to outsiders and maintained by servants through routine and more visible labor. Given that the public/private distinction was an important means of preserving class hierarchy, such subdivision was the surest way to maintain these hierarchies among a home's occupants.

The ability to restrict access to any given space, then, became the primary tool for reiterating class positions within a home. Perhaps not surprisingly, the 19th century saw the advent of the corridor as a design principle.[10] Prior to this point, domestic layouts typically relied on interconnection; people passed through one room to get to the next. Corridors enabled passage from place to place outside the living spaces, making it possible to instill rules of access for every room in the home and thereby maintain hierarchies between household members. Furthermore, as Robert Kerr's "Thoroughfare Plan" (Fig. 13.2) demonstrates, every corridor might be assigned to particular members of the

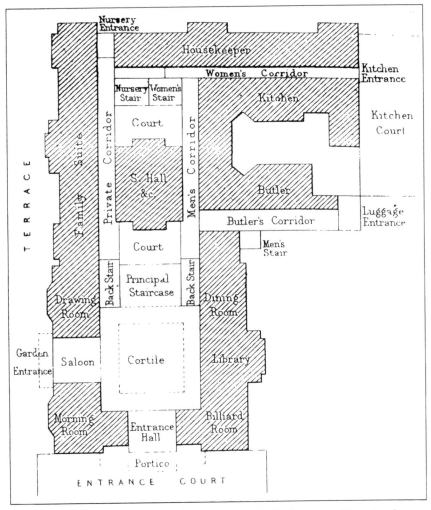

FIG. 13.2. "Thoroughfare Plan," from Robert Kerr's *The Gentleman's House*. London: John Murray, 1871, Plate 52, facing page 470.

household to avoid unsanctioned meetings on the way to and from the highly segregated places within the home.[11]

Corridors for "men" or "women" and discrete staircases throughout the house were designed to ensure the respectable behavior of servants by preventing male and female members of the staff from the temptations of encountering one another regularly, while the "Principal Staircase" and separate corridor for the "Private" use of the family and its guests helped keep the presence of servants as hidden as possible from the middle-class view. If one considers that before indoor plumbing became common throughout the house, bathing water, cleaning supplies, and the contents of chamber pots would have to be carried in buckets to or from every room, it is hardly surprising that families would not want to encounter their servants on the stairs in the course of the day. Yet such segregation also facilitated the spectacle of class position by locating servants and domestic labor in the least visible spaces of the house.

Illustrating how architecture can build these ideological elements into the walls of a home, many Victorian texts offered readers sample floor plans that demonstrated how to properly lay out a home to achieve both private convenience and the appropriate public spectacle of middle-class domesticity. Because homes in London and other cities were built up rather than sprawling across expensive real estate, even the small rooms of a modest house would occupy a minimum of three stories in addition to the basement kitchens, rendering it absolutely necessary to plan well in order to avoid endless trips up and down the stairs.

Figure 13.3 contains the plans for the family stories of a representative middle-class home in town, taken from J. H. Walsh's *A Manual of Domestic Economy* (1857). A typical ground floor (what Americans call the first floor) contained the dining room, a library and/or study, and an entrance hall that, as in this plan, was often separate from the main staircase hall. The back staircase on floor A of this plan created fairly uncomplicated access from the basement kitchen to the dining room. Associated with the man of the house, dining rooms, libraries, and studies were often described as "masculine" in their decor, and the easy access from these spaces to the outside world confirmed his manly need for public pursuits. By contrast, the first floor (American second floor) was the woman's floor, typically housing the drawing room, or suite of rooms, and perhaps her private boudoir. A woman's place was thus situated physically at the heart of the household, metonymically establishing her authority as the central manager of the domestic establishment and implying that one important job of a good home was to extend feminine succor to guests via the public drawing room space. In this plan for a relatively modest house, the primary bedroom, identified as "Bedroom No. 1," with its adjoining dressing room ("D.R.") and toilet ("W.C."), also occupies this floor. Subsequent floors generally contained more private places and include guest rooms and bedrooms for younger members of the family. At the top of the house, the bedrooms would be smallest; these might be for female servants, or, in a house with many children, they would serve as a nursery suite with accommodations for nursery staff as well as infant or school-age children. On the plans here, the small dressing room that opens directly off the servants' staircase on floor C would likely be a bedroom for the principle housemaid. Nursery space, if needed in this house, would be located on floor D, in order to afford a full story of space to serve as a sound barrier between the children's realm and the drawing room in which parents would entertain guests.

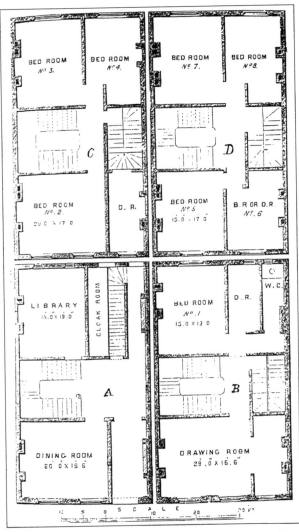

FIG. 13.3.   "Plans of Different Floors of Town House," from J. H. Walsh's *A Manual of Domestic Economy*, Second Edition. London: G. Routledge & Co., 1857, Figure 47, facing page 96.

One significant fact of household arrangements that this image would imply to a proficient Victorian reader is the importance of invisibility on the part of servants. Although the secondary staircase confirms their existence, the fact that there are no plans here for the basement or attic floors—which would contain kitchens, workrooms, and servants' quarters—highlights through absence how the servants ought to be relegated to the margins of the house.

Comparing Fig. 13.2 with Fig. 13.3, especially in the light of information provided in the text of Robert Kerr's book, identifies this as an important principle of home design. In the Preface to *The Gentleman's House* (1864), Kerr explains that "the fundamental idea of [my] treatise is that large houses and small houses, from the largest indeed to the smallest, if well devised as English Residences, have all alike the selfsame principles of plan, differing of necessity in scale, because they differ in size, but not differing in purpose" (viii–ix). That homes "well devised as English Residences, have all alike the selfsame principles of plan" implies the degree to which a domestic floor plan might embody social ideals. Thus, although a house with four major corridors and six staircases is a very large home indeed, Kerr's "Thoroughfare Plan" is significantly *not* intended to imply that one must have a tremendous income in order to design a respectable house. Instead, he assumes that the reader literate in middle-class ideology will see that this plan articulates the principle of segregating household occupants from one another as much as is practicable and that it should be "scaled" appropriately to suit individual requirements and budgets. By extension, this good reader would rightly understand that, although the floor plan in Fig. 13.3 shows a much smaller house, it is similarly well-designed in providing the necessary minimum of two staircases to segregate the working servants from the genteel family.

In addition to defining where each person in the house belonged, these physical boundaries within a home also provided a system by which people knew how to behave at all times. Thus, for example, a gentleman always knew what was expected from him in a lady's drawing room, even if he had never met his hostess before. These behavioral implications of floor plan images, however, are even less explicit on paper than the principles of hierarchical segregation that the plans suggest. As we saw, reading Kerr's "Thoroughfare Plan" too literally, as an inexperienced reader might, would seem to suggest that "respectability" requires an almost impossibly large house. Similarly, reading even the more modest plans in Fig. 13.3 simply as layouts for the dispersal of walls and windows, doors and fireplaces would not necessarily lead a reader to understand how the needs and pastimes of a home's occupants are answered by a floor plan or how their behavior should be shaped by specific places within the home. In order to understand these points, a reader would require some experience that enabled intertextual comparison—either with actual homes, in which other members of the middle class modeled and responded to appropriate behaviors, or with a wide range of other books whose directions and images collaborated with these floor plans to provide a more complete picture of the intricacies of middle-class home spaces.

Far from providing all the information that is necessary to create an ideal home, architectural books in fact require complementary information on the decoration of home spaces to suit one's class position. Indeed, Charles Eastlake's popular and influential *Hints on Household Taste* (originally appearing in 1868) proclaims that "half the effect of every room which is planned must ultimately depend on the manner in which it is fitted up; and if our national taste is ever to assume a definite character, let us hope that the interior of our dwellings will reflect it no less than the walls by which they are enclosed" (xxvii). Linking the principles built into the walls of a home with the "effect" produced by room decoration, Eastlake plays on the multiple meanings of the word "domestic" to assert that the character of the middle-class home is a matter of national interest. His emphasis on taste clearly indicates that a home was a marker of class position only if its decoration corresponded to the principles built into its layout. Indeed, there was substantial cultural attention to how to furnish and decorate a middle-class home properly. Architectural treatises that focus primarily on floor plans—such as Gervase Wheeler's *The Choice of a Dwelling*—also give some attention to topics like the appropriate color schemes for dining rooms and drawing rooms. Housekeeping sources, like *Cassell's Household Guide,* illustrate models of desirable furnishings. And texts devoted solely to interior design provide detailed images of good middle-class taste.[12]

Rather than offering here an overview of Victorian material culture, an issue addressed in voluminous detail by historians of the decorative arts, my interest is in how ideas of decoration were conveyed in images to the consuming public. A survey of texts that illustrate decorative processes and furniture reveals that there were two primary approaches to providing images of middle-class decor. Because color illustrations were extremely rare and costly, and fashionable colors and trimmings would likely change faster than books could be published, many authors preferred to draw on the distinction between taste and fashion, providing representative examples of "useful and tasteful" articles rather than aiming to offer readers a fashionable guide to the latest interior trends. Images in these texts tend to be generic, only occasionally with a designer's or manufacturer's name attached to suggest that this precise design was purchasable. Other texts offer readers detailed woodcut or line-drawn illustrations of a fully decorated room. These pictures, rather than giving readers samples of a variety of furniture options, locate the furniture in the room in which it would be used, thereby suggesting how to create an entire environment, from wallpaper to furniture to mantle ornaments. In both cases, there are intriguing patterns to what kind of information is and is not provided.

Thomas Webster's *Encyclopaedia of Domestic Economy,* a 10-volume set, is a good example of the multiple-samples approach to explaining home interiors. Devoting an entire book, about 150 pages, to "Household Furniture," Webster covers the make and materials of carpets, processes of decoration like gilding and japanning, and household items such as lamps, kitchen implements and china, as well devoting chapters to the furnishing of "the Principal Apartments." In the spirit of cataloguing all of the necessary items in a middle-class home, this book offers detailed information about every type of furniture it pictures. Items that might be unfamiliar are defined in terms of location, materials, and use. A *chiffonnière*, for example, is

> a French term applied to certain low moveable pieces of furniture ... generally made of an elegant form, and ornamented so as to suit a sitting room ... where they are often placed on the recesses on each side of the chimney as a substitute for closets and a sideboard ... In large apartments, as in libraries, ladies' sitting rooms, and even in drawing rooms, they are very convenient for holding a number of things that are often wanted; and the top may be ornamented with flowers, vases, ornamental china, minerals, or beautiful objects of art or nature. (240)

Such detailed definitions are followed by illustrations of more than one version of the item, with short captions explaining the primary differences in shape and function between them. Items like chairs and tea tables, which would be more self-explanatory, are not defined as if they were unfamiliar, as a chiffonnière most certainly would be to a newly wealthy family. Rather, Webster explains what constitutes good materials and workmanship in these furnishings, noting, for example, that "*In the cheapest kinds of chairs the legs* are held together by cross bars and rails; but in the best chairs these are omitted, the stoutness of the materials and the goodness of the workmanship permitting the legs to be sufficiently strong without" (245, italics in original). Thus providing information that would enable one to judge the quality of items for purchase and the range of furnishings necessary in a respectable home, Webster's book appears to tell readers everything they need to know about fitting out a middle-class home.

However, the illustrations are so plentiful as often to create a crowded appearance on the page, and the text at once explains the furniture in detail and leaves key points to the imagination of the reader. Fig. 13.4, for example, shows a sample page from Webster's book, on which a variety of "ladies' work tables" are illustrated.

The page immediately preceding this one offers a clear definition, as if to ensure that the item itself is no mystery to the reader. "*Ladies' work tables* are small tables for holding the lighter articles of their work, and are generally fitted up with convenient places for cottons, needles, pins, scissors, &c. They are sometimes plain, of mahogany, with small drawers, as *fig.* 209., or with a silk bag fluted with a fringe, as *fig.* 210., fixed to a frame that draws out for holding various articles of needlework that are in progress" (234, italics in original). In two facing pages, only one of which is reproduced in Fig. 13.4, ten varieties of work tables are illustrated, interspersed with short descriptions identifying the primary differences between them in terms of shape. Notably, however, these descriptions do not evaluate the tables in terms that would enable a reader truly unfamiliar with their use to decide which of the ten would be most appropriate for her needs in her drawing room. Identifying many of them as

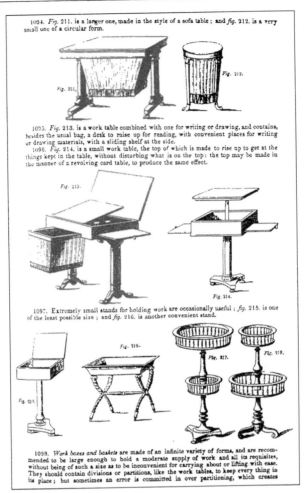

1094. *Fig.* 211. is a larger one, made in the style of a sofa table ; and *fig.* 212. is a very small one of a circular form.

1095. *Fig.* 213. is a work table combined with one for writing or drawing, and contains, besides the usual bag, a desk to raise up for reading, with convenient places for writing or drawing materials, with a sliding shelf at the side.
1096. *Fig.* 214. is a small work table, the top of which is made to rise up to get at the things kept in the table, without disturbing what is on the top: the top may be made in the manner of a revolving card table, to produce the same effect.

1097. Extremely small stands for holding work are occasionally useful ; *fig.* 215. is one of the least possible size ; and *fig.* 216. is another convenient stand.

1098. *Work boxes and baskets* are made of an infinite variety of forms, and are recommended to be large enough to hold a moderate supply of work and all its requisites, without being of such a size as to be inconvenient for carrying about or lifting with ease. They should contain divisions or partitions, like the work tables, to keep every thing in its place ; but sometimes an error is committed in over partitioning, which creates

FIG. 13.4.   Illustrations of ladies' work tables, from John Webster's *Encyclopaedia of Domestic Economy.* London: Longman, Brown, Green, and Longmans, 1844, page 235.

"convenient" without defining what makes them so, the text and illustrations here provide an almost overwhelming array of choices without offering the necessary tools to distinguish between them.

Webster's pages of dining tables, drawing-room chairs, and indeed every other major article of furniture similarly present a wide array of options. Some of them are identified as suiting various purposes, such as tables that will telescope to accommodate dinner parties of many different sizes, if one entertains often; however, many pages offer images that seem to differ in style more than anything else. The pages of chairs show ones with padded backs and others with wooden ones, some with silk and tassel upholstery and others with woven seats, and some heavily ornamented with carving while others have clean, sweeping lines. (See Fig. 13.5 for one such page; there are several other pages like this in Webster's book.)

There is no information explicit on these pages about how to choose between "good" chairs. The text notes, for example, that the front legs of chairs are typically straight and elaborately carved by being turned on a lathe, while the rear legs are curved, rendering lathe carving impossible and undesirable: less visible back legs need no ornamentation, "good taste requiring that labour shall not be thrown away" (245). Yet even while invoking "good taste" to explain chair design, Webster does not mention what kinds of upholstery are tasteful or how to tell the "antique style" from the modern, or what constitutes too much orna-

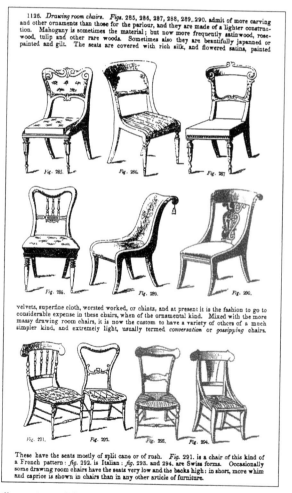

FIG. 13.5. Illustrations of chairs, from John Webster's *Encyclopaedia of Domestic Economy*. London: Longman, Brown, Green, and Longmans, 1844, page 247.

ment (although the warns against this vulgarity). Thus, although the plethora of images and the tiny-print text amongst which they are interwoven would seem to suggest that there could be no other possible detail necessary to know, in fact, reading these images requires careful interpretation by the reader. The multiple-samples format of book doesn't explain the mysterious concept of *taste* even when picturing it, making it difficult for a newly middle-class reader to tell *why* the objects are pictured at all. Although the information on the page provides facts, definitions and models, a reader still must figure out based on these pictures what the rules of proper taste are so that he or she is able to go to a shop and buy a good chair. Thus such books preserve the exclusivity of middle-class taste even as they present copious images that would seem to suggest that such taste can be learned in the pages of these volumes.

In contrast to the multiple-samples mode, the images in books like Rhoda and Agnes Garrett's *Suggestions for House Decoration in Painting, Woodwork and Furniture* provide visions of complete rooms decorated with good taste (see Fig. 13.6 and Fig. 13.7.)

In the "View of a Drawing-Room," the Garrett sisters bring together many of the elements that are catalogued in books such as Webster's. Thus, here, one can see how to array the furniture in the room, how to decorate the walls using wallpaper, dado, paint and pictures, what style of curtains might suit a modest room, and how many decorative objects provide a pleasing diversion to the eye without being overwhelming. In addition, the picture of the "Drawing-Room Chimney-Piece" illustrates not just principles for use but also the feeling such a room should be designed to convey.

Suggesting cozy comfort and conversation through the facing chairs pulled up to the fire, and signaling a lack of pretension in the fact that the easy chairs are not distinctly of the same style or too carefully matched, this chimney piece in effect takes the elements Webster enumerates and creates a narrative out of them. In order to gain the most from either book, however, it would be in a reader's best interest to consult them both. Webster offers variety; the Garretts put a much smaller selection of objects into use; and taken together, these books provide a more complete lesson in creating the image of home than either offers on its own. The visual rhetoric is thus not fully articulated by any single text: it requires multiplicity and repetition with variation to complete the picture in the readers' minds. Thus, proper consumption of these goods requires, in part, continued consumption of the books that explain these goods, since a middle-class reader has to buy book after book in order to get the complete image of domesticity.

In addition to decorative samples and architectural efforts to normalize the "principles of plan" and "purpose" of middle-class homes, many books provided directions aimed at the women who would manage such houses. Isabella Beeton's *The Book of Household Management* (1861) is perhaps the best-known example of such housekeeping guides, although many other similar

FIG. 13.6. "View of Drawing-Room," from *Suggestions for House Decoration* by Rhoda and Agnes Garrett. Philadelphia: Porter & Coates, n.d., Frontispiece.

volumes helped institutionalize the construction of domestic spaces and the relationships among household occupants that such homes intended to fix.[13] With the advent of books that address *The Practical Housewife* (1855; see Editors of the "Family Friend"), the concepts of "household management ... domestic economy ... and the comfort of home" are linked through a series of charts and tables that provide graphic images of the information necessary for running a household ("Dedication"). *Cassell's Household Guide* (1871) and *The Household Encyclopaedia* (1860), for example, explain that domestic economy requires maintaining the maximum of comfort within the means a husband can provide, and these books offer tables of sample monthly and annual budgets for household supplies. Walsh's *A Manual of Domestic Economy* warns newly married couples to live within their financial means and aids them by providing dozens of pages containing a meticulous table of household fur-

FIG. 13.7. "Drawing-Room Chimney-Piece," from *Suggestions for House Decoration*
by Rhoda and Agnes Garrett. Philadelphia: Porter & Coates, n.d., page 61.

nishing and supplies that would be wanted on each of four budgets ranging
from £.100 to £.1000 per year.[14] This table operates much like the pictorial catalogue of furniture we saw in Webster's book, offering readers a laundry list of
every conceivable item that might be wanted and leaving it up to individual
judgment to scale the list to an appropriate size.

Figure 13.8 shows one example of the type of visual image housekeeping
guides might provide. It is taken from Isabella Beeton's *The Book of Household
Management*, which opens by asserting her intention to "point out the plan
which may be the most profitably pursued for the daily regulation of affairs" (2).
Her efforts to provide women a "plan" that will enable them to regulate their
days are complemented by visual images that offer a quick reference for skills
and information a woman would require to run a proper middle-class house-

hold. Her book includes, for example, tables of servants' wages, pictorial comparisons between ancient and modern kitchen equipment, and menus for dinner parties arranged graphically to show women how to lay the dining table. Figure 13.8 does not simply tell a reader what ought to be served at a large dinner party. It tailors that information to the month of the year, to take into account what foods are in season in November, and it demonstrates how the food ought to be presented on the table for the most efficient and pleasing display. For the reader who might need some help in understanding the movement of courses through the meal, these table layouts also indicate what dishes should replace others—as in the Third Course diagram, where we learn that the place occupied by partridges will be later filled by plum pudding. Beeton provides similar graphics for each month of the year, and modified lists follow each graphic to explain how to trim the menu for dinners for twelve, eight, or six people respectively.

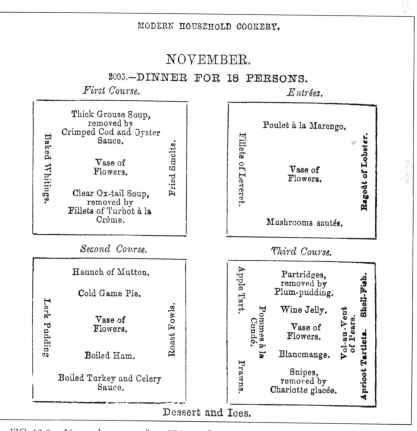

FIG. 13.8.   November menu for a "Dinner for 18 Persons," from Mrs. Isabella Beeton's *The Book of Household Management*. London: S.O. Beeton, 1869, page 946.

Providing a very different kind of information from the pictures of furniture available in Webster's guide, Beeton emphasizes menus and medicine, managing servants, and entertaining guests. In effect peopling the rooms that Walsh's plans built, *Cassell's Household Guide* budgeted, Webster's catalogues furnished, and the Garretts' book decorated, Beeton completes the picture of middle-class domesticity offered by all of these other texts. It is extremely important to recognize, then, how heavily these works depend on one another. No single one of them offers a comprehensive image of how to construct and live in a proper middle-class home. Rather, each provides for one set of concerns, offers one type of image, and relies on a reader to place these images alongside the many others available within the culture in order to get an accurate mental picture of the deceptively simple concept, home.

That each of these books contains encyclopedic detail about its chosen topic, and yet withholds a concrete definition of the sensibility and taste required to take these details and put them into three-dimensional practice in a home is, I would argue, a purposeful visual rhetorical strategy. Seeming to show a reader how to become middle class, while simultaneously mystifying the single most important but intangible quality of that position, these books ensure their own continued marketability. As readers continue to seek that elusive information, they will buy other similar books, hoping ultimately to be able to envision for themselves how to turn these floor plans and diagrams, room layouts and chair models into a three-dimensional home that will properly signify middle-class respectability.

Through this careful balance of education and silence, these books also sidestep potential anxieties about how their imagistic directions might inadvertently advocate an unseemly performance of identity. First and foremost, they position themselves not as sanctioning a disingenuous performance, but rather as providing the standards by which readers should judge their own and others' displays. In addition, although their illustrations may seem to serve as a primer of middle-class standards that enables even the most uneducated readers to envision domesticity, the sheer multiplicity of these texts reshapes their cultural impact. Relying on readers' knowledge that many other similar books exist, these countless texts depend on this implied intertextual reference to make their meaning. Each illuminates domestic ideology only in conjunction with the other texts that take up different aspects of homemaking. Hence, no single text might be accused of betraying the selectivity that differentiates the middle class.

The diligent reader will perceive, however, that careful attention to the implications of intertexual reading may ultimately have a life-shaping benefit. For, with so many texts available, readers could consume as many works as it took for domestic ideals to become second nature, so that eventually the well-read, middle-class consumer (even one whose parents were in trade) might "naturally" be able to display a properly domesticated identity. Brilliantly relying on intertextuality to solidify their meaning, however—an intertextuality that comes not just from reading these principles but from putting them into practice—these images deny that they undermine the value of naturally occurring middle-class sensibility. Through reiteration of images that alone *cannot* teach this sensibility, these individual texts situate themselves as articulating well-known principles rather than teaching readers how to create a proper home. Claiming a descriptive rather than prescriptive function, they manage to avoid the problem of appearing to teach the unteachable by ultimately relying on readers to understand how to consolidate these images into a fully functioning, properly signifying home.

CODA: ENVISIONING HOME IN THE TWENTY-FIRST CENTURY

Teaching domesticity by offering directions that must be internalized and naturalized to be useful, the visual rhetoric of these 19th-century housekeeping texts serves a careful, ideological purpose: making middle-class ideals seem at once accessible and exclusive. Significantly, these texts have implications for the study of contemporary images as well. First, they serve as reminders that heavy reliance on visual culture for shaping and disseminating ideology is a tradition that predates the 20th-century's multimedia, multicolored, technology-driven onslaught of visual images. Second, in a more specific context, we might see these 19th-century texts as the forerunners of publications like *Architectural Digest, Martha Stewart Living, House Beautiful, Metropolitan Home,* and *Better Homes and Gardens.* Despite their vastly different target markets, these magazines appeal to a diverse array of consumers who might all argue that they are "middle class" and who are united by their interest in creating an ideally desirable home space.

Moreover, operating on the very same principle as Kerr's *The Gentleman's House,* at least some of these magazines present images of homes that are distinctly beyond the means of their target readers. *Architectural Digest,* for example, offers a vision of domestic luxury that is unattainable for any but the extraordinarily wealthy. Creating desires that their readers may not have the power to fill, such publications enable commodity culture through the promise that there are always more, new ways to improve on one's home. Playing to the concept of *personal image* in a way that 19th-century publications would have found distressingly performative, these publications tout the perfect home as a revelatory marker of selfhood. They uphold a value system in which it is most desirable to have a mansion in Greenwich, Connecticut and a summer home in the Hamptons, but barring that, it is acceptable to make your own more modestly scaled home look as though it could *belong* in these places. And, by extension, they imply that the individual reader—through his or her home—partakes in the identity politics that require domesticity to complete the self. Just as 19th-century texts relied on the savvy consumer to realize that any single book on homemaking simultaneously provided useful information and revealed informational gaps that could only be filled by purchasing and reading another book, contemporary home magazines similarly play off one another. The message is that if you can't afford to order your silk lampshades through the top interior designer whose rooms are pictured on the pages of *Metropolitan Home*, at least you have *Martha Stewart Living* to teach you how to look as though you are part of the right crowd.[15]

Offering visual images of domestic ideals, reiterating the intersections of family, home, and class position, disseminating the ideological significance of home as a marker of selfhood, contemporary publications are surprisingly close to their Victorian predecessors. Yet these magazines are explicitly focused on consumable products, implicitly creating a commodity fetish, rather than emphasizing the moral value of those objects for the culture as Victorian texts did. Thus it is hardly surprising that whereas Victorian books on homemaking contained no advertising at all, their modern-day counterparts have glossy, color-rich advertisements that are often indistinguishable from their feature story illustrations. Yet while the contemporary culture of homemaking has moved beyond the moral imperative that drove the visual rhetoric of 19th-century domesticity, our culture is fascinated with all things (we imagine to be) Victorian. To whit: the BBC production *1900 House* ran repeatedly on PBS, consumer demand in both England and the United States has compelled the William Morris Company to reissue his most popular Arts and Crafts wallpaper designs of the 1860s, and the magazine *Victoria* was created specifically to teach us how to achieve the perfect "Victorian" home with all the modern conveniences. Thus at a moment when 21st-century consumers are undeniably lured by the imaginative power of the Victorian home, it becomes particularly important to highlight the disjunction between the Victoriana of today and the realities of the Victorian visual rhetoric of home.

NOTES

1. For example, there was a series of articles entitled "How to Build a House and Live in It" in *Blackwood's Edinburgh Magazine* from 1846–1847.
2. Although many recent scholars of 19th-century culture have thoroughly explored the degree to which this binary broke down in practice, cultural investment in upholding this ideal played a tremendous role in Victorian conceptions of home. Significant work investigating this issue has been done by the following cultural historians, literary scholars, and geography theorists: Monica Cohen, Catherine Gallagher, Elizabeth Langland, Mary Poovey, Gillian Rose, and John Tosh.

3. The first volume of this poem, "The Betrothal," was issued in 1854; three subsequent volumes continued the story, ending with "The Victories of Love," published in 1861.

4. Chapter Three of Lenore Davidoff and Catherine Hall's *Family Fortunes* traces the development of domestic ideology in terms of its reliance on cultural constructions of womanhood and offers a useful overview of how these terms are interrelated.

5. See also John Tosh for a historical overview of how the conception of home changed with increasing industrialization. He concurs that middle-class domestic ideology, based on the value of separate spheres, had become well-established by the early 1840s.

6. F.R.C.S. stands for Fellow, Royal College of Surgeons and indicates a man has a university medical education; R.I.B.A. stands for Royal Institute of British Architects—the professional association of architects created in 1837. Many female authors of similar manuals purposefully used "Mrs." on the cover of their books to authenticate their advice; their credentials were often also detailed by male co-authors in Prefaces to their books as further legitimation.

7. See George P. Landow's *Replete with Meaning: William Holman Hunt and Typological Symbolism* (originally published by Yale University Press in 1979, and now available as a Victorian Web Book) for a sustained reading of the religious implications of this painting.

8. The most widely cited conduct manuals today are the series by Mrs. Sarah Stickney Ellis, including such titles as *Wives of England, Women of England, Mothers of England, Daughters of England*. Her books, published in the late 1830s and early 1840s, focused on domestic life in terms of individual conduct, thereby offering a bridge between the etiquette-based conduct manuals of the previous century and the more practical housekeeping manuals that appeared in the 1850s and beyond.

9. This formulation clearly supports Pierre Bourdieu's argument that taste serves as the primary marker of class position. It is particularly useful also to consider this in light of Michel de Certeau's arguments about the role of everyday objects in cultural practice. In Victorian texts, the notion that taste is part of one's inheritance rather than learnable is implied by countless architectural and housekeeping texts that offer cautions against "over-ornament" and "vulgar" decoration. (See, for example, Kerr; Orrinsmith; and Wheeler, passim.) While these texts advocate *moderation* as a factor of *taste*, they do not define these terms.

10. See Robin Evans's "Figures, Doors and Passages" for a comprehensive history of changes in home design and fuller discussion of the move to a corridor-based model.

11. In addition to extremely detailed descriptions of all aspects of home layout and design, Kerr's *The Gentleman's House* contains dozens of oversized plates, such as this one, with detailed plans of grand country houses.

12. In addition to Eastlake's *Hints on Household Taste*, for example, Macmillan Publishing Company issued an "Art at Home" decorating series, with such titles as *The Drawing-Room* (Mrs. Orrinsmith), *The Dining-Room* (Mrs. Loftie) and *Suggestions for House Decoration in Painting, Woodwork, and Furniture* (Rhoda and Agnes Garrett).

13. I am indebted to Daphne Spain, and her book *Gendered Spaces*, for the notion that "once spatial forms are created, they tend to become institutionalized and in some ways influence future social processes" (6).

14. On £.100 per year, one could afford only the youngest kind of maidservant of all work. This was not enough money to maintain a growing family in middle-class style, which is why some banks, for example, routinely fired clerks who married before their salaries reached £.150 per year, on the grounds that such an impractical move might incite a man to turn to embezzlement when his income proved insufficient (see Sally Mitchell 36). However, £.100 was a sufficient income on which an unmarried middle-class man or woman might maintain him / herself without losing class position.

15. Although it is beyond the scope of this chapter to discuss television shows, the proliferation of home decorating shows on the *Home and Garden Network* sends precisely the same message. The show, *Designer's Challenge*, for example, showcases exclusive rooms and asks its designers to make a reasonable facsimile of the room on a budget that would be affordable for a "regular" person—turning a $20,000 bedroom makeover into one that "you too" could achieve with $1,000 and some elbow grease.

WORKS CITED

Beeton, Mrs. Isabella. *The Book of Household Management*. London: S.O. Beeton, 1861.

Bourdieu, Pierre. *Distinction: A Social Critique of the Judgment of Taste*. Trans. Richard Nice. Cambridge: Harvard U P, 1984.

Cassell's Household Guide: Being a Complete Encyclopaedia of Domestic and Social Economy. London: Cassell, Petter, and Galpin, 1869–1871.

Cohen, Monica F. *Professional Domesticity in the Victorian Novel: Women, Work, and Home*. New York: Cambridge U P, 1998.

Davidoff, Lenore, and Catherine Hall. *Family Fortunes: Men and Women in the English Middle Class, 1780–1850*. Chicago: U of Chicago P, 1987.

de Certeau, Michel. *The Practice of Everyday Life*. Berkeley: U of California P, 1984.

Eastlake, Charles. *Hints on Household Taste*. 2nd ed. Boston: James R. Osgood and Company, 1878.

Editors of the "Family Friend." [Robert Kemp Philip.] *The Practical Housewife, Forming a Complete Encyclopaedia of Domestic Economy*. London: Ward and Lock, 1855.

Ellis, Mrs. Sarah Stickney. *The Wives of England*. New York: D. Appleton, 1843.

Evans, Robin. "Figures, Doors and Passages," *Architectural Design* (April 1978): 267–278.

Gallagher, Catherine. *The Industrial Reformation of English Fiction: Social Discourse and Narrative Form, 1832–1867*. Chicago: U of Chicago P, 1985.

Garrett, Rhoda, and Agnes Garrett. *Suggestions for House Decoration in Painting, Woodwork, and Furniture.* Philadelphia: Porter & Coates, n.d.

The Household Encyclopaedia; or Family Dictionary of Everything Connected with Housekeeping and Domestic Medicine. London: W. Kent & Co., 1858–1860. Vol. I, A–F, 1858, Vol. II, G-Z, 1860.

"How to Build A House and Live in It," *Blackwood's Edinburgh Magazine: 59.368 (June 1846): 758–65; No. II, 60.371 (Sept. 1846): 349–57; No. III, 61.380 (June 1847), 727–34.*

Kerr, Robert. *The Gentleman's House; Or, How to Plan English Residences from the Parsonage to the Palace.* 3rd ed., rev. London: John Murray, 1871.

Landow, George P. *Replete With Meaning: William Holman Hunt and Typological Symbolism.* London and New Haven: Yale UP, 1979. *A Victorian Web Book.* 20 November 2002 <http://65.107.211.206/victorian/painting/whh/replete/contents.html>.

Langland, Elizabeth. *Nobody's Angels: Middle-Class Women and Domestic Ideology in Victorian Culture.* Ithaca: Cornell UP, 1995.

Loftie, Mrs. *The Dining-Room.* London: Macmillan and Co., 1878.

Mitchell, Sally. *Daily Life in Victorian England.* Westport, CT: The Greenwood P, 1996.

Orrinsmith, Mrs. *The Drawing-Room: Its Decoration and Furniture.* London; Macmillan and Co., 1878.

Patmore, Coventry. *The Angel in the House.* London: John W. Parker & Son, 1854–1861.

Poovey, Mary. *Making a Social Body: British Cultural Formation, 1830–1864.* Chicago: U of Chicago P, 1995.

—. *Uneven Developments: The Ideological Work of Gender in Mid-Victorian England.* Chicago: U of Chicago P, 1988.

Rose, Gillian. "As If the Mirrors Had Bled: Masculine Dwelling, Masculinist Theory and Feminist Masquerade." *Body Space.* Ed. Nancy Duncan. New York: Routledge, 1996: 56–74.

—. *Feminism and Geography: The Limits of Geographical Knowledge.* Minneapolis: U of Minnesota P, 1993.

Ruskin, John. "The Pre–Raphaelites: Letter To the Editor." *The Times,* 21.733 (May 25, 1854): 7.

Spain, Daphne. *Gendered Spaces.* Chapel Hill: U of North Carolina P, 1992.

Tosh, John. *A Man's Place: Masculinity and the Middle-Class Home in Victorian England.* New Haven: Yale U P, 1999.

Walsh, J. H., F.R.C.S. *A Manual of Domestic Economy: Suited to Families Spending from £.100 to £.1000 a Year.* 2nd ed. London: G. Routledge & Co., 1857.

Webster, Thomas, F. G. S. &c, assisted by the late Mrs. Parkes. *Encyclopaedia of Domestic Economy: Comprising Such Subjects as are Most Immediately Connected with Housekeeping.* London: Longman, Brown, Green, and Longmans, initiated 1844.

Wheeler, Gervase. *The Choice of a Dwelling: A Practical Handbook of Useful Information on All Points Connected with Hiring, Buying, or Building a House.* London: John Murray, 1871.

CHAPTER FOURTEEN

Framing the Study of Visual Rhetoric: Toward a Transformation of Rhetorical Theory

Sonja K. Foss

As the chapters in *Defining Visual Rhetorics* suggest, recent work in rhetoric has taken a pictorial turn. Three exigencies are prompting this move from exclusive attention to discourse to the study of visual images and material objects as rhetoric. One is the pervasiveness of the visual symbol and its impact on contemporary culture. Visual artifacts constitute a major part of the rhetorical environment, and to ignore them to focus only on verbal discourse means we understand only a miniscule portion of the symbols that affect us daily.

The study of visual symbols from a rhetorical perspective also has grown with the emerging recognition that such symbols provide access to a range of human experience not always available through the study of discourse. As Jean Y. Audigier explains, human experiences that are spatially oriented, non-linear, multidimensional, and dynamic often can be communicated only through visual imagery or other nondiscursive symbols. To understand and articulate such experiences requires attention to these kinds of symbols, as Marguerite Helmers and Charles Hill eloquently suggest in their analysis of the Thomas Franklin photograph that has come to be known as *Ground Zero Spirit*.

For me, the most important reason for studying visual rhetoric is to develop rhetorical theory that is more comprehensive and inclusive. Throughout rhetoric's long tradition, discursive constructs and theories have enjoyed ideological hegemony, delimiting the territory of study to linguistic artifacts, suggesting that visual symbols are insignificant or inferior, and largely ignoring the impacts of the visual in our world. Because rhetorical theory has been created almost exclusively from the study of discourse, rhetoricians largely lack sophisticated understanding of the conventions through which meaning is created in visual artifacts and the processes by which they influence viewers.

As studies of visual rhetoric generate rhetorical theory, then, they challenge and question the linguistic boundaries of our rhetorical theories and provide a more holistic picture of symbol use.

In response to the pervasiveness of visual rhetoric, access to multidimensional human experiences, and a desire for comprehensiveness in rhetorical theory, rhetorical scholars are analyzing photographs, drawings, paintings, graphs and tables, interior design and architecture, sculpture, Internet images, and film. The diversity that characterizes these efforts is exciting and energizing, but it also can be bewildering, as Helmers and Hill note in the beginning of their chapter, for those seeking to understand the role of visual elements in rhetorical theory. The studies in this book provide an opportunity to propose a frame that might order (but not unnecessarily confine) the study of visual rhetoric. They suggest that three major pillars create the frame within which the study of visual rhetoric currently is configured: (1) Definitions of *visual rhetoric*; (2) Areas of focus in the study of visual rhetoric; and (3) Approaches to the rhetorical study of visual artifacts. This is a frame, I will argue, that has the potential to transform rhetorical theory in significant ways.

DEFINITIONS

Bewilderment concerning the rhetorical study of visual symbols can begin at the definitional level, so that is perhaps a good place to start in my proposal of a frame that loosely organizes the indiscipline of visual rhetoric. The chapters in this book suggest that the term, *visual rhetoric*, has two meanings in the discipline of rhetoric. It is used to mean both a visual object or artifact and a perspective on the study of visual data. In the first sense, visual rhetoric is a product individuals create as they use visual symbols for the purpose of communicating. In the second, it is a perspective scholars apply that focuses on the symbolic processes by which visual artifacts perform communication.

Visual Rhetoric as a Communicative Artifact

Conceptualized as a communicative artifact, *visual rhetoric* is the actual image or object rhetors generate when they use visual symbols for the purpose of communicating. It is the tangible evidence or product of the creative act, such as a painting, an advertisement, a photograph, or a building and constitutes the data of study for rhetorical scholars interested in visual symbols. *Visual rhetoric* as artifact, then, is the purposive production or arrangement of colors, forms, and other elements to communicate with an audience. As Cara A. Finnegan suggests, it is a product that names a category of rhetorical discourse that relies on something other than words or text for the construction of its meaning.

Three characteristics appear to define artifacts or products conceptualized as visual rhetoric: They must be symbolic, involve human intervention, and be presented to an audience for the purpose of communicating. Visual rhetoric is symbolic action in that the relationship it designates between image and referent is arbitrary, in contrast to a sign, where a natural relationship exists between the sign and the object to which it is connected. Visual rhetoric also involves human action of some kind in that the creation of an image involves the conscious decision to communicate as well as conscious choices about the strategies to employ in areas such as color, form, medium, and size. In its address to an audience, visual rhetoric is also communicative. Visual elements are arranged and modified by a rhetor not simply for the purpose of emotional discharge but for communication with an audience, even if the creator is the sole audience for the image or object.

The chapters in this book represent the breadth of visual objects that now are conceptualized as visual artifacts appropriate for study as visual rhetoric. Two-dimensional images are the subjects of the chapters by Helmers and Hill, Finnegan, Helmers, and Janis L. Edwards, who study photographs, paintings, and cartoons. Three-dimensional artifacts are analyzed in Greg Dickinson and Casey Malone Maugh's chapter on the embodied space of a grocery store, while moving images receive attention by J. Anthony Blair in his analysis of television commercials and by David Blakesley in his study of film. That artifacts included under the rubric of visual rhetoric are equally broad in terms of their functions also is highlighted in these chapters. Both aesthetic and utilitarian images constitute visual rhetoric, with the utilitarian a more dominant emphasis; the aesthetic images studied by Helmers, in contrast to the explicitly persuasive and utilitarian biographical candidate films analyzed by J. Cherie Strachan and Kathleen E. Kendall, the advertising images studied by Diane S. Hope, the atlases explored by Charles Kostelnick, and the decorative home-making texts examined by Andrea Kasten Tange exemplify such work.

Maureen Daly Goggin's chapter on needlework as a semiotic practice complicates and most thoroughly explores the definition of *visual rhetoric* as artifact. She notes that a focus on the materiality of semiotic practice challenges a clear division of rhetoric into the image and the word because when images and words appear together, written verbal rhetoric is visual rhetoric. She uses the history of sampler making to demonstrate the ways in which the relationship between rhetoric of the word and rhetoric of the image is more fluid than is typically theorized. She suggests that *rhetoric of the visual* might be a better term to use than *visual rhetoric* to label meaning-making material practices and artifacts that engage in graphic representation.

Visual Rhetoric as a Perspective

Visual rhetoric refers not only to the visual object as a communicative artifact but also to a perspective scholars take on visual imagery or visual data. In this meaning of the term, *visual rhetoric* constitutes a theoretical perspective that

involves the analysis of the symbolic or communicative aspects of visual artifacts. It is a critical–analytical tool or a way of approaching and analyzing visual data that highlights the communicative dimensions of images or objects.
Finnegan provides an excellent definition of this sense of the term when she
suggests that visual rhetoric is "a mode of inquiry, defined as *a critical and theoretical orientation that makes issues of visuality relevant to rhetorical theory*" (197).
*A rhetorical perspective on visual artifacts constitutes a particular way of viewing im-
ages—a set of conceptual lenses through which visual symbols become knowable as
communicative or rhetorical phenomena.*

Key to a rhetorical perspective on visual artifacts is its focus on a rhetorical
response to an artifact rather than an aesthetic one. An *aesthetic response* consists of a viewer's direct perceptual encounter with the sensory aspects of the
artifact. Experience of a work at an aesthetic level might mean enjoying its
color, sensing its form, or valuing its texture. There is no purpose governing
the experience other than simply having the experience. In a *rhetorical response*,
in contrast, meaning is attributed to the artifact. Colors, lines, textures, and
rhythms in an artifact provide a basis for the viewer to infer the existence of
images, emotions, and ideas. Understanding these rhetorical responses to visual artifacts is the purpose of visual rhetoric as a perspective, exemplified in
Helmers's chapter on the fine arts. Her purpose is not to develop insights into
the aesthetic effects of paintings but to discover how they function rhetorically. A rhetorical response, she suggests, is a process of accrual in which past
experiences merge with the evidence of the canvas to construct a meaning.

Another major feature of the rhetorical perspective on visual symbols is a
particular conception of the audience for the artifacts studied. Visual rhetoricians are interested in the impact of visual symbols on lay viewers—viewers
who do not have technical knowledge in areas such as design, art history, aesthetics, or art education. Lay viewers' responses to visual artifacts are assumed
to be constructed on the basis of viewers' own experiences and knowledge, developed from living and looking in the world. Hill's chapter illustrates such a
focus on the ways in which visual symbols communicate to lay audiences. He
begins with the question of how images persuade and describes the psychological processes involved in viewing, including aspects such as visual perception and the effects of images on emotional reactions and analytical thought.
The processes he describes are not dependent on viewers' possession of art
protocols that privilege the art expert's knowledge of art conventions for attributing meaning to images but are processes that are universal for all viewers. His chapter illustrates how visual rhetoric functions as a perspective to
discover the nature of rhetorical responses to images by lay audiences.

As the authors of the chapters in this volume do, most scholars of visual
rhetoric employ the term *visual rhetoric* in both senses in their studies. They analyze visual data of some kind—visual artifacts, objects, or images—and
also use visual rhetoric as a perspective on their data. What they do in their

analyses of visual data and the nature of the perspective they take on those data are developed as they focus on particular aspects of visual artifacts—areas of focus that then function to transform rhetorical theory.

AREAS OF FOCUS

The chapters in this book suggest that rhetorical scholars tend to study visual objects with a focus on one of three areas—nature, function, or evaluation. In this pillar of the framework for studies of visual rhetoric, *nature* deals with the components, qualities, and characteristics of visual artifacts; *function* concerns the communicative effects of visual rhetoric on audiences; and *evaluation* is the process of assessing visual artifacts.

Nature of the Artifact

Essential to any study of visual rhetoric is explication of the distinguishing features of the visual artifact itself. This area of focus is primary and is part of all studies of visual rhetoric because to explicate the function of or to evaluate images or objects requires an understanding of the substantive and stylistic nature of the artifacts being explored. Description of the nature of the visual rhetoric involves attention to two primary components—presented elements and suggested elements. Identification of the presented elements of an artifact involves naming its major physical features, such as space, medium, and color. Identification of the suggested elements is a process of discovering the concepts, ideas, themes, and allusions that a viewer is likely to infer from the presented elements; for example, the ornate gold leafing found on Baroque buildings might suggest wealth, privilege, and power (Kanengieter 12–13). Analysis of the presented and suggested elements engenders an understanding of the primary communicative elements of an image and, consequently, of the meanings an image is likely to have for audiences.

An analysis focused on nature of the artifact is exemplified in the chapter by Hope on gendered environments in advertising. She suggests that the creation of gendered environments is a dominant strategy of image-based advertising. She identifies the components of this rhetoric to suggest how advertising overcomes the resistance of environmentally aware audiences to advertising by appropriating images of nature. Because of the presented elements of these ads and their suggested links to femininity and masculinity, she concludes, they are able to construct a denial of connection between consumption and environment.

Studies of visual rhetoric with a focus on the nature of the visual symbol play a critical role in the expansion or transformation of discourse-based rhetorical theory by reconceptualizing the basic elements of rhetoric. Such studies encourage rhetorical scholars to explore how traditional rhetorical elements can be translated into forms that apply to visual rhetoric—elements such as metaphor, argument, enthymeme, *ethos*, evidence, narrative, and stasis. At the same time, these studies push rhetorical theory to deal with an entirely new set of visual constructs, such as color, space, texture, and vectoriality. A rhetorical theory once restricted to linear linguistic symbols thus explodes into one characterized by multidimensionality, dynamism, and complexity as visual units of meaning are taken into account in rhetorical theory.

Function of the Artifact

A second focus for scholars who adopt a rhetorical perspective on visual symbols is the function or functions the visual rhetoric serves for an audience. The function of a visual artifact is the action it communicates (Foss). Functions of visual artifacts, for example, might range from memorializing individuals to creating feelings of warmth and coziness to encouraging viewers to explore self-imposed limitations. Function is not synonymous with purpose, which involves an effect that is intended or desired by the creator of the image or object. Scholars who adopt a rhetorical perspective on visual artifacts do not see the creator's intentions as determining the correct interpretation of a work. Not only may the scholar not have access to evidence about the intentions of the creators of artifacts, but a privileging of creators' interpretations over the interpretations of viewers closes off possibilities for new ways of experiencing the artifact. Once an artifact is created, these scholars believe, it stands independent of its creator's intention.

Edwards's chapter on the construction of cultural memory through images illustrates a focus on function in the study of visual rhetoric. She notes that one use of iconic images is their appropriation to new contexts, where they function to create analogies that recall past moments and suggest future possibilities. Focusing her analysis on the photograph of John F. Kennedy, Jr. saluting his father's funeral cortege, Edwards explores how it was used at the time of the deaths of Jackie Kennedy and the son, John Kennedy. She concludes that the photograph connected the past and the present through its symbolic twin expressions of outrage and regret.

Two chapters analyze visual rhetoric for ideological functions that construct viewers' identities in particular ways. In Dickinson and Malone Maugh's analysis of the Wild Oats Marketplace, they seek to discover how Wild Oats responds to the abstractions and discomforts of globalized postmodern consumer culture. They suggest that the store repackages the possibilities of globalization to convert individuals who normally would be resistant to such culture into consumers comfortable with the wide range of goods available to them as a result of it. The analysis by Kaston Tange of the images in Victorian books devoted to teaching home arts highlights a similar function. Books that contained floor plans, pictures of furniture, drawings of window treatments, and diagrams of how to set a table, for example, not only gave directions on how to achieve the home the readers desired but also helped create the desire for a home and, consequently, a middle class.

Studies such as these that have function as their focus have the capacity to transform rhetorical theory in that they encourage a conceptualization of a broader array of functions for symbols. Although discursive rhetoric can serve an infinite number of functions, the functions explored in rhetorical theory tend to be persuasive functions, with symbols designed to change audience members in particular ways. Such a singular function is much more difficult to attribute to many visual symbols given their greater ambiguity over verbal discourse. Exactly what the message is of an artifact is often open to myriad interpretations, limiting its persuasive potential but expanding its potential to communicate functions that may be less dominating and more invitational (Foss and Griffin), more eclectic, and more fragmented. Study of the visual, then, may help move rhetorical theory away from a focus on changing others to attention to a much broader array of functions for symbols and thus to a greater understanding of the infinitely varied actions that symbols can and do perform for audiences.

Evaluation of the Artifact

A third area in which scholars focus as they analyze visual rhetoric is evaluation or assessment. Some scholars choose to evaluate an artifact using the criterion of whether it accomplishes its apparent function. If an artifact functions to memorialize someone, for example, such an evaluation would involve discovery of whether its media, colors, forms, and content actually accomplish that function. Other scholars choose to evaluate visual symbols by scrutinizing the functions themselves that are performed by the symbols, reflecting on their legitimacy or soundness determined largely by the implications and consequences of those functions—perhaps, for example, whether an artifact is congruent with a particular ethical system or whether it offers emancipatory potential.

Strachan and Kendall's analysis of political candidates' convention films is an example of a focus on evaluation in rhetorical studies of visual artifacts. They are interested in understanding the nature of the biographical candidate films aired at political parties' conventions and analyze and evaluate the films of George W. Bush and Al Gore in the 1998 presidential campaign for this purpose. The Gore film, they assert, failed to live up to the full potential of its genre because it did not address the audience's patriotic values and thus did not evoke strong emotional reactions to the candidate. They evaluate the Bush film more positively as an artifact of the genre of the convention film because it celebrated values through emotional appeals and presented Bush as a rugged individualist standing for America. Like other scholars who focus on function, Strachan and Kendall are interested in understanding how the quality of the rhetorical environment is affected by various kinds of images and other visual artifacts.

A focus on evaluation, like those on nature and function, also has the potential to transform rhetorical theory. In particular, such a focus encourages a questioning of the traditional notion of effectiveness. Discourse at the interpersonal or small-group level typically is evaluated on the basis of whether an audience has changed in the direction desired by the rhetor after exposure to the rhetor's message. How such a criterion would be applied to visual rhetoric that is non-representational and perhaps baffling for audience members is unclear. Certainly, standard rhetorical criteria for assessing the potential of messages to create change such as clarity of thesis, relevance of supporting materials, vividness of metaphors, appropriateness of organizational pattern, dynamism of style, and credibility of the rhetor are largely irrelevant.

In the context of public discourse, an additional criterion for effectiveness often is added to the criterion of audience change—contribution to rationality. From this perspective, rhetoric is supposed to contribute to rational debate about issues in the public sphere, and visual rhetoric often is judged to be lacking according to this criterion. Neil Postman, for example, argues that the visual epistemology of television "pollutes public communication" (28) and contributes to a decline in "the seriousness, clarity and, above all, value of public discourse" (29). Similarly, David Zarefsky suggests that rhetorical forms such as visual images "stand in for a more complex reality" (412), contributing to the deterioration of "a rich and vibrant concept of *argument*, of public deliberation" (414).

Visual rhetoric may not be used to persuade audiences in directions intended by a rhetor and may not be contributing to standard definitions of rational public communication, but its effects are significant and certainly not always negative. The world produced by visual rhetoric is not always—or even often—clear, well organized, or rational, but is, instead, a world made up of human experiences that are messy, emotional, fragmented, silly, serious, and disorganized. Such experiences are not often captured in rhetorical theory that posits criteria for assessment that require that visual rhetoric be judged negatively or ignored entirely. Studies of visual rhetoric that focus on evaluation, then, expand rhetorical theory to include broader criteria for the evaluation of rhetoric that more accurately capture and acknowledge the role of the visual in our world.

APPROACHES

The chapters in this volume add a third pillar of the frame of the current study of visual rhetoric to definition and areas of focus in that they suggest how studies of visual images and objects approach their areas of focus to transform rhetorical theory. Some scholars deductively apply rhetorical theories and constructs to visual symbols to investigate questions about rhetoric and to contribute to existing rhetorical theories generated from the study of discourse. A second approach involves an inductive investigation of visual artifacts designed to highlight features of the artifacts themselves as a means to generate rhetorical theory that is expanded to include the visual.

Deductive Application of the Rhetorical to the Visual

Scholars who apply a rhetorical perspective to visual symbols deductively use visual artifacts to illustrate, explain, or investigate rhetorical constructs and theories formulated from the study of discourse. They begin with rhetorical constructs and theories and use them to guide them through the visual artifact. Underlying this approach is the assumption that visual symbols possess largely the same characteristics that discursive symbols do. These studies produce a contribution to a rhetorical theory focused on verbal discourse and thus one that tends to be unidirectional. The theory affects the understanding of the artifact, but what is discovered in the artifact has less effect on the nature of the theory in that analysis of the visual largely affirms the discursive features of the theory. Affirmation is not insignificant, however, because it suggests which aspects of rhetorical theory apply to both the visual and the verbal, thus marking areas of study where attention to the visual is likely to be less productive because, in those areas, verbal and visual rhetoric are functioning similarly.

Finnegan's chapter on photographs exemplifies the approach in which a rhetorical theory or construct generated from discourse is applied to visual data to generate insights into that rhetorical theory. She explores the place of rhetorical history in visual rhetoric and demonstrates how the rhetorical historian might engage visual images. Her chapter models a rhetorical history of the visual based on her analysis of Farm Security Administration photography of sharecroppers published in *LOOK* magazine. As Finnegan's chapter demonstrates, the deductive, rhetoric-based approach offers ease of connection to existing rhetorical theory. Because it begins with rhetorical theory and applies existing theory to visual data, theoretical connections are easily made between the visual and the verbal in the development and elaboration of rhetorical theory.

Inductive Exploration of the Visual to Generate the Rhetorical

A second approach to the study of visual rhetoric is the investigation of the features of visual images to generate rhetorical theory that takes into account the distinct characteristics of the visual symbol. Scholars who pursue this route begin with an exploration of visual artifacts and operate inductively, generating rhetorical theories that are articulate about visual symbols. An assumption of scholars who proceed inductively from visual objects is that these visual objects are different in significant ways from discursive symbols. They focus on the particular qualities of visual rhetoric to develop explanations of how visual symbols operate in an effort to develop rhetorical theory from visual symbols to insure that it takes into account the dimensions of visual forms of rhetoric.

Two chapters exemplify the inductive approach to the study of visual rhetoric. Blair asks whether there can be visual arguments when arguments as we usually know them are verbal. He articulates the two primary reasons offered against the possibility of arguments as visual—that the visual is inescapably ambiguous and that arguments must have propositional content—and answers both objections. He concludes by offering a definition of visual arguments that expands traditional definitions of argument and goes on to assert that the particular qualities of the visual image make visual arguments different from verbal ones in that the visual has an immediacy, a verisimilitude, and a concreteness that help influence acceptance in ways not available to the verbal. He thus expands an understanding of argumentation rooted in the particularities of the visual.

David Blakesley's analysis of Hitchcock's film, *Vertigo*, is another example of an approach that begins with a focus on characteristics of the visual. He proposes four approaches to film rhetoric derived from the characteristics of films—language, ideology, interpretation, and identification. Film identification is the focus in his analysis, and he suggests that Hitchcock employs a variety of visual techniques to focus attention on the psychological consequences of the desire for identification or identity. Because of its visual qualities, he notes, film makes identification even more inviting than it might be in a verbal text.

The inductive, artifact-based approach exemplified by Blair and Blakesley, because it begins with the characteristics of artifacts and builds rhetorical theory on the basis of those characteristics, offers the most opportunities for rhetorical expansion. It has the greatest potential to expand rhetorical theory beyond the boundaries of discourse as it offers rhetorical qualities, characteristics, and components for which current rhetorical theory cannot account.

CONCLUSION

The chapters in this volume represent the variety that exists in the analysis of visual rhetoric and provide models for the study of the rhetorical workings of visual artifacts. More important, however, these chapters lay out the primary components of the current framework for such study—definition of *visual rhetoric* as artifact or perspective; areas of focus as nature, function, or evaluation; and methodological approaches as deductive or inductive in their movement between visual artifact and theory. This framework is not simply a framework for an understanding of visual rhetoric, however, but also for transforming discourse-based rhetorical theory. As rhetorical theory opens up to visual rhetoric, it opens up to possibilities for more relevant, inclusive, and holistic views of contemporary symbol use.

WORKS CITED

Audigier, Jean. Y. *Connections*. New York: Lanham, 1991.

Foss, Sonja K. "A Rhetorical Schema for the Evaluation of Visual Imagery." *Communication Studies* 45 (1994): 213–224.

Foss, Sonja K., and Cindy L. Griffin. "Beyond Persuasion: A Proposal for an Invitational Rhetoric." *Communication Monographs* 62 (1995): 2–18.

Kanengieter, Marla R. *"Message Formation from Architecture: A Rhetorical Analysis."* Diss. U of Oregon, 1990.

Postman, Neil. *Amusing Ourselves to Death: Public Discourse in the Age of Show Business.* New York: Viking Penguin, 1985.

Zarefsky, David. "Spectator Politics and the Revival of Public Argument." *Communication Monographs* 52 (1992): 411–414.

About the Contributors

J. Anthony Blair is a University Professor at the University of Windsor in Windsor, Ontario, Canada. Over the past 25 years, he has contributed to the new field called "informal logic" by co-authoring two textbooks (*Logical Self-Defense* [McGraw-Hill, 1994] and *Reasoning, A Practical Guide* [Prentice Hall, 1993]), founding and co-editing the journal, *Informal Logic*, publishing numerous articles, and organizing several conferences in Windsor and in Amsterdam, where he is on the board of the International Society for the Study of Argumentation. He is currently developing a pluralistic theory of argument that incorporates logic, dialectics, and rhetoric, and in which visual argument finds a theoretically grounded place.

David Blakesley is Associate Professor of English and Director of Professional Writing at Purdue University. He is the author of *The Elements of Dramatism* (Longman, 2002) and the forthcoming *Illuminating Rhetoric: A Guide to Seeing, Reading, and Writing* (Mayfield / McGraw-Hill, 2003). He is the editor of the forthcoming collection, *The Terministic Screen: Rhetorical Perspectives on Film* (SIU Press, 2003) and the co-editor and publisher, with Dawn Formo, of *The Writing Instructor,* a networked journal and digital community.

Greg Dickinson is Assistant Professor of Speech Communication at Colorado State University. His research focuses on the material practices of everyday life. His essays on urban space, consumer culture, and gender have been published in the *Quarterly Journal of Speech, Rhetoric Society Quarterly,* and the *Journal of Women's History.* He is currently working on the spatial and visual rhetorics of whiteness, and the intersections among memory, postmodernity and consumer spaces in Los Angeles.

Janis L. Edwards is Associate Professor of Communication Studies at the University of Alabama. Her work focuses on the intersections of political discourse and visual rhetoric, especially with regard to candidate image, national self-image, and the cultural implications of image circulation. She is the author of *Political Cartoons in the 1988 Presidential Campaign: Image, Metaphor, and Narrative* (Garland Press, 1997) and her work in political and visual rhetoric has appeared in such journals as the *Quarterly Journal of Speech, Communication Quarterly*, and *Women's Studies in Communication*. She has also won numerous awards for her creative work in visual art, but claims to possess no talent at cartooning.

Cara A. Finnegan, Assistant Professor in the Department of Speech Communication at the University of Illinois at Urbana-Champaign, studies the rhetorical history of photography in the United States. She is the author of *Picturing Poverty: Print Culture and FSA Photographs* (Smithsonian Institution Press, 2003), and has published in scholarly journals such as *Rhetoric and Public Affairs*, *Argumentation and Advocacy*, and *Rhetoric Society Quarterly*. She is currently working on a new book project, a series of essays about public controversies that involved the photograph's status as evidence. She is also an amateur photographer.

Sonja K. Foss is Professor in the Department of Communication at the University of Colorado at Denver. The focus of her research is on the methodological and ideological boundaries constructed around rhetorical theories and the impacts they have on conceptions of rhetoric. She explores this question through work in visual rhetoric and feminist perspectives on rhetoric. Her work on visual rhetoric includes essays on visual argumentation, appeal in visual images, and the rhetorical evaluation of visual images. Her work in feminist rhetoric includes *Women Speak, Feminist Rhetorical Theories*, and *Inviting Transformation*, and essays on invitational rhetoric, feminine spectatorship in Garrison Keillor's monologues, and sewing as an emancipatory ritual.

Maureen Daly Goggin is Associate Professor of Rhetoric in the English Department at Arizona State University, where she teaches courses in the history and theories of rhetoric. She is author of *Authoring a Discipline: Scholarly Journals and the Post-World War II Emergence of Rhetoric and Composition* (netlibrary, 2000) and editor of *Inventing a Discipline: Rhetoric Scholarship in Honor of Richard E. Young* (NCTE, 2000). Her publications on the history of rhetoric and composition as well as on visual and material rhetoric appear in *Rhetoric Review, Rhetoric Society Quarterly, Composition Studies* and various edited collections.

Marguerite Helmers is Professor in the Department of English at the University of Wisconsin Oshkosh. She received a PhD in Rhetoric and Composition from the University of Wisconsin–Milwaukee. She is the author of *Writing Students* (SUNY, 1995) and editor of *Intertexts: Reading Pedagogy in College Writing Classrooms* (Erlbaum, 2002). She has contributed articles to *College English, The Journal of Advanced Composition*, and the electronic journals, *Enculturation* and *Kairos*. She has received the James Berlin Outstanding Dissertation Award from the National Council of Teachers of English, the Distinguished Teaching Award at UW Oshkosh, and the Kimball Foundation Award for Excellence. She was also a Fellow of the Center for Twentieth Century Studies in 1999–2000.

Charles A. Hill is Associate Professor in the Department of English at the University of Wisconsin Oshkosh. His work has appeared in *Written Communication, The Journal of Computer Documentation*, and *Computers and Composition*. His recent publications include "Reading the Visual in College Writing Classes," in *Intertexts: Reading Pedagogy in College Writing Classrooms*, edited by Marguerite Helmers (Lawrence Erlbaum Associates, 2002).

Diane S. Hope is the William A. Kern Professor in Communications at the Rochester Institute of Technology and is the Editor of the interdisciplinary journal, *Women's Studies Quarterly*. She has published critical essays on the rhetoric of the women's movement, the civil rights movement, the environment, and visual rhetoric. Her most recent publications include guest editing a special issue of *WSQ: Earthwork: Women and Environments* (Feminist Press, 2001), and "Environment as Icon in Advertising Fantasy" in *Enviropop: Studies in Environmental Rhetoric and Popular Culture*, edited by Mark Meister and Phyllis Japp (Greenwood Press, 2002).

Kathleen E. Kendall is Visiting Professor in the Department of Communication at the University of Maryland, College Park, and Professor Emerita from the University at Albany, SUNY. She has published two books: *Communication in the Presidential Primaries* (Praeger, 2000), and *Presidential Campaign Discourse* (SUNY Press, 1995). Her current research focuses on political debates and speeches, media coverage of political messages, and conversations about politics.

Charles Kostelnick is Professor in the English Department at Iowa State University, where he has taught business and technical communication and a graduate and an undergraduate course in visual communication in professional writing. He is the co-author of *Designing Visual Language: Strategies for Professional Communicators* (Prentice Hall, 1997).

Casey Malone Maugh is a doctoral candidate in the Communication Arts and Sciences Department at The Pennsylvania State University. She received her Master's degree in Speech Communication and an interdisciplinary graduate certification in Women's Studies from Colorado State University.

J. Cherie Strachan is Assistant Professor of Political Communication at the University at Albany, in Albany, New York. She is the author of *High-Tech Grass Roots: The Professionalization of Local Elections* (Rowman & Littlefield, 2003), which explores the consequences of using communication consultants and technology in local political campaigns. Her current research projects, which explore messages in civic education efforts and in gubernatorial candidates' campaign rhetoric, continue to address the way communication patterns affect average citizens' abilities to participate in the political process.

Craig Stroupe is Assistant Professor of Composition at the University of Minnesota Duluth, where he teaches courses in information design and visual rhetoric. He previously worked as Associate Director of San José State University's Online Campus, advising faculty in the pedagogy of designing Web-based courses. He writes about the relations of visual and verbal discourses, the influence of technology on university curricula, and the borders between academic and mass cultures. His work has appeared in *College English* and is forthcoming in *Pedagogy* and *Computers and Composition*.

Andrea Kaston Tange is an Assistant Professor of English at Eastern Michigan University, where she teaches graduate and undergraduate courses on 19th-century British literature. She is currently in the final stages of a book project, tentatively entitled *Architextural Identities: Literature, Domestic Space, and the Victorian Middle Class*, which examines how representations of domesticity in architectural and literary texts helped construct middle-class identities in 19th-century England. Long interested in visual culture, she has also published an essay on the relationship between illustrations and text in Victorian fairy tales in the *Journal of Narrative Technique*.

Author Index

A

"Acura" Advertisement, 161, 175
Albrecht, Sheri A., 225, 240, 241
Allen, Chris T., 37, 39
Althusser, Louis, 68, 69, 85
Anderson, Benedict, 4, 8, 16, 22
Anderson, Carolyn, 131, 132
Andrews, Malcolm, 165, 175
Aristotle, 41, 60
Armada, Bernard J., 273, 274
Asen, Robert, 209, 212
Attridge, Derek, 92, 108
Audigier, Jean Y., 303, 313
Auiler, Dan, 131, 132
"Auto Kills Women Before Your Eyes!" 203, 212

B

Baesler, E. James, 32, 38
Bakhtin, Mikhail, 245, 246, 256, 257, 257
Bal, Mieke, 15, 16, 22
Barber, Benjamin, 4, 22
Barringer, Tim, 164, 177
Barthel, Diane, 173, 175
Barthes, Roland, 16–17, 22, 29, 38, 156, 168, 175, 204, 212, 212
Barton, Ben F., 225, 232, 237, 240
Barton, Marthalee S., 225, 232, 237, 240
Baty, S. Paige, 4, 22
Baughman, James L., 212, 212
Baxandall, Michael, 68, 71, 82, 85
Beeton, Mrs. Isabella, 292, 294, 295, 296, 300
Bellafante, Gina, 173, 175
Benjamin, Walter, 200, 212, 213
Bennett, Tony, 82, 85

Benson, Thomas W., 113, 116, 131, 132, 212, 213
Berger, John, 157, 175
Berkman, Brenda, 12, 22
Bernhardt, Stephen A., 87, 108
Berry, Wendell, 173, 174, 175
Bertin, Jacques, 238, 240
Betten, Neil, 208, 213
Biagra, Jello, 254, 257
Biderman, Albert D., 216, 227, 240
Birdsell, David S., 60, 60
Blair, Carole, 273, 274
Blair, J. Anthony, 60, 60
Blakesley, David, 114, 116, 131, 132, 198, 213
Bledstein, Burton J., 107, 108
Bleich, David, 66, 85
Block, Lauren G., 32, 38
Boorstin, Daniel J., 217, 240
Bordwell, David, 116, 131, 132, 132
Borgerson, Janet L., 171, 173, 177
Bourdieu, Pierre, 299, 300
Braidotti, Rosi, 262, 274
Brandt, Deborah, 173, 175
Brewer, W. H., 227, 240
Brinton, Willard C., 240, 240
Bristor, Julia, 173, 175
Brittain, Judy, 91, 108
Brooke, Collin, 198, 213
Brown, Shirley Ann, 94, 108
Browne, Clare, 107, 108
Brummett, Barry, 116, 131, 132
Bryson, Norman, 15, 16, 22
Buck, Ross, 30, 32, 39
Buhl, Claus, 171, 176
Burke, Kenneth, 28, 36, 38, 64, 85, 106, 108, 112, 114, 117, 124, 132, 156, 175, 268, 274
Bush, Clive, 165, 175

319

Subject Index